McGraw-Hill Reading

Wonders

McGraw Hill Education

Bothell, WA • Chicago, IL • Columbus, OH • New York, NY

Cover and Title Pages: Nathan Love

www.mheonline.com/readingwonders

 The *McGraw-Hill* Companies

Education

Copyright © 2014 The McGraw-Hill Companies, Inc.

Send all inquiries to:
McGraw-Hill Education
Two Penn Plaza
New York, New York 10121

ISBN: 978-0-02-118712-6
MHID: 0-02-118712-6

Printed in the United States of America.

4 5 6 7 8 9 DOW 17 16 15 14 13

C

McGraw-Hill Reading Wonders

CCSS Reading/Language Arts Program

Program Authors

Diane August

Donald R. Bear

Janice A. Dole

Jana Echevarria

Douglas Fisher

David Francis

Vicki Gibson

Jan Hasbrouck

Margaret Kilgo

Jay McTighe

Scott G. Paris

Timothy Shanahan

Josefina V. Tinajero

McGraw Hill Education

Bothell, WA • Chicago, IL • Columbus, OH • New York, NY

UNIT 1

 Go Digital! http://connected.mcgraw-hill.com

THE BIG IDEA

Excursions Across  Time

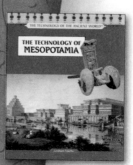
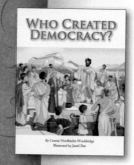

 Go Digital! http://connected.mcgraw-hill.com

THE BIG IDEA

Challenges

Franklin D. Roosevelt Library; Jamie Bloomquist Photography; Stockbyte/Getty Images

UNIT 5

THE BIG IDEA

Discoveries

Bettmann/Corbis; Vladimir Piskunov/Netta/Getty Images

 Go Digital! http://connected.mcgraw-hill.com

THE BIG IDEA

Taking *ACTION*

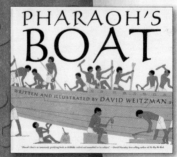

LITTLE BLOG ON THE PRAIRIE

by Cathleen Davitt Bell

illustrated by Craig Orback

Essential Question

How do new experiences offer new perspectives?

Read how an experience at a unique summer camp gives a teenage girl a whole new perspective on her life.

 Go Digital!

Imagine for a moment that the year is 1890. No indoor plumbing. No refrigerators. No electricity, period! This is the life that 13-year-old Genevieve Welsh and her younger brother Gavin have to endure for the whole summer, since their mother has decided that the family's vacation will be spent at a frontier fantasy camp near Laramie, Wyoming. When the Welsh family arrives, all their modern conveniences—even, to Gen's horror, her shampoo— are taken away and placed in storage by the camp's owners, Ron and his daughter Nora. Genevieve even has to wear the fashions of the 1890s, including long dresses and something called "pantaloons."

Will the family survive, living together in a tiny log cabin? Mr. Welsh is afraid of almost all animals, but Genevieve, at least, has a head start. Before they left she decided to hide her cell phone in order to keep in touch with her friends. Little does she know they will turn her text messages into a blog called …

… Little Blog on the Prairie.

Gavin opened the front door, and the room was suddenly flooded with light. I could see colors outside: a bright blue sky, the intense green of the woods, the packed-down dirt in front of the house, and some yellow weeds poking up through it. It looked cold—you can always tell—like at early Saturday soccer games in the fall, when the field is almost silver-colored with dew, and you get clumps of grass clippings stuck in your cleats when you run.

"Don't go out to explore yet," Mom called before Gavin crossed the **threshold**. "First wood! You too, Genevieve," she said. "We need a lot to keep this fire going."

I called back, "How am I supposed to button this dress?" I couldn't reach behind my back to get it fastened.

My mom took a break from the stove to come help, gathering her skirts in one hand and using the other to hold herself steady as she climbed the ladder.

"You mean in 1890 you couldn't even get dressed without someone to help you with your buttons?" I said.

"I guess not," my mom answered. "Your dad got a little impatient this morning helping me with mine." And when she turned I noticed he'd missed every other one.

"Here," I said, but just as I was slipping the last button through its hand-sewn hole, we heard shrieking coming from outside. Before we could even start to wonder what it was, Gavin burst in.

"You won't believe the chickens," he said, breathless, wild eyed, his fingers splayed—he was shaking them out like they were wet.

"Gavin?" my mom said. "What happened?"

"They tried to kill me," he said.

"Who?" answered my mom, making her way down the ladder as fast as she could.

"Gavin!" she exclaimed once she was standing on the floor again and could focus on what he was saying. "Where's the wood you went to get?"

"I got too scared," he said.

"Scared?"

"Of the chickens." He was mumbling now, like he was a little embarrassed. And he should have been. Who's afraid of a couple of chickens? Well, besides Dad.

"Look," my mom said. "You can't all be **phobic**. Farm kids need to be tough, and you two are farm kids now. Those chickens are more afraid of you than you are of them." She pointed to a box next to the woodstove. "This is the wood box. In 1890, kids would have kept this box filled to the top all day long, without ever having to be reminded. I know you are hungry and cold right now, but let's get off on a good footing. If you can take this on as a project, we'll all be warm and fed very soon."

"But—," Gavin started.

"Oh, fine," I said. "I'll get the wood." I was thinking that if I could get out of the house, I'd warm up in the sunshine.

But from the moment I took a step off the porch, I was pretty much attacked. Wings flapping, feathers flying, clawed feet leaping so high I was afraid for my face. There were screeches and squeals. I covered my eyes, tripping backward onto the porch, scrambling to stand up again, reaching blindly behind me for the door.

It was the chickens.

Gavin was right. They were going to poke out my eyes or peck off my toes. They would stop at nothing.

"I think they're hungry," said Gavin when I was safely inside, panting, untangling my skirt from my legs. I swore my dress had been in on the attack, whipping this way and that, trapping me. "It took them a minute to find me," he continued. "They came from over by the barn. But now they know where we are, they're just waiting for us to come out again. They're guarding the door."

"I don't think it's hunger," I said. "I think they *hate* us."

"Here," said my mom. "Give them this." She was holding some cornmeal in a tin cup.

"You give it to them," I said. "I'm not going back out there."

"Do chickens eat that?" asked Gavin. "What if that isn't something they even like? What if it makes them angrier?"

"It does look a little thin," Mom said. "I'm not sure how they'd be able to peck it up off the ground."

STOP AND CHECK

Visualize How does Gen's description of the area around the cabin help you to picture the location of the frontier fantasy camp?

13

"Can I try a pinch?" asked Gavin.

"You want it raw?" said my mom.

Gavin just shrugged. "I'm hungry."

"I'll try to light the fire with what we have inside," my mom said.

"What time is it anyway?" I said. I was starting to get the feeling that it was really early in the morning. Like, bus-stop early.

"I don't know," my mom confessed, kind of laughing. "I don't know how you tell time out here. Ron gave your dad a watch yesterday, but he forgot to wind it, and now it's off. It's funny, all these little things, isn't it?"

"Ha," I said in a way that I hoped communicated that "funny" was dead last in the list of words describing all these little things—with "annoying," "unnecessary," and "unfair" coming closer to the top.

Just then my dad approached the cabin. I could tell because I heard the chickens start screaming and squealing followed by Dad letting out a surprised "Oh!" Then he must have started to run, because the screaming and screeching got louder and I could hear wings flapping. My dad burst through the door, out of breath, feathers floating in a cloud around his legs. He slammed the door behind him.

"They're just chickens," my mom said. "I don't know why you all are so afraid."

My dad didn't answer her. His face was white. "I think one of them was foaming at the mouth," he said.

"Beak," my mom corrected.

"Birds carry disease," he said. He placed the bucket of water on the table and held out his hand to examine it. "I guess it didn't break the skin." My mom rolled her eyes, reaching behind herself to straighten her bun, then peering into the bucket of water.

"It's only half filled," she said.

"Some of it spilled while I was running the gauntlet just now," he said. "I hope there's enough for coffee."

"I was going to make grits," my mom said. "It's fast, and we have cornmeal."

"Do I like grits?" Gavin asked.

"What are grits?" I said.

"You're going to make coffee first," my dad said. "Because I need coffee before I can take on one more thing today." His teeth were chattering. He pointed to the cookbook from 1882. "Does that show you how to make coffee? Do we even have coffee?"

My mom lifted the lid on a trunk. There were some bags and a few tins in it. She pulled out a wooden box with a crank on the top and a tin box with a lid. "Coffee!" she said brightly. It was pathetic how she was trying to act like she was in a good mood and trick the rest of us into agreeing with her.

"Is there orange juice?" Gavin asked.

"How can there be orange juice if there isn't even a refrigerator?" I said.

"How can there be no refrigerator?" Gavin asked.

"We've got to light this fire," my mom said.

"We've got to get me some coffee," said my dad.

My mom had put a match to the fire in the stove and after a few smoke-filled attempts finally got it going when we had our first visitor. Those hungry chickens were like a doorbell, squealing and squawking. I knew somebody was in the yard.

My mom was too busy flapping air into the stove with the bellows to notice, but I opened the door a crack to peek out.

It was Nora.

I watched her, wanting to see how an experienced farm person managed around killer fowl. A muzzle? A shotgun? But the thing is, when the chickens saw it was Nora, they didn't even attack.

"Hey, Pumpkin," I watched her say to one of the chickens. Just the sound of her voice seemed to calm them down. "Hey, Daisy." She pulled a handful of something out of her pocket and tossed it on the ground. Daisy and Pumpkin scrambled to peck at it. It didn't look like cornmeal.

I would have stepped into the yard and asked her what she was giving them, but when she looked up, there was a **glimmer** of something in her eyes that made me afraid to talk to her.

Instead of saying hi to me or anything like that, Nora shook her head like I wasn't there and said, "The new folks never feed

those poor chickens. And if you'd fed them and shut them in the coop like my dad told you to last night," she added, meeting my gaze, "you'd be eating eggs for breakfast this morning, instead of what all it is you're planning to make without milk or eggs."

With that, she stepped inside and walked around the cabin like she owned it, which I guess, technically, she did, but still. She pulled the drawer out of the coffee grinder and looked inside, nodding briefly to show my dad that she approved. My mom had finally closed the door to the stove, and Nora opened it again, inspected the fire, added two pieces of kindling, then closed the door and changed the vents in the door and the side of the stove until they met her approval.

"Breakfast plans?" she asked my mom, not even bothering to expand that thought into a full sentence.

"Grits," my mom said, and Nora nodded, neither approving nor disapproving.

"Better with a little salt pork if you can spare it," she said. Then she jutted her chin toward a shelf where all the dishes were stacked—tin plates, a stack of tin cups. Nora said, "Coffeepot's up there."

I looked over at my dad, hoping to get some kind of a reading from him on

Nora. He didn't disappoint. He had a kind of **sarcastic** expression on his face. Nora turned to me like a teacher who hears a kid talking in the middle of class.

"You're Genevieve, right?" she said. "How old are you?"

"I'm thirteen," I said. "But I turn fourteen in September. I'll be in high school." I don't know why I needed to tell her that, other than the fact that the term "high school" felt comforting. It was nice to remind myself that Nora or no Nora, at some point all of this would be over and I'd be back with Kristin and Ashley in the world where I belonged.

"I'm fourteen," Nora said. "But I'll be fifteen in October. So I guess that makes me a full year older than you."

"Almost," I said.

"What?"

"Almost a full year," I said. I knew I was being picky about it, but she was wrong and that should count for something when you're acting like you are the biggest expert on everything in someone else's house. "My birthday's in September. So we're actually eleven months apart."

As if I hadn't said a word at all, Nora reached up to the dish shelf, pulled down a tin cup, and used it to scoop water from the bucket and pour it into the pump mounted on the counter. She pumped vigorously and poured more water into the pump, until water started flowing out of the pump on its own. "You've got to prime the pump in the mornings," she said. "Especially when the place stands empty a few days."

Meanwhile, my mom had put the coffee grounds in the pot, and was starting to heat up the water for the grits. "Will you stay for breakfast?" she asked Nora.

"Nah." Nora shook her head. "I've got chores and lessons, and shoot, we get up at 4:30 in the summer. For me, it's closer to dinnertime than it is to breakfast."

"It's almost nighttime?" Gavin asked.

"Did you really just say *shoot*?" I asked.

Nora ignored my question. "No, dinner's what you eat at the noon meal," she said. "And we're having chicken and dumplings."

I wish I had been stronger. I wish we all had. But at the mention of chicken and dumplings—and I didn't even know what that was, except something they had for dinner in the song "She'll Be Comin' Round the Mountain"—I felt my spine go limp. It was as if all the bones in my body had been replaced by longing for whatever chicken and dumplings were. One look at Gavin, Mom, and Dad told me they were feeling exactly the same way. We were all leaning toward Nora as if we might smell the hot food coming off her.

"I'm sure you'll be having stuff like that in no time," she said, and I knew that what she really meant was that we probably wouldn't have a meal like that until we got home and drove straight from the airport to a restaurant.

Grits, which we sat down to eat as soon as Nora was gone, taste exactly like what they are—cornmeal mixed with water. I don't think they're supposed to be crunchy, or have a smoky flavor, but these did.

"Why did we come here again?" I said after taking my first bite.

My mom said, "They're better with butter."

My dad said, "And when they're not burnt."

My mom pushed her dish away and stood up to pump water in a bowl to do the dishes, and my dad said, "You're going to boil some for that washing, right? The only thing that would make it worse out here is if one of us got dysentery."

My mom said, "Don't you have some work to do outside?" and Dad stood, took one more bite, then left the cabin. My mom turned to me. "Genevieve," she said. "It will be your job to clear the table, scrape the food off the plates into a bowl for the animals, and clean the dishes after the meal. You can also make the beds, and I'll expect you to set the table and sweep out the house after every meal. When you're done you can help your dad in the fields."

I stood there and stared at her.

Week 1 – Monday

11:16 am

I am standing in the middle of a cornfield. I am holding a hoe. As my mom said when we were setting off to work in the field, we are farmers now.

Week 1 – Monday

11:17 am

Here's the thing: being a farmer is BORING. I am halfway down one row, there are ten rows to go, and it's already taken TWO HOURS.

I turned the phone off and slipped it into my pocket. I did this every time I sent a text, promising myself I wouldn't get it out again until much later. I didn't want to get caught. And I didn't want to run down the battery. But then two seconds would pass and I'd find myself reaching for it again. I couldn't help it. It was like the way Gavin sneaks his candy from the jar on top of the fridge where my mom makes him keep it.

I had to have some weeding done when my dad got back, though, so I swore that this time I'd keep the phone in my pocket. My dad had gone to get us water, taking Gavin along with him.

Before we'd headed out to the cornfield, my dad sat Gavin, my mom, and me down on the edge of the porch to tell us what we needed to know about bears.

"I assume you're not talking about the Chicago football team," my mom had said.

"They could be anywhere," my dad replied.

When Gavin said, "Seeing a bear would be so cool," my dad hunched his shoulders up toward his ears, drew his bushy eyebrows together, and stood over him.

"Bears are no joke," he growled. "You have to be careful. Especially in the woods."

STOP AND CHECK

Visualize How does visualizing Gen's father's warning about bears make his character more comical?

Gavin had been swinging his legs, but now he stopped.

"You're scaring him," said my mom.

"You kind of look like a bear right now," Gavin said.

"You should be scared," Dad said to Gavin, but he backed away. "If you want to avoid a bear, the best thing to do is make sure they know where you are. Call out to them as you walk. Call out 'Bear, bear.'"

"They speak English?" I asked.

"Do you know what you do if you see a bear?" my dad asked.

"Run?" I said.

"Never run. I'm telling you . . ." He looked at each one of us hard. "If you see a bear, stay put. Wave your hands above your head. It will make the bear think you're bigger than you are, that you're not worth attacking." He was demonstrating, but with the sun behind him, he looked like he was performing a rain dance. "And if they come for you anyway, what you do is you crouch down on the ground." He showed us this too, his forehead in the dirt, his knees tucked under his chest, his arms covering the back of his head. His voice was muffled, but he still managed to shout out, "The idea here is that you're using your body to protect your vital organs. Better to have the bear rip some meat off your back than to puncture your lungs or heart."

Now, all alone in the cornfield, I thought, "Ugh. Meat."

Week 1 – Monday

11:41 am

ARE there really bears out there? My dad said if you're all by yourself you should sing to keep them away.

Week 1 – Monday

11:42 am

But the way I sing, a bear might attack me just to make me stop.

I heard something rustling behind me and I jumped. I stashed the phone thinking it must be my dad. But then when I called out "Dad?" and the sound of my voice died unanswered in the great openness of the field, with the mountains beyond, I started to get a little freaked out.

"They told him don't you ever come around here," I started, my voice warbly and small. "Beat It" was the only song I knew all the words to because my sixth-grade gym teacher had made us learn a dance to it. I went on a little bit louder. I wanted to be sure a bear could hear.

Holding the hoe in two hands, I brought the blade down on a clump of weeds growing up around a cornstalk. You have to hit them at the root and it's not always easy to figure out where they are. This time I took down the corn plant as well. I'd been doing that a lot.

The next time, I didn't hit the corn. I started doing a little dance in time to the song, hacking away at the weeds. I was

belting it out, but who cared? Except for the bears, I was completely alone.

I was already on the third verse when I noticed Gavin and my dad ten feet away, listening. Gavin said, "Yeah, the '80s!" and I felt my face go hot. I went back to my weeding in silence.

Week 1 – Monday

1:24 pm

You know what's worse than being caught by your little brother singing "Beat It" at the top of your lungs while you do a little corn-weeding dance? Having him follow you down the row, doing a little dance of his own, and stopping only to say, "Come on, Gen, you know you're feeling it." All morning long.

Week 1 – Monday

1:29 pm

My one consolation is that last night Gavin got a mosquito bite on his eyelid, and it's swollen so bad he can't open that eye. Actually, it kind of makes me feel bad for him.

After lunch that day—grits again, because my mom hadn't figured out how to cook anything else—we went back into the field. I was able to text again when it was my turn to fetch water, and that's how it went over the next few days—**heinous** chores, stolen moments to text, lots of singing and calling out to bears who may or may not have been listening.

About the Author

Cathleen Davitt Bell

started writing books when she was nine years old because she loved to read. She wanted her favorite stories to "keep on going." However, Cathleen admits that her early attempts never really got off the ground. She just wasn't able to put down on paper the grand images and full story lines she had in her head. Over time, though, she learned to start small and build on each spurt of writing until what she put down on paper more closely resembled her original ideas.

Little Blog on the Prairie has the honor of being selected for the Texas Lone Star Reading List. Cathleen lives with her husband, two children, and two dogs in Brooklyn, New York.

Author's Purpose

The author includes text messages in the story. How are these messages set apart from the rest of the text, so readers can easily tell when Gen is sending a message to her friends?

Flo Lunn

Respond to Reading

Summarize

Summarize the important events that helped change Gen's perspective in *Little Blog on the Prairie*. Information from your Character, Setting, Plot Chart may help you.

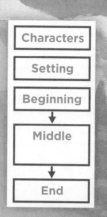

Characters
Setting
Beginning
Middle
End

Text Evidence

1. How do you know that *Little Blog on the Prairie* is realistic fiction? Identify at least two features the author includes to support your answer. **GENRE**

2. How is Genevieve's life at home different from her life at fantasy frontier camp? Give three examples that contrast her home life with life at the camp. **COMPARE AND CONTRAST**

3. What is the meaning of the word *vital* on page 21? Use context clues to help you figure out the meaning. **SENTENCE CLUES**

4. Authors often compare and contrast the similarities and differences between characters in order to create tension in the plot. Write about how the author creates tension between Nora and Gen by comparing and contrasting these two characters. **WRITE ABOUT READING**

Make Connections

How have Genevieve's experiences at camp given her a new perspective on the life she left behind in the city? **ESSENTIAL QUESTION**

Genevieve sends text messages at the end of the story. How does this help to reveal Gen as more of a "typical" teenager than Nora, and make it easier to have readers identify with her? **TEXT TO WORLD**

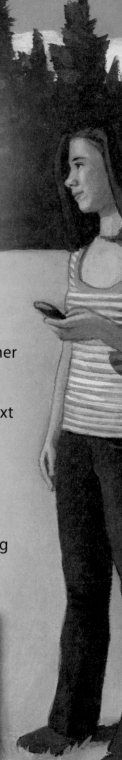

Compare Texts
Read how two weeks in New York City affect one young artist.

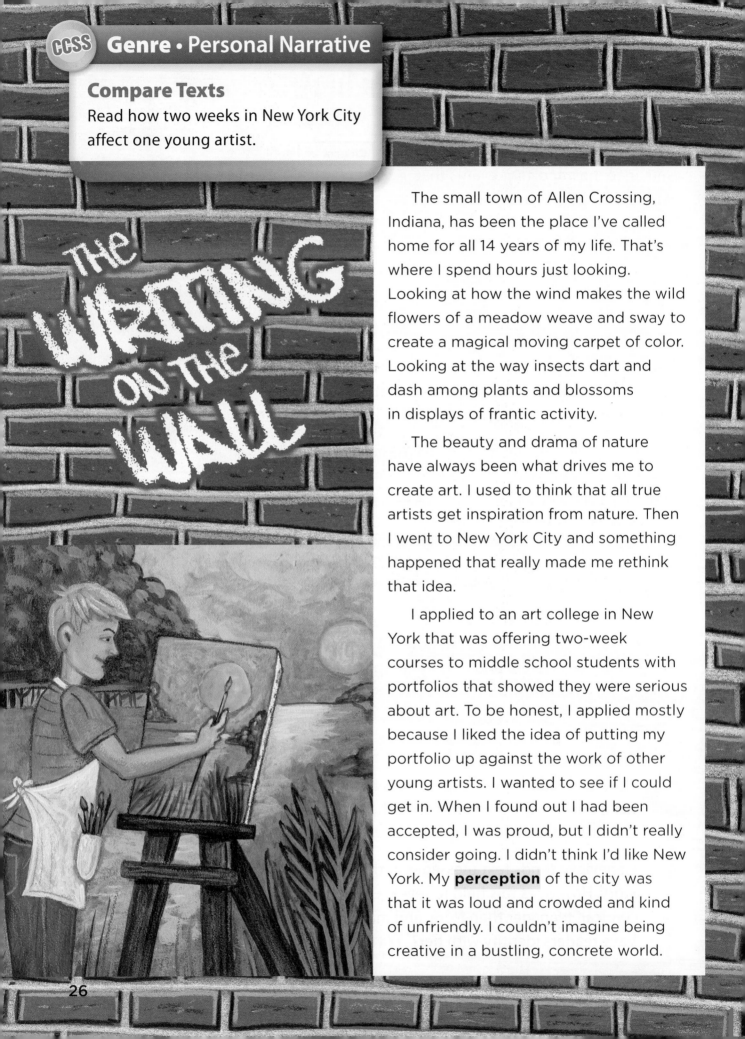

THE WRITING ON THE WALL

The small town of Allen Crossing, Indiana, has been the place I've called home for all 14 years of my life. That's where I spend hours just looking. Looking at how the wind makes the wild flowers of a meadow weave and sway to create a magical moving carpet of color. Looking at the way insects dart and dash among plants and blossoms in displays of frantic activity.

The beauty and drama of nature have always been what drives me to create art. I used to think that all true artists get inspiration from nature. Then I went to New York City and something happened that really made me rethink that idea.

I applied to an art college in New York that was offering two-week courses to middle school students with portfolios that showed they were serious about art. To be honest, I applied mostly because I liked the idea of putting my portfolio up against the work of other young artists. I wanted to see if I could get in. When I found out I had been accepted, I was proud, but I didn't really consider going. I didn't think I'd like New York. My **perception** of the city was that it was loud and crowded and kind of unfriendly. I couldn't imagine being creative in a bustling, concrete world.

When my mother reminded me that the classes in New York would be taught by real, working artists, I felt a glimmer of excitement about going. And when she told me I could stay with my aunt and her family, who live in the city, it seemed sort of crazy not to go.

I arrived in early July. New York was just as noisy and teeming with people as I thought it would be. When my older cousin Ken and I took the train to the college for the first time, I had some serious doubts about whether I had made the right choice about coming. I was so used to the quiet countryside. There I could just let the sights inspire me by letting them seep gently into my awareness. In New York, nothing seeps gently. People pushed past us to squeeze through the doors of the subway cars. Everything had hard edges and moved at a supersonic pace. It all came at me so quickly that I felt I had no time to process it all.

Art classes were another story. Once I was able to start making art, I felt like myself again. Working from memory, I made sketch after sketch of landscapes and other natural scenes. Each stroke of the brush or scratch of the pencil brought me closer to remembering why I had come. The teachers walked around the room and made comments on what each student was doing.

"Your images are very realistic and accurate," one teacher told me. "Why don't we see what happens if you loosen them up a little? Try using brighter colors and bolder shapes and motions." She told me I should go to the Museum of Modern Art to look at the paintings of artists like Vincent Van Gogh and Georges Seurat, so after class Ken and I went to the museum. I saw several paintings by Van Gogh. Using brash, flowing strokes of rich color, he painted forms found in nature in ways I had never seen. Seurat applied paint in a variety of multi-colored dots that allowed a viewer's eye to blend the colors. When I tried applying some of these same techniques to my own art,

I was amazed at the change. My careful images gained a new movement.

Toward the end of my two weeks, I was going back to my aunt's house with Ken, and my head was so full of the colors and shapes I was making in class that I took out my sketchbook to work on one of my drawings.

"Can I see that?" Ken asked. When I handed him the sketchbook, he began flipping through the pages. Finally he said, "Dude, these are great; they remind me of graffiti."

I looked at my sketches and was confused because to me graffiti was not art, it was just messy, unreadable writing scrawled on walls—and you weren't supposed to do it. In most places it was against the law.

"Hey!" A loud voice broke my reverie.

I looked up to see three tall teenage boys staring at us across the aisle. I sat up straighter and tried to look like I wasn't intimidated, but then Ken said, "Hey, Myles!" and I realized that my cousin knew them. He introduced me to Myles, LeShawn, and Pete.

Myles had seen us looking through my sketchbook. "What's in the book?" he asked, so I showed it to the three boys.

"Cool," Myles said. "If you're into art, you should come with us," and with that he opened his backpack and I saw it was filled with cans of spray paint. As far as I was concerned, art was not made with spray paint.

I started to protest that I didn't want to proceed when the train pulled into the subway station, Ken grabbed me, and we followed Myles, LeShawn, and Pete up the steps to the street.

Suddenly we turned the corner and standing in front of us was a huge factory that was completely coated with graffiti. The walls were covered with colors so bright they looked like neon; detailed portraits appeared next to cartoon-like creatures and words and calligraphy-like symbols were emblazoned in six-foot high characters. Everywhere I looked there was something new to see.

"What is this place?" I muttered as I looked around to see if anyone was watching us.

"It's a legal graffiti exhibit space," Myles said, "like a big gallery for street art." He explained that he and LeShawn and Pete had been selected to paint there in a contest their school had held before summer recess. They showed me sketches of what they planned to paint, and then I turned my gaze to the factory again. What I saw was art not unlike what I had been making. The big difference was, along with images from nature, the artists also drew images from city life. There was a subway train crammed with people rushing off to work and there were tall, shiny buildings stretching up into the sky. In every sketch, there was an energy that reminded me of that first subway ride, only it was a creative energy, not a panicky energy.

What I learned that summer in New York was **indispensable** to me, for now I know that inspiration is different for everyone. What drives one person crazy can be the thing that drives another person to create. I may not look at the city the way Myles, LeShawn, and Pete do, but they may not see nature the way I do. I respect the way the city's energy inspires them. And now I use that energy wherever I am to create my own art.

Make Connections

How did this student's trip to New York City change his perspective on art?
ESSENTIAL QUESTION

What kinds of experiences gave the characters you have read about a new perspective on their lives? **TEXT TO TEXT**

29

THE MOSTLY TRUE ADVENTURES of HOMER P. FIGG

BY RODMAN PHILBRICK

ILLUSTRATED BY MARK PENNINGTON

Essential Question

Why do people form alliances?

Read what happens when a 12-year-old boy, searching for his brother, plummets into one of the biggest conflicts in American history.

Go Digital!

32

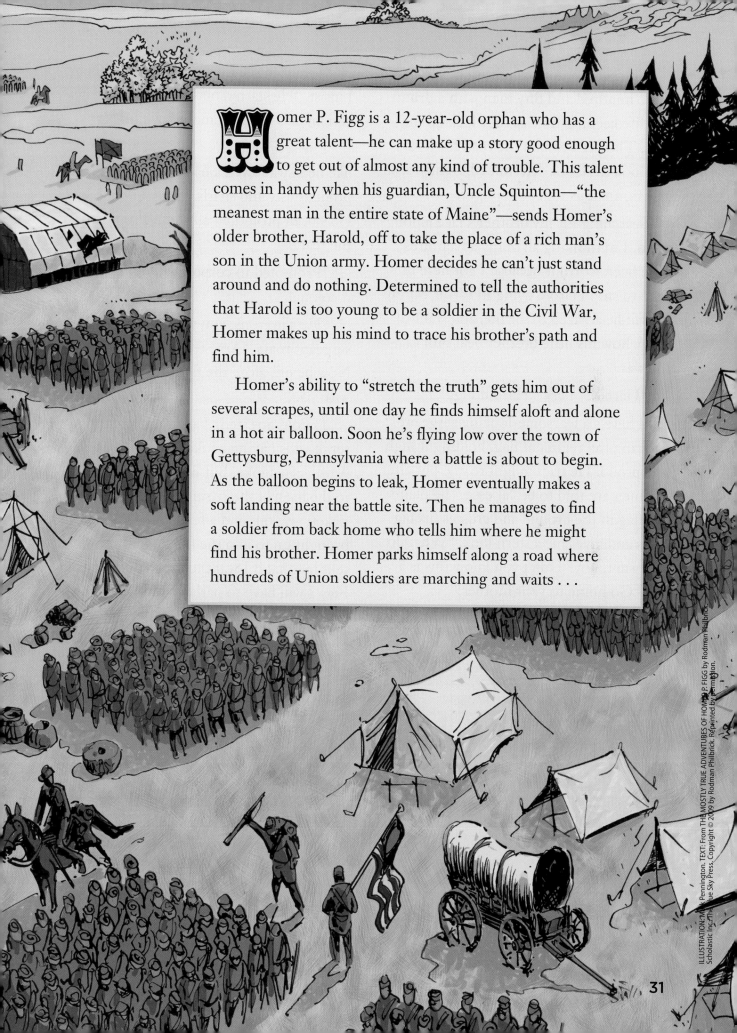

omer P. Figg is a 12-year-old orphan who has a great talent—he can make up a story good enough to get out of almost any kind of trouble. This talent comes in handy when his guardian, Uncle Squinton—"the meanest man in the entire state of Maine"—sends Homer's older brother, Harold, off to take the place of a rich man's son in the Union army. Homer decides he can't just stand around and do nothing. Determined to tell the authorities that Harold is too young to be a soldier in the Civil War, Homer makes up his mind to trace his brother's path and find him.

Homer's ability to "stretch the truth" gets him out of several scrapes, until one day he finds himself aloft and alone in a hot air balloon. Soon he's flying low over the town of Gettysburg, Pennsylvania where a battle is about to begin. As the balloon begins to leak, Homer eventually makes a soft landing near the battle site. Then he manages to find a soldier from back home who tells him where he might find his brother. Homer parks himself along a road where hundreds of Union soldiers are marching and waits . . .

They come along at a brisk march, three hundred and fifty men with a drum and fife keeping time as they kick up the dust. They've been on the road for hours and look tired but determined. Some raise cheers, anxious to join the fight.

Searching for my brother's face among them, I'm thinking all of my adventures have been worth it because I got here in time to stop Harold dying in battle. Surely he will be amazed to see me, and want to know how his little brother beat him to the war.

"Harold!" I cry. "Harold Figg!"

There's a fearsome-looking sergeant carrying the regiment flag, holding it high and proud. He tries to ignore me, but after the men are told to be "at ease," he plants the flag in the ground and crosses his big arms and gives me a stern look. "What do you want, boy? Don't you know this is a war? Go home to your mother!"

"I want to see my brother, Harold Figg!" I insist. "He started out as a private but it's certain he's been promoted by now."

The sergeant gets a look on his face like he's swallowed a bad egg. He spits prodigiously and snarls. "Harold Figg, bah! He's been promoted all right. Promoted to the rear!"

"Promoted to corporal? Or is it colonel?"

"He's in irons, you young fool!" the sergeant roars. "Arrested and under guard! Now be off, afore the fighting starts! Away with you!"

Harold arrested? I assume the burly sergeant is having a joke at my expense. A bad, cruel joke. But when I go around to the back of the regiment, where some rickety wagons and a few horses have been brought up to join the fight, another soldier tells me that if I want to see Private Harold Figg I will have to parlay with the guards.

In one of the wagons, under guard of three armed soldiers, are five or six prisoners, each with a large, crude M chalked upon his blue uniform.

"*M* is for mutineer," a guard tells me, showing me his piece of chalk. "That's my idea. The *M* will be something to aim at if they try running away, ha-ha."

The guard's laughter is cruel, as if he thinks he's made a funny joke and doesn't care who it hurts.

One of the prisoners, a scurvy-looking fellow with a black eye, is my brother, Harold. When I call his name he covers his face and weeps.

All my life, I never knew Harold to be scared or ashamed, and seeing him this

way is like stepping backward off a cliff. Or discovering the world has gone inside out and upside down. I sit next to where he crouches in the wagon and try not to look at his black eye, or notice the sickly unwashed smell of him.

"Homer, what are you doing here?" he asks, his voice catching.

"Thought I'd take a stroll behind the barn and this is where I ended up." I give him a playful nudge. "I come looking for you silly! To tell you it was nothing but a trick, making you enlist in the army. Squint sold you for a substitute and kept the money. They fooled you into enlisting. It ain't legal."

Harold hangs his head. His voice is so small I have to lean in close. "Don't matter now, Homer. I went and done it and will be court-martialed."

"What happened?" I ask. "Did you run from the bullets? Did you run from the cannon? From men with bayonets?"

My brother shakes his head. Somewhere in all his sorrow there comes a slight chuckle. "Disobeyed my squad sergeant.

I swear he's worse than Squint."

"Is that what happened to your eye?"

He nods. "At first I liked it, being in the regiment. The fine uniform and the drilling. Shooting rifles. Three good meals a day. Sleeping in tents. I even liked the marching, and folks cheering as we went by. But I never did like the sergeant telling me what to do without so much as a 'please' or 'thank you,' and one day I told him so. When he objected I slung him down in the mud, just like I did to Squint. It got worse from there," he adds. "He took it upon himself to make my life a misery. Said I was swamp trash not fit to serve."

"So you ran away?"

"Didn't get far, as you can see."

"What will happen?"

"It doesn't matter, little brother. I am disgraced. You must leave here and forget you ever knew me."

"Don't be stupid. That sergeant has knocked the sense right out of you."

"I mean it, Homer. You need to get away from here! Whatever happened yesterday, whatever you might have seen, it's nothing to what will happen today and tomorrow, and every day until one side or the other is defeated."

"Couldn't be worse than yesterday," I tell him.

"Oh yes, it could! The Union has ninety thousand men and will use them all. The rebels a similar number. Can't you hear the artillery pounding away? It has started already."

"It ain't fair," I say.

"Fair doesn't signify. I swore an oath and disobeyed. I must be punished."

"Do they hang mutineers?"

"Sometimes. Mostly not. Likely they'll send me to prison."

Up to now I've been trying to act cheerful, pretending things ain't so bad. But the prospect of Harold being sent off to prison in disgrace makes me gloomy and quiet. Probably they won't let me go off to prison with him. I'll have to visit, and **smuggle** in a saw so he can make his escape. Then we'll run away, as far as we can get. As far as the Western Territories, maybe, where land is free and nobody cares what happened in the war. We'll grow so much corn that we'll get fat as ticks, and build us a fine house with a fireplace and windows and a proper privy. We'll fish in mountain streams for trout as big as dogs, and someday we'll sit in rockers on the porch and **reminisce** about the silly old days when the stupid rotten sergeant blacked his eye, and how we made our great escape. Maybe on horseback, or in a silk balloon, I ain't decided yet.

"It will be all right," I tell him. "Our Dear Mother always said things work out for the best."

Harold gives me a sorrowful look. "You were barely four years old when Mother passed. How can you know what she said, or what she believed?"

"I know because you told me."

He nods to himself, as if he already knew what I would say. "I am sorry, Homer. I have to let you down."

"Don't be silly. Squint sold you into the army. It ain't your fault."

"You don't understand," he says, sounding mournful. "I let it happen. I knew it was a sham, and could have said so before I joined the regiment. But I wanted to be shut of the farm, and our hard life. I wanted to breathe air that had never been dirtied by Squinton Leach."

"Oh," I say.

"There's worse." He hesitates, then takes a deep breath and continues. "For once in my life I wanted not to have to take care of you. Not to be your brother and your mother and your father all rolled into one. I wanted out, Homer. I saw my chance and took it."

Poor Harold looks so miserable I can't hardly stand it. Besides, the things he's telling me don't exactly come as a big surprise. I sort of knew it all along, that he wanted to get away from Squint, and not to always be having to look after his little brother.

I say, "It don't matter because you don't have to take care of me no more. It's my turn to take care of you."

Harold studies me and shakes his head and smiles a little. "How'd you get here, really? A boy your age that never left the farm?"

I'm about to tell him the story of my true adventures, and all the fun and sorrows I had along the way, when an officer starts shouting out commands.

"Men of the Twentieth Maine, move out! We are shifting to the left! Keep formation! Keep formation!"

The guards kick me out of the prisoner wagon, but chase me no farther than a few yards. It is easy enough to follow as the regiment picks up and moves, along with the rest of the brigade.

There are thousands of soldiers below the crest of the hill, awaiting orders. Men from Maine and New York, Pennsylvania and Vermont, Massachusetts and Connecticut, Michigan and Illinois, and just about everywhere in the Northern states. The sound of rifle and artillery fire coming from the other side of the ridge is more or less continuous, and the men seem eager to join the fight.

This is the day, they tell one another. Today we stand our ground. Today we turn the tables on Robert E. Lee. Today we win the war.

I feel like tugging on sleeves and saying don't be in such a hurry, the bullets are faster than you. But I keep my mouth shut and my eyes on the prisoner wagon, trying to scheme up a plan to break Harold out of his **confinement**.

A little while later I see the wounded being carried back from the top of the hill, and it comes to me that maybe being a prisoner and mutineer ain't such a bad thing to be. Nobody's shooting at them. Could be worse.

Then worse himself comes charging up on a big gray horse. Colonel Joshua Lawrence Chamberlain, the young commander of the 20th Maine, all fitted out with his sword and pistols and his fancy big mustache, and his eyes glowing.

"Men of the Twentieth, look to me! See that small hill?" He points with his sword. "We must hold that with our lives! It guards the left of the Union Army and cannot be allowed to fall into rebel hands! Every man! Every man on the double! Run for the hill and take position! Follow the flag! Quickly now!"

He makes to wheel away and then thinks better of it. Instead he sidles up to the prisoners and shows them the flat of his sword, tapping it against his boot. "Gentlemen! Those willing to fight will get a good word from me. Obey your orders and I'll do my best to get the charges dropped."

To my dismay, the prisoners stand as one, including my brother, Harold Figg, begging to be allowed to fight.

The guards release them, and they dust away the *M* so cruelly chalked upon their uniforms. The prisoners and guards grab rifles and cartridge boxes and run for the hill, following the flag of the 20th Maine.

All is confusion, but I manage to get to Harold just as he picks up a rifle.

"Now's our chance!" I say. "There's no one to stop us! We can run for it! We'll be miles away before they notice!"

Harold looks at me like I got two heads. "I gave my word," he says.

"Words won't stop the bullets!" I say as he wrenches himself loose from my grasp. "Words won't keep the shells from exploding! Words won't stop you getting killed and leaving me alone in this world!"

He shoves me to the ground.

"Stay there!" he orders me. "Crawl under the wagon and keep yourself safe. I will see you after the battle, Homer, after the fight is done."

Then he's running up the hill, a rifle in one hand and a cartridge pouch in the other.

"Harold, stop!"

He won't stop. He keeps on going, running toward the sound of gunfire.

What choice do I have? I haven't come all this way for nothing. So I follow my brother up the hill, into the fight, into the Battle of Gettysburg.

The top of the little hill is strewn with rocks and boulders and a few **spindly** trees. The men from the 20th Maine spread out along the ridge, quickly finding shelter among the rocks. From here they may fire down upon the enemy and still be afforded some small protection.

STOP AND CHECK

Visualize As the battle rages, what details does the author include that help you realize why Homer and Harold's situation is so dangerous? Use Visualize as a strategy to help you as you read.

They don't have long to wait. Ten minutes after occupying the hill a full regiment of Alabama men attack from below, waving their regimental flag.

Suddenly gray uniforms swarm among the rocks and into the open, surging upward with that terrible cry that is called a rebel yell. The *ki-yi-yip-yip* of the rebel yell being partways an owl-like screech and partways a high-pitched yelp that makes your skin crawl if you happen to be on the receiving end.

The bullets start flying before I can locate Harold or find a place to hide. Bullets spitting off rocks and scudding up the dirt and making little smacking noises as they hit skinny trees that are too small to hide behind.

Everywhere I turn there are more bullets striking all around, like hornets swarming, *snick-snick-snick*.

Finally Harold scoots out from behind his rock and drags me to safety. "What are you doing, you little fool? Do you want to be killed, is that it?" he asks, panting.

"I want to go home."

Harold grunts, then takes aim between the rocks and fires his Springfield rifle. His leather cartridge pouch lies open at his side and he swings the rifle around, tears the paper cartridge in his teeth, rams it down the muzzle, swings the rifle back around, inserts the primer cap, and cocks the hammer—all as quick as you can count.

Then he takes careful aim and fires and does it all over again.

There are forty cartridges in his leather pouch, which means when he fires thirty-seven more times he'll be out of ammunition. Figure twenty minutes or less, if he keeps up to speed.

"Where are you going?" he cries.

"To get more ammunition!"

And that's what I do, scampering down the back slope of the hill, out of the line of fire. I follow the others and locate the powder wagons, hoisting a wooden ammunition box that looks like a little casket and dragging it up to where Harold is still loading and firing his rifle, steady as a clock, a bullet fired every count of twenty.

After seeing that Harold is well supplied, I make myself useful hauling ammunition to some of the others, who are strung out all the way to the southern end of the little hill, and under vicious fire from the troops below.

Time and again the Alabama men scream out their wild rebel yell and swarm up the hill, only to be turned back at the last moment, punished by the men of the 20th Maine, who hold their ground, hunkered down among the rocks like smoking barnacles, refusing to let go.

For an hour or more the bullets fly. Men are wounded, men scream, men die, but still the bullets fly.

Colonel Chamberlain is everywhere.

He strides along the ridge, in direct line of the rebel sharpshooters firing from below, ordering where his men should be placed and how they might best repel the next desperate charge of the troops from Alabama.

Bullets crease the air around him, close enough to part his hair, but he never flinches from his purpose.

Later I heard he was a college professor who knew nothing of war excepting what he'd read in books, but that fateful day upon the little hill he seems to be Napoleon himself, never in doubt as to what must happen next. He orders where the men should move, when the line should be extended, and when the wounded should be dragged back to safety and carried by stretcher away from the withering fire.

The bodies of the fallen have to be left where they fall, to be **retrieved** when the battle concludes, if it ever does.

Seeing me scurrying along with a load of ammunition, Colonel Chamberlain pauses in his purposeful stride and says, "You there, boy! Do you know the risk you take?"

"Yes, sir!"

"Very good! Carry on!" he commands. "And keep your head down!"

Then his attention is drawn elsewhere as one of his officers falls, wounded in the neck, and he must see to a replacement.

In the first few minutes of the assault the rebels almost gain the top of the hill, where they are met with pistol shot and sword. A few soldiers fight hand to hand, rolling among the rocks, but most of the casualties are **inflicted** at a distance of thirty yards or so.

All to gain advantage on a rocky little spur of a hill that happens to stand at the far end of the line, where the Confederates hope to sweep around and crush the Union Army from both sides. A small hill shrouded in gray gun smoke and running with the blood of the wounded and the dead.

The steady hail of lead chops little bits out of the trees, like they are being attacked by small, invisible axes.

I keep down, like Harold and the colonel suggested, and find myself a good boulder to hide behind.

All the ammunition has been taken from the wagons and distributed. It can't last forever, the way the men are using it up, each taking two or three shots a minute, but for now the gunfire spits and pops like a full load of popcorn in a hot pan of grease.

There comes a lull when only a few guns are popping off and I hear Harold call out for more ammunition.

"All gone!" an officer shouts back. "Find cartridges where you can!"

Already they are borrowing cartridge cases from the many who have fallen. The dead men don't object.

In my hiding place, curled up small, I'm praying the cartridges will run out soon, so we can fall back.

It comes to this: I care not if the rebels take the hill. There are a million hills in Pennsylvania, let them have this one if they want it so bad!

A little distance away, half obscured by the clouds of gun smoke, the colonel confers with his officers. From what I can see of their faces the news must be very grim indeed.

Good, I'm thinking, sound your retreat! An army can't fight without bullets, can it? We are outnumbered, outgunned, and outfought. The only sensible thing to do is run for it.

Then, clear as a bell that tolls through the fog, comes his order.

"Fix bayonets!" he roars.

All down the line soldiers eagerly slip bayonets onto the muzzles of their empty rifles and ready themselves for what happens next.

Ahead of me, crouching behind his rock, my brother, Harold, shakes his head at me.

"Homer, get back!" he shouts above the din. "Go home! Save yourself!"

Then Colonel Chamberlain's voice booms out, louder than the crack of artillery.

"Charge!" he commands, lifting high his sword.

Harold leaps to his feet and follows him down the hill, into the guns of the enemy.

To this day I cannot say what made me follow my brother down that hill. It was not ignorance, because I had seen what war does, and hated it. It was not courage, because fear of dying made me scream out loud.

All I know is, there I was, running after Harold and begging him to take shelter. And as I come over the top of the hill the air itself is hot enough to catch afire from the heat of flying lead.

STOP AND CHECK

Visualize Visualize how the author describes the fight to gain possession of the hill. How does he reveal the intensity of the battle?

Go home!
Save
yourself!

CHARGE

Fast as I'm running over that rough ground, I can't seem to catch up to Harold. Soldiers on either side of him fall like rag dolls but he keeps on going.

Just ahead of him is the burly sergeant with the regimental flag, the one who cussed Harold and said he was swamp trash. The sergeant stumbles, clutching at his stomach, and the flag starts to fall.

Without breaking stride Harold drops his empty rifle and seizes the flag from the wounded sergeant.

"Harold, no!"

Now all rebel eyes—and rebel guns—will be upon him. My brother holds up the flag as he advances, leaning into the lead-filled air as if he is leaning into warm summer rain.

"Harold, get down!" I scream. "Get down or be killed!"

Holes appear like stars in the billowing flag, but still he will not take shelter.

I search for a rock to throw at him, to bring him to his senses, but the first thing my groping hand encounters is the fallen sergeant who passed the flag to Harold. He lies on his side, grinning at his pain, hands clawing at his wounded stomach. I want to ask him why he blacked my brother's eye, and if he's sorry now, but it don't seem right to ask.

Instead I lift the pistol from his holster and take aim, intending to fire at Harold's feet to get his attention.

I pull the trigger.

The bullet strikes the ground. Harold falls.

At first I think he has finally been struck by rebel lead and then I see what has happened. My own shot has splintered away

a chunk of rock that has stuck itself in his leg like a dart in a board.

As Harold falls, he tries to keep the flag upright.

Without thinking I drop the sergeant's pistol and somehow the flag ends up in my hands and my brother lying at my feet.

By rights I should toss aside the flag and drop to the ground and try to get under the flying lead, but something in me won't let go. Now that the flag is in my hands it don't seem right to let it fall on bloody ground.

A dumb idea. Dumb enough to get me killed, but there it is.

The strangest thing is happening. All around me, all down the hillside, rebel soldiers are throwing down their rifles and surrendering.

STOP AND CHECK

Visualize Why are Homer and Harold both heroes as the battle ends? Visualize the events in the story to help you respond.

Beneath me Harold is groaning and trying to pry loose the sliver of stone imbedded in his leg. I am sorry he is hurt but glad that he is alive.

Then I notice that not all the Alabama soldiers have surrendered. I notice because one of them has risen from the ground with his sword in both hands. His eyes moving from the flag to me, as if deciding what to strike first, the hated Yankee flag or the boy holding it.

He hesitates.

At that moment exactly, Colonel Joshua Lawrence Chamberlain appears and aims his pistol at the swordsman's head with a steady hand.

"Surrender or die," he suggests.

The man drops the sword and falls to his knees.

"I'll take the flag," the colonel says. "See to your brother."

That day the battle ends for us, but not for others.

45

ABOUT THE AUTHOR AND ILLUSTRATOR

RODMAN PHILBRICK

grew up in a small town on the New England coast. He began writing short stories when he was in the sixth grade, and finished his first novel when he was only 16 years old. Until Rodman could make a living writing full time, he worked as a boat builder and longshoreman, loading cargo onto ships.

The Mostly True Adventures of Homer P. Figg won Rodman many awards, including a Newbery Honor medal. Like Homer, Rodman trusts in the power of imagination: "I believe that we have the ability to change our lives using our imaginations," he says. "Imagination is a muscle—the more you use it, the stronger it gets."

MARK PENNINGTON

has been working in the commercial art field for over twenty years. He graduated from the Kubert School, formerly the Joe Kubert School of Cartoon and Graphic Art, in Dover, New Jersey, in 1985. He then went on to work as a toy designer. In 1988, Mark got his first assignment as an illustrator and has been hard at work ever since.

When he's not working, Mark likes to spend time helping his wife Cathy and playing with their three children. In his free time he gets away from the drawing board and out into the sunshine where he enjoys playing golf and tennis.

AUTHOR'S PURPOSE

In this selection, the author writes about a boy's extraordinary adventure in a battle that took place long ago. How does his word choice help you to visualize both the event and the time period?

RESPOND TO READING

SUMMARIZE

Use what you learned about character, setting, the story problem, and the events that lead to a solution in *The Mostly True Adventures of Homer P. Figg* to summarize the important events in the story. Information from your Character, Setting, Plot Chart may help you.

Character
Setting
Problem
Events
Solution

TEXT EVIDENCE

1. What text features help you know that *The Mostly True Adventures of Homer P. Figg* is historical fiction? **GENRE**

2. What effect does the setting of this story have on the sequence of events in the plot? **SEQUENCE**

3. What is the meaning of the word *repel* in the first paragraph on page 41? Use context clues to help you figure out the meaning. **PARAGRAPH CLUES**

4. Write about the specific event in the story that you feel is the turning point in the plot. Use text evidence to support your choice. **WRITE ABOUT READING**

 Make Connections

Talk about how the alliance between Homer and his brother helped both of them survive the Battle of Gettysburg. **ESSENTIAL QUESTION**

Do you feel that forming an alliance can make a difference in people's lives? Explain why or why not. **TEXT TO WORLD**

Compare Texts
Read how bullying can
create conflicting feelings
in one of its victims.

ENOUGH!

I finish, glance at the clock.
There are fifteen minutes left.
Should I turn in my test? No.
Because I can hear Ernesto already. Ernesto and his friends.
The snide laughter. The smirks. **Adversity** in all its forms.
Hey Brainiac! Finished already?
Too bad the Olympics don't have an event for geeks!
The bell finally rings. We turn in our papers.
Do I bolt out the door to avoid a cruel jeer?
Stay glued to my seat admitting my fear?
How much longer do I have to deal
   with this?

Ernesto and his easy banter,
coasting through school without a care in the world.
Good at most sports, he is self-assured,
winning loyalty from everyone.
So easy to loathe him but I have to admit
I envy him too.
How can you want to be liked by somebody you don't like?
A question I ask myself.
A question I cannot answer.
And so another day ends.

Early morning. Ms. Simmons smiles and her eyes beam.

I want to introduce Sean, who is joining our class today.

Sean nods politely, but looks at no one.

He clings to his notebook,

a life preserver keeping him afloat.

The school bell rings for lunch.

Sitting by myself, pretending to read, I suddenly see Sean.

His tray is piled high with food.

The freshly waxed floor is a sheet of glass.

Sean slips, swerves, stumbles. Food is everywhere.

Hey Sean! Auditions for Waltzing with a Star *are next door!*

It is Ernesto. Everyone laughs. Sean slinks away.

I'm oddly grateful. Why?

Because Ernesto has finally inflicted his teasing on someone else?

On my way out my eyes meet Ernesto's eyes.

Suddenly, arms flailing, I make goofy faces, imitating Sean's fall.

Ernesto points at me. *Good one Jonas!* he says.

My mind is in a whirl.

I feel bad about what I did.

But then I say to myself, what does it matter?

Sean did not see me.

And I also feel as if a large burden has been lifted off of me.

But why do I need to tear someone down to feel worthwhile?

The next morning is warm and sunny. A hint of spring.

I arrive at school early and sit outside.

The first students arrive.

And then I see Sean. I shout out
    his name and smile.

We shake hands.
    An **alliance** is formed.

Then there is a loud noise behind us.

Hey Sean! It's Ernesto. A voice laced
    with disdain.

Hey Ernesto! I shout back. ***Enough!***

Make Connections

Why does Jonas form an alliance with Sean? **ESSENTIAL QUESTION**

Explain what you have learned about alliances, why people make them, and how they can be of benefit to the people involved. **TEXT TO TEXT**

ILLUSTRATIONS: Christian Slade

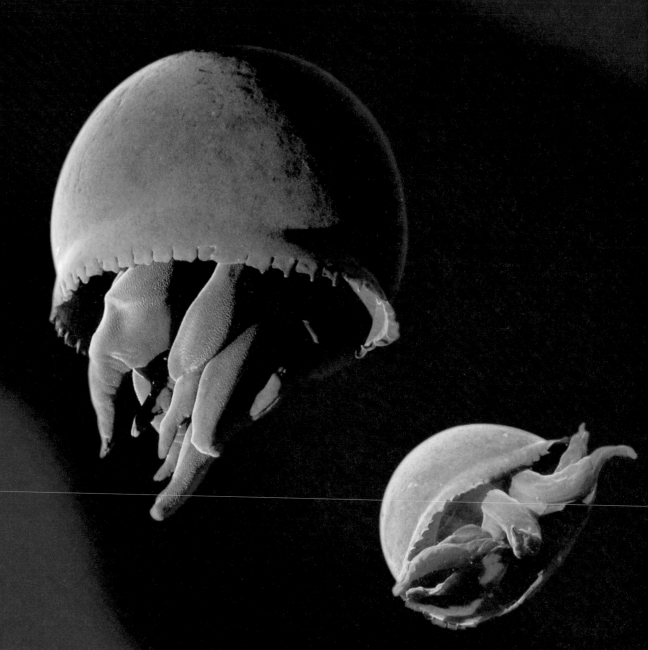

Essential Question

How do life forms vary in different environments?

Read how animals in the world's oceans vary, all the way down to the deepest, darkest depths.

 Go Digital!

50

Journey into the Deep

By Rebecca L. Johnson

Like a spaceship from a distant galaxy, the massive jellyfish hovers in the frigid water. Its meaty dome-shaped bell is as wide as a doorway and the color of a bad bruise. Beneath the bell, fleshy arms twist and sway. The bell contracts, and the jellyfish glides backward. It relaxes, then contracts again. Contract, glide, relax. Contract, glide, relax. With a steady rhythm, the jellyfish pulses through the utter darkness of the deep sea.

Until a few years ago, no one even knew that this species, or kind, of jellyfish existed. The scientists from California's Monterey Bay Aquarium Research Institute who discovered it nicknamed it Big Red. Big Red jellyfish have probably been living in the deep ocean for hundreds of thousands of years. So why hadn't anyone seen one before?

The answer is that even in the twenty-first century, the ocean remains largely unexplored. What we call the Atlantic, Pacific, Indian, Southern, and Arctic oceans are all connected. Together, they form one enormous world ocean that covers about 70 percent of Earth's surface. On average, the ocean is 13,123 feet, or 2.5 miles (4,000 meters) deep. We know less about this huge watery kingdom than we do about many planets in our solar system.

In 2000 scientists from around the world set out on a ten-year quest to learn more about the ocean and everything that lives in it. They called their quest the Census of Marine Life. Several thousand researchers from dozens of countries began the largest ocean exploration in history.

The scientists weren't just looking for new species. They wanted to get a better picture of ocean biodiversity. To do that, they needed to learn more about familiar species as well as any new ones they might find. They also needed to find out which species are common and which ones are rare. Finally, the scientists hoped to discover more about how different species are distributed in the ocean, from the surface to the seafloor and from pole to pole.

How did Census scientists explore something as immense as the ocean? They worked in teams. Different teams

During the Census, scientists got a closer look at many unusual creatures, like the barreleye. This unique fish has a transparent head and huge eyes that can roll in many directions.

studied different parts of the ocean environment. Some teams focused on life in the shallow regions. Many others headed into deeper water.

Studying the ocean can be almost as challenging as exploring outer space. You need ships and lots of special equipment. The hours are long, and the work is hard. But you get a chance to be a true explorer. And you never know what you might find.

In these pages, you'll have the chance to explore the ocean alongside teams of scientists working around the globe. You'll visit parts of the ocean few people have ever seen. You'll travel from the ocean's sunlit surface to its deepest, darkest depths. Best of all, you'll get a firsthand look at amazing creatures Census scientists discovered in their quest.

Scientific Classification

Scientists classify, or group, living things based on their similarities. The smallest scientific category is the species. Living things that belong to the same species are very much alike. They can mate and produce offspring. Similar species are grouped together into a large category called a genus. Together, a living thing's genus name and species name make up its scientific name.

Similar genera (more than one genus) make up a family. Families are grouped to form a class. Several classes make up a phylum, and several phyla together make up a very large, broad category called a kingdom. The Animal Kingdom, for example, includes all the different kinds of animals on Earth.

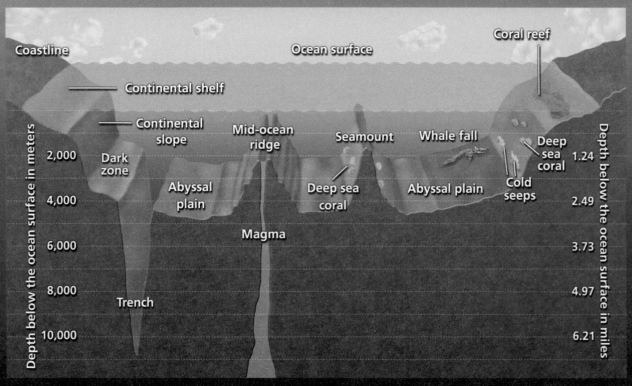

Deep Slopes

Propped up on one elbow, you're lying on your side. Your neck is twisted. Your forehead is pressed hard against the glass. Your muscles are cramping, and you're getting cold. But none of that matters. As amazing as it is to explore the ocean with an ROV (remotely operated underwater vehicle), this is better. This is the real thing.

Scrunched inside a submersible that has just passed 1,476 feet (450 meters), you're descending though a dark world few people have seen. You stare out the small porthole, hardly daring to blink. Zooplankton drift and dart past the glass every few seconds. Many are bioluminescent.

Somewhere below is your destination. You're with a team of Census scientists who are studying a site on the continental slope of North America that stretches south into the Gulf of Mexico. Continental slopes are the **submerged** edges of continents. Some slant sharply down, forming steep cliffs. Others angle more gradually to the sea bottom.

Your headset crackles. From the forward **compartment**, the pilot announces that there's coral dead ahead. Where? You can't see anything but black water. Then the submersible turns so your porthole faces the slope.

A deep-sea coral reef, as it looks from a submersible's front compartment.

This diagram tells you where you are in the ocean. The top shows you how deep you are. The globe shows where you are in the world.

The sub's bright lights illuminate the scene. Outside is a pink coral as big as a tree. It's covered with electric blue worms.

The sub moves slowly along the slope, past a garden of deep-sea corals. They have formed a huge reef here, like their shallow-water cousins do near the ocean's surface. Yellow, pink, orange, red – the colors of the corals are amazing. Of course, if the pilot turned off the sub's lights, you wouldn't see anything at all. These corals grow in total darkness, in water that's just a few degrees above freezing.

How fast do deep-sea corals grow? The scientist sitting up with the pilot tells you that most species grow only 0.04 inches (1 millimeter) a year. Your fingernails grow that much in less than two weeks. Scientists have analyzed samples of deep-sea corals to estimate their age. Some are hundreds, even thousands, of years old. That makes these beautiful animals among the oldest living things on Earth.

Water Pressure

It's not just cold and dark in the deep sea. The water pressure is also enormous. Water pressure is the force of water pressing in from all sides. The pressure increases the deeper you go.

At 13,123 feet (4,000 meters) —the ocean's average depth —it's 5,846 psi (411 kilograms per square centimeter). If you were subjected to that kind of pressure, it would be like having a large pickup truck parked on every square inch of your skin.

Most animals in the deep sea have hard or rubbery bodies with no air spaces. Even under great pressure, they can't be crushed. When scientists bring these deep-sea creatures to the surface, the change in the pressure doesn't affect them very much.

STOP AND CHECK

Reread How have animals that live in the deep slope ocean environment adapted in order to thrive there? Reread to check your understanding.

The sub moves slowly toward a clump of what the scientist says is bamboo coral. It has slender branches that divide again and again.

As the sub gets closer, the pilot turns out most of its lights. The sub has a mechanical arm that can collect things underwater. The pilot uses it to reach out and touch the coral. A soft blue glow flickers up and down its delicate branches. This bamboo coral is bioluminescent.

Next, you cruise over a massive patch of branching coral that's nearly as white as snow. The scientific name of this coral is *Lophelia pertusa*. It may be the most common reef-building deep-ocean coral in the world – or at least on the deep reefs that scientists have explored so far.

Image courtesy of Lophelia II 2009: Deepwater Coral Expedition: Reefs - Rigs - and Wrecks.

In this close-up of **Lophelia** *pertusa, you can see the tiny, fleshy tentacles of the coral animals sticking out from the branches. They use these tentacles to snag bits of food from the water.*

Deep-sea coral reefs are home to many other kinds of living things. Almost every coral you see has at least one animal perching on it. Brittle stars and basket stars wind their long arms around and around coral branches. Long-legged squat lobsters and orange-headed shrimp hold on with pointed claws.

The sub's cameras flash, recording different scenes. The pilot uses the mechanical arm to collect small samples of several different corals and put them into containers mounted on the front of the sub. Then you're leaving, heading farther down the slope. The coral garden fades to black as the darkness **engulfs** it.

Chemosynthesis

Plants, algae, and some microorganisms use energy from sunlight to turn water and the gas carbon dioxide into sugars that they use for food. This process is called photosynthesis. Living things that carry out photosynthesis form the first link in most of the food chains on Earth. Much of what you eat, for example, either comes from plants or something that eats plants.

In the deep ocean, where sunlight cannot reach, some food chains start with living things that carry out chemosynthesis. These organisms – mostly bacteria – use chemicals such as methane as an energy source for making their own food. Some animals living around cold seeps survive by keeping chemosynthetic bacteria in their bodies and sharing the food the bacteria make. Others live by eating the bacteria directly.

A tiny species of squat lobster—new to science—sports rainbow colors. Census scientists found it on an Australian coral reef.

Tube worms (Lamellibrachia luymesi) *at a cold seep extend their feathery tops into the dark water. The rest of a tube worm's body is protected by a tough, flexible tube that's made of a substance similar to your fingernails. Tube worms like these may live to be as much as two hundred years old.*

Farther down the continental slope, bubbles start fizzing past the porthole. For one terrifying moment, you're sure the submersible is leaking air. The scientist calmly explains that you've arrived at a cold seep, a place where gases are bubbling up from the seabed. The gases are methane and hydrogen sulfide. If you could smell the water outside the submersible, it would stink like rotten eggs.

Microscopic bacteria use these stinky gases as a source of energy in a food-making process called chemosynthesis. Billions of chemosynthetic bacteria live around cold seeps. What look like patches of white stuff on the seafloor are actually dense clusters of these bacteria.

From the porthole, you spot what looks like a bush growing up from the seafloor. But as the sub gets closer, it's obvious that this is no shrub. It's a cluster of spindly, red-topped tube worms.

The worms have no mouth or stomach. Tucked inside their long bodies are special organs packed with bacteria. The worms take in chemicals from the water and the seafloor that the bacteria need for chemosynthesis. The bacteria use them to make food for themselves and their worm hosts.

Fist-sized mussels huddle in groups near the tube worms. Chemosynthetic bacteria live inside their bodies too.

Several minutes later, and deeper still, the submersible glides over what looks like a small, dark lake. Thousands of mussels surround it, crowding right up to the edge. These are similar to the bacteria-hosting mussels you saw at the cold seep. The fact that the mussels are here is a sign that the area around the lake is rich in methane.

The pilot says the lake itself is a brine pool. The dark water is four or five times saltier than ocean water. Being so salty, it's much denser and heavier than seawater. The salty water has settled into a low spot here on the seabed.

The water in the brine pool is too salty for the mussels. That's why they live around but not in it.

At depths below about 1,970 feet (600 meters), the water pressure is so great that methane gas freezes as it comes out of the seabed, forming methane ice. Here the orange ice is covered with dozens of little hollowed-out spots. Nestled in each one is a slithery pink worm. The worms have a row of bristles on each side of their bodies. The bristles are moving, but the ice worms are not. They look as if they're all running in place.

Methane ice worms (Hesiocaeca methanicola), *each about 1 to 2 inches (2.5 to 5 centimeters) long, sit in the depressions they've carved out for themselves in a solid chunk of orange methane ice.*

STOP AND CHECK

Reread Why is methane such an important resource in this part of the ocean? Reread the text on pages 58–59 for clues.

Countless mussels live around the edge of a brine pool.

Ian R. MacDonald

Ridges and Vents

First, the ship sailed east. Then it sailed west. Now it's heading east again. You ask one of the scientists on this expedition to the Southeastern Pacific Ocean what's going on. He explains that the ship is towing an instrument back and forth above the ocean floor. It's searching for signs of hydrothermal vents.

A hydrothermal vent is a place in the ocean floor where hot, chemical-rich water comes blasting out. The towed instrument is searching for traces of this vent water. Judging by the excited shouts that suddenly fill the air, it's just found some.

Several hours later, crew members ready the submersible for a dive. Your destination is a spot 7,500 feet (2,286 meters) below, on a part of the mid-ocean ridge called the East Pacific Rise. As the sub descends, a scientist explains that most hydrothermal vents are found along mid-ocean ridges. These are chains of undersea mountains on the ocean floor. They all connect to form the longest mountain range on Earth. Like stitching on a baseball, the mid-ocean ridge system winds for 40,400 miles (65,000 kilometers) around the planet.

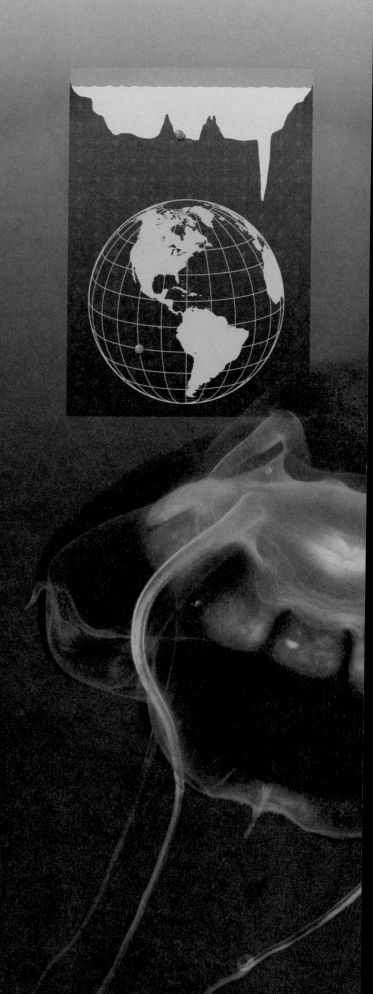

STOP AND CHECK

Visualize What details does the author provide to help you visualize the chains of mountains on the ocean floor?

Your first glimpse of the mid-ocean ridge is a surprise. There's no soft mud here. The submersible's lights pick out masses of barren volcanic rock. These rocks are new pieces of Earth's crust. They formed when magma, or melted rock, surged up through a crack in the ocean floor and cooled in the near-freezing water.

Slowly the submersible clears a jagged ridge. On the other side, jets of what looks like black smoke stream up from chimney-like vents among the rocks.

Moving Plates

Earth's crust is made up of about two dozen gigantic rocky plates that fit together like pieces of a jigsaw puzzle. Mid-ocean ridges mark the places where these massive plates are slowly moving apart. Magma from beneath the crust comes up at these spreading plate boundaries. It cools to form a new crust. In some areas, this new crust is riddled with hydrothermal vents, underwater geysers of dark, chemical-laden seawater that's as hot as 750°F (400°C)!

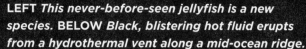
LEFT *This never-before-seen jellyfish is a new species.* BELOW *Black, blistering hot fluid erupts from a hydrothermal vent along a mid-ocean ridge.*

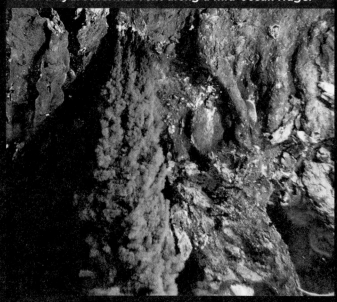

"MY FIRST DIVE TO A VENT SITE WAS IN THE FRENCH SUBMERSIBLE *NAUTILE,* ON THE MID-ATLANTIC RIDGE. TRAVELING DOWN THROUGH THE DARK WATER, I STARED AND STARED OUT THE TINY PORTHOLE. AND THEN SUDDENLY, THE BLACK SMOKERS WERE IN FRONT OF US."
– Eva Ramirez-Llodra, Institut de Ciències del Mar, Spain

just as it does at cold seeps. These giant tube worms (Riftia pachyptila) *take up chemicals from the water through their fluffy, plumed tops. Chemosynthetic bacteria inside the worms turn the chemicals into food.*

Mounds of mussels cluster so thickly at some hydrothermal vents that they completely obscure the ocean bottom.

Around the vents, giant tube worms—as tall as a person—grow in great clumps. The scientist wants to get a closer look at these strange animals. The pilot carefully guides the sub through a maze of black smokers. Passing directly over one would be a serious mistake. The dark fluid is hot enough to melt parts of the submersible. Outside, the water pressure is enormous. If the sub cracked, you'd be crushed in an instant.

After a few minutes of careful **maneuvering**, the sub is **flanked** by tube worms on both sides. Their feathery plumes sway just outside the portholes. Like their cousins at cold seeps, the worms harbor billions of chemosynthetic bacteria inside their bodies.

The tube worms share their space with other animals. Snail-like limpets the size of mini jelly beans are inching their way up the outsides of the tubes. Scuttling among them are pink worms covered with scales that overlap like shingles on a roof.

The sub moves out of the forest of tube worms and over a field of large mussels. They lie in heaps on the bottom, crowding out everything else. Ghostly white squat lobsters scurry over and around them.

(l) V. Tunnicliffe, University of Victoria; image from ROV ROPOS, CSSF; (r) Pacific Ring of Fire 2004 Expedition. NOAA Office of Ocean Exploration; Dr. Bob Embley - NOAA PMEL - Chief Scientist

The yeti crab (Kiwa hirsuta) *was a major discovery during the Census of Marine Life made by scientists with the French ocean research institute Ifremer. Scientists gave it that nickname because its white color and hairy legs reminded them of the mythical abominable snowman, or yeti. Like some deep-sea crabs, the yeti crab is blind. But it is so different from other crab species that scientists created a new genus and a new family to classify it. The yeti crab in this picture is about as long as your hand.*

Michel Segonzac

"HOW DO LARVAE FIND NEW VENTS? THAT'S THE MAIN QUESTION! THEY CANNOT ACTIVELY SWIM IN A PARTICULAR DIRECTION, ESPECIALLY AGAINST A CURRENT. AT THIS POINT, WE SIMPLY DO NOT KNOW HOW THEY DO IT."
– Paul Tyler, National Oceanography Centre, Southampton, United Kingdom

"IN SCIENCE, WHAT IS PERHAPS MOST IMPORTANT IS TO KNOW HOW TO ASK GOOD QUESTIONS. ONCE YOU KNOW THE QUESTIONS, YOU CAN GO ABOUT TRYING TO ANSWER THEM."
– Myriam Sibuet, Institut Océanographique, Paris, France

Something else that's white catches the pilot's eye. He eases the sub closer and lets out a triumphant cry. It's a yeti crab, a strange, newly discovered species with remarkably hairy legs.

Yeti crabs have only been found at a few vent sites. They may be rare, but scientists can't really say for sure. The reason is that no two vents are exactly alike, even in the same part of the ocean. They'll have many species in common. But they won't be identical.

What's even more puzzling are the differences scientists have found between vents in different ocean basins. Pacific Ocean vents like this one are home to giant tube worms, mussels, and clams. Vents in the Atlantic and Indian oceans swarm with blind shrimp.

Mid-ocean ridges are nearly continuous all the way around the world. So why don't vents in every ocean basin have pretty much the same collection of animals? During the Census of Marine Life, scientists studied vents all over the world trying to answer that question. They still don't know.

Just as baffling is how new vent communities form. Tube worms and other animals that cannot move produce eggs that hatch into larvae. Larvae drift off in search of new vents where they can settle down and grow into adults. But how the larvae find the vents remains a mystery. Solving these deep-sea puzzles is an enormous challenge. Every dive to a hydrothermal vent, however, yields a few more clues.

When the time comes for the sub to ascend, it's hard to leave the vents behind. But you know you've just become a member of a small group of very lucky people who have seen them firsthand.

(t) Courtesy of Paul Tyler; (b) Courtesy of Myriam Sibuet/Institut Océanographique

About the Author

Rebecca L. Johnson's

favorite book as a child was *Alice in Wonderland*, because she liked the idea of visiting an unusual place where strange creatures lived. As an adult, she has traveled to many unusual places all over the Earth, visiting and writing about some of the world's most extreme and interesting environments.

Rebecca has gone scuba diving near Australia's Great Barrier Reef, and once spent nine months in Antarctica. But it was her trip more than 2500 feet below the ocean's surface that finally made her feel like a real-life Alice in Wonderland. Rebecca wrote *Journey into the Deep* because she wanted readers to share the journey with her.

When Rebecca is not exploring she's in South Dakota, where she lives with her husband and Bengal cats.

Author's Purpose

The author includes photos and captions as well as diagrams in the selection. What do these features add to the text to help you understand what life is like in the deepest parts of the ocean?

Respond to Reading

Summarize

Use the key details from *Journey into the Deep* to summarize what you learned about sea creatures that live in the ocean's depths. Information from your Main Idea and Key Details Chart may help you.

Main Idea
Detail
Detail
Detail

Text Evidence

1. Identify two text features that help you identify *Journey into the Deep* as an example of expository text. **GENRE**

2. Examine key details in the first two paragraphs on page 52. Use them to identify the main idea. **MAIN IDEA AND DETAILS**

3. Use clues in the second paragraph on page 56 and the root *bio-*, which means "life," to help you figure out the meaning of *bioluminescent*. **GREEK ROOTS**

4. Identify the key details in the text under the subhead *Ridges and Vents* on pages 60–61. Then write about how the details support the main idea. **WRITE ABOUT READING**

Make Connections

How do different life forms interact with their changing environments? **ESSENTIAL QUESTION**

Describe the most interesting fact you learned about how sea creatures adapt to changing environments. What are some questions you would like to ask the scientists who worked on the Census of Marine Life? **TEXT TO WORLD**

Compare Texts
Read about a scientist who took part in the Census of Marine Life.

Extreme Exploration:

An Interview with Dr. Eva Ramirez-Llodra

Imagine being eleven-years-old and having your parents announce one day that your family is about to take off on an eight-year adventure, sailing around the world. That's exactly what happened to Dr. Eva Ramirez-Llodra. She literally grew up at sea, and then when she turned nineteen Eva returned to her native Barcelona, Spain to study biology. She couldn't have imagined then that the love for the sea she developed during that incredible trip would lead her to become a marine biologist.

In 1999 Dr. Ramirez-Llodra was chosen to become one of five coordinators for the Census of Marine Life project. Eva worked on this global effort with more than 2,500 other scientists. They explored deep-sea ecosystems all over the world for over

(inset) Courtesy of Dr. Eva Ramirez-Llodra; (bkgd) Ewa Ahlin/Getty Images

ten years. The project's goal was to create a record of the biodiversity, or the different kinds of life, that can be found in the world's oceans. In this interview, Dr. Ramirez-Llodra answered questions about the unique organisms that live in the bottom-most depths of Earth's oceans.

Q: How is it possible to do research in this kind of environment?

Dr. Ramirez-Llodra: Deep-sea exploration is not easy. It's expensive and requires complex planning. There are several pieces of high-tech equipment that are needed. Cameras, video recorders, and communication equipment are just some. We need smaller vehicles called submersibles that scientists can maneuver easily down at the bottom of the ocean. These vehicles must make it possible for scientists to see the organisms they find up close. All of this equipment must be able to withstand conditions that are hostile to humans.

Q: What kind of habitat is the deep-sea environment?

Dr. Ramirez-Llodra: The deep-sea is an extreme habitat! It's extremely cold. There's constant darkness. The water pressure is powerful as it increases further and further down in the ocean.

Q: How can anything live in such an extreme habitat?

Dr. Ramirez-Llodra: Actually, this habitat is not extreme or unfriendly to the creatures that live there. All living things adapt to their habitat. If they didn't, they wouldn't be able to survive. Deep-sea organisms are no different. An enormous variety of life forms have successfully adapted to the darkness, high water pressure, limited food supply, and icy cold waters. These organisms could never live in water close to the surface.

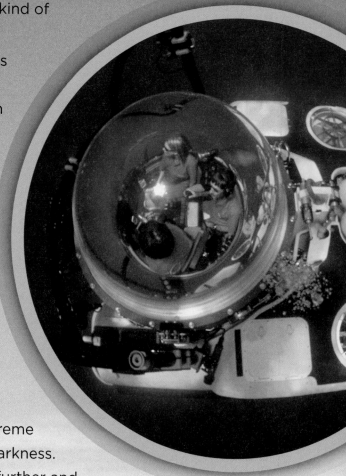

Q: Are there many creatures living in this unusual habitat?

Dr. Ramirez-Llodra: There are scientists who work on identifying different species. They analyze the different organisms and create a scientific **classification** so that types of creatures that are similar are grouped together. Scientists believe there may be over a million kinds of deep-sea life forms!

Q: How have these organisms adapted to life in this unique environment?

Dr. Ramirez-Llodra: These organisms don't suffer from the changing pressure underwater. That's because they don't have air inside their bodies. They have no difficulty moving in complete darkness. Some even use sound or light that they generate themselves to communicate with others of the same **species**. These special sounds and lights also distract predators, and attract prey. Many deep-sea species also have a reduced body density similar to the density of seawater. As a result, they neither sink to the sea floor nor float to the surface.

Q: How do changes to the ecosystem affect deep-sea species? What causes these changes?

Dr. Ramirez-Llodra: Changes in the ecosystem can certainly impact the deep-sea species that live there. A variety of things can cause these changes. Two examples are underwater landslides and storms of rapidly moving water currents. They can wipe out whole communities of organisms just as a tsunami or a landslide can affect people on land.

Q: How does global climate change affect the deep sea?

Dr. Ramirez-Llodra: Warmer water temperatures, for example, can affect the survival of smaller species. It can cause fish to migrate and affect the production of organic matter in water close to the surface. This matter is important because it sinks to the bottom and provides food for deep-sea organisms. Less organic matter near the surface means less food for the organisms that live far below.

Q: Why is the study of deep-water ecosystems so important?

Dr. Ramirez-Llodra: Deep-water ecosystems help maintain the natural cycles of our planet. They hold a wealth of biological and mineral resources. These resources include fish for food, compounds for medicines, and hidden reserves of oil, gas, and minerals. We're using up many of the natural resources on land and in surface waters. It's not surprising, then, that the idea of mining the depths of the ocean becomes increasingly appealing. However, the deep-sea is the largest ecosystem on our planet. It's also one of the most fragile. Having a good understanding of how the ecosystem works is essential if we are going to conserve our natural resources and use them wisely.

Make Connections

How have deep-sea creatures adapted to their environment? **ESSENTIAL QUESTION**

What have you learned about the ways life forms vary in different environments? **TEXT TO TEXT**

INTO THE VOLCANO

A VOLCANO RESEARCHER AT WORK

By Donna O'Meara
Photographs by Stephen and Donna O'Meara

Essential Question

How do natural forces affect Earth?

Read how erupting volcanoes continue to change the landscape of planet Earth.

Go Digital!

Kilauea volcano, on the southeastern side of Hawaii's big island, is one of the world's most active volcanoes. Not only has it erupted over forty times in the past century, but it has been erupting almost nonstop since 1983. In the following memoir, volcano researcher and photographer Donna O'Meara describes the first time she was able to explore Kilauea on her own. She was hoping she would be able to photograph the volcano in action . . . and she wasn't disappointed.

Alone on Kilauea

I zigzagged down the Chain of Craters Road to sea level and parked in front of a deep lava flow that had covered the highway—and several houses—a few months earlier. As I arrived, the sun broke through the clouds at last. I heaved on my backpack and climbed up the hardened lava rock.

Kilauea's lava flows originate high up on the flank of the volcano. Gravity sends the lava flowing down to the sea in red rivers. The chillier air quickly cools and hardens the tops of these rivers, creating sealed tubes through which the hot lava rushes. Shield volcanoes like Kilauea often form underground plumbing systems with dozens of these lava tubes. The tubes can be miles long.

A Hawaiian Hot Spot

The Hawaiian Islands were all formed by a hot spot under the Pacific Plate. Each island formed separately as the plate moved northwest over the hot spot at about the rate your fingernails grow—36.5 mm (1.5 in.) per year. First came Kauai, then Oahu, Molokai and Maui.

Now the Big Island of Hawaii sits over the hot spot that formed its six volcanoes: Kohala, Mauna Kea, Hualalai, Mauna Loa, Kilauea and Loihi sea mount. Kohala is extinct (it will never erupt again). Mauna Loa, Mauna Kea

and Hualalai are dormant (sleeping) but could erupt again. Scientists estimate little Loihi will have to be about 6,000 m (20,000 ft.) tall before it even breaks the ocean's surface and becomes the Big Island's newest volcano, and that could take tens of thousands of years. Feisty Kilauea, still fed by the hot spot, is one of the most active volcanoes in the world.

TEXT: *Into the Volcano* written by Donna O'Meara with photographs by Stephen and Donna O'Meara used by permission of Kids Can Press Ltd., Toronto. Text © 2005 Donna O'Meara. Photographs © Stephen James O'Meara and Donna O'Meara.

How Volcanoes Form

The Earth's crust is made up of huge, solid chunks, called tectonic plates, that float atop Earth's fluid mantle. Volcanoes form when magma from Earth's mantle breaks through the plates or oozes out at the edges. This can happen in different ways.

Subduction

When two plates smash against each other, one plate is forced under the other. (above, right) The underlying plate melts into magma and can erupt through the overlying plate as a volcano. Central America's volcanoes, including Arenal in Costa Rica and Pacaya in Guatemala, were formed this way.

Mid-Ocean Rift

When two plates drift apart, magma fills the gap between them and submarine (under the ocean) volcanoes can form as shown above. Iceland's Surtsey is a good example of a volcano that grew slowly until it emerged from the ocean.

Hot Spot

Sometimes there is a weak spot in one of Earth's plates and a stationary plume of magma erupts through it. The Hawaiian volcanoes were all formed this way.

Sometimes the lava tubes crack and red lava squeezes out. This is called a surface breakout. For a short period of time the red lava flow is visible, then it cools and hardens again.

A surface breakout is a rare and wonderful sight. I hoped to find one and photograph it before the lava hardened again. But walking around lava tubes can be treacherous. It's hard to know when you're right over one, and the crust over a tube can be thin. You're at risk of breaking through and **plummeting** into the molten lava below. I planned to be careful, but I was also determined. I wanted to photograph molten red lava.

> **STOP AND CHECK**
>
> **Reread** What are three different ways volcanoes can form? Reread to check your understanding.

Volcano Types

Just like people, volcanoes come in all shapes and sizes. There are more than twenty-five different kinds of volcanoes on Earth. The lava's viscosity (stickiness) plays a big role in the type and shape of a volcano and how the volcano erupts. The stickier (more viscous) the lava, the more pointed and cone-shaped the volcano. The more fluid (less viscous) the lava, the more rounded and low the volcano. Here are a few of the most common types of volcanoes.

Shield Volcanoes

Shield volcanoes have very fluid basalt lava flows that can travel relatively quickly. Over time, thousands of syrupy lava flows can pile up like pancake batter to form these gently sloping, shield-shaped volcanoes. Kilauea is a shield volcano.

Stratovolcanoes

The classic Hollywood cone-shaped volcano is created as explosive eruptions of ash, lava and cinders build up in layers. Arenal and Stromboli are stratovolcanoes. Because the ash and lava form layers, these volcanoes are sometimes called composite volcanoes.

Compound Volcanoes

A compound volcano has frequent eruptions that form more than one cone, dome or vent. Pacaya is a compound volcano.

Cinder Cone Volcanoes

Cinder cones are formed when a vent (a hole through which lava erupts) tosses lava cinders and spatter skyward. When these fall back to Earth, they build an oval hill with a circular depression on top.

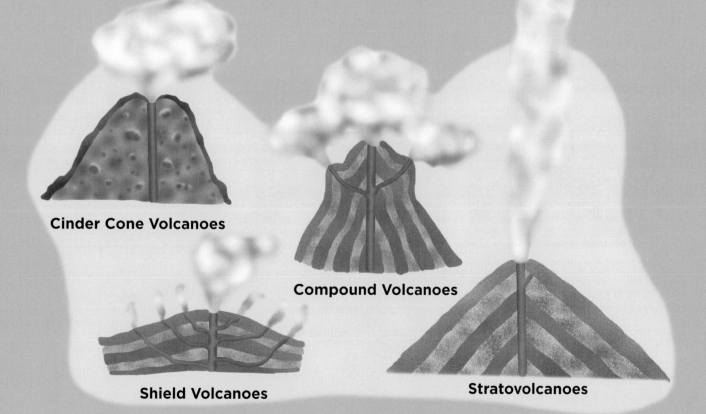

Cinder Cone Volcanoes

Compound Volcanoes

Shield Volcanoes

Stratovolcanoes

To find my way back after sunset, I stuck white sticks into lava cracks about every hundred feet and tied white pieces of cloth to them like little flags. Later on, in the dark, the white markers would glow in my flashlight beam and lead me back to my car.

On my right, the coast dropped off sharply in a steep cliff. Saltwater droplets sprayed my face, and I could hear huge waves pounding the cliff. At high tide, the Pacific's waves were enormous!

I was thirsty. I needed some water. I sat down, but before I took a sip, I noticed that my seat was getting hot. I felt the hardened lava with the palm of my hand. It was hot. Very hot. Too hot. Uh-oh! Was I sitting right on top of a lava tube?

Types of Lava

Molten rock below Earth's surface is called magma. Once it breaks through Earth's crust it is called lava. As soon as lava erupts, it begins to cool, causing gas in the lava to escape and minerals to crystallize and harden. The chemical composition, gas content and temperature all dictate what the lava will look like and how it will behave.

pressure builds on gases trapped in the magma until... *Kaboom!* A huge explosion occurs. (It's a bit like when you place your thumb over the opening of a soda bottle, shake it and release it.) The gases expand and explode violently, shattering the lava into smaller particles of cinders and ash.

Aa Lava

Aa lava, (shown above) is also made of basalt, but it clumps as it cools. Aa looks like chunky blocks that have been lumped together in a long pile. When the flow moves, these blocks tumble slowly forward as if a bulldozer were pushing the pile from behind. The moving blocks make sounds like glass breaking and fingernails screeching on a blackboard.

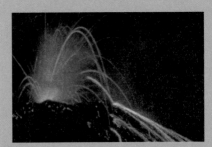

Viscous Lava

Viscous (sticky and slow-moving) magma (shown above) of andesite, dacite and rhyolite sometimes plugs a volcano's vent like a cork. Then,

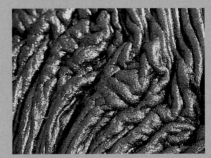

Pahoehoe Lava

Pahoehoe lava (above) contains the igneous rock basalt and is hot and smooth. It moves like spilled pancake batter. When it hardens, it can be smooth or ropey.

To get a better view, I hiked inland and scrambled up a mound of lava called a tumulus, a big pimple made when lava pressing up from beneath pops open, leaving a broken hill. From it, I could see an amazing sight. Steam and gases wisped up from the ground in crisscrossing lines. These were probably the outlines of lava tubes.

Off in the distance, I saw something even more amazing—a strange pink cloud. What was it? I wanted to investigate, but the gassy outlines of lava tubes were in my way.

Here's an old photo of my husband, Steve O'Meara, standing inside an empty lava tube. Just imagine this tube filled with lava.

Gases and steam can signal an underground lava tube.

I was looking for a route around the lava tubes when I came to a wall of lava rocks. I had stumbled upon Wahaula Heiau. A heiau is an ancient Hawaiian temple. Wahaula means "red mouth" in Hawaiian.

Some Hawaiian temples are considered sacred, and I certainly didn't want to disturb this one. Plus, it looked as though the lava tubes went under the heiau as well.

I was sandwiched between a raging sea cliff on the right and a sacred temple on the left. If I hoped to find out what was causing the pink cloud, there was only one way to go—straight across the tops of the steaming lava tubes.

Would the hardened tops of the tubes support my weight? There was only one way to find out. I held my breath and ran.

Kilauea: A Shield Volcano

Shield volcanoes like Kilauea have surfaces that are cracked by earthquakes. These weakened areas are called rift zones. Kilauea has two rift zones: the Southwest Rift Zone and the East Rift Zone. For the last twenty years most activity has occurred along the East Rift Zone, which extends east from the summit to a point about 55 km (35 mi.) offshore.

Kilauea's East Rift Zone is walloped with up to a hundred earthquakes a day. They severely crack the rock in the area. As magma rises from below, it **exerts** even more pressure on these shattered rocks. Finally, the pressure is too much. The rock cracks open, allowing molten magma to erupt to the surface. Rift zones aren't the only places magma erupts. It could surprise us and erupt in a new weakened area at any time.

Kilauea's fluid lava flows are so universally recognized that the phrase "Hawaiian type" eruption is an accepted scientific term used to describe similar volcanic activity around the world. Kilauea usually oozes pahoehoe or aa lavas but a more explosive eruption is possible.

A Walk on the Wild Side

I ran across the smoking tops of the lava tubes as if my life depended on it. Because it did!

I made it . . . or had I? The pink cloud now loomed in front of me. And it was tossing chunks of lava right at me.

I had read about these steam clouds but never seen one. They happen when hot lava pours into cold seawater and instantly boils the water into steam. As it hits the cold ocean the hot lava is blasted into chunks called lava bombs and spatter. Huge explosions rocket the lava bombs higher and higher up into the **scalding** plume. Then, thanks to gravity, the heavy lava bombs and spatter hurtle back to Earth.

Most people would have run by now, but I wanted to see the lava pouring into the sea. That meant getting to the cliff edge. And *that* meant running right through the steam cloud—and the falling lava bombs.

I dodged and ran as hot lava bombs rained down around me. Blasts of steam blew some of the flowing lava into tiny **shards** of glass that pricked my bare arms like bee stings. Each step crunched. It was like running over black crystal snowflakes made of glass.

STOP AND CHECK

Visualize What words help you to visualize what happens when hot lava pours into cold seawater?

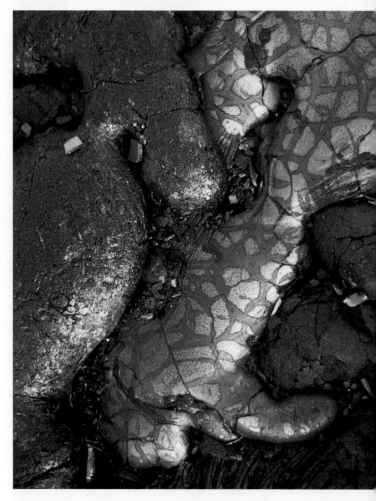

When pahoehoe lava cools quickly, it forms a crunchy black crust that shatters like glass if stepped on.

*Two black lava tubes empty their molten contents into the Pacific Ocean, causing big steam clouds to rise as the seawater vaporizes. Waves **pulverize** the lava into black sand, which washes ashore and creates a black sand beach.*

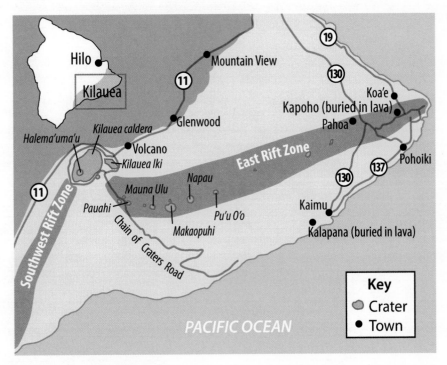

Kilauea Volcano, Hawaii

The steam was hot. Worse, hydrochloric acid in the steam cloud stung my eyes, nose and throat. Coughing, I hastily poured water onto my bandana and tied it around my mouth and nose. I put on goggles to protect my eyes.

When I got to the cliff edge, I could hardly believe my eyes. Pounding waves had wrenched off a huge piece of the cliff. The lava tube and the entire river of orange lava was exposed as it poured into the ocean. But it wouldn't be visible for long. The cold seawater might seal the tube in minutes.

I grabbed my camera and began shooting. Ouch! The camera was getting hot. I wrapped the bottom of my shirt around the camera like a pot holder and worried that my film might be cooked.

I could see a small ledge jutting out about 2 m (6 ft.) down on the cliff face. If I could make it down there, I could get out of the heat. I carefully lowered myself. If I missed the ledge I'd boil in the lava/sea/steam cauldron below me.

I dropped onto the ledge and had a ringside seat for the best lava show in town. An incandescent torrent of fiery lava **cascaded** from a gaping tube in the black cliff and poured furiously into the turquoise sea. *Kaboom!* Another blast as hot lava sputtered into a whirlpool of steam. The noise was deafening.

The sun was setting and the light was magical. I began to shoot my film. I was lucky. It was almost twenty minutes before the sea won the battle and cooled the top of the lava river into a filmy black crust. The tube sealed over again and the show ended. The air grew still. All I could hear was the waves smacking against the cliff.

I took a deep breath and realized I might have been the first person to photograph this kind of volcanic event. I looked down and saw that my arms had a pink lava sunburn. I could feel my face glowing, too.

As I climbed back up, my left foot shattered the thin ledge I stood on. I could see pounding waves through the hole. Do not look down! Do not look down! I clung to the cliff face and heaved myself up. In the scramble, my leg caught on sharp lava, and it sliced into my calf muscle like a razor. I ripped a piece of T-shirt and tied a tight tourniquet below my knee to slow the blood flow. Then I stuffed some absorbent photo lens wipes into the wound and duct-taped the whole thing tight to my leg.

The pink cloud was made up of vaporized seawater, lava spatter and lava bombs. It was the bombs that worried me.

Lava bombs are chunks of hardened lava. Some can be as big as a football—not something you'd want crashing down on your head.

U.S. Geological Survey/photo by J.P. Lockwood

A chunk of cliff fell off, exposing this beautiful lava river flowing from its tube. A rare moment, and one I was lucky enough to photograph.

In the dark the hike back was long. Thankfully my little white flags were there to guide me. When I got to the car I celebrated with a candy bar. The sugar gave me energy to drive the two hours to a clinic in Hilo.

The doctors cleaned my wound as well as they could, but to this day there are still tiny shards of lava embedded in my calf. Some people believe that lava is the physical form of Kilauea's volcano goddess, Pele. When my leg hurts, I wonder if that is true.

My lava sunburn was gone in about a week, and I was relieved that all my film was fine. Those dramatic images, one of which you can see above, were some of the hardest I have ever had to work to get. I feel that I really earned them. After almost twenty years of shooting volcanoes, they are still my favorites.

RIGHT: Donna O'Meara, volcano researcher.

STOP AND CHECK

Reread What makes the work that Donna O'Meara does so risky?

ABOUT THE AUTHOR

DONNA O'MEARA

figured out a way to combine her love of art and science after studying journalism and business at Harvard University. She started a career taking photos of active volcanoes. In addition to publishing her photographs in the award-winning books and articles she writes, Donna and her husband, Steve, use them to teach people about volcanoes.

In 1994, Donna and Steve founded Volcano Watch International (VWI), a research organization that helps people better understand Earth's active volcanoes. VWI uses Donna's photographs to help educate people around the globe about volcanic dangers and what can be done to help people who live in or near unsafe areas. Part of Donna's work includes finding out ways to predict when volcanoes might erupt.

Over the years, Donna has seen about 100 volcanoes, including Mt. Erebus, Antarctica's most active volcano. She says it looks like a giant vanilla ice cream sundae!

When they're not visiting volcanoes, Donna and Steve make their home in the rain forest on top of Hawaii's Kilauea with their dog, Daisy Duke.

AUTHOR'S PURPOSE

The author uses models to illustrate important information about volcanoes. How do these text features help you understand the text?

RESPOND TO READING

SUMMARIZE

Use main ideas and key details from *Into the Volcano* to summarize what you learned about volcanologist Donna O'Meara, and how volcanoes affect both the people who live near them and Earth as well. Information from your Main Idea and Key Details Chart may help you.

Main Idea
Detail
Detail
Detail

TEXT EVIDENCE

1. What features and text details in *Into the Volcano* help you to recognize that this selection is narrative nonfiction in the form of a memoir? Identify the text features. **GENRE**

2. Identify the important details in the sidebar captioned *Kilauea: A Shield Volcano* on page 78. Then classify them to find the main idea. **MAIN IDEA AND KEY DETAILS**

3. To what does O'Meara compare the tiny shards of lava that pricked her bare arms? How does recognizing the simile O'Meara uses on page 79 help you understand how she felt during the experience? **METAPHOR AND SIMILE**

4. Identify the key details in the sidebar about lava on page 76. Then write about how these details support the main idea. **WRITE ABOUT READING**

Make Connections

In what ways do volcanoes change the surface of Earth? **ESSENTIAL QUESTION**

Identify the most interesting fact you learned about volcanoes in this selection. What can people learn about how the surface of Earth changes from this information? **TEXT TO WORLD**

Compare Texts
Read how one scientist investigates one of the natural forces that affect Earth.

Donna O'Meara

Donna O'Meara:
The Volcano Lady

After a blistering hot day, a cold storm suddenly whipped around the top of Mt. Stromboli, a volcano on an island off the coast of Sicily. The temperature quickly dropped over 60 degrees. Donna O'Meara and her husband, Steve, didn't dare try to climb down the steep slopes in the dark. They were stuck on a narrow ledge just 200 feet above a fiery, smoking pit. They huddled together, shivering nonstop in the cold air. Thundering blasts from the volcano and falling rocks the size of basketballs kept them awake and fearful. When the sun came up, Donna felt cinder burns on her face. There were sharp pieces of rock tangled in her hair.

Frightening experiences on top of a volcano are not unusual for Donna O'Meara. For over 25 years, she has worked with Steve to photograph and study volcanoes all over the world. They hope their **documentation** will someday be a written and visual record of information that helps scientists to better predict volcanic eruptions.

O'Meara grew up in the New England countryside. There are no volcanoes in Connecticut, but in the spring and summer there were fierce thunder and lightning storms that thrilled Donna. In school, her favorite classes were earth science and biology. However, instead of turning her love for

science into a career after graduation, she became an artist, photographer, and writer. As she worked on different magazines and books, she gradually began to realize that something was missing in her life.

When Donna went back to school at the age of 32 to study science, her passion for volcanoes began. She took geology classes to learn more about what rocks and soil tell us about the earth. She found out that volcanism is one of the most **dynamic** forces in nature. Volcanoes constantly shape and change the earth. Many islands, such as the islands that make up Hawaii, were formed by volcanic activity.

In 1986, Donna visited her first volcano as Steve's research assistant. After dodging lava bombs and feeling the heat from underground lava melting her shoes, Donna was hooked. The following year, she and Steve were married on lava that had oozed from Kilauea on Hawaii and hardened. Lava that hardens creates new landforms, and some volcanoes, such as Surtsey off the coast of Iceland, actually create new islands!

Today, Donna can't imagine what her life would be like without volcanoes. She loves them so much she lives on one. Her home is on top of Kilauea, where she was married. This is one of the most active volcanoes in the world.

From their home, Donna and Steve run Volcano Watch International. (VWI) The O'Mearas' organization is dedicated to understanding how Earth's active volcanoes work. VWI uses photos and video to educate people about the dangers of volcanoes. Their mission is to travel to active volcanoes and document the eruptions.

The first volcano Donna studied was Kilauea, which is a shield volcano.

Mt. Stromboli is a stratovolcano. A stratovolcano has the common cone shape people usually picture when they think of a volcano. It is formed from explosive eruptions that build layers of ash, lava, and cinders at the top of the mountain.

Donna says the experience of being stranded on Mt. Stromboli for one freezing night was the scariest experience of her life. Since the sides of

A village is quite close to the volcano on the island of Stromboli. Millions of people around the world live near active volcanoes.

this volcano are steep, it was impossible for the O'Mearas to travel down the slopes until the sun rose in the morning. So they were trapped on a ledge in the freezing cold with scalding rocks flying around them.

Donna O'Meara escaped from her scary night on Mt. Stromboli safe and sound. Now she and Steve hope that the knowledge they gather photographing and studying volcanoes will help save the lives of people who live near them. The O'Mearas' volcano photographs, videos, and samples of volcanic rock are part of the permanent collection of the Smithsonian Institution located in Washington, D.C.

Donna believes they have the best jobs on earth, even though their work may be the most dangerous as well.

Stratovolcano

Pyroclastic flow is made up of hot ash, chunks of rock, and fiery gases that explode out of an erupting stratovolcano. It flows in two layers. The heavier layer carries big rocks along the ground. The lighter, top layer is called an upsurge. It contains lighter, burning ash.

Make Connections

How have volcanoes helped to change Earth? **ESSENTIAL QUESTION**

What have you learned about the natural forces that affect Earth? In what ways do these forces sometimes affect one another? **TEXT TO TEXT**

THE ECONOMIC
Roller Coaster

Essential Question

What factors influence how people use money?

Go Digital!

What forces control the ups and downs of a nation's economy?

When people talk about a nation's economy, they mean everything a country and its citizens own. This also includes the goods and services that are made, provided, bought, and sold there. **Basically**, the economy is about buying and selling. This can include buying the services of workers to build houses. It can also include selling nails and power tools at the do-it-yourself store.

As a student, still in school, you may think you have no effect on the economy. But have you ever bought a slice of pizza, had a haircut, shopped for shoes or a baseball glove? If you do anything that requires the exchange of money for goods and services, you are affected by the economy. One way or another, the economy affects everyone. To understand why, it helps to think of the economy as the engine of a country. As long as it's running smoothly, society keeps moving forward.

When the Price Is Right

The United States has what is called a *free-market* economy. This means that people, rather than the government, control the buying and selling of goods and services. Prices change based on a principle called *supply and demand.* "Supply" refers to how much of something is **available**, whether it's a natural resource, such as oil or crops, a **manufactured** product, such as a cell phone, or a service, such as a dry cleaner. "Demand" refers to how many people want a resource, product, or service. This principle is the foundation of a free-market economy.

An economy is said to be in good shape when demand is slightly higher than supply, because that keeps businesses working hard to make what people want. Businesses hire workers and pay them **salaries** for their services. The workers have cash in their pockets to buy the products and services of other businesses. That keeps the demand high, keeps businesses running, and lets people keep earning—and spending—money. When supply and demand are in balance, prices are stable and the system functions smoothly.

An economy can falter when demand is low. Businesses can't sell their products. When that happens, they will lay off workers or won't hire workers to make the products. The workers, in turn, won't have money to spend on other products. Prices may go down as businesses try to do whatever they can to sell the goods they have. But low prices don't help very much when most people don't have money to spend.

> **STOP AND CHECK**
>
> **Reread** How does the concept of supply and demand affect an economy? Reread to check your understanding.

The Right Formula

The **factors** behind supply and demand influence lots of economic decisions, and these decisions affect what you can afford to buy. Suppose that a very popular athlete issues a new athletic shoe. He says he'll only produce 1,000 copies of the shoes. The demand for these shoes will be really, really high and the supply will be very low, so people who want them will be likely to pay a lot. The same idea is behind what makes gold and diamonds so expensive. If an item is rare, then the supply is low. When a lot of people want the item, the demand is high. That's the **formula** for high prices.

Sometimes you'll walk past a store that's putting a product on sale. You might see a big sign saying "Computers 1/3 Off!" Supply and demand is often the force behind such low prices. If a company wants to sell off its huge **inventory** of outdated computers before a new one comes on the market for sale, then the situation is high-supply, low-demand. That's a formula for a very low price.

Bad weather such as a drought (left) or a flood (right) can affect the prices of certain crops.

Natural disasters and bad weather can sometimes destroy crops. That means prices for certain grains, fruits, or vegetables might go up. On the other hand, favorable conditions for growing crops mean plenty of food, and not only for people. Feed for livestock is also less expensive. If the price of feed is low, ranchers will raise a lot of cattle. This means the price of beef will go down.

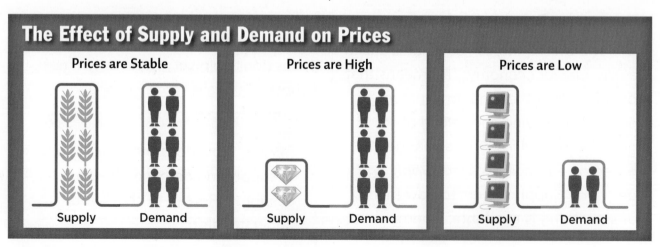

The Effect of Supply and Demand on Prices

Prices are Stable	Prices are High	Prices are Low
Supply　Demand	Supply　Demand	Supply　Demand

If You Ask Me...

by L.D.

POINT COUNTERPOINT

Even in a free-market economy like ours, the federal government sometimes takes actions to affect supply and demand. For example, it might step in to establish price controls to stop prices from rising too fast or too high. Another strategy is for the government to tighten the money supply, which means making it more costly to borrow money.

These situations have happened many times over the last century. The government's actions are seen by some people as necessary to keep the economy balanced. Those in favor of government action believe it is the government's job to keep the economy healthy, and that this is the way to do it. If you ask me, however, I think government actions like these don't help a free-market economy.

The principle of supply and demand shows us that things change over time. Costs, prices, and income go up and down as a natural part of the free-market environment. Over time, I believe, everything will sort itself out. Supply and demand will find balance again, and the economy will keep rolling along like a well-oiled machine.

Randall Fung/Spirit/Corbis

Emotions can affect the economy as much as supply and demand does. If people feel confident that the economy is doing well then they will spend more money. If they are worried about the future, or feel prices may **fluctuate**, they may not spend as much, and the economy will slow down. In cases like these, it is sometimes beneficial for the government to step in and provide tax cuts and other measures to help get the economy moving again.

Respond to Reading

1. What details help you recognize that "The Economic Roller Coaster" is an example of an informational text? **GENRE**

2. Evaluate the argument the author makes in "If You Ask Me . . ." Is it supported with evidence, as in the article "The Economic Roller Coaster"? Explain your answer. **AUTHOR'S POINT OF VIEW**

3. What is the meaning of *smoothly* on page 93? Use the meaning of the suffix added to the root word to help you. **ROOT WORDS**

4. How do the actions of both buyers and sellers affect the U.S. economy? **TEXT TO WORLD**

Compare Texts
Read one person's essay about why the Federal Reserve System is so important to the economy of the United States.

Our Federal Reserve at Work

Who are you going to call when the economy of the United States is in trouble? The answer is, and should be, the Federal Reserve. The Federal Reserve System is the central bank of the United States government. Sometimes called "The Fed," it was established by Congress in 1913.

Historically, one of the most important roles of the Fed has been using its power to adjust interest rates. An interest rate is the price that people pay to borrow money. When you pay back money you have borrowed from a bank, called a loan, you return the amount you borrowed plus the interest the bank charged you to borrow the money.

The amount of interest is usually based on a number of **factors**. They can include the amount of the loan, the amount of time a person needs to pay it back, and the qualifications of the borrower. For example, say a person has borrowed money before and paid it back on time. He or she might get a

The headquarters of the Federal Reserve is located in Washington, D.C., our nation's capital.

lower interest rate than a person who borrowed money before and was late paying it back.

Interest rates, like other prices, can **fluctuate**. They are determined by the forces of supply and demand. Higher interest rates provide a good reason for people to save more and borrow less. This is because a bank will pay them more interest for the money they put in a savings account. When interest rates become too high, however, businesses and people are not likely to borrow money from a bank. This is because it will cost them too much to pay it back. As a result, people are likely to spend less on housing, cars, and other major purchases that might require a loan. This can hurt businesses that sell and make certain products.

Likewise, lower interest rates provide reasons for people to borrow more and save less. A low interest rate is likely to cause businesses to invest more and expand. It will also encourage people to make more purchases. In this way, interest rates affect how much economic activity takes place in an economy.

I believe that when the economy slows down the Federal Reserve must take action. It should lower interest rates and keep money moving through the economic system. I also believe the Fed should raise interest rates if people start borrowing too much.

The flow chart below helps explain this sound monetary position.

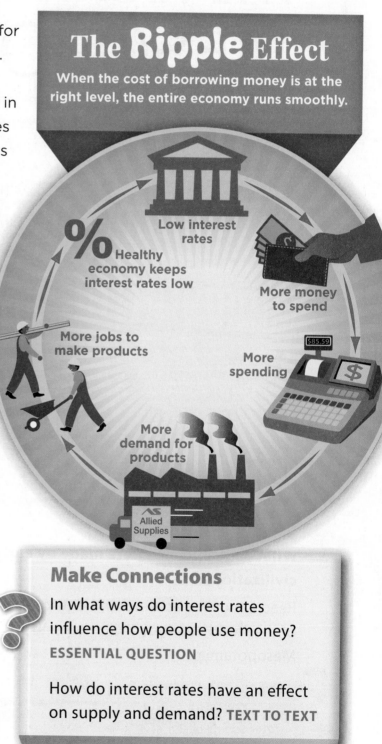

The Ripple Effect

When the cost of borrowing money is at the right level, the entire economy runs smoothly.

% Healthy economy keeps interest rates low

Low interest rates

More money to spend

More spending

More demand for products

More jobs to make products

Allied Supplies

Make Connections

In what ways do interest rates influence how people use money? **ESSENTIAL QUESTION**

How do interest rates have an effect on supply and demand? **TEXT TO TEXT**

CCSS **Genre • Expository Text**

THE TECHNOLOGY OF MESOPOTAMIA

By Graham Faiella

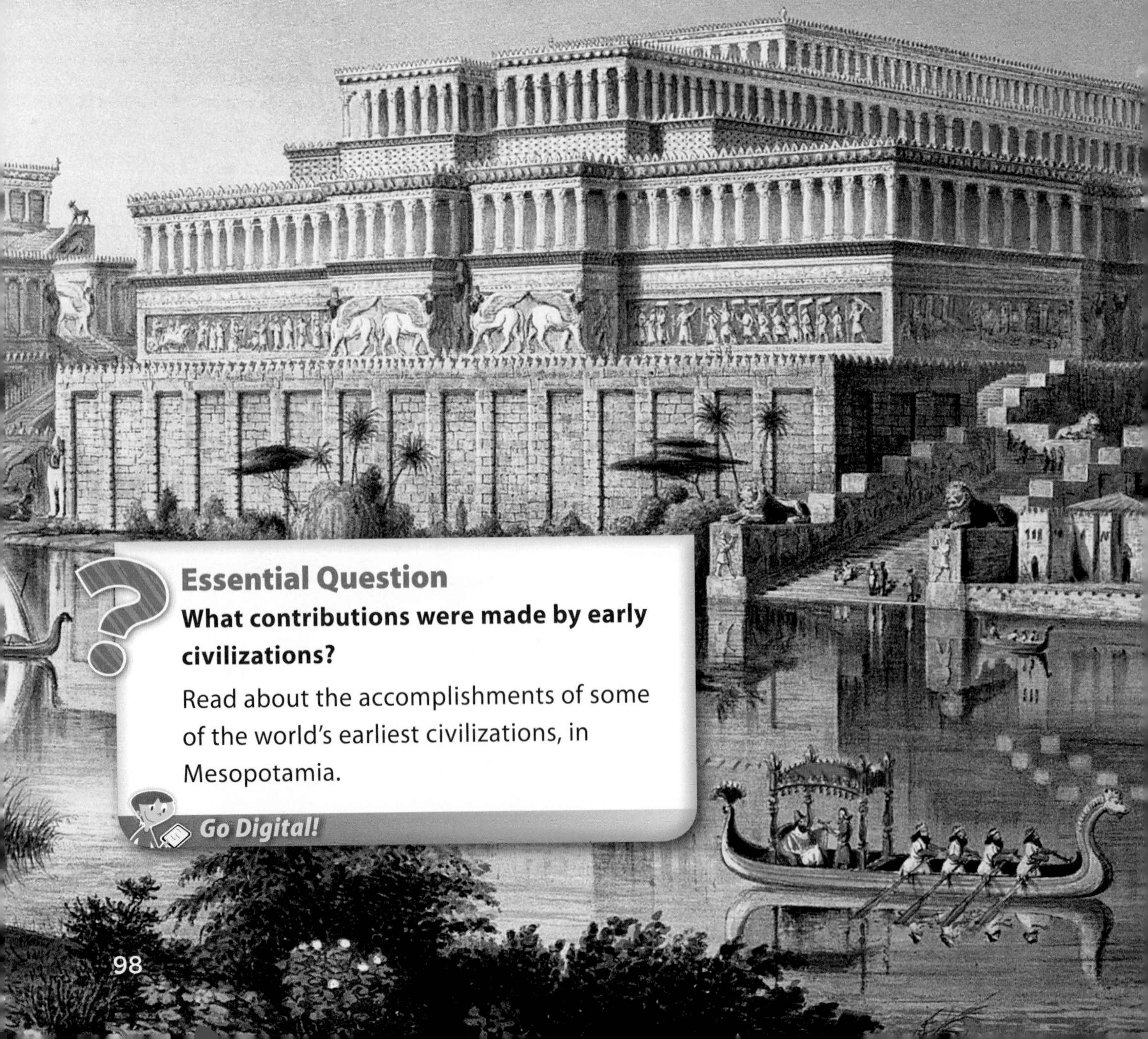

Essential Question

What contributions were made by early civilizations?

Read about the accomplishments of some of the world's earliest civilizations, in Mesopotamia.

Go Digital!

People first began settling the area we know today as Iraq, northern Syria, and southwestern Iran between 8,000 and 9,000 years ago. Their farming communities grew bigger and more complex. They built towns and cities. They developed technologies and made important inventions that we still use today. (The word "technology" comes from the Greek words *techne*, meaning "art" or "craft," and *logos*, meaning "word" or "study." It has come to mean the use of science and engineering to perform practical tasks.)

This was the land of Mesopotamia. The word "Mesopotamia" means "the land between the rivers" (the Tigris and the Euphrates). It was the first place in the world where large, complex societies used **communal** technology to organize themselves efficiently. Mesopotamia was the cradle of civilization.

The Mesopotamian civilization was the first to build cities. The Mesopotamians' inventions and technologies evolved with their urban life. They learned how to manufacture things; keep written records; count things and measure time; govern people; construct buildings, from ordinary houses to royal palaces; produce food efficiently in large amounts; irrigate their desert fields; and transport things—and people—across long distances.

Mesopotamia was a region dominated at different periods by various groups of people for more than 4,500 years. Each new period had its own civilization, its own capital cities, languages, gods, and dynasties of kings. Sumer, in the south, was the first great civilization of Mesopotamia, beginning around 3500 BC. The Sumerians were followed by the Akkadians (2334–2193 BC). From about 1900 BC until 539 BC, Assyria in the north and the city of Babylon in the south were the main centers of Mesopotamian civilization.

LEFT: This illustration shows a palace along the Tigris River in the city of Nineveh. RIGHT: Mesopotamian artists made this baked clay model of a chariot over 4,000 years ago.

(t) Leemage/Universal Images Group/Getty Images; (l) DEA/G. DAGLI ORTI/De Agostini Picture Library/Getty Images; (l) Erich Lessing/ Art Resource, NY. TEXT: From: The Technology of Mesopotamia Copyright © 2006 by The Rosen Publishing Group, Inc. and reprinted with permission.

A lion made of glazed bricks is part of the decoration on a city gate.

DATES FOR EVENTS IN MESOPOTAMIAN HISTORY

It is very difficult to determine accurate dates for the oldest events and periods of time in Mesopotamia. Dates have to be **derived** from archaeological evidence. In some cases it can only be said that an event or development happened within a thousand-year period, which is called a **millennium**. In those cases, it is common to date the development or event in a particular millennium BC. However, no one can say accurately, for example, when Mesopotamian cities were first built. We know only that they appeared in the fourth millennium BC (4000–3001 BC), meaning between 5,000 and 6,000 years ago. The first writing also appeared sometime in the fourth millennium, although probably closer to 3000 BC than 4000 BC.

1000 BC – 1 BC	First millennium
2000 – 1001 BC	Second millennium
3000 – 2001 BC	Third millennium
4000 – 3001 BC	Fourth millennium
5000 – 4001 BC	Fifth millennium

IRRIGATION AND AGRICULTURE

People settled around "the land between the rivers" for one reason: water. Water from the Tigris and Euphrates was necessary for life to survive in that otherwise dry desert region. It enabled people to grow crops and provided water for drinking.

The two rivers of Mesopotamia overflowed when rain in the north increased the flow of water running south to the sea. The overflowing rivers flooded the surrounding land. At those times of flood there was plenty of water to irrigate crops. The problem was that the rivers did not flood regularly. They could flood anytime between April and June. And a flood could be so overwhelming that it destroyed crops. Mesopotamians had to invent ways of getting water out of the rivers more regularly, and in controlled amounts, to irrigate their crops.

They mastered the technology of irrigation. They built not only canals but underground aqueducts. They also built levees, or raised banks, along the rivers to protect against damaging floods. The basic materials used in water-supply projects were simple: baked brick and reeds. The design and organization of these projects, however, required sophisticated planning and engineering.

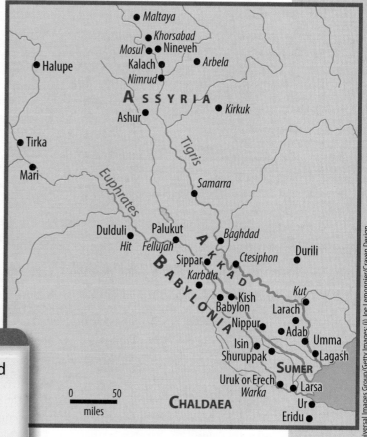

Mesopotamia around 1750 BC. Later names are in italics.

(t) Leemage/Universal Images Group/Getty Images; (i) Joe Lemonnier/Craven Design

STOP AND CHECK

Ask and Answer Questions How did technology help the Mesopotamians irrigate their crops, and what problems did it solve? Support your answer with evidence from the text.

101

The Shadoof

The simplest form of irrigation was the shadoof (also spelled "shaduf"). It was invented in Mesopotamia and Egypt around 2000 BC, and is still used today in parts of the Middle East and Egypt. The shadoof consisted of a long pole with a bucket on one end and a counterweight on the other. The middle of the pole was set up on a wood framework. The farmer used his own weight to pull the bucket down into the river. When it filled up with water, the farmer let go of the bucket. The counterweight at the other end of the pole lifted the bucket up. The farmer could then swing the bucketful of water around and empty it into the canal used to irrigate his field. The system could also be used to transfer water from one big canal to another smaller one. A series of shadoofs could lift water in steps from a lower source of water to a higher level.

The Greek geographer Strabo (circa 64 BC–AD 23), in book 16 of his major work *Geography*, described a system used to irrigate the famous Hanging Gardens of Babylon (one of the Seven Wonders of the Ancient World). He described "water engines, by means of which persons, appointed for the

The Egyptians and Mesopotamians first used the shadoof around the same time, about 2000 BC. The long pole with a bucket on one end and a counterweight on the other was used mainly to irrigate fields.

purpose, are continually employed in raising water from the Euphrates into the garden." We cannot be certain what the "water engines" were. They may have been a series of shadoofs. Or they may have been part of a "bucket-and-chain" system. For this, a chain would be wound around two large wheels, one above the other. The wheels (and the chain) would revolve continuously. Buckets attached to the chain would lift water from the river in a continuous loop. They might have emptied directly into the gardens or into a channel leading into the gardens.

Aqueducts

In the eighth century BC, an Assyrian king, Sargon II (ruling 721–705 BC), discovered how to build underground aqueducts to transport water long distances. A surveyor first had to mark out a line on the ground in the direction the water had to travel. At intervals along the line, vertical holes were dug into the ground at different depths. Teams of diggers then dug out horizontal channels underground between the holes. Many teams could dig out the underground channel faster than one digger burrowing along by himself like a mole. Workers then smoothed out the walls of the underground channel to turn the tunnel into an underground aqueduct.

This technology only worked in the hard rock of northern Mesopotamia. In the south the ground was muddy clay and could not be tunneled into without collapsing. Where they needed to build aqueducts in the south, they built them aboveground.

MESOPOTAMIAN "FARMER'S ALMANAC"

Around 1700 BC, a farmer's almanac of nearly 100 lines was written on a clay tablet. In it, a farmer gives his son instructions about how to grow good crops, including instructions about how to use the seeder plow and how to manage workers. Farmers in Mesopotamia knew about the benefits of crop rotation (periodically leaving fields fallow), to increase the soil's fertility. It seems, however, that they did not know the technique of fertilizing their fields to increase crop **yields**.

THE TECHNOLOGY OF WRITING

The Mesopotamians invented writing 5,000 years ago. Scribes (writers) used a pointed stick or reed, called a stylus, to scratch pictures of things on damp clay tablets. This kind of writing was called cuneiform. The clay hardened, either baked by the sun or in a kiln. The writer's **inscription** lasted until the tablet crumbled or broke. For the duration of their civilization, throughout thousands of years, Mesopotamians wrote mainly on clay tablets. If scribes wanted to write something important, they used a stylus made from metal or bone to inscribe the writing on a more durable material such as stone. It was harder to do, but it lasted longer than clay tablets.

Hundreds of thousands of pieces of clay tablets with cuneiform writing have been found among the ruins of Mesopotamia. They show how cuneiform writing developed over thousands of years. At first the tablets recorded mostly activities revolving around agriculture or the economy of early Mesopotamian cities. Some tablets contain lists of cuneiform words to teach others what the symbols meant. (At the time, there was no such thing as an alphabet. The world's first alphabet was invented in Palestine and Syria around 1700 BC.) Cuneiform was the standard form of writing throughout almost the entire period of Mesopotamian civilization.

Mesopotamian scribes used a stylus to practice writing.

From Pictograms to Cuneiform

The earliest Mesopotamian writing on clay tablets dates from about 3500 to 3000 BC. It features pictures of things like sheep or cattle or grain stored in a warehouse. Each picture symbol was a pictogram. A picture of an ox's head would be the pictogram for an ox. The pictogram for a day would be a picture of the sun coming over the horizon. Barley was represented as an ear of barley. The main reason writing was invented was to keep accounts and official records. It was only much later that writing was used for literary or artistic purposes.

Gradually, over hundreds of years, the Mesopotamians made their picture writing more abstract. They found it was easier to write a simplified symbol of an ox, for example, rather than a picture of it. They began using the end of a cut reed as a stylus to make standard marks to represent the object, rather than using a sharp point to draw a picture of it. The blunt end of a reed stylus was a wedge shape. The wedge-shape writing they produced was called cuneiform (from *cuneus*, the Latin word for "wedge").

The three tablets pictured here represent the progression of the technology of writing in Mesopotamia. The top limestone tablet shows pictograms of proper names, including a landowner, and dates from the end of the fourth millennium. The middle clay tablet shows the grain counts at a temple. It dates from around 2900 BC, just before cuneiform writing was common, and uses pictures and symbols. The bottom clay tablet lists in cuneiform barley rations for seventeen gardeners for one month. The tablet dates from about 2000 BC.

STOP AND CHECK

Ask and Answer Questions Why do you think writing was first developed to keep accounts and records, and only used later for artistic purposes? What clues in the text can help you answer this question?

(t) Sophie Kittredge; (t) Réunion des Musées Nationaux/Art Resource, NY; (c) The Metropolitan Museum of Art/Art Resource, NY; (b) Erich Lessing/Art Resource - NY

At first, cuneiform writing only represented objects or numbers. There was no grammar and no representation of the sounds of the spoken language. By around 2500 BC, cuneiform signs used for objects began to represent sounds, too. The sounds they stood for—syllables—were from the language of the dominant people of the time, the Sumerians. This was the beginning of writing that represented the spoken word. From then on, the different languages of people all around Mesopotamia began to be written in cuneiform script.

Clay Envelopes

The Mesopotamians not only invented writing, they invented **stationery**, too. From around 2000 BC, they started using clay envelopes in which to put the clay tablets they wrote on. The information inscribed on a clay tablet could easily be changed by wetting the clay and rewriting on it. Clay envelopes, sealed with an official clay seal, kept the documents safe. Personal "letters," written on a clay tablet and sealed, could also be put in clay envelopes. The address ("To my brother, Awil-Adad," for example) would be inscribed on the outside of the envelope. This would have been the world's first postal service!

A scene from a stone relief from Nineveh, from about 700 BC, shows scribes with hinged writing boards and scrolls counting enemy heads after a battle. The Mesopotamians invented writing more than 5,000 years ago. They first used a stylus, which was a simple pointed water reed, to draw pictures of objects on wet clay tablets.

Hammurabi's Legal Code

Hammurabi (who ruled from 1792 to 1750 BC) was king of Babylon. He was one of the greatest of all Mesopotamian rulers. During his reign, 282 "laws" were engraved on a block of black granite stone that was 6.5 feet (2m) tall. The laws, written in cuneiform in the Babylonian language, are known as the Code of Hammurabi. In fact, they were not laws as such. They were a series of people's rights, responsibilities and obligations, and legal judgments. Punishments for offenses were based on the concept of "an eye for an eye, a tooth for a tooth."

The Code of Hammurabi is the single most important written document of Mesopotamia. It gives us a clear view of everyday life and the organization of Babylonian society in the eighteenth century BC. It is the longest and most complete legal document in the history of Mesopotamia yet discovered. The stone on which the code was written was discovered by French archaeologist Jean-Vincent Scheil in 1901. Today it is housed in the Louvre Museum in Paris, France.

The Code of Hammurabi (1792-1750 BC) is a collection of 282 case laws (violations of the law and their corresponding punishments), inscribed on a 6.5-foot-tall (2-m-tall) stela, discovered at Susa, in southern Iran, in 1901. At the top of the stela is a carving that shows Shamash (left), the sun god, handing the law to Hammurabi.

THE TECHNOLOGY
OF MATHEMATICS AND NUMBERS

Our knowledge of the Mesopotamians' counting systems comes mainly from
Babylonian times (2000-600 BC). Earlier, the Sumerians and Akkadians
had used a counting system based on units of sixty (called a base-sixty, or
sexagesimal system; today we mainly use a system based on units of ten, the
decimal system). The Babylonians inherited the sexagesimal system and
developed very complex mathematics from it. Today we still use the old
Babylonian base-sixty system for some units of measurement; for example,
there are sixty minutes in an hour and 360 degrees in a circle.

Before Babylon

Babylonian mathematics evolved over thousands of years from number
systems in Mesopotamia. The earliest, from the seventh millennium BC,
involved the use of simple clay tokens. The number of tokens represented a
number of sheep, or bundles of grain, or some other agricultural commodity.
Tokens later came to represent a fixed number of something. A cone-shaped
token might mean ten sheep. Two cone tokens would represent twenty sheep.
A round token might represent fifty bundles of grain. Three round tokens
meant 150 bundles of grain.

The invention of cuneiform writing around 3000 BC brought an important
change in Mesopotamian counting. In the past, one symbol would represent a
number and the thing being counted; for example, one symbol for five sheep,
and a different symbol for five bundles of grain. Now the symbol for the
quantity of something could be written in cuneiform. That would be followed
by a separate symbol for the item being counted.

This was the beginning of numbers and measuring systems. Over
the third millennium BC, the Mesopotamians developed many different
systems of weights and measures. (Even today we use different measuring
systems; for example, kilograms and pounds, meters and feet, and acres and
hectares.) They used cuneiform tablets to record not only amounts but also
mathematical calculations, such as the formula for the area of a field, or the
length of a city wall. They also made up conversion tables with solutions

This Sumerian clay tablet gives the calculations of the surface area of land at the city of Umma, and dates from 2100 BC. The Mesopotamians used cuneiform tablets to write down complex mathematical problems by 1700 BC.

to all kinds of complicated mathematical problems. By 1700 BC there were thousands of clay tablets showing multiplication tables, square roots, and other complex mathematics, including trigonometry.

We have inherited important features of Mesopotamian counting systems. The division of the hour into sixty minutes and the minute into sixty seconds, as well as the 360 degrees of a circle, come from the Mesopotamian sexagesimal system. The division of the day into twenty-four hours, and the year into 365 days, also comes from Mesopotamia.

STOP AND CHECK

Reread What are some important elements of Mesopotamian mathematics that we still use today? Reread the text on pages 108–109 to find the answer.

Conclusion

The Mesopotamian civilization ended around AD 650. The great cities and structures built by the Mesopotamians were abandoned. They remained covered by the desert sands until their discovery by archaeologists in the nineteenth century. Technologies that evolved in Mesopotamia over many thousands of years, however, survived the passage of time. They were passed on and developed by later civilizations of ancient Greeks and Romans, Persians, North Africans, and modern Europeans. Today many of the most basic technologies that we take for granted—for example, the wheel, writing, and counting systems—were born thousands of years ago in "the land between the rivers," that cradle of civilization that we know as Mesopotamia.

This reconstruction of the Ishtar Gate was built in Baghdad, Iraq, to become the entrance to a museum that was never completed. The original Ishtar Gate (Ishtar was the goddess of war and love) was the eighth gate to the inner city of Babylon and was constructed around 575 BC by King Nebuchadnezzar II (circa 630-562).

TIME LINE

10,000–9000 BC	Permanent settlements begin in the region around Mesopotamia.
7000 BC	First farming communities are created.
7000–6000 BC	Earliest counting system (clay tokens) is used.
6000 BC	Handmade pottery and clay stamp seals are made.
3500–3200 BC	The wheel is invented for pottery making and transportation.
circa 3500 BC	First picture writing appears; cylinder seals are used.
3200–2000 BC	Early Bronze Age takes place in Mesopotamia.
circa 3200 BC	Earliest Mesopotamian city, Uruka, flourishes.
circa 3000 BC	Cuneiform writing is invented.
circa 2500 BC	Cuneiform symbols begin to represent sounds and speech.
2100 BC	Ziggurat of Ur is constructed.
circa 1755 BC	Code of King Hammurabi (1792 – 1750 BC) is engraved in cuneiform on a stone slab.
circa 604–562 BC	The reign of King Nebuchadnezzar II and the construction of the Hanging Gardens of Babylon occur.
539–331 BC	Babylon is ruled by Persians.
331–126 BC	Mesopotamia is ruled by the Greeks.

ABOUT THE AUTHOR

GRAHAM FAIELLA

believes that geography means much more than just maps and mountains—it should also include information about the rich cultures that have contributed to the development of a region. His books have taken readers on fascinating journeys through England and Spain and into America's distant past.

In addition to cultural geography, Graham has written about everything from whales and fishing to nutrition and ancient inventions. No matter what he's writing about, though, Graham knows that careful research is an important part of a writer's job. After carefully investigating a topic, he enjoys sharing his discoveries with readers of all ages. Graham lives in London, England.

AUTHOR'S PURPOSE

In this selection, the author describes tools and inventions that came into use thousands of years ago. How does he use precise, specific language to help you understand how ancient technology worked?

RESPOND TO READING

SUMMARIZE

Use important details from *The Technology of Mesopotamia* to summarize what you have learned about how early inventions helped people solve problems. Information from your Problem and Solution Chart may help you.

Problem	Solution

TEXT EVIDENCE

1. Describe the text features the author uses. How do they help you determine that *The Technology of Mesopotamia* is an example of expository text? **GENRE**

2. Identify three problems that the people in Mesopotamia faced and the inventions that helped solve them. **PROBLEM AND SOLUTION**

3. The Latin root *contra-* means "opposite" or "against." How does this root help you figure out the meaning of the word *counterweight* on page 102? **LATIN ROOTS**

4. Review the pictures on page 105 of *The Technology of Mesopotamia* that show how cuneiform writing changed over time. Write about how later forms of cuneiform helped Mesopotamians solve problems that earlier forms could not have solved. **WRITE ABOUT READING**

Make Connections

Talk about the early Mesopotamians and their contributions to civilization. **ESSENTIAL QUESTION**

In what ways are we still influenced by Mesopotamian technology? **TEXT TO WORLD**

Compare Texts
Read about the discovery of what
may be the first story ever to be
written down.

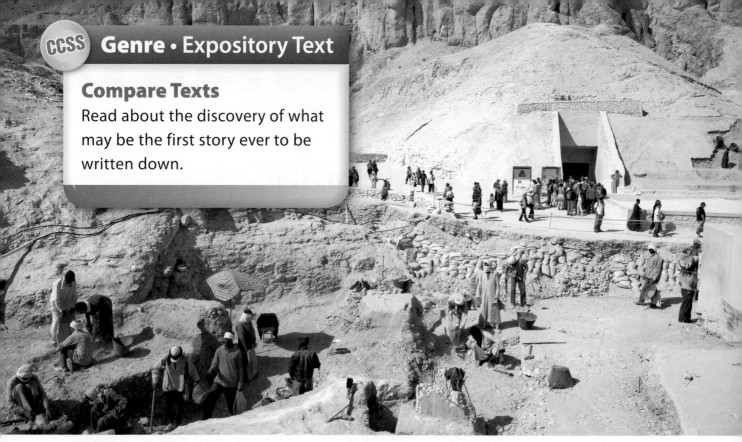

GILGAMESH LOST AND FOUND

*The search for ancient
artifacts can be a long
and difficult process.*

A Stunning Discovery

A dozen clay tablets tell what may be the first fictional story
ever written on Earth. Yet the story was nearly lost forever. In 1853,
archaeologists in Iraq discovered fragments of tablets covered with
cuneiform writing. They turned out to be the remains of a vast
Assyrian library that had been buried for more than two thousand
years. But the cuneiform writing they contained was a mystery.

Then an amateur researcher named George Smith started
studying the tablets. He taught himself all about cuneiform, and
spent his free time piecing together and translating the fragments.
He discovered that most of the tablets **utilize** cuneiform to record
names, dates, and farming information. But then he found an
artifact that was different from the rest. It told a story, the epic
saga of King Gilgamesh. Epics are long narrative poems about the
adventures and deeds of traditional or historical heroes or heroines.

Gilgamesh and Enkidu

The Epic of Gilgamesh

The epic begins in the Mesopotamian city of Uruk, where King Gilgamesh is a strong, brave, and handsome ruler. But he is also a selfish tyrant who mistreats his subjects and abuses his power. No one will challenge him, so the gods decide to send Enkidu to befriend Gilgamesh and hopefully bring peace.

In this excerpt, Enkidu and Gilgamesh meet for the first time.

Gilgamesh and Enkidu's friendship grows stronger as they travel and share many adventures. Returning at last to Uruk, Gilgamesh becomes a fair and compassionate king.

Ivy Close Images/Alamy; (bkgd) Siede Preis/Photodisc/Getty Images

from The Epic of Gilgamesh

retold by Elizabeth Poreba

Crowds clustered around Enkidu as he entered the city gate.

"As tall as the king," the people said, "but is he as strong as Gilgamesh?"

They told Enkidu about Gilgamesh and his cruelty.

And then the king himself appeared.

Quick as thought, Enkidu shot out a foot and blocked the king's way.

Furious, Gilgamesh threw himself upon the impressive stranger.

The two men grappled by the gate and clashed in the public square.

The doors and walls of Uruk shuddered with the force of their fight.

Finally, Gilgamesh wrestled Enkidu to the ground, for he was the stronger champion. Yet as soon as the fight was over, Gilgamesh immediately lost his anger and spoke to Enkidu with respect and admiration.

"Your mother's son is a man like no one else," said the king. "You are mightier than others and destined for greatness."

Thus began a noble friendship. Who knows the ways of men?

Make Connections

Discuss why a written record of the first fictional story was an important contribution by Mesopotamian civilization. **ESSENTIAL QUESTION**

How did the technology of writing that the Mesopotamians developed help preserve *The Epic of Gilgamesh* for future generations? **TEXT TO TEXT**

Essential Question
How did democracy develop?

Read how democratic concepts that began in ancient Greece and Rome served as a foundation for the development of American democracy.

Go Digital!

WHO CREATED DEMOCRACY?

By Connie Nordhielm Wooldridge
Illustrated by Jamil Dar

Before we ask the question *Who created democracy?* perhaps we should ask another question first. Just what exactly is democracy? A democracy is a form of government in which the people take part in governing themselves. The word *democracy* comes from two Greek words: "demos" meaning "people" and "kratos" meaning "power" or "authority." When you put these two words together, *democracy* can be translated to literally mean "people power," or "rule by the people."

Thousands of years ago, when people first began to live in communities and cities, they looked for ways to create rules and laws for everyone to follow. Many of these early cities and civilizations had autocratic governments. The word *autocracy*, the opposite of democracy, comes from the Greek words "kratos" and "autos," meaning "self." In an autocratic government, one person holds all the power. Sometimes he or she governs without the consent of the people.

So how did people win the right to govern themselves? In other words, who created democracy? To find the answer to this question we must journey back in time, to the city-state of Athens in the fifth and fourth centuries B.C.

In 700 B.C., there was no Greek word for "democracy." It didn't exist for the same reason that the Greek word for "computer" didn't exist. It had not yet been imagined. For the wealthy citizens of Athens, there was no reason to imagine it. The social system of the city was based on wealth rather than aristocratic birth. Rich landowners relaxed on enormous estates. They grew olives, grapes, and other crops, their fields attended to by slaves. And they made the laws for everyone else.

Only the rich were part of the oligarchy that ruled Athens. An *oligarchy* is a government that is ruled by only a few people. Yet most Athenians were not rich. Many struggled to grow crops on their tiny farms and plots of land. If they could not pay their taxes they were forced to borrow the money. If they couldn't pay back their debts, family members were often sold into slavery.

By 630 B.C. the poor of Athens were becoming angry and frustrated. In the weekly marketplace they met and traded not only food but stories of broken families. They grumbled about debts that could never be repaid. In time, the conversation turned into action.

The wealthy members of the oligarchy knew they could not fight the poor. They were outnumbered. They had to make changes before Athens headed straight for a civil war.

Taxation Without Representation

Over a thousand years later, in 1765, debt was also on the mind of Britain's King George III. He had just fought an expensive war to defend his American colonies in the French and Indian War. Instead of being grateful, however, the colonists were aspiring to rule themselves. They began by forming assemblies that hadn't been approved by the British Parliament. So Parliament passed the Stamp Act. This required colonists to buy a stamp and attach it to every piece of paper they used, from newspapers to magazines to playing cards. The king believed this would refill the British treasury. It would also remind the colonists who was in charge.

WHAT IS A POLIS?

Thousands of years ago, when people who had been nomads and wanderers began to settle in particular places, they had to figure out how they would live with one another and who would be in charge of the government. In ancient Greece, several hundred small city-states formed, each one called a polis ("city"). The word *politics* comes from this Greek word. Each polis had its own army, government, and culture.

The colonists, however, became furious. Not over the amount of the tax but over the idea that Britain thought it had the right to tax citizens who could not vote for their representatives in Parliament. The colonists **withstood** this assault on their freedom by demanding that the king repeal the Stamp Act. This was followed by protests in the streets of Boston, Philadelphia, and New York. Many people burned the hated stamps. Seeing the hostile reaction in the colonies, the British government repealed the Stamp Act in March 1766. But at the same time it passed the Declaratory Act, which said that Great Britain was superior to the American colonies "in all cases whatsoever." In other words, Britain could raise taxes on the colonies whenever it felt like it.

Anger in the 13 American colonies began to bubble over. If the colonists didn't have a vote in Britain's Parliament, why should they follow the laws that it approved? Soon whispers of war were passed from person to person in the shops and harbors of America's cities and villages. The situation was spinning out of control.

STOP AND CHECK

Ask and Answer Questions In what way were taxes a part of the fight for democracy in both the American colonies and ancient Athens?

A New Government for Athens

By 600 B.C. the situation in Athens was also spinning out of control. The wealthy landowners knew they had to find a way to calm the city and quiet the protests that erupted almost daily. In 594 B.C., for reasons that remain obscure, they turned to a man named Solon for help.

Solon was a landowner. He had built a fortune working for many years as a trader. But he had also once been poor. For this reason he was able to build a bridge between the classes.

At first, there was great **speculation** about what Solon would do with the power that had been given to him. But Solon surprised everyone. First, he changed the debtor's laws. Athenians would no longer have to sell family members into slavery to settle debts.

Then Solon began to change government and society. He divided citizens into four classes based on how much their farms produced. Now people were able to move into another class by growing more food. In the new system, people in the first three classes were able to run for government office. The wealthy were no longer in charge of making laws for everybody.

Many people liked what Solon had done, but not everyone. The wealthy were not happy about having to share power. The lowest class still could not participate in government and make laws. Would the new Athenian government survive?

The Revolutionary War Begins

In contrast to the Athenian crisis of 594 B.C., the colonial crisis in September 1774 could not be solved by one person. In the months that had **preceded** the crisis, Britain had closed Boston Harbor thinking it would teach the colonists a lesson. Without their harbor, the people of Boston could not send or receive goods. But instead of giving in to Britain the American colonies boldly sent representatives to a general Continental Congress in Philadelphia. The colonists fired off a letter to King George III asking for a voice in Parliament. In April, 1775, the King sent British troops to Massachusetts to seize colonial weapons that had been stored there.

The colonists saw only one way forward: they began preparations to wage war against the most powerful country in the world. It was a war based on the **principal** idea that citizens should have a say in their government. Thomas Jefferson argued the case elegantly when he wrote the Declaration of Independence. Every man who signed that document, on July 4, 1776, was guilty of treason in the eyes of the British.

As the British army marched toward Lexington, Massachusetts, a small band of colonists gathered to meet them. A British officer ordered the colonists to drop their weapons and leave. Suddenly, as the colonists turned to go, a shot rang out. The Revolutionary War had begun.

True Democracy for Athens

In 561 B.C. another powerful man sent troops, this time to Athens. Peisistratus was rich and powerful, and with the help of his soldiers he took control of the city from Solon. A short 34 years after Solon's reforms, Athenian democracy stumbled. The people had no control over what Peisistratus did, and he began to **restrict** their rights. When his son Hippias took control after his death, the wealthy landowners of Athens hired an army to remove Hippias from power. Then they asked a man named Cleisthenes, who helped defeat Hippias, for his ideas about a new government.

Cleisthenes wanted a government run by the people, and he made sweeping changes. First, he formed what he called an Assembly, which became the city's lawmaking body. Every citizen, rich or poor, got a vote there. Assembly meetings occurred on a hillside outside Athens every ten days where laws and taxes were debated. No laws were passed in Athens unless they were approved by the Assembly.

In 507 B.C. Cleisthenes also formed the Council of the Five Hundred to run the daily business of Athens. Ideas for laws and taxes started in the Council and were then brought to the Assembly for a vote.

After almost fifty years, the people of Athens had a true democracy – government run by the people.

A Republic for Rome

While Cleisthenes was hard at work forming the Council of Five Hundred, across the Mediterranean Sea the Romans were busy establishing their own republic. In 509 B.C., King Lucius Tarquinius Superbus was driven from Rome and the Roman government was eventually divided among three separate branches: the Senate, the Assembly, and the Consuls:

Senate - The Aristocratic or Patrician Branch of Government

Roman Senators (from the Latin word *senex* meaning "old man") were patricians (or aristocrats) chosen by the Consuls as advisors. Their number started at 300 but grew over the years of the republic. The Senate controlled how much money the government spent and because its members served for life, it became more powerful over time.

Assembly - The Democratic Branch of Government

The earliest Roman Assembly was made up only of patricians so the plebeians, or working class, established an assembly of their own. They were tired of having only a limited say in government. By 287 B.C. the plebeian Assembly included a few patricians and created laws for all Roman citizens. Since the Assembly elected the Consuls and all Consuls became Senators, the Assembly became a powerful branch of the government over the years.

Consuls - The Monarchical or King-like Branch of Government

Two men were nominated by the Senate and elected by the Assembly each year to rule Rome. They had veto power over one another, they took monthly turns ruling over the Senate, and they commanded the Roman army. After 367 B.C., at least one of the two had to be a "plebeian" or common person. Consuls automatically became Senators at the end of their terms.

STOP AND CHECK

Ask and Answer Questions
How did the reforms of Cleisthenes change the concept of Greek democracy developed under Solon?

We the People

In 1783, after eight years of fighting, the British surrendered and a government ruled by the people finally became a reality in America. But for a few years following the peace treaty with Great Britain the very foundation of the newborn United States of America was threatened. As some powerful state governments tried to **promote** their ideas and force their wills on the nation, many people realized that a compromise between state governments and a new federal government would be necessary.

When a delegation of men finally gathered in Philadelphia for a Constitutional Convention in May 1787 to address the problem, they had done their homework well. They had studied Solon, Cleisthenes, and the government of ancient Athens. They were familiar with Rome's three-branch model of government.

But if they agreed on the three-branch plan, they disagreed on how the two houses of the legislative branch ought to look: should each state send an equal number of representatives as the New Jersey Plan urged? Or should the Virginia Plan, which proposed representation based on a state's population, be adopted?

The Convention was near collapse when a solution was proposed: The Senate would have the same number of representatives from each state while the members of the House of Representatives would be chosen based on the population of their state. So today Texas would have more representatives than a state such as Rhode Island. With the crisis averted, the Convention produced a government much like the Republic of ancient Rome:

The **executive branch** is headed by the president who executes, or carries out, laws and directs national defense and foreign policy.

The **legislative branch** is headed by the two houses of Congress, the House of Representatives and the Senate. Congress passes laws, approves treaties, and creates spending bills.

The **judicial branch** is headed by the Supreme Court which interprets the Constitution.

How did democracy develop? It began when the ancient Greeks and Romans tried to answer the question *Who should be in charge of government?* Influenced by the Greeks and Romans, the writers of the U.S. Constitution answered the question in the first three words of the document they wrote in 1787: *We the people.*

ABOUT THE AUTHOR

CONNIE NORDHIELM WOOLDRIDGE

loves taking historical events and finding ways to "translate" them into nonfiction stories that will engage readers. Sometimes she zeroes in on a small event, but more often she reads stacks of books on a large, sweeping subject, searching for a factual storyline that will carry her readers on a journey through fifty or a hundred or even several thousand years of time. Her book *When Esther Morris Headed West* tells the true story of a 55-year-old woman who settled in the Wyoming territory in 1869, and almost single-handedly convinced the local government to allow women the right to vote.

Before she started writing, Connie studied Greek culture and archaeology in Greece – a great introduction to the beginnings of Greek democracy! Today she lives with her husband in Richmond, Indiana.

AUTHOR'S PURPOSE

In writing *Who Created Democracy?*, Connie Nordhielm Wooldridge wanted to help readers compare and contrast the beginnings of democracy in ancient Greece, Rome, and colonial America. What signal words and graphic devices did she use?

RESPOND TO READING

SUMMARIZE

Use key details from *Who Created Democracy?* to summarize the most important facts and events in the selection. Information from your Venn diagram may help you.

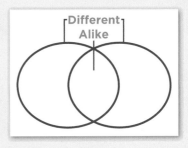

TEXT EVIDENCE

1. Identify at least two text features that help you recognize *Who Created Democracy?* as an example of expository text. **GENRE**

2. In what ways were the Senate and Assembly of ancient Rome similar to and different from the House of Representatives and the Senate in the U.S. Congress? **COMPARE AND CONTRAST**

3. The Latin prefix *re-* means "anew." How does knowing the meaning of this prefix help you to understand the meaning of *reform,* as in "after Solon's reforms, Athenian democracy stumbled"? **GREEK AND LATIN PREFIXES**

4. A compare and contrast text structure explains the similarities and differences between two or more topics. Write about whether you think this was an effective way for the author to present information about the development of democracy. **WRITE ABOUT READING**

Make Connections

How does studying the past help us to understand how concepts such as democracy developed over time? **ESSENTIAL QUESTION**

Describe the most interesting fact you learned about the history of democracy. What does this fact help you understand about why different forms of government succeed or fail? **TEXT TO WORLD**

How *Ideas* Become LAWS

Charlie Hill

A Rocky Ride

Americans, young and old, can help bring about change. Take, for example, the theoretical case of Steve Kresky. One day he was racing the wind along the bike path near his home. Steve felt like he was flying. Then, suddenly, Steve *was* flying. The front tire on his bike grazed a rock and, knocked off balance, Steve landed hard on the ground. Luckily he wasn't hurt because he was wearing a bicycle helmet.

Later, when he got home, Steve talked about what had happened with his dad. "It's so easy to have an accident," Steve said. "There should be a law that states everyone has to wear a helmet."

Then Steve had an idea; maybe he could help to create a law. His dad said that the first step was to contact their state representative. "Representatives are the people we elect to make laws in our state," his father explained.

Democracy in Action

National laws apply to everyone in the United States, while state and local laws are for people who live in a particular state or city. Almost anyone can suggest a law.

Steve and his dad contacted Marta Ortiz, who was a member of the state assembly. Along with representatives in the state senate, assembly members make laws. After speaking with Steve, Ms. Ortiz agreed that bicycle helmets were an important safety issue, so she said she would propose and sponsor a bill, or a plan for a law.

An Idea Becomes a Law

During a committee hearing with assembly members, Steve and Ms. Ortiz explained why they felt the law was necessary. The committee rewrote the bill to include only people younger than 18 years of age, and then passed it on to the assembly. The assembly and the senate approved it, and the governor signed it!

The process of transforming an idea into a law is nearly the same in our national government and in many states across the country. Cities and towns also apply many of the same democratic ideas. When our country's founders created the Constitution, they borrowed ideas from the ancient Greek and Roman systems of government. The **foundation** of these systems was based on the belief that ordinary citizens should not be discouraged from **aspiring** to suggest laws.

A Law Takes Shape

Ms. Ortiz displayed the following chart to show Steve the process a bill takes to become a law in their state.

Step 1: The bill goes to a clerk, who reads the bill to the state assembly.

Step 2: The bill goes to a committee. If the committee approves the bill, it goes to the full state assembly.

Step 3: Representatives debate the bill then vote on it. If it passes in the assembly, it goes to the state senate.

Step 4: A state senate committee votes on the bill. If it passes, the full senate debates the bill then votes on it. If it is approved, it goes to the governor.

Step 5: The governor can sign the bill into law, do nothing so that it automatically becomes law after 5 to 14 days, or veto it. A veto means the law is rejected. Most state assemblies and senates can override a veto by a two-thirds majority vote.

Make Connections

What role does democracy play in the lawmaking process?
ESSENTIAL QUESTION

In what ways has lawmaking changed since ancient times?
TEXT TO TEXT

ROMAN DIARY

THE JOURNAL OF ILIONA OF MYTILINI, WHO WAS CAPTURED
BY PIRATES AND SOLD AS A SLAVE IN ROME, AD 107

By Richard Platt, illustrated by David Parkins

Essential Question

**What was life like for people in
ancient cultures?**

Read about the experiences of a
young slave girl in ancient Rome.

Go Digital!

When Iliona and her family sail to Egypt from their home on the Greek island of Mytilini, their ship is attacked by pirates. Iliona's parents are killed, and she and her younger brother Apollo are taken to Rome where they are sold as slaves. But Iliona still has in her possession the ink, pen, and papyrus her mother gave her before they left on their trip. She uses them to keep a diary of her new life, with its hardships and adventures. But one question is always on her mind: Will she ever be free again?

MY THIRD DAY IN ROME

We reached this strange and enormous city two days ago—not directly, but by hopping like frogs, for we were bought and sold three times on the way.

At each auction, Apollo and I clung to each other, in case we should be sold apart, but—praise be to Zeus—it has not happened. Instead, other children have joined our miserable band. At each auction, our price rises (though mine more than Apollo's, for I can speak **fluent** Latin and read a few words, but he struggles to write even in Greek). Finally we came into the port of Ostia on a stinking barge, which I think must have carried rotten fish before us.

We were herded quickly through the streets to some dark, cramped lodgings. We had food to eat—bread, oil, and olives—but we were all filthy from our long journey. Creatures moved in my hair; my clothes were like rags, and my eyes were red from crying.

Today two women came to the room in which we were locked with the other children. They took us out and gave us water and oil to wash with. Then they cleaned our hair with fine-toothed combs to remove the lice and gave us new garments to wear. I could not help but enjoy this, until one of my companions snapped, "Idiot! Can't you see that they are preparing us for sale again?"

During the journey to Rome, we traveled on foot (much) . . .

by ship (also much) . . .

in a cart (twice) . . .

and on donkeys (once).

THE SIXTH DAY

My parting from Apollo came sooner than I had dreamed possible, for, seeing me sob all the way from the auction, the overseer clearly decided he'd have no peace until we were separated.

When we reached the house, he pushed me into a little room and bolted the door. I hammered with my fists but simply got bruised and splintered. I lay on the bed and tried to forget I was a prisoner by writing everything that had happened that morning in this journal.

I must have slept afterward, for when I awoke, the door was open and a little lamp burned in an **alcove** in the wall, casting shadows across the room. When one of them moved, I sat up quickly.

"Don't be afraid," the shadow said, and I saw its owner, a girl a couple of years older than me. She told me she was a slave too and that I would be happy here, for the master was a kind and generous man. "And his wife doesn't whip us unless we deserve it!" she added. I asked her name, but before answering, she leaned out of the door and bellowed, "She is awake!"

She had just told me she was called Cytheris when a tall and finely dressed woman swept into the room and shooed her out.

"Iliona—that is your name, isn't it?" the woman asked, turning to me. "I want you to know how welcome you are," she said, but didn't smile.

I asked if I could see Apollo. She looked puzzled, then left the room. A moment later, my little brother shuffled in.

I jumped up and threw my arms around his neck. We sat for a moment on the bed together, but before we had time to say much, the woman came back. In her arms was a sleeping child, about a year old.

The overseer followed her in, so I guessed what was to come. I screamed and begged him not to take Apollo, but it made no difference. He pushed us roughly apart.

Seeing my tears, the woman sat down and put her arm around my shoulder. This started me sobbing again, and the child awoke. I thought she would cry too, but instead she grabbed my hand and began sucking on my little finger.

Apollo's hands were untied now, so he could hug me.

More gently this time, her mother—my new mistress—began talking to me again. I was to be a companion and teacher for little Lydia, she said. I would also teach Greek to Lydia's half brothers, Marcus and Lucullus. "We wanted to buy you because you already knew some Latin," she explained.

Her arm around my shoulder, the warmth of the room, the child in her arms—all these things reminded me of home and my own mother—not in a sad way but (to my surprise) in a way that comforted me. And for a moment I forgot my sorrow and began to wonder if I might be happy here.

DAY III OF THE MONTH OF MAIUS*

I had imagined that a slave's life here in Rome would be one of locks and chains, but there is nothing like that to keep me from running away.

Yet where would I run to, and why would I try? I am beginning to see that in Rome, slavery and freedom are not opposites, like night and day or winter and summer. The poorest Roman citizens are worse off than many slaves. Here I have clothes (though it's true they are simple linen), my stomach never aches with hunger (though the food is plain), and I can rest when I am tired.

*Latin for May

I sleep in a room with Cytheris, and in this I feel I am lucky. She keeps me company and is teaching me much about Rome. Last night I learned about the calendar. Romans count the years from the date Rome was founded. The months are about thirty days long and are each differently named. The days are more difficult, and for now I will just make my diary by counting up from the first day of each month.

STOP AND CHECK

Make Predictions Do you think Iliona will be happy in her new surroundings? Cite text evidence to support your prediction.

It would be simple to distract the doorman and slip into the street.

DAY IV

This day I began my studies. It was also the first time I had set foot outside since the auction. I had expected to study at home, as girls always do in Greece. But instead I went to school with Marcus and Lucullus. The three of us walked there through the streets with Cestius, the boys' pedagogus*.

I was surprised at how humble the school is. On Mytilini, Apollo studied in a grand building with a hundred other boys. This one was just a tiny room with a few stools and an armchair for the teacher. Cestius made fun of my surprise: "This is one of the better ones!" he told me. "Most boys sit in the street to study."

Our class was not so different from my brother's school in Mytilini. Mostly we write on the same wax-coated tablets, though my stylus is shaped like the letter T. With its flat end I can smooth out the wax when I make mistakes, which I think is a fine idea, for I make many.

We studied reading and writing from early morning until noon, when Cestius came back. We walked home along Etruscan Street, which is lined with the most **exotic** kinds of shops. In fact, my nose found the street before my eyes did, because all the incense and perfume sellers have their stalls here.

The street is very busy, and Cestius took my hand. "Keep your eyes peeled," he told us, "for there are thieves around every corner here. They will skin you alive and

Cestius is an old slave: part tutor, part guardian.

sell you back your own hide before you realize you've been robbed."

We saw no thieves, but we did have to flatten ourselves against the wall as a huge cart rumbled past, carrying building stone and timber. Our limbs seemed to be more at risk than our purses!

DAY XX

A fortnight ago, I wrote a letter to Apollo and gave it to my mistress. She promised that the overseer, who regularly travels between Rome and the farm, would take it to him, but I have had no reply.

DAY XXV

This morning I awoke with a thundercloud around my head. I had dreamed that Apollo and I were back on Mytilini, doing the things we used to do together before we were captured—running on the open hills and swimming in the sea. When I awoke, the walls around me felt like a prison.

My master saw my long face, and I told him about my dream. He tried to make me feel better about living here in Rome, finishing by saying, "There is always a chance of manumission." I didn't understand this Latin word, so he explained that good and obedient slaves may be freed through the kindness of their masters or may buy their freedom with the money they earn.

His words lifted my **stifling** gloom, and I began to hope that I might not live my whole life as a slave.

DAY XX OF IUNIUS*

I am soon to see my brother again! As I sat with Lydia this afternoon, Cytheris came and told me that in one month we shall be traveling to my master's estate in the Sabine Hills. We shall stay there through the hottest weeks of the summer—and I shall have the chance to spend some time with Apollo, if his work allows. I am glad, for he has not replied to any of the letters I have sent him.

*Latin for June

DAY XXII

This day our master went to sit in the Senate, which always causes much **upheaval**. He dreads going but loves it when he gets there. Making Rome's laws makes him feel important, and he sees all his friends. Most are very old, and I suspect that they take secret bets on which of them will die first.

In the Senate, my master wears a purple-edged toga.

It was halfway through the morning when my mistress let out a shriek. "He's left his medicine behind!" I looked around, and sure enough, in a niche by the door was my master's flask of sea-grape potion. "Iliona, take it to him, or truly he will cough his lungs up."

I dashed to the Forum and rushed through the door of the Senate House without stopping. Too late, I realized that the passageway led straight into the Senate chamber. I found myself surrounded by Rome's greatest, richest men.

The room fell silent.

"Young lady," a senator finally

addressed me, "I assume that your dramatic appearance is of the **utmost** importance, since the very future of Rome hangs upon the debate it interrupted."

Scanning the rows of seats, I spotted my master and held up the flask. "Senator Martius, you forgot your sea-grape potion."

There was another unbearable silence. Then I heard a stifled snicker from a younger senator at the back. One of his neighbors guffawed, and at length laughter echoed around the chamber. When it died down, someone shouted, "Take your potion, Gaius. Your coughing has been driving us all mad!"

As the laughter started again, a hand pulled the vial from my grip, and it was passed back to my master.

I didn't wait to see him drink, but fled the chamber as quickly as I had entered it.

DAY 1 OF THE MONTH OF IULIUS*

This morning there was silence from the kitchen, which normally rings with the sound of water flowing endlessly from a pipe on the wall into a stone basin below.

"The aqueduct has burst once more!" my mistress exclaimed when she came down.

In Mytilini, water always came from a well, never from a spout in the wall. She explained that our water here comes from springs four days' journey away.

"It's beautiful, clear water, but to flow here, it crosses deep valleys on high, arched bridges. In other places it flows underground, through tunnels. Because of its length—more than 60,000 paces—the channel is always leaking."

In my first week in Rome, I had marveled at the luxury of having water running in the house but soon took it for granted. Now I appreciate it once more, for I have to pick up an amphora* and join a long line of slaves at the fountain in the street outside.

DAY V

We still have no water in the house, and today an errand took me past the aqueduct. From a gap in its side spills a torrent of water that rushes down onto the roofs of the houses below. On the bridge I saw stonemasons at work trying to block the hole with bags full of sand. Quite a crowd had gathered to watch, and I listened as a man shouted angrily at the supervisor of the water repairs. Judging from his fine new toga, he was very wealthy.

"Why do the street fountains still flow when the water in my house has dried up?" the rich man demanded. "Beggars may drink, while my fountain is silent!"

The supervisor of the water repairs let out a deep sigh before replying with exaggerated respect: "Because, sir, inside the castellum** there is a barrier. Normally there is enough water to flow over it and

*Latin for July

*a vase for carrying water ** storage part of an aqueduct

into the pipes that lead into your fine abode"—here he made a little bow—"but if the aqueduct bursts or leaks, the level falls. Then your pipes are cut off, but water continues to flow to the public fountains. In this way"—he paused before delivering his crushing last line—"the poorest citizens in Rome do not have the free water taken from them by those who can afford a supply to their own homes."

This bold response brought a round of applause, for we had all expected the official to grovel to such a wealthy, important man.

Sniffing defeat, the man edged away, muttering, "Ah, yes, I see. Thank you for that clear explanation," as he tried to hide his embarrassment.

DAY XX

We were supposed to leave for the country today, but during a thunderstorm last night, lightning bolts flashed in the direction of the Sabine Hills and everyone (but me) feared it was a sign that we should not travel.

To check whether it was truly a bad omen, my mistress went to the temple of Jupiter Tonans, a thunder god, taking with her an offering of a chicken. (Cytheris says she cannot think the omen too serious, or she would have taken a pig at least.) She came back saying that it is safe to travel, so we depart tomorrow.

I returned past Cloaca Maxima, the city's biggest sewer, which stank in the summer heat.

STOP AND CHECK

Confirm and Revise Predictions
Is Iliona happy in her new surroundings or has she simply adjusted to them? Cite evidence from the text to confirm or revise your prediction.

My master's villa in the Sabine Hills is very grand.

DAY XXII OF IULIUS

From the moment I awoke this morning, I could think only of finding Apollo. Yet this was the very thing I could not do, for the villa is a very different place from our house in Rome. There, my master and mistress lead busy lives and hardly notice if one of us is missing. Here, they are idle, with nothing better to do than to count us and ask, "Where's Cytheris?" or "I haven't seen Iliona for some time. Where's she gone?"

So instead of searching for my brother, I had to be content with glancing from the windows to see if I could spot him. When I finally plucked up the courage to ask whether I could see Apollo, my mistress said curtly, "Perhaps tomorrow," and sent me to put the baby to bed.

Here Cytheris and I have separate rooms. We all retired early to bed this evening, which has given me plenty of time to write in this diary.

DAY XXV

I have finally met Apollo! Having seen me sulking and kicking my heels about my tasks, my master asked me what the matter was, and I said I longed to see my brother.

"Then you shall!" he said, and sent a message that the bailiff, who runs the farm, should fetch him.

I hardly recognized Apollo—his hair was matted and greasy, and he stank like a goat.

When the bailiff finally arrived with a boy, I stared and blinked. Was this Apollo? Only when he spoke my name was I sure, and I ran and threw my arms around him. Then I stood back and gazed at him. He was quite changed. He wasn't just thinner; he had bruises on his arms and a red scar around one ankle. Worse, perhaps, were his eyes. They darted left and right, and he had the expression that I once saw on the face of a stag as it fled from the hunt.

I asked him if he was all right, and before answering, Apollo turned to the bailiff.

Only when the man nodded did he reply—and then in stuttering Latin. "I'm fine," he said. "They treat us well here. The work is not too hard, and we get enough to eat…."

All this came without expression, like the worst actors I had seen in the theater on Mytilini. Then he said in Greek, "I've missed you, but I cannot stay long. We are weeding the vines, and if I don't return, my friends will have to do my row as well as their own. Good-bye."

He kissed me and was gone.

DAY XXVI

I have made friends with the house dogs. They are huge and black—whereas the herders' dogs are all white. I was curious about this and asked the bailiff, who told me, "Why, think about it, girl. A guard dog must be black so that thieves who come in the night cannot see him. A herder's dog is better off white so that he is not mistaken for a wolf."

The house dogs scared me at first.

DAY XXVII

Last night I was woken by the small noise of something dry and hard falling on the floor of my room. Outside, I heard the slap of bare feet running from my window. I crawled around to try to find whatever had been thrown in, but it was too dark. In the morning, I found a short piece of bone. One side was scratched in a pattern. I took it to the window, and in the sunlight, I realized I was holding it upside down.

There, in tiny Greek letters, was a message:

COME TO OUR HUTS IN 2 NIGHTS.

My mistress pointed down the hill to a row of low shacks.

I didn't know how Apollo found out which room was mine. Nor did I think I could wait that long to see him again, but I had no choice. So I continued with my tasks as if I were still in Rome.

Here, though, time seems to crawl past, for in fact, there is little for us to do. This morning my mistress decided that she would like to take a walk with the baby while Cestius was teaching the boys. What this really meant was that she walked while I carried Lydia.

From the road we could look down at row upon row of vines stretching down into the valley—and up, to the steeper slopes lined with olive trees. My mistress's conversation was mostly about how difficult it was to make money from a vineyard. I paid little attention until I heard her saying, "And that's where the laborers live."

DAY XXIX

Zeus must have been smiling on me last night, for there was a full moon. Once everyone was in bed, I had no difficulty slipping out the window and running down the drive through the moon shadows of the olive trees. Now I have learned the truth about Apollo's life on the farm.

"Iliona, I can't begin to describe how awful it is here," he told me. "We are prisoners. We live mostly on coarse bread and olives and work eight days in every nine from dawn until dusk."

I asked him what happened to his ankle.

"One of us tried to escape. They picked him up, whipped him, shaved his head, and branded his leg with an F for *fugitivus*—a runaway."

"But your ankle?"

"I'm coming to that. The overseer said we must all have known about the escape, so for a month we worked in chains. Then Gaius Martius arrived without warning one day and saw what we were enduring. He fired the overseer and put an old slave in his place. Now things are not as bad as they were—we have new clothes and time to rest in the hottest hours."

A dog began to bark, and I was glad I had made friends with them. Apollo poked his head out of the hut. "You had better go. Don't try to come here again. It will be trouble for both of us." He pushed me out, and I sprinted back to the villa.

Only this morning did I realize how close I had come to discovery, for the daylight revealed my dusty footprints, leading from the drive to my window!

DAY XV OF THE MONTH OF AUGUSTUS*

Our stay in the hills finished yesterday, and we are back in Rome. I did not see Apollo again, apart from when we came only close enough to wave. My mistress frowned a silent warning when I asked if we could talk.

We had one exciting moment when rumors spread of slaves deserting a nearby farm. The shutters went up. In the end, though, it turned out to be false gossip.

Latin for August

> **STOP AND CHECK**
>
> **Ask and Answer Questions** Why are living conditions for Iliona and Apollo so different? Find evidence in the text to support your answer.

DAY XX

Yesterday I nearly lost my life—and became a heroine (though I am not sure I deserve the glory heaped on my shoulders)!

The day began normally enough: we set out for Agrippa's baths (not as nice as Nero's, for the water is less clear). We did not linger as long as usual, but instead went to the house of my mistress's friend nearby. Lydia was sleeping, and I took her crib to the other end of the house.

Not long after, there was a smell of smoke. Nobody was concerned, for there is always smoke in Rome from people lighting cooking or heating fires with small wood, to set the charcoal alight. But the conversation turned to fires, such as the great fire fifty years ago that destroyed most of Rome.

Even when we heard cries in the street, there was no alarm. Our hostess looked out but returned, saying, "The fire is distant, and the wind blows it away from here."

It seems that I stumbled from the smoke and flames, dropped the crib and its squealing passenger, and fainted.

But then came a loud hammering at the door. A boy hardly older than me, his face black with soot, asked for buckets, adding, "Look out! The flames are attacking your walls!" At this exact moment, a billow of smoke blew into the room, as if Adranos, the fire god himself, had heard him.

Everyone rushed toward the peristylum.* As soon as we got outside, we heard loud crackling and felt heat on our faces. Hungry flames licked toward the room where Lydia slept, but nobody did anything. While my mistress sobbed, all the other women wrung their hands. One muttered, "At least it isn't a male child."

Their stupidity made me furious and foolhardy. I plunged into the pool in the middle of the peristylum to soak my clothes and covered my face with my wet scarf. Then I dashed toward the open door.

For the rest of my story, I rely on others, for all I remember is waking up in bed at home and immediately retching a foul black paste onto the bedclothes. When the room ceased to spin around me, I saw Cytheris, who whispered, "I fetched our master from the Senate," and pointed to where he stood with my mistress at the end of the bed. They beamed, and my mistress said quietly, "You did a brave and fine thing, Iliona. We shall not forget this."

*courtyard

DAY XXIX OF SEPTEMBER

Our small quiet world was turned upside down yesterday. My master seemed weak and ill when he rose in the morning. When he complained of pains in his chest and numbness in his left arm, my mistress tried gently to persuade him not to attend the Senate. But he was determined to go and set off in a litter, gripping his vial of sea-grape potion.

We learned later that at the Senate House he had to be almost carried to his favorite seat. The blow came when he stood to speak: his legs would not hold him, and he fell to the ground, clutching his chest.

DAY XXX

During the night, a physician came to examine my master. The man was a Greek like me. He arrived with four attendants but took only my mistress into the bedchamber where my master was lying.

When they came out, he was holding my mistress's hand and reassuring her. However, as they passed a torchbearer, I glimpsed his eyes clearly and could see from their empty, hopeless look that he did not believe his own words.

An hour later, my master suffered another blow like the one that struck him yesterday. This time he did not recover.

Even though he was one of the best in Rome, the physician could not help my master.

Now my master is dead.

DAY I OF THE MONTH OF OCTOBER

In the middle of the misery and mourning for my master, I have a reason to be joyful! The reading of his will has brought a fantastic and wonderful surprise.

Yesterday my master's brother fetched the will from a temple nearby where it had been stored for safekeeping. He took it into the dining room to break the seals and read the wax panels to the family.

After about half an hour, my master's brother called me over to sit with him in the peristylum. There he read to me the words that follow (for I borrowed the wax tablets and copied them):

For her bravery in saving my baby daughter from certain death in the flames of a house fire, I set free my slave Iliona immediately. I also set free her brother, Apollo, who shall be brought from my country estate to be reunited with his sister. In addition, I give to Iliona each year the sum of one hundred denarii. *

I am free at last!

DAY III OF THE MONTH OF NOVEMBER

Now that I am free, my mistress treats me better than she did before and even says "please" and "thank you" if she remembers.

Cytheris did not speak to me for a fortnight. Thankfully, though, we are friends once more.

I am spared some of the tasks I hated most, but I am still studying and looking after little Lydia.

Lydia now seems just like a baby sister to me.

Apollo and I have talked about returning to Greece. We could perhaps save enough from our earnings to pay the fare. However, our parents are at the bottom of the sea, and we have few relatives on Mytilini.

Furthermore, if pirates were to attack our ship on the journey, we might swiftly find ourselves back in Rome. Then our story would start again, just as it began a year ago, with chalk on our feet and wooden signs around our necks.

No, for the present we shall stay here, for my mistress's home is now our home, and her family has become our family, too.

* *Roman coins*

145

ABOUT THE AUTHOR AND ILLUSTRATOR

RICHARD PLATT

first explored engineering, graphic design, and photography before he realized that he loved to write. Platt likes to investigate a complex topic and then try to explain it simply. More than 60 nonfiction books later, Platt still loves writing, exploring, and the fascinating research that goes along with it. He has written on a wide variety of subjects including spiders, plagues, rain forests, shipwrecks, space travel, and the histories of cities like New York and London.

Platt and his wife live in Kent, England where five chickens call the Platt backyard home.

DAVID PARKINS

first began making illustrations of wildlife before he moved on to illustrating textbooks. Ultimately, Parkins ended up creating artwork for a wide variety of children's books, magazines, comic books and comic strips. Born in England, Parsons recently moved to Canada, where he is proud to say he has learned to ice skate.

AUTHOR'S AND ILLUSTRATOR'S PURPOSE

The author and illustrator have collaborated on many of the illustrations and captions in *Roman Diary*. What additional facts and details do these features provide readers?

RESPOND TO READING

SUMMARIZE

Use important details from *Roman Diary* to summarize what you have learned about daily life in ancient Rome. Information from your Point of View Chart may help you.

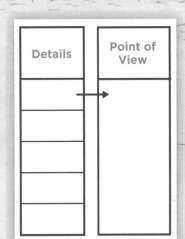

Details	Point of View

TEXT EVIDENCE

1. What features in the text help you to identify *Roman Diary* as a work of historical fiction? **GENRE**

2. The author tells the story from Iliona's point of view. How does this help readers better understand what life was like for a slave in ancient Rome? **POINT OF VIEW**

3. On page 132 of *Roman Diary* it says that a finely dressed woman shooed Cytheris out of the room where Iliona had been taken. What connotation does the word *shooed* have that indicates how Cytheris was asked to leave the room? **CONNOTATIONS AND DENOTATIONS**

4. The narrator tells us everything we know about the other characters in *Roman Diary*. Write on what we might learn about a character such as Cytheris if the story was written from another point of view. **WRITE ABOUT READING**

Make Connections

? What was life like for slaves in Ancient Rome? **ESSENTIAL QUESTION**

Describe one aspect of life in ancient Rome that interested you. How is it similar to or different from the way we live today? **TEXT TO WORLD**

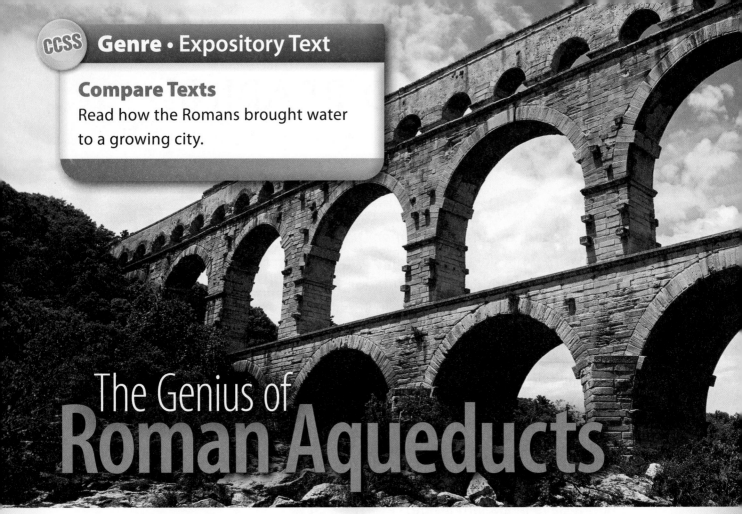

Compare Texts
Read how the Romans brought water to a growing city.

The Genius of Roman Aqueducts

Many ancient Roman aqueducts, such as this one [pictured] are still in use.

It's a hot and muggy day and you've been outside all afternoon, maybe playing catch or jumping rope. Naturally, you're thirsty and a long drink of cold water would certainly hit the spot. You pick up a glass, walk to the faucet and turn it on. You experience first a trickle and then a steady stream of cool, clear water. Ah, that tastes good!

Did you know that many children in ancient Rome did the same thing? In fact, they played many of the same games you do, jumping rope or playing catch, and when they were thirsty they came inside for a drink or went to any number of public drinking fountains around the city.

Most children in Rome knew how water was transported to their city. But did you ever wonder where the water you drink comes from? Or how it got to your faucet?

The fact is, if you do not have a well in your own backyard, the water you use at home may come from a long distance away. However, it doesn't travel by truck or train. Water is transported to you via a complex system of connected pipes and tunnels. These pipes and tunnels channel water from reservoirs and transport it to you. We call the system that carries water an aqueduct. In Latin, this word means "a conductor of water."

Apply Pictures/Alamy

148

What Did People Do Long Ago?

Thousands of years ago, if you wanted water there was often a river nearby. For a city or civilization to thrive, water is essential. People need water for **domestic** purposes like bathing and cooking. It is also used to irrigate farms and for **commerce**, the transportation, buying, and selling of goods. Many early civilizations, such as those in Egypt, Mesopotamia, and India, grew up alongside rivers such as the Nile, the Tigris and the Euphrates, and the Indus.

The city of Rome was no different. It also grew up alongside a river, the Tiber, one of the longest rivers in Italy. But as Rome grew and became the capital of a large empire, it needed more water than the Tiber could provide. So how did the ancient Romans obtain and transport this water?

Aqueducts in Rome

The Romans didn't invent the idea of aqueducts. They had been used in Mesopotamia to supply water to crops some distance from the Tigris and Euphrates. However, the aqueducts the Romans built were far more complex than anything that had come before them. Long, long before engines had been invented that could pump water, the ancient Romans figured out how to use natural forces to do the same thing. They used

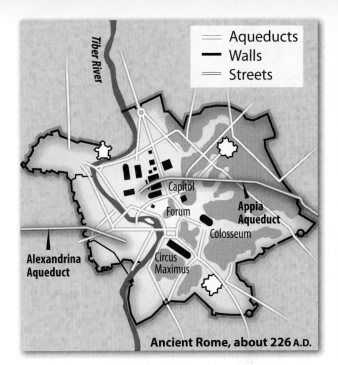

Ancient Rome, about 226 A.D.

the water pressure created by gravity to move water hundreds of miles. It would travel from mountaintop lakes, down the sides of mountains, across valleys and into cities and towns.

Over a period of 500 years, from approximately 300 B.C. to 200 A.D., Roman slaves and paid laborers built 11 major aqueducts throughout the city of Rome. Every stage of the aqueduct had to be carefully planned to make sure that the water, pulled by gravity, made its way gradually downhill to the city. Roughly four of every five miles of Rome's aqueducts ran underground, to protect Rome's water supply from possible enemies. When water had to travel through a valley that was lower than the surrounding countryside, Roman engineers would construct arcades, or bridges with a series of arches. Many of these

arcades can still be seen near Rome. Today they are what most people picture when they hear the word *aqueduct.*

Millions of Gallons of Water

The aqueducts worked because they enabled water to flow downward at a specific angle. The angle had to be steep enough to propel the water forward, but it couldn't be so steep that it would make the water burst through the pipes or make channels overflow. Although the route of the water might seem indirect, it always moved in a way that would allow gravity to get it where it had to go. It might first run downward and then level off as it travelled across the top of an arcade. Then it might proceed downward again in a stepped fashion. Regardless, the force of gravity was central to the design.

At the height of Roman civilization there were more than one million citizens of Rome. All of them relied on the aqueducts to provide more than 40 million gallons of water each day. For a privileged few, such as the emperor, senators, and military leaders, water pipes connected directly into their homes. However, while outdoor fountains today are merely decorative, in ancient Rome, they were actually the main source of water for most Romans. People rarely lived or worked more than a couple of hundred feet from a fountain.

Fountains in ancient Rome allowed all people access to running water.

Rome would have been very different if the aqueducts had not existed. It is hard to imagine what the city would have looked like without a fountain on every square. Many historians believe that without running water, the culture of Rome might never have reached its extraordinary heights.

Make Connections

Why were aqueducts an important contribution of the ancient Romans? **ESSENTIAL QUESTION**

What have you learned about the technologies developed by ancient cultures? **TEXT TO TEXT**

Replicating Water Pressure in a Roman Aqueduct

Question: How does water pressure affect the way water moves? With this science activity you can see the effect of water pressure. Use your science lab safety equipment and ask an adult to help.

Materials:

- A clean, empty, two-liter soda bottle
- A thin nail with a relatively dull point
- Plastic tub or bowl
- Access to running water or large pitcher filled with water
- Duct tape and scissors
- Marker, pencil, and sheet of paper

Step 1: Ask yourself this question before you begin the activity: *What do you think will happen when you fill the bottle with water after making a small hole on the side?*

Now make a second prediction based on this question: *What will happen if two more holes are added on the side of the bottle—one above and one below the first?* Do you think the flow of the water will change depending upon the placement of the holes? In what way? Why?

Step 2: With the marker, carefully make dots on the side of the bottle. The marks will indicate where you should make the three holes. Start about 1/4 away from the bottom of the bottle and make sure that the marks for the three holes are evenly spaced.

Step 3: Take the nail and carefully make the holes. Be sure that the holes are both evenly spaced and sized.

Step 4: Cut off a piece of duct tape large enough to easily cover the three holes. Carefully place the tape over the holes.

Step 5: Fill the bottle to the neck by going to the sink or using water from a pitcher. Make sure you have a tub or bowl placed below the bottle.

Step 6: Pull off the duct tape in one even movement. What do you observe about the flow from the three holes?

Explanation: The more water there is to press down, the further the water will go. As a result, the arc of water from the hole closest to the bottom travels further.

(l, t to b) Comstock/Getty Images; McGraw-Hill Companies - Inc./Richard Hutchings; Stockbyte/Getty Images; Stockbyte/Getty Images; Siede Preis/Getty Images; Burke/Triolo/Brand X Pictures/Jupiterimages; (r, t to b) McGraw-Hill Companies - Inc./Ken Cavanagh - photographer; McGraw-Hill Companies - Inc./Richard Hutchings; Alex Cao/Digital Vision/Getty Images

Essential Question

What influences the development of a culture?

Read about a boy's quest to learn about the art of making pottery in 12th-century Korea.

 Go Digital!

A Single Shard

by Linda Sue Park

illustrated by Julie Kim

Korea is an ancient country located on a peninsula on the eastern edge of Asia. In the 1100s, Korea was a kingdom of farmers and nobles. However, it also had potters, people who made beautiful vases and other objects from clay. The potters were considered to be artists. Tree-ear, the hero of this selection, has only one wish—to become a potter and make works of art from clay.

Tree-ear was so called after the mushroom that grew in wrinkled half-circles on dead or fallen tree trunks, emerging from the rotten wood without **benefit** of parent seed. A good name for an orphan, Crane-man said. If ever Tree-ear had had another name, he no longer remembered it, nor the family that might have named him so.

Tree-ear shared the space under the bridge with Crane-man— or rather, Crane-man shared it with him. After all, Crane-man had been there first, and would not be leaving anytime soon. The shriveled and twisted calf and foot he had been born with made sure of that.

Tree-ear knew the story of his friend's name. "When they saw my leg at birth, it was thought I would not survive," Crane-man had said. "Then, as I went through life on one leg, it was said that I was like a crane. But besides standing on one leg, cranes are also a symbol of long life." True enough, Crane-man added. He had outlived all his family and, unable to work, had been forced to sell his possessions one by one, including, at last, the roof over his head. Thus it was that he had come to live under the bridge.

Once, a year or so earlier, Tree-ear had asked him how long he had lived there. Crane-man shook his head; he no longer remembered. But then he brightened and hobbled over to one side of the bridge, beckoning Tree-ear to join him.

"I do not remember how long I have been here," he said, "but I know how long *you* have." And he pointed upward, to the underside of the bridge. "I wonder that I have not shown you this before."

On one of the slats was a series of deep scratches, as if made with a pointed stone. Tree-ear examined them, then shook his head at Crane-man. "So?"

"One mark for each spring since you came here," Crane-man explained. "I kept count of your years, for I thought the time would come when you would like to know how old you are."

Tree-ear looked again, this time with keen interest. There was a mark for each finger of both hands—ten marks in all.

Crane-man answered before Tree-ear asked. "No, you have more than ten years," he said. "When you first came and I began making those marks, you were in perhaps your second year—already on two legs and able to talk."

Tree-ear nodded. He knew the rest of the story already. Crane-man had learned but little from the man who had brought Tree-ear to the bridge. The man had been paid by a kindly monk in the city of Songdo to bring Tree-ear to the little seaside village of Ch'ulp'o. Tree-ear's parents had died of fever, and the monk knew of an uncle in Ch'ulp'o.

When the travelers arrived, the man discovered that the uncle no longer lived there, the house having been abandoned long before. He took Tree-ear to the temple on the mountainside, but the monks had been unable to take the boy in because fever raged there as well. The villagers told the man to take the child to the bridge, where Crane-man would care for him until the temple was free of sickness.

"And," Crane-man always said, "when a monk came to fetch you a few months later, you would not leave. You clung to my good leg like a monkey to a tree, not crying but not letting go, either! The monk went away. You stayed."

When Tree-ear was younger, he had asked for the story often, as if hearing it over and over again might reveal something more—what his father's trade had been, what his mother had looked like, where his uncle had gone— but there was never anything more. It no longer mattered. If there was more to having a home than Crane-man and the bridge, Tree-ear had neither knowledge nor need of it.

STOP AND CHECK

Make Predictions Do you think Tree-ear will one day try to find out what happened to his uncle? Cite evidence from the text to support your prediction.

Breakfast that morning was a feast—a bit of the rice boiled to a gruel in a castoff earthenware pot, served up in a bowl carved from a gourd. And Crane-man produced yet another surprise to add to the meal: two chicken leg-bones. No flesh remained on the arid bones, but the two friends cracked them open and worried away every scrap of marrow from inside.

Afterward, Tree-ear washed in the river and fetched a gourd of water for Crane-man, who never went into the river if he could help it; he hated getting his feet wet. Then Tree-ear set about tidying up the area under the bridge. He took care to keep the place neat, for he disliked having to clear a space to sleep at the tired end of the day.

Housekeeping complete, Tree-ear left his companion and set off back up the road. This time he did not zigzag between rubbish heaps but strode purposefully toward a small house set apart from the others at a curve in the road.

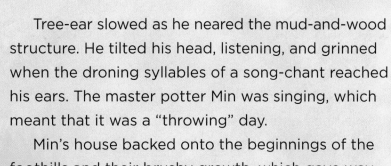

Tree-ear slowed as he neared the mud-and-wood structure. He tilted his head, listening, and grinned when the droning syllables of a song-chant reached his ears. The master potter Min was singing, which meant that it was a "throwing" day.

Min's house backed onto the beginnings of the foothills and their brushy growth, which gave way to pine-wooded mountains beyond. Tree-ear swung wide of the house. Under the deep **eaves** at the back, Min kept his potter's wheel. He was there now, his gray head bent over the wheel, chanting his wordless song.

Tree-ear made his way cautiously to his favorite spot, behind a paulownia tree whose low branches kept him hidden from view. He peeped through the leaves and caught his breath in delight. Min was just beginning a new pot.

Min threw a mass of clay the size of a cabbage onto the center of the wheel. He picked it up and threw it again, threw it several times. After one last throw he sat down and stared at the clay for a moment. Using his foot to spin the base of the wheel, he placed dampened hands on the sluggardly lump, and for the hundredth time Tree-ear watched the miracle.

In only a few moments the clay rose and fell, grew taller, then rounded down, until it curved into perfect **symmetry**. The spinning slowed. The chant, too, died out and became a mutter of words that Tree-ear could not hear.

Min sat up straight. He crossed his arms and leaned back a little, as if to see the vase from a distance. Turning the wheel slowly with his knee, he inspected the graceful shape for invisible faults. Then, "Pah!" He shook his head and in a single motion of disgust scooped up the clay and slapped it back onto the wheel, whereupon it collapsed into an oafish lump again, as if ashamed.

Tree-ear opened his mouth to let out his breath silently, only then realizing that he had been keeping it back. To his eyes the vase had been perfect, its width half its height, its curves like those of a flower petal. Why, he wondered, had Min found it unworthy? What had he seen that so displeased him?

Min never failed to reject his first attempt. Then he would repeat the whole process. This day Tree-ear was able to watch the clay rise and fall four times before Min was satisfied. Each of the four efforts had looked identical to Tree-ear, but something about the fourth pleased Min. He took a length of twine and slipped it **deftly** under the vase to release it from the wheel, then placed the vase carefully on a tray to dry.

As Tree-ear crept away, he counted the days on his fingers. He knew the potter's routine well; it would be many days before another throwing day.

The village of Ch'ulp'o faced the sea, its back to the mountains and the river edging it like a neat seam. Its potters produced the delicate celadon ware that had achieved fame not only in Korea but as far away as the court of the Chinese emperor.

Ch'ulp'o had become an important village for ceramics by virtue of both its location and its soil. On the shore of the Western Sea, it had access both to the easiest sea route northward and to plentiful trade with China. And the clay from the village pits contained exactly the right amount of iron to produce the exquisite gray-green color of celadon so prized by collectors.

Tree-ear knew every potter in the village, but until recently he had known them only for their rubbish heaps. It was hard for him to believe that he had never taken the time to watch them at work before. In recent years the pottery from the village kilns had gained great favor among those wealthy enough to buy pieces as gifts for both the royal court and the Buddhist temples, and the potters had achieved new levels of prosperity. The pickings from their rubbish heaps had become richer in consequence, and for the first time Tree-ear was able to forget about his stomach for a few hours each day.

During those hours it was Min he chose to watch most closely. The other potters kept their wheels in small windowless shacks. But in the warm months Min preferred to work beneath the eaves behind his house, open to the breeze and the view of the mountains.

Working without walls meant that Min possessed great skill and confidence to match it. Potters guarded their secrets jealously. A new shape for a teapot, a new inscribed design— these were things that the potters refused to reveal until a piece was ready to show to a buyer.

Min did not seem to care about such secrecy. It was as if he were saying, *Go ahead, watch me. No matter—you will not be able to imitate my skill.*

STOP AND CHECK

Confirm Predictions Is Tree-ear interested in finding out about his past? Confirm or revise your prediction with text evidence.

It was true, and it was also the main reason that Tree-ear loved watching Min. His work was the finest in the region, perhaps even in the whole country.

Tree-ear peered between the leaves of the paulownia tree, puzzled. Several days had passed since his last visit to Min's house, and he had calculated that it was time for another throwing day. But there was no sign of Min at his work, nor any wet clay on the wheel. The workshop area was tidy, with a few chickens in the yard the only signs of life.

Emboldened by the silence, Tree-ear emerged from his hiding place and approached the house. Against the wall was a set of shelves holding a few of Min's latest creations. They were at the stage the potters called "leather-hard"—dried by the air but not yet glazed or fired. Unglazed, the work was of little interest to thieves. The finished pieces were surely locked up somewhere in the house.

Tree-ear paused at the edge of the brush and listened hard one last time. A hen clucked proudly, and Tree-ear grinned—Min would have an egg for his supper. But there was still no sign of the potter, so Tree-ear tiptoed the last few steps to stand before the shelves.

For the first time he was seeing Min's work at close range. There was a duck that would have fit in the palm of his hand, with a tiny hole in its bill. Tree-ear had seen such a duck in use before. A painter had been sitting on the riverbank, working on a water scene. The painter had poured water from the duck's bill onto a stone a single drop at a time, mixing ink to exactly the correct consistency for his work.

Tree-ear stared at Min's duck. Though it was now a dull gray, so detailed were its features that he found himself half listening for the sound of a quack. Min had shaped and then carved the clay to form curve of wing and tilt of head. Even the little tail curled up with an **impudence** that made Tree-ear smile.

He tore his gaze away from the duck to examine the next piece, a tall jug with ribbed lines that imitated the shape of a melon. The lines were perfectly symmetrical, curving so gracefully from top to bottom that Tree-ear longed to run his finger along the smooth shallow grooves. The melon's stem and leaves were cleverly shaped to form the lid of the jug.

The last piece on the shelf was the least interesting—a rectangular lidded box as large as his two hands. It was completely undecorated. Disappointed in its plainness, Tree-ear was ready to turn away when a thought struck him. Outside, the box was plain, but perhaps inside . . .

Holding his breath, he reached out, gently lifted the lid, and looked inside. He grinned in double delight at his own correct guess and at Min's skill. The plain box held five smaller boxes— a small round one in the center and four curved boxes that fit around it perfectly. The small boxes appeared to completely fill the larger container, but Min had left exactly the right amount of space to allow any of them to be lifted out.

Tree-ear put the lid of the large box down on the shelf and picked up one of the curved containers. On the underside of its lid was a lip of clay that held the lid in place. Tree-ear's eyes flickered back and forth between the small pieces in his hand and the larger container, his brow furrowed in thought.

How did Min fit them together so perfectly? Perhaps he made the large box, then a second one to fit inside, and cut the smaller boxes from that? Or did he make an inside box first and fit the larger box around it? Maybe he began with the small central box, then the curved ones, then—

Someone shouted. The chickens squawked noisily and Tree-ear dropped what he was holding. He stood there, paralyzed for a moment.

It was the old potter. "Thief!" he screamed. "How dare you come here! How dare you touch my work!"

Tree-ear did the only thing he could think of. He dropped to his knees and cowered in a deep formal bow.

"Please! Please, honorable sir, I was not stealing your work—I came only to admire it."

The potter stood over the boy.

"Have you been here before, beggar-boy?"

Tree-ear's thoughts scrambled about as he tried to think what to answer. The truth seemed easiest.

"Yes, honorable sir. I come often to watch you work."

"Ah!"

Tree-ear was still doubled over in his bow, but he allowed himself a single sigh of relief.

"So is it you who breaks the twigs and bruises the leaves of the paulownia tree just beyond?"

Tree-ear nodded, feeling his face flush. He had thought he was covering his tracks well.

"Not to steal, you say? How do I know you do not watch just to see when I have made something of extra value?"

Now Tree-ear raised his head and looked at Min. He kept his voice respectful, but his words were proud.

STOP AND CHECK

Ask and Answer Questions Do you think Tree-ear would like to become a potter? Cite evidence from the text to support your answer.

165

"I would not steal. Stealing and begging make a man no better than a dog."

The potter stared at the boy for a long moment. At last, Min seemed to make up his mind about something, and when he spoke again, his voice had lost the sharpest edge of its anger.

"So you were not stealing. It is the same thing to me—with one part damaged, the rest is of no use." He gestured at the misshapen pottery box on the ground, badly dented from its fall. "Get on your way, then. I know better than to ask for payment for what you have ruined."

Tree-ear stood slowly, shame hot in his breast. It was true. He could never hope to pay Min for the damaged box.

Min picked it up and tossed it on the rubbish heap at the side of the yard. He continued to mutter crossly. "*Ai*, three days' work, and for what? For nothing. I am behind now. The order will be late . . . "

Tree-ear had taken a few dragging steps out of the yard. But on hearing the old potter's mutterings, he lifted his head and turned back toward him.

"Honorable potter? Sir? Could I not work for you, as payment? Perhaps my help could save you some time . . . "

Min shook his head impatiently. "What could you do, an untrained child? I have no time to teach you—you would be more trouble than help."

Tree-ear stepped forward eagerly. "You would not need to teach so much as you think, sir. I have been watching you for many months now. I know how you mix the clay, and turn the wheel—I have watched you make many things . . . "

The potter waved one hand to cut off the boy's words and spoke with **derision**. "Turn the wheel! Ha! He thinks he can sit and make a pot—just like that!"

Tree-ear crossed his arms stubbornly and did not look away. Min picked up the rest of the box set and tossed it too on the rubbish heap. He muttered under his breath, so Tree-ear could not hear the words.

Min straightened up and glanced around, first at his shelf, then at the wheel, and finally at Tree-ear.

"Yes, all right," he said, his voice still rough with annoyance. "Come tomorrow at daybreak, then. Three days it took me to make that box, so you will give me nine days' work in return. I cannot even begin to think how much greater the value of my work is than yours, but we will settle on this for a start."

Tree-ear bowed in agreement. He walked around the side of the house, then flew off down the road. He could hardly wait to tell Crane-man. For the first time in his life he would have real work to do.

About the Author and Illustrator

Linda Sue Park

began to earn money for her writing when she was just nine years old. She received a check for one dollar in payment for a haiku poem that was published in a children's magazine. Her proud father promptly framed the check.

Linda was born in Urbana, Illinois to Korean parents. Her novel *A Single Shard* was awarded the Newbery Medal in 2002. Since then, the author has published several other novels. Today, Linda lives with her husband and two children in New York State.

Julie Kim

sees things that aren't there. At least, she sees the things she plans to draw before she puts anything on paper. Julie carefully researches costumes and other period details of the story settings for her illustrations. Julie has illustrated several magazines and books for children and lives in Seattle, Washington, with her family.

Author's Purpose

In *A Single Shard*, Linda Sue Park goes into great detail about the ceramics produced in Ch'ulp'o, as well as the delicate features of Min's pottery. How does this information help you to understand the culture of 12th-century Korea?

Respond to Reading

Summarize

Use key details from *A Single Shard* to summarize what you have learned about the influences behind the development of a culture. Information from your Point of View Chart may help you.

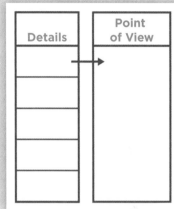

Details	Point of View

Text Evidence

1. What details in the text help you to identify *A Single Shard* as a work of historical fiction? Give at least two details from the story to support your answer. **GENRE**

2. From what point of view is the story told? How does using this point of view help the author develop the character of Tree-ear? **POINT OF VIEW**

3. The Latin-derived suffix *-ance* means "state of." How does this suffix, along with the description of Min's feelings on page 166, help you figure out the meaning of *annoyance* on page 167? **GREEK AND LATIN SUFFIXES**

4. Write how *A Single Shard* would be different if the scene in which Min finds Tree-ear in his yard was written from Min's point of view, in the first person. **WRITE ABOUT READING**

Make Connections

How did the location of the village and the type of clay found in its soil influence the development of its culture? **ESSENTIAL QUESTION**

Explain whether or not you would like to work for a potter or other artist as an apprentice. What part of the work would or would not appeal to you? **TEXT TO WORLD**

Compare Texts

Read how the results of an exam can change the fortunes of a family in China long ago.

A Scholar in the Family

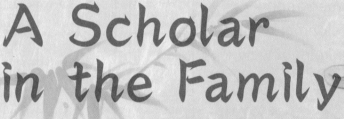

家庭中的學者

Julie Wu

Introduction

The history of China is filled with the struggles of leaders who tried to unite the people of this enormous country. Since the Sui Dynasty (581-618), it had been possible to become a government official by passing a series of written exams. It was only during the Song Dynasty (960-1279), however, that the examination system came to be considered the ladder to success.

Beginning around 1000, for the first time, Chinese commoners were permitted to have jobs within the government. These jobs were called civil service jobs. In order to qualify for a civil service job, men had to take a very grueling civil service exam.

Characters

Narrator

Grandfather (of Cheng and Mei)

Cheng (a young student)

Mei (Cheng's younger sister)

Ying (neighbor and friend of Cheng)

Mother (of Cheng and Mei)

Messenger

Narrator *(Stands alone in front of curtain.)*: Permit me to introduce you to Cheng. *(Cheng walks onto stage and bows.)* Cheng is a young scholar. He has studied very hard in order to take the civil service exam. He is far from home, taking this very difficult test right now. *(Cheng runs off stage quickly and when the Narrator is satisfied that he is gone he nods—as if to say "okay." Then he continues speaking.)* His family awaits his return.

(Curtain opens.)

Mei: Grandfather, do you hear that? *(Mei leans out a window)* It sounded like a horse and cart. Perhaps Cheng is on his way home!

Grandfather: No, it is much too early. Cheng and Ying walked many miles to the city to take the examination, and it lasts for several days. And when he returns, he will make the journey on foot, not by cart.

Mei: I want to take the examination too, when I am older!

Grandfather: A girl's place is at her mother's knee, learning how to tend the fire and prepare meals. It was not long ago that even a boy like Cheng could not take the examination.

Mei: Why is that, Grandfather?

Grandfather: Years ago, only men born to noble families could take the civil service examination. Commoners could not move up in the world. Today, any scholar may try his luck. Now, government jobs will come to those who have proven skill, and not because they were born into a noble house.

Mother: Only one scholar in 100 passes the test! But Cheng has worked so hard. His eyes would grow so tired, learning how to print thousands of Chinese characters. And he has spent years studying the teachings of Confucius, the great educator.

Mei: I know. I helped him study by doing his chores sometimes, remember? *(She smiles brightly.)*

Grandfather: Yes, and I was very proud of you. You were a great help to your brother. In my day if the earth trembled and our homes collapsed or if the great river overflowed, swollen with too much rain, and swept our fields away we peasants lost everything. We had no other work we could do—no way to earn money and rebuild our lives. If Cheng and Ying are accepted into civil service, it would be the beginning of a great **legacy** for our village.

Mei *(looking worried)*: What if they fail?

Grandfather: If they fail . . . *(Grandfather shrugs)* I don't know. We will be no worse off than we were before I suppose.

Narrator: We will soon find out how the boys did! After traveling for many miles along numerous dusty roads, they have finally arrived at the entrance of Cheng's home.

Mother: You look so thin! *(She embraces her son.)*

Mei: Did you pass?

Cheng: I do not know yet, but the examination was very difficult. We each sat in our own small stone cell and wrote about Confucius's writings for three days and three nights!

Mei: You wrote the whole time? Were you allowed to use your books?

Cheng: Oh, no! They even made sure we were not carrying any notes.

Ying *(who has been standing quietly next to Cheng)*: Don't forget. You promised. *(Ying exits.)*

Mother: Promised what?

Cheng *(looking embarrassed and shaking his head)*: It is nothing. *(Cheng turns away from his family and stares in the direction of the front door, where Ying has just exited.)*

Grandfather: It will be a miracle if your score is among the highest. People have invented so many ways to cheat on this exam. Some even pay the officials to get a better score.

Mother: What is wrong, my son?

Cheng *(speaking softly)*: I promised not to tell.

Grandfather *(beginning to get angry)*: You should not keep secrets from us.

Cheng *(Quietly, almost whispering)*: Ying cheated on the exam.

Mother *(gasping)*: Cheated?

Cheng *(Hesitating)*: It became hot on the walk home. Ying pulled a small fan out of his bag to fan his face. As he fanned himself I could see tiny notes on the fan's folds. I accused him of cheating and he admitted to me that he had. He simply opened his fan, pretending to cool himself, and copied his notes!

Julie Wu

Grandfather (*angrily*): If Ying secures a position and you don't, I will have something to say to those officials!

Mother: I would rather have my son fail honestly than cheat.

Cheng: But mother, someone from our village must develop **expertise** beyond being a simple farmer! It's the only way we will be protected if disaster destroys our crops.

Mei (*who has been looking out the window*): Look! A messenger has arrived on horseback. He looks like a soldier. I wonder what he wants.

Messenger: Is this the home of scholar Cheng?

Grandfather: It is.

Messenger: I bring news of the civil service examination exam.

Mother (*anxiously*): What is it?

Messenger: Cheng's score is among the highest of all those who took the exam. Confucius would be proud!

Mei: Here comes Ying. He must have heard the messenger arrive.

(*Cheng and his family all look angrily at Ying as he approaches.*)

Ying: What about me, Ying? Didn't I score well?

Messenger (*consulting his list*): Ying, Ying. Wait a moment. Ah, here it is. (*He scowls.*) You were observed using a small fan in your chamber. You were seen cheating on the exam. Your examination was thrown out.

Mother (*turning and embracing Cheng*): I am so proud of you, my son. We will have a feast to celebrate.

Messenger: After your feast, Cheng will accompany me to the city to begin his new position.

Mei: I wish I could take the exam. I've already learned 1,000 Chinese characters!

Cheng: Maybe by the time you learn all the others you will be permitted to be a civil service worker too!

[Curtain comes down]

Narrator: All is well with the family of Cheng tonight. Not so for the family of Ying. (*Ying frowns, bows his head, and walks off stage. Cheng watches him go, shaking his head.*)

Make Connections

How did allowing Chinese commoners to compete for civil service jobs influence Chinese culture? **ESSENTIAL QUESTION**

In what ways can learning new things and developing new opportunities for people influence the development of a culture? **TEXT TO TEXT**

MAJESTIC

Essential Question
What can the past teach us?
Read how poets reflect on the past and how it affects them.

Go Digital!

It has been years since guests have spent the night,
yet here it sits, majestic in its state
of disrepair, a shadow of the sight
it once projected, ill-aware of fate.
When gold ran out the miners laid in wait,
and word got out, which slowed the westward drift,
migration stalled while those in stead debate
decided if economies would lift.
With nothing else to draw, the end was swift,
more vacancies, the empty rooms were cold.
No longer could the owners man the shift,
and nothing left—the hotel hadn't sold.
The long abandoned property, forlorn,
displays its fading windows as we mourn.

—Jack Huber

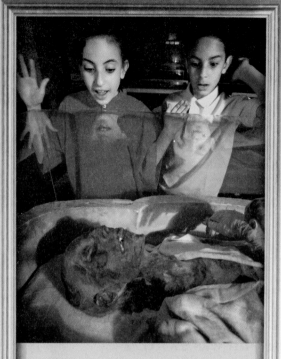

Mummy

So small a thing
This mummy lies,
Closed in death
Red-lidded eyes,
While, underneath
The swaddled clothes,
Brown arms, brown legs
Lie tight enclosed.
What miracle
If he could tell
Of other years
He knew so well;
What wonderment
To speak to me
The riddle of
His history.

— Myra Cohn Livingston

Clay

It all goes back to clay
Beads and bowls and bricks
    baked and built into houses
Pots and paints and possibly poetry
    scratched on terrene tablets
    all those many years ago
Jars to hold cool water
Jars to hold dry bones
A legend of lives lived
    plain or fancy
    foolishly or well
A history of the world
    in this earth unearthed
It all goes back to clay

—Marilyn Singer

RESPOND TO READING

SUMMARIZE

Think about what the speaker of "Majestic" wants to commemorate. Then use important details to summarize the poem. Information from your Theme Chart may help you.

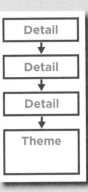

Detail
↓
Detail
↓
Detail
↓
Theme

TEXT EVIDENCE

1. Is "Majestic" an example of a sonnet, lyric poetry, or both? Explain your answer. **GENRE**

2. What is the rhyme scheme in the first four lines of the poem "Mummy," and what is the meter, or the pattern of stressed and unstressed syllables in each line? **LITERARY ELEMENTS**

3. How does the poet use personification in the beginning of the poem "Majestic"? **PERSONIFICATION**

4. Reread "Clay." Use details from the text to explain the message the author is trying to communicate to the reader. **WRITE ABOUT READING**

Make Connections

? The poets contemplate some aspect of the past. What are some important things we could learn from the mummy in Myra Cohn Livingston's poem, or the jars and tablets described in "Clay"? **TEXT TO WORLD**

Compare Texts
Read how two different poets contemplate the past.

Maestro

He hears her
when he bows.
Rows of hands clap
again and again he bows
to stage lights and upturned faces
but he hears only his mother's voice

years ago in their small home
singing Mexican songs
one phrase at a time
while his father strummed the guitar
or picked the melody with quick fingertips.
Both cast their music in the air
for him to snare with his strings,
songs of *lunas* and *amor**
learned bit by bit.
She'd nod, smile, as his bow slid
note to note, then the trio
   *voz, guitarra, violín***
would blend again and again
to the last pure note
sweet on the tongue.

— Pat Mora

* *Lunas* (lōō´ näs) and *amor* (a mōr´)
means "moons" and "love" in Spanish.

**The phrase *voz, guitarra, violin* (vōs, gē tä´ rrä, vē ō lēn´)
means "voice, guitar, violin" in Spanish.

TEXT: "Maestro" is reprinted with permission from the publisher of "Borders" by Pat Mora (© 1986 Arte Público Press-University of Houston) PHOTO: (t) Library of Congress Prints and Photographs Division: [LC-DIG-ppmsc-00343]; (b) Bettmann/Corbis; (frames) Stockbyte/Getty Images ; (bkgd) Brand X Pictures/Getty Images

Tradition

From *Under the Sunday Tree*

Pineapples! pumpkins! chickens! we
carry them on our heads you see
we can glide along forever
and not drop a thing, no never
never even use our hands
never put a finger to it
you know how we learned to do it?
knowledge came from other lands
Africans of long ago
passed it down to us and so
now we pass it on to you
for what is old is also new
pineapples, pumpkins, chickens, we
carry more than the things you see
we also carry history

— Eloise Greenfield

Make Connections

What do these poets remember and celebrate from the past? Why is it important to them? **ESSENTIAL QUESTION**

What have these poems added to your knowledge about the past that you might not have learned in other texts? **TEXT TO TEXT**

Essential Question
What happens when people share ideas?

Read how people from two different cultures clash and then learn from one another.

Go Digital!

How Tía Lola Came to ~~Visit~~ Stay

by Julia Alvarez
illustrated by Lester Coloma

Miguel and Juanita Guzmán have moved to Vermont
from New York City because their mother has taken a job at
a local college. Their mother's aunt, Tía Lola, arrives for a
visit from the Dominican Republic. Tía Lola soon impresses
Miguel's friends and Rudy, the owner of a local restaurant
and the coach of Miguel's baseball team. At the restaurant,
Tía Lola also charms the difficult Colonel Charlebois who
owns the farmhouse that Miguel's family rents.

The long, sweet, sunny days of summer come one after another after another. Each one is like a piece of fancy candy in a gold-and-blue wrapper.

Most nights, now that school is out, Tía Lola tells stories, sometimes until very late. The beautiful cousin who never cut her hair and carried it around in a wheelbarrow. The grandfather whose eyes turned blue when he saw his first grandchild.

Some nights, for a break, they explore the old house. In the attic, behind their own boxes, they find dusty trunks full of yellowing letters and photographs. Miguel discovers several faded photos of a group of boys all lined up in old-fashioned baseball uniforms. Except for the funny caps and knickers and knee socks, the boys in the photos could be any of the boys on Miguel's team. One photo of a boy with a baseball glove in his hand is inscribed, *Charlebois, '34.*

Miguel tries to imagine the grouchy old man at Rudy's Restaurant as the young boy with the friendly smile in the photograph.

But he can't see even a faint **resemblance**.

* * *

Since the team doesn't have a good place for daily practice, Miguel's mother suggests they use the back pasture behind the house. "But let me write Colonel Charlebois first, just in case."

Their landlord lives in a big white house in the center of town. He has already written them once this summer, complaining about "the **unseemly** shape of the vegetation," after Tía Lola trimmed the hedges in front of the house in the shapes of pineapples and parrots and palm trees.

"Can't you just call him and ask him, Mami?" Miguel asks. After all, the team is impatient to get started with practice. A letter will take several days to be answered.

"You try calling him," Miguel's mother says, holding out the phone. Miguel dials the number his mother reads from a card tacked on the kitchen bulletin board. The phone rings once, twice. A machine clicks on, and a cranky old voice speaks up: "This is Colonel Charles Charlebois. I can't be bothered coming to the phone every time it rings. If you have a message, you can write me."

STOP AND CHECK

Make, Confirm, Revise Predictions Do you think the Colonel will let the team practice on his property? Look for text evidence to help you make your prediction.

183

"Let's write that letter, shall we?" Mami says, taking the phone back from Miguel.

Two days later, Colonel Charlebois's answer is in their mailbox. It has not been postmarked. He must have driven out and delivered it himself.

"I would be honored to have the team practice in my back pasture," he replies in a shaky hand as if he'd written the letter while riding in a car over a bumpy road.

"Honored!" Miguel's mother says, lifting her eyebrows. She translates the letter for Tía Lola, who merely nods as if she'd known all along that Colonel Charlebois is really a nice man.

And so every day Miguel's friends come over, and the team plays ball in the back field where only six months ago, Miguel wrote a great big welcome to Tía Lola. Twice a week, Rudy drops by to coach. They play all afternoon, and afterward when they are hot and sweaty, Tía Lola invites them inside for cool, refreshing smoothies, which she calls *frío-fríos.* As they slurp and lick, she practices her English by telling them wonderful stories about Dominican baseball players like Sammy Sosa and the Alou brothers and Juan Marichal and Pedro and Ramón Martínez. The way she tells the stories, it's as if she knows these players personally. Miguel and his friends are **enthralled**.

After a couple of weeks of practice, the team votes to make Miguel the captain. José, who is visiting from New York, substitutes for whoever is missing that day. Tía Lola is named manager.

"*¿Y qué hace el manager?*" Tía Lola wants to know what a manager does.

"A manager makes us *frío-fríos,*" Captain Miguel says.

Every day, after practice, there are *frío-fríos* in a tall pitcher in the icebox.

It is a happy summer—

Until Tía Lola decides to paint the house purple. Miguel and his friends have been playing ball in the back field—their view of the house shielded by the maple trees. As they walk back from practice, they look up.

"Holy cow!" Miguel cries out.

The front porch is the color of a bright bruise. Miguel can't help thinking of the deep, rich purple whose name he recently learned from his father in New York. "Dioxazine," he mutters to himself. The rest of the house is still the same color as almost every other house in town. "**Regulation** white," Papi calls it whenever he comes up to visit and drives through town.

In her high heels and a dress with flowers whose petals match the color of the porch stands Tía Lola, painting broad purple strokes.

For a brief second, Miguel feels a flash of that old embarrassment he used to feel about his crazy aunt.

"Awesome," his friend Dean is saying.

"Cool!" Sam agrees.

They wave at Tía Lola, who waves back.

"¡Frío-fríos!" she calls out. Today she has chosen grape flavor in honor of the new color of the house. By the time Miguel's mother comes home from work, he and his friends look like they have helped Tía Lola paint the house: their mouths are purple smudges. When they open their mouths to say hello, their tongues are a pinkish purple.

"Okay, what is going on?" Mami asks, glancing from Miguel to Tía Lola. She looks as if she is about to cry, something she has not done in a long time.

Tía Lola speaks up. Don't the colors remind her of the island? *"La casita de tu niñez."* The house where Mami spent her childhood.

Miguel can see his mother's face softening. Her eyes have a faraway look. Suddenly, Mami is shaking her head and trying not to laugh. "Colonel Charlebois is going to throw a fit. Actually, he's going to throw us out."

"El coronel, no hay problema," Tía Lola says, pointing to herself and Miguel and his friends. Miguel's mother looks from face to face as if she doesn't understand. Miguel and his friends nod as if they understand exactly what Tía Lola is up to.

The next afternoon, when Miguel's friends come inside from practice, Tía Lola takes their measurements. She has bought fabric with the money the team has collected and is making them their uniforms.

When it is Miguel's turn, he stands next to the mark that his mother made on the door frame back in January. He is already an inch taller!

"Tía Lola, what are you up to?" the team keeps asking. "Are we going to lose our playing field if Colonel Charlebois takes back his house?"

"No hay problema," Tía Lola keeps saying. Her mouth curls up like a fish hook that has caught a big smile.

"Are you going to work magic on him?" Miguel asks his aunt that night.

"The magic of understanding," Tía Lola says, winking. She can look into a face and see straight to the heart.

She looks into Miguel's eyes and smiles her special smile. As the house painting continues, several neighbors call. "What's happening to your house?" farmer Tom asks Miguel. "I don't believe I've ever seen a purple house. Is that a New York style or something?"

Their farming neighbors think of New York as a foreign country. Whenever Miguel and his family do something odd, Tom and Becky believe it is due to their having come from "the city."

"I've never seen a purple house in my life," Miguel admits.

"Neither have I," José adds, "and I live in the city!"

"I've seen one!" Juanita speaks up, showing off.

"Where?" Miguel challenges.

"In my imagination." She grins.

Miguel has been trying to imitate Tía Lola, looking for the best in people. He stares straight into Juanita's eyes, but all he can see is his smart-alecky little sister.

One afternoon, soon after José has returned to the city, Miguel is coming down the stairs to join his teammates in the back field. He pauses at the landing. The large window affords a view of the surrounding farms and the quaint New England town beyond.

A silver car Miguel doesn't recognize is coming down the dirt road to their house. Just before arriving at the farmhouse, it turns in to an old logging road at the back of the property. Behind a clump of ash trees, the car stops and the door opens.

Later, as he stands to bat, Miguel can make out a glint of silver among the trees. Who could it be? he wonders. He thinks of telling his mother about the stranger, but decides against it. She would probably think an escaped convict was lurking in the woods and not allow the team to practice in the back field anymore.

The next afternoon, Miguel watches from behind the curtain as the same silver car he saw in the woods yesterday comes slowly up the drive. His friends have already left after their baseball practice, and his mother is not home from work yet. He can hear Tía Lola's sewing machine humming away upstairs.

"Who is it?" Juanita is standing beside him, holding on to her brother's arm. All her smart-alecky confidence is gone.

"I think it's him—Colonel Charlebois," Miguel whispers. Now that the car is so close, he can make out the old man behind the wheel. The hood has a striking ornament: a little silver batter, crouched, ready to swing. "I'm going to pretend no one is home," Miguel adds.

But Colonel Charlebois doesn't come up to the door. He sits in his car, gazing up at the purple-and-white house for a few minutes, and then he drives away. Later that day, a letter appears in the mailbox. "Unless the house is back to its original white by the end of the month, you are welcome to move out."

"*Welcome* to move out?" Miguel repeats. He wrote ¡BIENVENIDA! to his Tía Lola when she moved in. It doesn't sound right to *welcome* someone to move out.

"We've got three weeks to paint the house back or move," their mother says in a teary voice at dinner. "I'm disappointed, too," she admits to Tía Lola. After all, she really loves the new color. That flaking white paint made the place look so blah and run-down. "But still, I don't want to have to move again," Mami sighs.

Tía Lola pats her niece's hand. There is something else they can try first.

"What's that?" her niece asks.

They can invite *el coronel* over on Saturday.

"But that's the day of our big game," Miguel reminds his aunt. They'll be playing against another local team from the next county over.

Tía Lola winks. She knows. *"Pero tengo un plan."* She has a plan. Miguel should tell his friends to come a little early so they can change.

"Change what?" Miguel's mother asks. "Change the color of the house?"

Tía Lola shakes her head. Change a hard heart. She'll need more grape juice from the store.

STOP AND CHECK

Confirm and Revise Predictions Was your prediction correct? What text clues did you use to help you make your prediction?

The day dawns sunny and warm. The cloudless sky stretches on and on and on, endlessly blue with the glint of an airplane, like a needle sewing a tiny tear in it. Every tree seems filled to **capacity** with dark green rustling leaves. On the neighboring farms, the corn is as tall as the boys who play baseball in the **fallow** field nearby. Tía Lola's garden looks like one of Papi's palettes. But now, after living in the country for seven months, Miguel has his own new names for colors: zucchini green, squash yellow, chili-pepper red, raspberry crimson. The eggplants are as purple as the newly painted house. It is the full of summer. In a few weeks, up in the mountains, the maples will begin to turn.

Miguel's friends and their parents arrive early. The boys head upstairs behind Tía Lola and Rudy. Their parents stay downstairs, drinking grape smoothies and talking about how their gardens are doing. At last, the silver car rolls into the driveway.

Slowly, Colonel Charlebois climbs out. He stands, a cane in one hand, looking up at the house. One quarter of the house is purple. The other three-quarters is still white. Which color will the whole house end up being?

Miguel looks down at the old man from an upstairs window. Suddenly, he feels a sense of panic. What if Tía Lola's plan doesn't work? He doesn't want to move from the house that has finally become a home to him.

> **STOP AND CHECK**
>
> **Visualize** Visualize the author's description of the garden. In what ways are the colors a symbol for the changes Tía Lola has brought to the Colonel and Miguel's family?

He feels his aunt's hand on his shoulder. *"No hay problema, Miguelito,"* she reassures him as if she can read his thoughts even without looking into his eyes.

Colonel Charlebois is still staring up at the house when the front door opens. Out file nine boys in purple-and-white-striped uniforms and purple baseball caps. They look as if the house itself has sprouted them! Miguel leads the way, a baseball in his hand. Behind them, Tía Lola and Rudy each hold the corner of a pennant that reads: CHARLIE'S BOYS.

Colonel Charlebois gazes at each boy. It is difficult to tell what is going through his mind. Suddenly, he drops his cane on the front lawn and calls out, "Let's play ball!" He stands, wobbly and waiting and smiling. Miguel looks into the old man's eyes and sees a boy, legs apart, body bent forward, a gloved hand held out in front of him.

He lifts his arm and throws the ball at that young boy—and the old man catches it.

About the Author/Illustrator

Julia Alvarez

was born in New York City, but she spent her early years in the Dominican Republic. She and her sisters were brought up, along with their cousins, by Julia's mother and her many aunts, or tías. They told her wonderful stories about their own childhood, which Julia has used in the many books and stories she has written.

When Julia was ten years old her family returned to New York. "Not understanding the language, I had to pay close attention to each word—great training for a writer," she explains.

"As a kid," Julia says, "I loved stories—hearing them, telling them. Since ours was an oral culture, stories were not written down. It took coming to this country for reading and writing to become allied in my mind with storytelling."

Lester Coloma

approaches all projects in the same way—by getting at the heart of them. He researches the subject, looking for as much information as he can. After drawing a series of tiny thumbnail sketches, Lester transfers the final sketch to canvas. He chooses colors, and then he adds paint. This is Lester's favorite part, since that is when, in his words, "the painting comes to life." He likes to leave brushstrokes and other marks on the surface to add dimension to his work.

Author's Purpose

How Tía Lola Came to Visit Stay includes some Spanish words. Why do you think the author included them, and how does she help readers understand these words in the story?

Respond to Reading

Summarize

Use important details from *How Tía Lola Came to ~~Visit~~ Stay* to summarize what you learned about what happens when people share ideas. Information from your Theme Chart may help you.

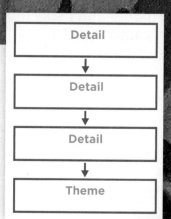

Detail
↓
Detail
↓
Detail
↓
Theme

Text Evidence

1. What details in the text help you to identify *How Tía Lola Came to ~~Visit~~ Stay* as an example of realistic fiction? Give at least two details from the story to support your answer. **GENRE**

2. Explain the theme of the story in your own words. Give two clues from the story to support your answer. **THEME**

3. What is the meaning of the word *glint* on page 190? Use context clues to help you figure out the meaning of the word. **CONTEXT CLUES**

4. The author provides several clues that hint at what Miguel and Colonel Charlebois have in common. Write how Tía Lola knows that the Colonel will not evict Miguel and his family from the house they are renting from him. **WRITE ABOUT READING**

Make Connections

What happens when the characters in *How Tía Lola Came to ~~Visit~~ Stay* share ideas about how to respond to Colonel Charlebois? **ESSENTIAL QUESTION**

How could following Tía Lola's ideas help you if you encounter a difficult person? **TEXT TO WORLD**

Compare Texts

Read about what happens when musicians gather and make music together.

The Music of Many

An allegory is a story that teaches a lesson about life by having characters or events stand for ideas or beliefs. Read "The Music of Many" to find out what a king learns about the value of working together.

One summer morning, a king sat by an open window in his castle. Outside, a chorus of birds chirped and warbled together. Each bird had a unique song, but the beautiful sounds blended together in exquisite harmony, delighting the king.

Listening to the beautiful birdsong soon became the king's greatest pleasure, and he looked forward to the birds' melodies. Yet in autumn, as the days began to shorten, the birds flew away one by one, leaving silence where their music had once graced the air.

The king was saddened by the loss of music. Upon seeing the king's glum face, his most loyal and humble servant said, "Your Majesty, perhaps in winter, a musician could play to while away the quiet." The king agreed, and he ordered his servant to find the most talented musicians in the world.

Soon a harpsichordist arrived from England. A sitar player brought his stringed instrument from India. A Peruvian pipe player arrived in a brightly woven shirt, bursting with color. In a short time, musicians from many lands had gathered in the courtyard of the king's castle to audition.

A flutist from France was first to play. She amazed the assembled court with her vibrato trills. At first the king smiled politely, but then he abruptly clapped his hands to dismiss the flutist.

Next, the servant escorted a drummer into the throne room that had sailed all the way from Africa. His hands hovered over the drums in an impressive blur, like hummingbird wings above a flower. But again, although the king was polite, he dismissed the drummer with a nod of his head.

A famous violinist tried out next. His pizzicato plucking stunned the audience—except for His Majesty, that is. "No," sighed the disappointed king, "something is not quite right." The violinist slumped as he left the throne room. He knew it would be useless to try to **negotiate** with a king.

Christiane Beauregard

194

The musicians waiting in the courtyard began to grow restless. The king seemed awfully picky.

As the sun began to ebb in the late afternoon, the musicians needed to keep warm, so the flutist decided to limber up and began to play a few notes. The drummer beat a slow tap to keep time with the flutist, and then the guitarist from Spain strummed a few chords and the Peruvian pipe player took up the tune and harmonized soulfully. The other musicians joined in.

Inside the throne room, the final musician finished her audition, but the king stared into space, dreaming of the birds that had sung so beautifully outside his window.

As the king sat, his ears strained to pick up a few notes that wafted through the thick castle walls. A grin slowly crept across the king's face. "At last!" he exclaimed. "That is the sound I have been seeking!" He looked at the members of the court and exclaimed, "Allow me to share an **insight** I have gained. It is not one sound but the music of many blended together that is truly beautiful."

With that, he commanded his servants to invite all of the musicians to enter and form a royal orchestra. Of course, they would have summers off, once the birds returned.

Make Connections

What happens when the individual musicians play together and share their music? ESSENTIAL QUESTION

What have you learned about the importance of sharing ideas from the characters in these selections? TEXT TO TEXT

Lizzie Bright and the Buckminster Boy

by Gary D. Schmidt
illustrated by Jago

Essential Question

What kinds of challenges transform people?

Read what happens when a boy must face the challenge of the sea in order to save his newfound friend after a terrible accident.

Go Digital!

In the summer of 1911, 13-year-old Turner Buckminster and his parents leave the busy city of Boston and settle in a small town on the coast of Maine, where Turner's father is the new minister. Turner feels lost until he meets a girl named Lizzie Bright. Lizzie lives on nearby Malaga Island in a community founded by former enslaved African Americans. She helps Turner learn about the sea and its inhabitants.

Every morning Turner walks to the shore where the New Meadows River meets the ocean, and where Lizzie waits for him. He begins to call these exquisite days of summer blue days, because of the beautiful blue sky that blends into the indigo-colored ocean horizon. But then one day a dreadful accident occurs, and Turner must use everything Lizzie has taught him to save his friend.

Every morning the sea breeze bustled up and called Turner until he followed it to the shore where Lizzie waited for him, her bucket half full of clams.

Blue days, as the tide washed away the twin footprints Lizzie and Turner left along the beach. Blue days, as they walked among the sharp-edged mussels, prying open their blue-black shells to tickle their orange tendons. Blue days, as they sprinted against the sea breeze and chased the gulls until Turner finally, finally, finally touched a tail feather. Blue days, as they dangled their legs over the granite ledges and felt the gigantic continent behind them.

And it was on one of their climbs, on one of those blue days that was gushing into a bright copper, that Turner reached up and put his hand on something wet and clammy and slimy and moving, **recoiled** with a yelp, and startled Lizzie beneath him. She tried but could not quite find her balance and fell down to the mudflats, striking her head on a granite outcropping just before she dropped to the bottom.

"Lizzie!" Turner cried, half falling himself until he was beside her, his hands under her head, startled by how quickly they were covered with her blood. "Lizzie!"

"Don't you get—" she said, then stopped. "Whatever you do," she started again, "don't get blood on that shirt." She put her hand up to her forehead, and it shook. "You better get me back to my granddaddy. I'm so dizzy."

She tried to stand up, Turner behind and holding on to her, but her feet didn't go where she wanted them to, and Turner had to steer her as she swayed and zigzagged to the dory. The blood leaked through her fingers and dripped to the sand.

"Almost there."

"I can hardly see," she said slowly, and Turner's stomach tightened.

When they reached the boat, Lizzie stood there stupidly, not quite sure what to do. "Climb in," said Turner, but he had to lift her front leg for her, and once she was in, she fell into a loose heap in the bow, and her eyes closed.

Turner figured that the more awake Lizzie was, the better she would be, so he hollered at her, and when she did not open her eyes, he splashed seawater into her face until she sputtered and opened them. "Keep them open, or I'll splash you again."

"If you splash me again, I won't help you get that blood off your shirt."

"Just keep your eyes open, Lizzie Bright." He shoved the dory out stern first into the New Meadows and noticed how choppy it had become, with even some whitecaps tumbling between him and Malaga. He settled himself, took the two oars and fixed them to the oarlocks, then dipped them in and was surprised at how the water took them, almost sweeping one oar under the boat and the other out of his hand. He imagined watching the oar drifting away out to the open bay and wondered how he would ever get across if that happened.

He kept turning around to look at Lizzie. "Are your eyes open?" he called. "Lizzie, open your eyes. Open your dang eyes."

"A minister's son . . . a minister's son shouldn't say . . . shouldn't say dang." Turner's stomach grew tighter and tighter with the slow sprawl of her words.

"Keep your eyes open," he said, and bent back to the oars, trying to get the stern steady and the bow pointed to the island. It was harder than he had realized. Much harder. The water was running out against him, and every whitecap that struck him broadside sent water into the bottom of the boat. The dory felt clumsy, and it would not keep its nose where it was supposed to go. Soon he was no longer trying to point it at the island's north end but at its south end, and with every stroke in toward the island, he felt the boat drifting down and away from it.

He began to row with a frantic energy, the oars chewing raggedly at the water. But the waves kept turning the bow from Malaga, and the oars kept slipping out of the locks, and by the time he had gotten them back in, the boat had **skewed** all around and was slipping up and down in the troughs.

"Head the dory . . . the dory into the waves," said Lizzie **feebly**.

Turner did not reply. He was watching the granite ledges slip past, the pines above them bending with the wind out to sea.

"Into the waves," said Lizzie again.

He turned around. "I know, Lizzie. I'll get it. Keep your eyes open. Both of them."

They were now well away from Malaga and heading stern first down the New Meadows. The waves chopped briskly as they rushed out to the bay and to the sea beyond, and Turner gave up any notion of trying to make it back to the island. Instead, he turned the bow against the running tide to maneuver the dory in close to the mainland, where he might find some mudflats to run up to. But now the ledges came right down to the New Meadows, and there were no open mudflats. The water was choppier in close, and twice he struck a stone ridge just beneath the surface, the second time so hard he was afraid it might bash in the boards. He moved the dory out farther again.

Lizzie, who had felt the bashing just beneath her, raised her head. "You missed the island."

"Yes."

"You missed the island. How could you miss the island?"

"The tide's too strong. It's taking us out with it."

Lizzie put her hand to her head, and Turner thought she might be sick. "I'm going to fall asleep," she murmured.

"You can't fall asleep, Lizzie. You've got to keep your eyes open."

"When you reach the point . . . when you reach Bald Head . . ."

"When I reach Bald Head," Turner repeated.

"The tide will slack some. You can ground. . . . The tide will slack some." Then Lizzie was quiet.

Turner looked ahead and saw the rock ledges streaking past and the shore bending away. He moved the dory in closer to the land and stopped rowing altogether except to keep the bow into the waves. His arms felt drained, and he wasn't sure he could make them do what he wanted them to do when the slack water came. But he waited and watched,

hollering back to Lizzie now and again to be sure she stayed awake.

But she wasn't hollering back.

The copper of the sky had deepened into a dark red, and the dark red was now deepening into the purple of early night. When Turner looked over his shoulder to the east, more than a few stars had already yawned themselves awake and were stretching to begin their run. On the ledges above him there passed a farmhouse, then another, and still another, where yellow lamps were glowing out the windows. He felt the air cooling quickly.

Then the rhythm of the waves changed. In a moment they had lost their choppiness and had lengthened into long swells that came slow and syrupy. The boat smoothed out, and it was easy to keep the bow to the low stretches of water that swiped at the dory's nose.

Turner thought immediately that they must be at the point. When he looked at the shore, it was hard to tell whether it was bending away or whether it just got lost in the gathering darkness. But he turned into it anyway, rowing with all the might he could **summon** in his drained arms, pushing back with his legs and grunting with each pull, not even calling to Lizzie because he could not speak and pull at the same time. He felt the dory skim across the swells, cutting through their rhythm, and figured that finally, finally he was setting their course.

STOP AND CHECK

Make, Confirm, Revise Predictions Will Turner gain control of the dory? Use text evidence to support your prediction.

As the purple of the sky spread all the way across to the west, he rowed. As more and more stars **roused** themselves, he rowed. And as the wind picked itself up and wrestled with the tops of the swells, he rowed.

He rowed until he realized he had missed the point and they were well out into the bay.

And then he stopped.

Now the purple spread from horizon to horizon, and the stars that had clustered in the east were fading with the early light of the rising moon. The swells lengthened even more, so that the dory rocked up and down as gently as ever it might, and if it had not been for the farmhouse lights on the shoreline, Turner would hardly have been able to tell that the dory was moving at all.

He was not afraid, and was surprised to find that he wasn't. As long as he could keep the shoreline lights from dipping under the waves, he knew that he was in sight of shore. And he knew that the tide would have to stop flowing sometime and head back up the New Meadows. Already he could sense it weakening when he dipped the oars into the water. He could even make some headway into shore before his tired arms gave out and he was pulled back to where he had started. He was thirsty and more than a little bit hungry, but without the panic of hopelessness.

If only Lizzie were awake, this would be something out of a dream, something that, had he known he might do it, he would have longed for. But when he looked at Lizzie, there was a sickening tug down deep in his gut. It was getting harder and harder to get her to keep her eyes even half open, and though the bleeding from the wound had stopped, she seemed to be fading from him.

He shipped the oars and turned to face her. "Lizzie? Lizzie Bright?" He shook her by the knee. "Lizzie?"

"We almost there?"

"Almost."

"Turner?" she asked.

"Yes?"

"You ever row a boat before?"

Turner hesitated. He wondered if being on the swan boats in the Public Garden counted and figured that probably it didn't. "Not hardly."

"Ever in your whole life?"

"Not until today."

"I thought so."

"Keep your eyes open, Lizzie." Turner went back to the oars, turned the bow toward shore—it wasn't hard in the long swells—and tried to row in again. He kept his strokes slow and long, and though, when he finally turned his head, it seemed the shore lights were not much nearer, they were a little nearer, and he held to the pace until his muscles buckled, and he shipped the oars and watched the lights very slowly withdraw again.

And that was when he first heard the water ripping near him.

The moon had roused herself fully out of the sea and was tossing her silver bedclothes all around. Turner was sure that in that light he should have been able to make out any rocks. But he couldn't see anything breaking the surface. He listened, not moving, and heard the ripping again, but behind him this time, and closer to shore, and ahead of him—one after another. In the moonlight he saw a silver spray burst up into the air, a shower of diamond dust. Then another, and another almost beside the boat, so that he could feel the spray of it against his face, and the dory rocked to the rhythm of the new swells as a great Presence broke the surface of the sea and Turner knew, or felt, the **vastness** of whales.

Now he almost did panic. One could come right up beneath them and turn the dory over as easily as a pine chip, and he would be floating in the sea, holding on to the upturned dory, holding on to Lizzie, who he was sure could not hold on by herself. That is, he would be holding on to her if he could find her after they capsized.

But though the dory rocked back and forth with the swell of them, the whales never came

203

so close that the boat might capsize. Turner heard them ripping the surface all around him, and felt the diamond spray sprinkle down on him in the moonlight like a benediction. He knew he was in the middle of something much larger than himself, and not just larger in size. It was like being in the middle of a swirling universe that could swamp him in a moment but had no desire to. He might put out his hand into the maelstrom and become a part of it.

But he didn't put his hand out yet, because as he watched, a whale five times as long as the dory surfaced, and rode quietly alongside him in the smooth swells. Turner could not breathe. The whale flipped its tail up a bit and began to roll from side to side, a great gargantuan roll like the roll of the globe, side to side, until it could slap the swells with the length of its flippers, gleaming silver-white in the moonlight. Turner held on to the sides of the dory and rolled side to side with it with this great vastness that had swum past the mountains and valleys of the sea. Together

STOP AND CHECK

Visualize How does the author's use of similes and metaphors help you to visualize the whales as a great "presence" in the water?

they rocked, and Turner wished that the rocking would never stop, that there would always be this moonlit moment.

But slowly the whale did stop rocking, and the seas calmed, and the rhythm of the swells took hold again. Quietly, more afraid than not, Turner slipped the oars into the water, and with gentle strokes, keeping the oars beneath the surface all the time, he eased the dory forward, hoping that the whale would wait on the surface.

It did. And so Turner reached the whale's eye, and they looked at each other. They looked at each other a long time—two souls rolling on the sea under the silvery moon, peering into each other's eyes. Turner wished with a desire greater than anything he had ever desired that he might understand what it was in the eye of the whale that shivered his soul.

He stretched his hand out across the side of the dory and reached over as far as he could without tipping the boat. But the whale kept a space of dark water between them, and they did not touch. Then slowly the whale sank, the water closing quietly along its black and white back.

And the whales were gone.

"Lizzie," whispered Turner.

There was no answer. He reached back and shook her leg, then her shoulder. Finally, he scooped up water and splashed it into her face—since saltwater will do for everything. "Lizzie, you've got to open your eyes."

"They're open," she said. "You splashed me."

"Lizzie, there were whales."

She didn't answer.

"Lizzie, whales."

"You touch one?"

"Tried."

She took a deep breath. "They only let you touch them if you understand what they're saying."

"What do they say?"

"You'll know when . . . when they let you touch them. Home yet?"

He set to rowing again. He did not know how long they had been with the whales. Maybe a century or two. But however long it was, he saw that the dory had not drifted out much from the shore lights, and that now, as he pulled steadily on the oars, the lights really

were coming closer. Even though he was as hungry and thirsty as he had been before the whales, he was not at all as tired. The pull of the water against his arms and back thrilled him as he felt the dory moving through the lowering swells, sensed the bow cutting quickly and truly back up into the New Meadows with a new tide.

But the whales were gone.

Soon the lights were much larger, and sometimes they blinked out as though someone had walked past a window for a moment. He wasn't quite sure if he would hit Bald Head right on or if he could find the mouth of the New Meadows and row up to Malaga itself. But he decided he would take the first landfall he could find, beach the dory, and go for help.

His arms felt strong. There was no panic in him.

He had looked into the eye of a whale.

STOP AND CHECK

Confirm Predictions Will Turner now gain control of the dory? Confirm or revise your prediction based on evidence in the text.

About the Author

Gary D. Schmidt

was born in Hicksville, New York, a diverse community that taught him to recognize and respect many different ways of life. Each summer while growing up Gary attended a camp in the Catskill Mountains, where he developed an appreciation of nature, a feature that shows up in many of his books. "You could lay on your back," he remembers, "and watch hawks play with thermal winds — never moving their wingtips. What could be better?" Well, perhaps winning two Newbery Honor Awards for his books *Lizzie Bright and the Buckminster Boy* and *The Wednesday Wars*.

Today Gary lives on a farm in Alto, Michigan, with his wife and six children. Here he splits wood, writes, feeds the cats that drop by, and wishes that sometimes the sea breeze Buckminster enjoyed came farther inland.

Author's Purpose

In *Lizzie Bright and the Buckminster Boy* the author includes detailed and almost poetry-like descriptions of the natural setting. How does this help you relate to the story's characters?

Respond to Reading

Summarize

Use important details from *Lizzie Bright and the Buckminster Boy* to summarize the most important events in the story. Information from your Theme Chart may help you.

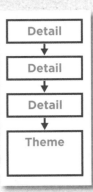

Detail → Detail → Detail → Theme

Text Evidence

1. Identify at least two features that help you recognize *Lizzie Bright and the Buckminster Boy* as an example of realistic fiction. **GENRE**

2. What are two challenges that Turner must face in the story? What steps does he take to meet each challenge? Give two examples in your answer. **THEME**

3. What is the meaning of the word *gargantuan* on page 204? Use context clues in the paragraph to help you figure out the meaning. **PARAGRAPH CLUES**

4. Write about the message the author is trying to communicate to readers by making the whale Turner encounters an important character. **WRITE ABOUT READING**

Make Connections

How does Turner's experience in the boat transform him? **ESSENTIAL QUESTION**

How might reading about Turner's experience help someone who is facing a challenge or a frightening situation? **TEXT TO WORLD**

Compare Texts
Read how the challenge of learning to skate changed the way a boy thought about friendship.

Confronting a Challenge

Last year, my family moved from Southern California. I'd loved everything about my life there—my friends, my school, and especially baseball.

Everything changed when my family moved to St. Paul, Minnesota, where the average winter temperature is around 10 degrees Fahrenheit. There were only a couple of months during the year when I could play baseball, and once summer ended, everyone went inside—to play ice hockey. I'd been on the ice only a couple of times, when I was much younger. During my second lesson, I'd fallen and broken my wrist, and after that, I'd vowed never to put on ice skates again. The fact is, I was afraid, but I didn't want anyone to know— including Ben, the one friend I had made in my new city.

Like everyone else, Ben was a hockey player, and for weeks I made up excuses not to play with him and his friends. Ben began to think that I was avoiding him. I had a **dilemma** and wondered if I should confess to him that I was afraid to skate.

When I finally told Ben I couldn't skate, he volunteered to teach me. Even though Ben was very patient, I was so embarrassed by my clumsiness that I began to make up more excuses for not skating.

About a month later, walking home from school, I discovered a faster route home. It took me past a large pond that was completely frozen over. One day I noticed a woman teaching a young girl to skate. The girl was attempting to jump and spin in the air. Over and over, she pushed off the ground with the toe of her skate. And over and over, she landed hard on the ice.

After I had been watching the girl practice for about a week, one Thursday afternoon she suddenly lifted off the ground, spun in the air, and landed on her feet! Her hard work and perseverance had paid off.

Scott Altmann

Later, alone in my bedroom, I started my social studies homework. I read a chapter in my textbook about Robert Peary, a Caucasian man, and Matthew Henson, an African-American, who explored the arctic together in 1909. I could only imagine the fears these explorers had to conquer in order to visit a remote region few people had ever traveled to before—a place much colder than Minnesota!

When I finished reading I made a pact with myself. The next day I used some money I had earned shoveling snow to buy myself some brand new skates. Every day on the way home from school I stopped at the pond, laced up, and wobbled onto the ice, right next to the figure skater who had landed her jump. As she perfected her twists and tricks, I taught myself to glide and turn. It was hard being a beginner, and when I fell I had to fight the urge to simply give up. Instead, every time I went down, I just picked myself up and started over

again. If nothing else, I was **persistent**.

Soon I was able to keep my balance and skate more confidently. In just a few weeks, I was actually ready to practice the speed skating, fast stops, and quick turns needed for ice hockey. When I was finally ready to show Ben my newfound skating ability, he was impressed. He told me I should join the local hockey league.

I tried out and was chosen for a team. By the end of the season, not only was I part of a winning team, but also I had a group of new friends, including Ben.

Make Connections

How can a role model help someone overcome his or her own challenges? **ESSENTIAL QUESTION**

How have the characters you have read about been transformed by the challenges they faced? **TEXT TO TEXT**

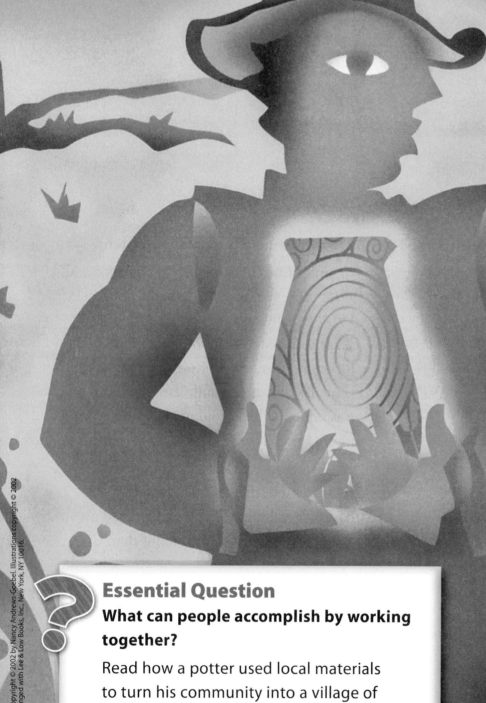

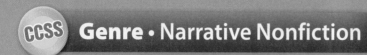

Essential Question

What can people accomplish by working together?

Read how a potter used local materials to turn his community into a village of successful artists.

Go Digital!

THE POT THAT JUAN BUILT

BY NANCY ANDREWS-GOEBEL

ILLUSTRATED BY DAVID DIAZ

Juan Quezada was born in Santa Barbara
Tutuaca, Mexico, in 1940. When he was one year
old, his family moved to Mata Ortiz, a village of
dirt roads and adobe houses on the **windswept**
plains of Chihuahua. It was there that Juan
rediscovered the pottery-making process of the
Casas Grandes people, who had vanished from
that part of Mexico six hundred years ago.

Juan became a professional potter in the 1970s. Before that he worked as a farm laborer, a railroad hand, a **sharecropper**, and even a boxer. He has never been afraid of hard work and takes pride in using ancient methods and natural materials in his pottery making. Juan taught eight of his ten brothers and sisters and many of his neighbors how to make pots. They all developed their own special styles. Juan's discovery changed Mata Ortiz from an **impoverished** village of poorly paid laborers into a prosperous community of working artists.

Cleaning the clay

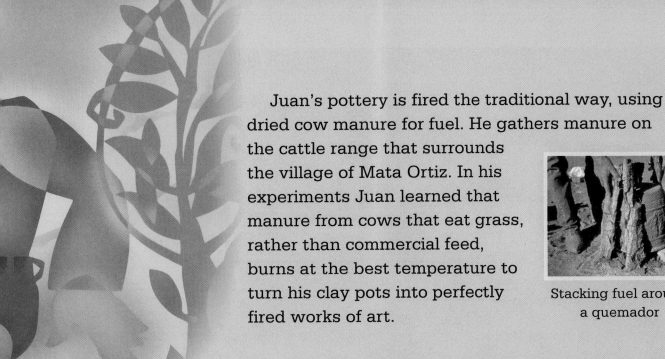

Juan's pottery is fired the traditional way, using dried cow manure for fuel. He gathers manure on the cattle range that surrounds the village of Mata Ortiz. In his experiments Juan learned that manure from cows that eat grass, rather than commercial feed, burns at the best temperature to turn his clay pots into perfectly fired works of art.

Stacking fuel around a quemador

STOP AND CHECK

Summarize Summarize how Juan was able to change the lives of the people who live in Mata Ortiz.

Michael Wisner

215

Juan makes paint out of local minerals such as black manganese and red iron oxide. He makes paintbrushes from human hair. He says that some of his best brushes are fashioned from children's hair, especially his granddaughter's. Since very little hair is used to make a paintbrush, no one minds giving Juan just a snip to design a pot.

Painting a pot

Grinding minerals
for paint

When he was twelve years old, while bringing firewood down from the hills on his burro, Juan found his first potsherds. They were pieces of broken pottery from the ancient Casas Grandes city of Paquime, which was located fifteen miles from present-day Mata Ortiz. The potsherds inspired Juan to create something similar. Even though he had never seen a potter at work, Juan began experimenting with local materials. His mother declared that he was always covered in dirt of many colors from his experiments with minerals and clay.

After his clay pots dry Juan polishes them before he applies the paint. To polish his pots, Juan uses animal bones, smooth stones, and even dried beans. Animal bones are **abundant** because of the deer hunting and cattle ranching that help feed the people of Mata Ortiz. Smooth stones are available in the Palanganas River, which runs along the eastern boundary of town. Of course dried beans can be found in any kitchen in the village.

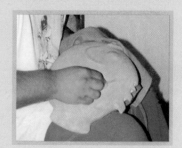

Polishing a pot.

Juan hand builds all his pots. He begins by patting out a flat piece of clay he calls a "tortilla," which becomes the bottom of the pot. He then rolls out a sausage-shaped piece of clay called a "chorizo" and presses it onto the edge of the tortilla, pinching and pulling it up to become the walls of the pot. Juan makes his pots in a small workroom behind his house, often in the company of chickens and his calico cat.

Adding the chorizo

Shaping a pot

STOP AND CHECK

Summarize Summarize the process Juan goes through to make one of his pots.

Michael Wisner

Juan says his painted designs look best on *barro blanco*, a pure white clay he digs in the Sierra Madre Mountains above Mata Ortiz. He uses the ancient designs of Casas Grandes potters for inspiration, but he doesn't copy them. Juan never plans the decoration in advance. He lets the pattern develop as he paints it onto the clay pot.

Digging for clay

One day while Juan was out searching for minerals and clay, he noticed a colony of ants burdened with tiny cargoes of white material. Looking closely, Juan realized that the ants were transporting bits of clay from underground up to the edge of their anthill. So Juan dug a hole near the anthill and **unearthed** a vein of white clay, the finest clay he had ever seen.

A pot cooling

Juan gave away his first pots as gifts to family and friends. Today his work is exhibited in museums and art galleries all over the world. In 1999, Mexico's president, Ernesto Zedillo, presented Juan with the National Arts and Science Award, the highest honor for any artist in Mexico. Pope John Paul II received a Juan Quezada pot as a gift from the people of Mexico. In spite of his fame and wealth, Juan cherishes most of all the time he spends in **solitude**, exploring the hills above Mata Ortiz in search of minerals and clay. If he is very quiet, Juan says, the voices of the ancient potters can still be heard.

STOP AND CHECK

Make, Confirm, Revise Predictions How do you think the success of Juan's pots will affect the future of Mata Ortiz? Look for text evidence to support your prediction.

Reflecting on the changes the art movement has brought to Mata Ortiz, Juan Quezada observes with characteristic enthusiasm, "People in the village are happy. They no longer have to leave their hometown to find jobs. Their work is here with their families." He further adds, "The pottery is so important! To me, all the world's pottery is wonderful, but especially when it is produced naturally, in the traditional manner, the way we do it here in Mata Ortiz. I really do believe that it's what makes our pottery so interesting. We'll pass this work on to our children and our grandchildren for their futures, for the future of Mata Ortiz. My hope is that one day the village will have a nice art history museum here in the old train station. It will have big shade trees all around, a pleasant place for people to sit quietly and reflect on their lives and on the past, the present, and the future of our village."

Juan Quezada with one of his pots.

ABOUT THE AUTHOR AND ILLUSTRATOR

NANCY ANDREWS-GOEBEL
met the artist Juan Quezada when she was on vacation in Mexico in 1995. His fascinating pottery and life inspired her and her husband to make a documentary video about Mata Ortiz. Two years later, she got the idea to turn the story into a book. She realized that this was "an engaging and important story worth researching and refining."

Travel has always motivated Andrews-Goebel's books. She says that her ideas often come from "interesting, out-of-the-way places I visit and from the extraordinary people I've had the privilege to know."

Nancy and her husband live in the California town of Cayucos with their three cats: Kitty, Flanna, and Alice.

DAVID DIAZ
was excited to create artwork about Mata Ortiz not only because he was inspired by Juan Quezada's story but also because he shares a personal connection with Juan. They are both expert potters. For his illustrations, Diaz combines traditional materials and modern tools. He used a computer to create some of the vivid illustrations for *The Pot That Juan Built*. David won the Caldecott Medal in 1995 for illustrating the book *Smoky Night*. He lives in Carlsbad, California.

AUTHOR'S PURPOSE

The author uses photographs as well as drawings in the book. How do these two kinds of images work together to tell the story of Juan Quezada and Mata Ortiz?

RESPOND TO READING

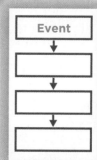

SUMMARIZE

Use important details from *The Pot That Juan Built* to summarize what you learned about Juan Quezada's village and what it accomplished when the people who live there worked together. Information from your Sequence Chart may help you.

Event

TEXT EVIDENCE

1. Identify at least two details that identify *The Pot That Juan Built* as an example of narrative nonfiction **GENRE**

2. What steps does Juan follow to make a pot? Identify at least two signal words from the text that the author uses to help you recognize each step in the sequence. **SEQUENCE**

3. The noun *tradition* means "a custom or belief that is handed down from one generation to the next." How does adding a suffix affect the meaning of the word *traditional* on page 223? **PREFIXES AND SUFFIXES**

4. Write about three events in Juan Quezada's life that helped to change the history of Mata Ortiz. Describe them in the order that they occurred. **WRITE ABOUT READING**

Make Connections

Talk about how the people of Mata Ortiz worked together to make their community more prosperous. **ESSENTIAL QUESTION**

How might other communities follow the example set by Mata Ortiz? **TEXT TO WORLD**

Compare Texts
Read about four students who work together to raise money for their school.

A BOX OF IDEAS

Characters

Inés, a sixth-grader
Silvia, Inés's cousin and neighbor
Gil and **Chris**, Inés's neighbors
Ms. Cerda, Inés's mother

Setting

The backyard of a house in a small town; the school fair three weeks later

Scene 1

Setting: Inés's backyard

(Ms. Cerda is working at a craft table in her backyard. Inés, Silvia, Gil, and Chris run into the yard.)

Inés: Hola, Mamá. Do you mind if we hold a meeting here? We got kicked out of Gil and Chris's place because their dad's studying.

Ms. Cerda: No problem. What's the meeting for?

Silvia: We want to come up with a plan to raise money for the school library.

Inés: The school doesn't have enough money to buy new books. We want to help.

Gil: We're trying to think up something original to do at the next School Fair.

Ms. Cerda: Sounds like a great cause. Talk all you want. A little noise always helps me work. It makes me feel even more creative.

Gil: Thanks, Ms. Cerda.

(The students sit on the ground and stare at one another.)

Inés: So? What are we going to do?

(They all shrug. No one has an idea.)

Chris *(watching Ms. Cerda)***:** What's that box you're making?

Ms. Cerda: It's called a nicho. This one celebrates my mother. First, I made a tin box. Then I punched out a design using a hammer and a tool called an awl, which is like a thick nail, but not so sharp. See how the dots look like a flower? It's a dahlia, my mother's favorite.

Chris: It's Mexico's national flower, too.

Ms. Cerda: That's right, it is.

Inés *(laughing)***:** Hey, Chris! Stop pestering my mom.

Gil: I told you he was too young to help out.

Silvia: We could do a car wash.

Inés: No way! My hands are still peeling from the last one.

Chris *(looking at Ms. Cerda's project)***:** What are those pictures?

Ms. Cerda: This one is a photo of my mother, and this one is the house where she grew up. It was a ranch about three hours west of Mexico City.

Inés: What about a bake sale?

Gil: Uh-uh. Mom says if she has to make any more muffins, she'll explode.

Chris *(still talking to Ms. Cerda)***:** What are those things on the sides?

Ms. Cerda: They're doors. Many nichos have them.

Chris: How'd you learn to make nichos?

227

Ms. Cerda: It's a tradition in my family. My grandmother sold them at the market every Saturday. She taught me how.

Silvia: Chris, are you going to help us or talk to Inés's mom?

Chris (*ignoring Silvia*): How do you decide what to put inside?

Ms. Cerda: That's the best part—you can put anything you like inside. Every nicho is unique. Since this one is for my mother's birthday, I added some special things just for her. This is a button from an old dress she loved.

Chris: I wish I could make a nicho.

Ms. Cerda: When I was your age, I used to make them out of cardboard boxes.

Gil (*annoyed*): Chris! Pay attention!

Chris: I am. Besides, I have a great idea for the School Fair. Let's make our own nichos! Only ours will celebrate our town instead of people.

(Inés, Silvia, and Gil look at each other and smile.)

Silvia: Hey, that's a pretty good idea.

Inés: Pretty good? It's terrific!

Gil (*sheepishly*): Didn't I tell you my little brother would be a big help?

Scene 2

Setting: The School Fair, three weeks later

(Inés, Silvia, Gil, and Chris stand behind a table with a hand-painted sign that says, "Neighborhood Nichos." There is one nicho on the table. Ms. Cerda comes by, picks up the nicho, and looks inside.)

Ms. Cerda: I'm impressed. You've all become expert nicho makers. This is beautiful.

Inés: I got the shoebox from you, mom!

Silvia: I added the doors—they came from a grocery store carton.

Gil: That one celebrates Main Street. I took pictures of the stores and cars. My uncle printed them out for us.

Chris: I got some wire for the tree trunks from Mr. Marsalis, the electrician next door. The treetops are made of green yarn that Ms. Miller gave us.

Inés: And I added bottle caps to make the car tires.

Ms. Cerda: Very clever. I'm really impressed by your **ingenuity**.

Silvia: Nichos are fun to make. The whole neighborhood got involved.

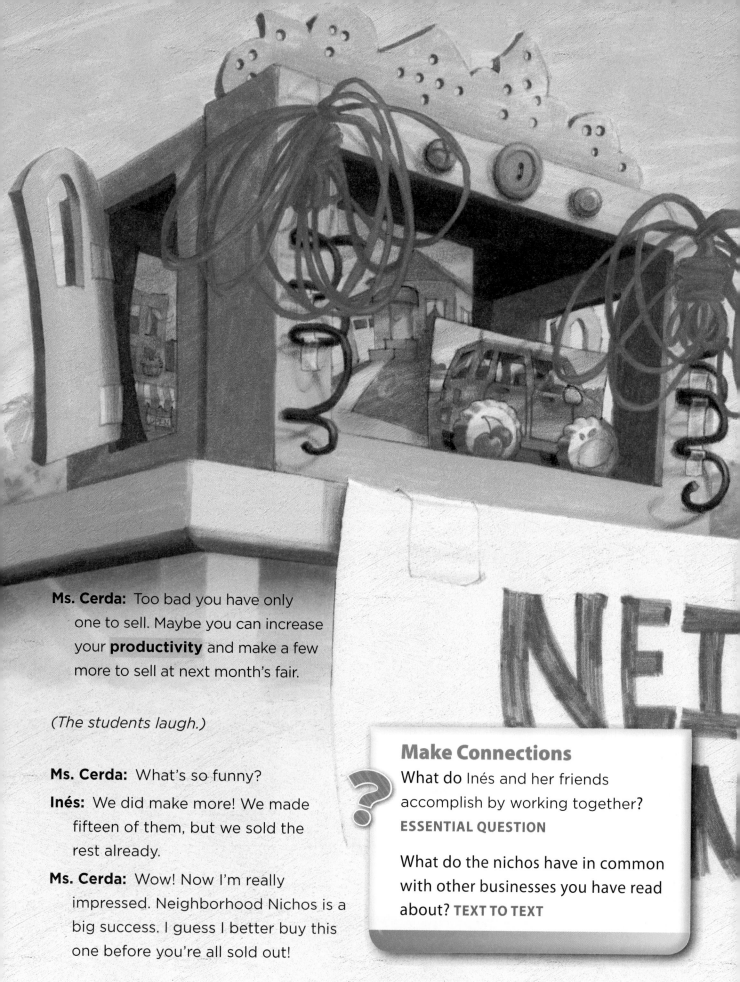

Ms. Cerda: Too bad you have only one to sell. Maybe you can increase your **productivity** and make a few more to sell at next month's fair.

(The students laugh.)

Ms. Cerda: What's so funny?

Inés: We did make more! We made fifteen of them, but we sold the rest already.

Ms. Cerda: Wow! Now I'm really impressed. Neighborhood Nichos is a big success. I guess I better buy this one before you're all sold out!

Make Connections

What do Inés and her friends accomplish by working together? **ESSENTIAL QUESTION**

What do the nichos have in common with other businesses you have read about? **TEXT TO TEXT**

229

? Essential Question

How can one person affect the opinions of others?

Read the true story of one of the world's first cycling champions.

Go Digital!

MAJOR TAYLOR
CHAMPION CYCLIST

BY **Lesa Cline-Ransome**
ILLUSTRATED BY **James E. Ransome**

In Indianapolis, Indiana, there was a street lined with bicycle shops from one end to the other. Visitors would marvel at each window displayed with the most up-to-date models along that stretch of North Pennsylvania Avenue locals called Bicycle Row.

Right at the center sat the Hay and Willits Bicycle Shop: Thomas Hay, Bert Willits, proprietors.

It was this shop young Marshall Taylor visited when his own bicycle needed fixing. Marshall was thirteen years old, and waiting patiently was not one of the things he did best. So while he waited, he kept himself busy trying out new stunts. Then, the repairs made, he used one of his fancy mounts to climb quickly onto his bicycle. If he hurried, he could still finish his newspaper route before supper.

As Marshall left, Mr. Hay shouted, "Hey, son, that was some stunt work."

"Oh, those," said Marshall. "I have a lot more, wanna see?"

And without waiting for an answer, he began his demonstration with an acrobatic mount. Round and round the store he rode, first backward, then forward on the handlebars, each move more daring than the last. By the time he'd finished, everyone in the store was applauding for more.

"How'd you get so good?" Tom Hay asked the boy.

Marshall explained that he'd taught himself quite a collection of tricks riding on the long stretches of country road between his newspaper stops.

"Are you looking for work? For six dollars a week, all you need to do is sweep, straighten, and show off some of those stunts, and you've got yourself a job."

"Six dollars to clean and do tricks?" Marshall asked. Why, that paid a dollar more than his paper route.

"Okay, okay, we'll throw in a new bike, too," countered Bert Willits.

"I'll take it!" Marshall shouted.

How did a thirteen-year-old black teenager in 1891 come to be such a crackerjack cyclist—or even to own a bicycle? Mr. Hay and Mr. Willits wondered. And so Marshall told them of his father's job as a coachman to the **prominent** Southard family and how at the age of eight he'd been hired as the live-in companion of their only son. It was then that Marshall began his new life of luxury: private tutoring, fine clothing, a playroom stacked with toys.

But what Marshall loved most was the bicycle the Southards had given him. He'd never seen anything like its smooth curved lines of metal, so shiny and new and so utterly modern. He jumped on at once, knowing those wheels could carry him faster than his legs ever could.

And sure enough, in no time he became the top cyclist in the neighborhood. Amongst stately Victorian houses and tree-lined streets, in each and every race, Marshall breezed by the other boys, aware only of the wind against his face and the road he left behind.

For the days when Marshall was to perform, Mr. Hay outfitted him in a uniform with elaborate braidings and shimmery gold buttons. Crowds gathered afternoons at 4:00 P.M. sharp to watch Marshall on the sidewalk outside the store. They were amazed by the young man in military uniform so **adept** on two wheels.

"He looks like a little major!" they would marvel.

Then they'd filter into the store to request private lessons and try out the bicycles that could make that little major do his tricks.

Hay and Willits Bicycle Shop had finally made a name for itself, and the owners had the kid everyone now called Major Taylor to thank for it.

The annual ten-mile road race, sponsored by Hay and Willits, was one of the biggest sporting events in Indianapolis. Each year an elaborate gold medal for the winner was displayed in their window, on view for all. Marshall liked to put down his cleaning rags and stop to admire it. He'd adjust it, polish it, and hold it up to the light to watch it sparkle. Once, he even tried it on, smiling at his own reflection in the window.

"Major Taylor, Champion Cyclist," he whispered to himself.

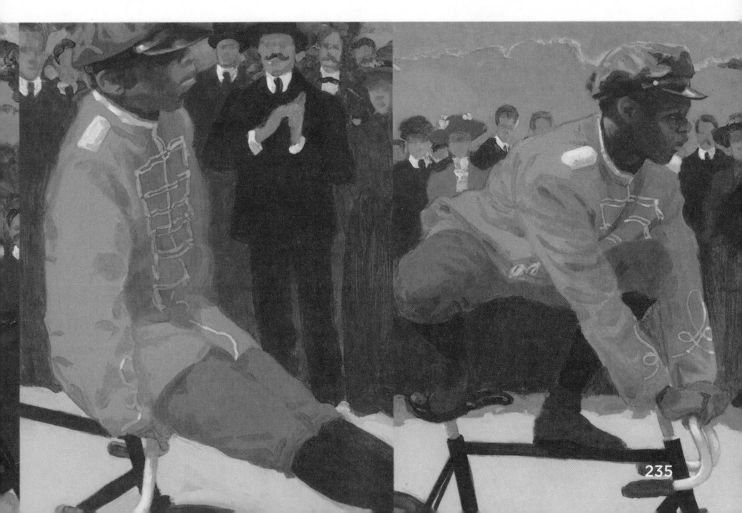

Early on the morning of the race, Marshall took his place among hundreds of **spectators**. He'd never seen a bicycle race up close and he didn't want to miss a single detail.

When Mr. Hay spotted Marshall, he waved to him. "Come on over here, young man; you must start in this race," he insisted.

"I don't think I can do it," Marshall protested.

"Why, it's no different than riding with your friends," he encouraged. "Look, just start up the road and come back when you're tired. The crowd will love it."

Bang! The starting pistol sounded, and Marshall was off, pedaling hard and fast, hoping only to keep pace with the others.

"Just till I get tired . . . just till I get tired . . . ," he kept repeating, his legs pumping as fast as his heart. Gradually the rhythmic creaks of the other bicycles faded and all he could hear was his own panting. Time fell away as he struggled to maintain speed, and the wind whipped his face. Out of nowhere Mr. Hay appeared, shouting and dangling the gold medal.

"You're a mile ahead! Keep going!"

Now he thought he could make out a swell of spectators gathered at the finish. Pushing, pushing with everything he had, his legs cramped with exhaustion, he burst through the winning tape . . . and then collapsed.

When he came to, sore, stiff, and exhausted, the crowd's cheers were ringing in his ears.

At thirteen years old, Marshall Taylor had won his first race.

Back at the shop, Marshall's dreams now stretched far beyond the walls of Hay and Willits. More than anything, he wanted to be a professional cyclist.

STOP AND CHECK

Summarize Summarize the events in the story that led Major Taylor to compete in his first bicycle race.

One by one, he committed to memory the names of racers who'd visited the shop—Arthur Zimmerman, Willie Windle of Massachusetts, and Louis "Birdie" Munger, who had recently opened a racing workshop in town.

As Marshall grew to know Munger, he began spending more and more time at his shop. He'd follow him to the track, pleading, "Tell me about the race when . . ."

Birdie was tickled by Marshall. In fact, the boy reminded him of a younger version of himself. "You've got talent, but you've got to keep working," Birdie instructed after one of Marshall's many wins. Soon Marshall had been hired as his assistant, running errands and doing chores.

When Birdie decided to move to Worcester, Massachusetts, he invited Marshall along. After a fond farewell to his family, Marshall set off with Birdie to begin training. To anyone who'd listen, he would boast, "I am going to make Major Marshall Taylor the fastest bicycle rider in the world."

Marshall's talent grew as fast as his popularity. It wasn't long before racing fans—although they may not have known the name Marshall Taylor—knew there was a young Negro causing quite a stir.

But by the time Marshall turned professional at age eighteen, challenges off the track began to trail him like a shadow. All of the large purses won in races all over the country couldn't buy him a meal in a restaurant or a room in a hotel.

Cities like Louisville, St. Louis, and even Indianapolis wouldn't permit a black man on their tracks—their entry forms read, "For White Riders Only." Still that couldn't keep Marshall down. As the only Negro granted membership in the League of American Wheelmen, he was entitled to compete on any track he chose.

"You're never going to finish this race!" riders would holler above the noise of the crowd, or "This race is going to be your last," they'd taunt. Working as a group, they'd box him out. Racing next to him, they'd poke and jab him. They agreed that if they defeated him, the winner would split the prize money with the others. But usually there was no prize money to split: For every trick they tried, Taylor had his own.

Marshall's style had always been to stay behind the pack. "Save it for the finish," he would recite to himself. Wearing his lucky number 13 armband, he'd keep pace, then ride full speed in the final yards. But when the competition turned crueler, he had to adjust his style. As soon as he'd spot a clearing in the pack, he'd cut through and make his way to the front. And that's where he stayed, all the way across the finish line.

The "Black Whirlwind," as he was called by the press, had his own set of rules: "Ride clean and ride fair." Asked by reporters how he managed to keep calm despite attacks by other cyclists, Marshall answered, "I simply ride away."

Munger's prediction years earlier had come true. Major Marshall Taylor was now the fastest bicycle rider in the world. After he won the 1899 World Championship title, beating out the Butler brothers, offers to compete abroad flooded his home. Promises of money and racing against the world's best cyclists were too much to resist.

In 1900 friends and family said good-bye as Marshall boarded the *Kaiser Wilhelm der Grosse*, proud to be representing his country on his first European racing tour.

From the moment he arrived in France, fans swarmed around him, welcoming "le Nègre Volant," the Flying Negro. At every Parisian café, hotel, and track, they followed for a chance to shake his hand. The press reported his every move, and he was invited into the homes of **aristocracy**. Halfway around the world, Marshall Taylor was finally getting the recognition and respect he had worked for his whole life.

It was not on a starting line but rather at the Café Esperance that Marshall met the French champion, Edmond Jacquelin. "Welcome to Paris, Monsieur Taylor!" he greeted, smiling broadly. And with that, the two became instant friends.

STOP AND CHECK

Summarize Summarize the examples of discrimination Taylor experienced before he left for Europe in 1900.

Jacquelin, winner of the 1900 World Championship, French Championship, and Grand Prix of Paris—the Triple Crown of racing—was a sharp contrast to the 1899 World Champion. Everyone wondered who would **prevail** in the next race—the quiet, gentlemanly Taylor or the explosive, larger-than-life Jacquelin?

Long before Taylor and Jacquelin arrived at Le Parc des Princes velodrome for their race, crowds had gathered, straining for a glimpse of the two rivals. Shivering against the cold, Taylor stood at the starting line dressed in layers to protect himself from the biting wind. Was this the Flying Negro from America the fans had heard so much about?

Meanwhile Jacquelin strode onto the track.

"Vive Taylor! Vive Jacquelin!" shouted the crowd as more fans huddled beyond the gates.

The race was on.

When it was over, roars of applause rang out to the beat of the French national anthem.

"Edmond Jacquelin, the victor in two straight heats," came the announcement.

To schedule a rematch so close to the first race was unheard of, but the crowds demanded it.

"Who will be king?" asked *L'Auto Velo*. Would it be the 1899 or the 1900 World Champion, America or France, Taylor or Jacquelin?

As the men took their positions at the start of the first heat and strapped their feet to their pedals, the crowd held one **collective** breath.

Bang!

Jacquelin jumped comfortably into the lead. Marshall concentrated on erasing all thoughts of their first race from his mind. He leaned lower over his handlebars, and from high in the stands fans looked down on the shadow of a figure lying almost flat, inching closer and closer to his rival.

> **STOP AND CHECK**
>
> **Make Predictions** Who will win the race, Major Taylor or Jacquelin? Base your prediction on clues from the text.

For one brief moment the two became one. Side-by-side and wheel-by-wheel they sped to the finish. It was only in the final lengths that one seemed to edge ahead.

In the blink of an eye, the heat was over. Taylor had come from behind to cross the finish line first. The crowd roared, yet the victor was still to be decided: The winner had to take the best of three heats.

In the second heat, again Marshall waited for just the right moment.

When he noticed a shift in Jacquelin's closely guarded position, he maneuvered his bike as adeptly as he had in front of Hay and Willits Bicycle Shop years ago. And once again all eyes were on little Major Taylor.

The wind, which Marshall had once so loved against his face, now pushed at his back, carrying him well ahead of his rival and first through the winning tape.

Two races and two straight heats brought American fans to their feet. While Jacquelin quietly rode off the track, Marshall tied the American flag to his waist. As he rode his victory lap, he heard the familiar tune of "The Star Spangled Banner," and all the world watched the colors red, white, and blue billow and fly in the wind.

About the Author and Illustrator

Lesa Cline-Ransome

grew up in Malden, Massachusetts. It was there that her mother helped her realize her love of reading and writing. When she was in middle school, Lesa decided she wanted to be a journalist, but she soon discovered that factual writing was not for her. "I wanted to create my own stories," she said, "or at least be able to put my own creative spin on the stories I wrote." She finally got that opportunity with her first book, *Satchel Paige,* about the famed African American baseball player. "I love finding the most interesting parts of a person's life, piecing them together and creating a new story for a new group of readers," says Lesa.

To write about Marshall Taylor, Lesa put herself in his shoes by visiting the Massachusetts town where he lived and trained. After researching and reading everything she could about Marshall, Lesa knew she could write about him in a way that felt authentic.

James E. Ransome

began drawing and writing books in elementary school. In high school, classes in filmmaking and photography helped him develop his style of illustration and taught him how to tell a story with pictures. James is married to Lesa Cline-Ransome, and the two have published several books together.

Author's Purpose

How does the author's use of dialogue give the story of Marshall Taylor a literary quality that not all biographies have?

Respond to Reading

Summarize

Use important details from *Major Taylor: Champion Cyclist* to summarize how Marshall Taylor's achievements influenced the opinions of those who watched him perform and race. Information from your Cause and Effect Chart may help you.

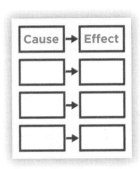

Cause	→	Effect
	→	
	→	
	→	

Text Evidence

1. What details in the text help you to identify *Major Taylor: Champion Cyclist* as a biography? Give at least two details from the selection to support your answer. **GENRE**

2. How did Marshall Taylor become a champion cyclist? Identify the cause and effect relationships that led to his career. **CAUSE AND EFFECT**

3. What is the meaning of the word *entitled* on page 238? Use context clues to help you figure out the meaning. Then use the meaning in the sentence to see whether it makes sense. **PARAGRAPH CLUES**

4. Write about the racism that Marshall faced during his career and the effect it had on his performance when he raced. Include an example from the text to support your answer. **WRITE ABOUT READING**

Make Connections

How was Marshall able to affect the opinions of others? **ESSENTIAL QUESTION**

Tell about a breakthrough achievement that you think influenced people in a positive way. How do you think this changed people's opinions? **TEXT TO WORLD**

Compare Texts
Read about a woman who changed people's attitudes about female photographers.

MARGARET BOURKE-WHITE:
Fearless Photographer

In 1904, girls weren't supposed to dream of careers that took them flying into the sky on airplanes, or climbing out onto ledges at the top of skyscrapers. And they certainly weren't encouraged to think about competing with men for the opportunity to photograph important people and events.

Joseph White and Minnie Bourke, however, never told their daughter what to think and dream about. Instead, young Margaret, or "Peg" as her friends called her, got plenty of attention and encouragement from her parents to explore her world. Early on, they taught her to work hard and to go after what she wanted. They even gave

her a motto: "You can." It's no wonder Margaret Bourke-White grew up to be one of the most accomplished women and talked-about photographers of the twentieth century.

Many photographers today owe thanks to Margaret. From the time she started taking photographs and recognized that they could stir up feelings to the culmination of her long career as a photojournalist, Margaret was a **trailblazer**. She shaped the art of photography and the profession of photojournalism and showed that women photographers could travel all over the world and work alongside men in dangerous situations.

Margaret Bourke-White with her camera atop the Chrysler Building in New York City in 1931.

A Star Photographer

Her mother gave Margaret her first camera in 1921, when she was 17 years old. Her interest in photography grew as a result of her father's enthusiasm for cameras. A few years later, Margaret's classmates at Cornell University became her first admirers when photos she took of the campus appeared in the school newspaper. A year after graduating, Margaret moved to Cleveland, Ohio and opened a commercial photography studio.

One of Margaret's first clients was the Otis Steel Company. Her success was due both to her technique and her skills in dealing with people. At first, several people at the company wondered if a woman could stand up to the intense heat and generally dirty and gritty conditions inside a steel mill. When Margaret finally got permission, the technical problems began. Black-and-white film at that time was sensitive to blue light, not the reds and oranges of hot steel. The pictures came out all black. Margaret solved this problem by bringing along a new style of flare (which produces white light) and having assistants hold them to light her scenes. Her abilities resulted in some of the best steel factory pictures of that era, and these earned her national attention.

The city's powerful businessmen soon began calling on her to take pictures of their mills, factories, and buildings. In the steel mills, she wanted to be right next to the melted metal. The extreme heat sometimes burned her face and damaged the paint on her camera. In her first well-known photographs, Margaret made the production of steel look magnificent, mysterious, and awe-inspiring. Her photos, filled with streams of melted steel and flying sparks, caught the eye of someone who would change her life.

A New Sort of Storytelling

Henry Luce was a powerful and important American publisher. In the 1920s and 1930s he started a series of magazines that would change journalism and the reading habits of Americans. Luce's magazine called *Time* summarized and interpreted the week's news. *Life* was a picture magazine of politics, culture and society that became very popular in the years before television, and *Fortune* explored the economy and the world of business. *Sports Illustrated* investigated the teams and important players of popular sports such as baseball and football.

In 1929 Henry Luce invited Margaret to work at *Fortune* Magazine. She

jumped at the chance and became the first woman in a new field called photojournalism, in which photographers reported the news through images.

As Margaret snapped artistic shots of workplaces, she was able to find beauty in simple objects. Over time she adapted her techniques to photograph people and was adept at catching expressions and showing hardship. In 1930, she was the first photographer from a Western country to be allowed into the Soviet Union (now Russia), where she took pictures of the workers in what was then a communist country.

World War II and After

When World War II broke out in 1939, Margaret became the first female war correspondent. This is a journalist

Ready for anything, Margaret prepares to leave on a bombing raid with the U.S. Army at the height of World War II in 1943.

who covers stories first hand from a war zone. In 1941, she traveled to the Soviet Union again and was the only foreign photographer in Moscow when German forces invaded. Taking shelter in the U.S. Embassy, she then captured much of the fierce battle on camera.

As the war continued, Margaret joined the U.S. Army Air Force in North Africa and then traveled with the U.S. Army in Italy and later Germany. She repeatedly came under fire in Italy as she traveled through areas of intense fighting.

After the war, Margaret continued to make the world's most complex events understandable. Her photos reflected stirring social issues of the time. She photographed South Africans laboring in gold mines and civil rights leader Mahatma Gandhi's nonviolent work in India.

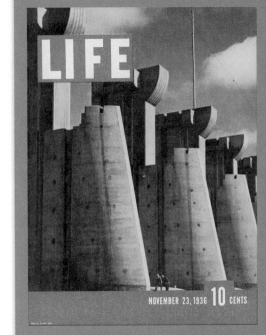

In 1936, Margaret had the honor of shooting the first cover for Luce's new *Life* magazine. To many, her image of Fort Peck Dam in Montana represented a strong United States. It said that Americans were ready to pull themselves out of the Great Depression. Margaret soon left *Fortune* and joined the staff of *Life* Magazine.

A Lasting Influence

During the 1930s and 1940s, Margaret's adventurous attitude and **perseverance** paved the way for women to take on roles beyond the norm. Rather than snapping photos of high-society parties as other female photographers had done before her, she marched into steel plants and combat zones. She proved to women that they had every right to pursue the careers they wanted.

Through her work, Margaret became a role model for working women as well as a strong voice for the poor and powerless. She earned the respect of powerful businessmen when women were discouraged from working. When she died in 1971, she left behind not only an amazing photographic record of the human experience. She also left a message for women all over the world who wanted to make an impact: "You can."

Make Connections

How did Margaret Bourke-White's achievements influence others? **ESSENTIAL QUESTION**

Why is it sometimes difficult to break down professional barriers? **TEXT TO TEXT**

TIME FOR KIDS®

Stewards of the Environment

LayneKennedy/Corbis

? **Essential Question**

What steps can people take to promote a healthier environment?

Read about how some people across the country approach solving environmental problems.

Go Digital!

How can using a different approach help solve different problems?

In an address to Congress in 1905 President Theodore Roosevelt said, "Conservation means development as much as it does protection. I recognize the right and duty of this generation to develop and use the natural resources of our land. But I do not recognize the right to waste them, or to rob, by wasteful use, the generations that come after us." Many of Theodore Roosevelt's **initial** achievements as president were in the area of conservation. Roosevelt used his authority to protect wildlife and public lands by creating the U.S. Forest Service. He also established bird reservations, 150 National Forests, and five National Parks.

It has been over 100 years since Roosevelt made this statement before Congress. The fight for conservation and a cleaner environment, however, goes on. Here are some ways a variety of people have chosen to earn the title "Steward of the Earth."

Chad Pregracke poses with some of the rubbish he has collected along America's waterways.

STOP AND CHECK

Ask and Answer Questions
In what way did Chad Pregracke honor the statements Theodore Roosevelt made in 1905?

Cleaner Rivers

As a boy growing up in the Quad Cities in Illinois, you might say that the Mississippi River was Chad Pregracke's backyard. He grew up just a few feet from the legendary waterway. While attending high school and college, Chad worked as a commercial fisherman. During the summers, he was also a barge hand on the Mississippi and Illinois rivers. It was during this period that Chad began to notice their deteriorating condition. This was due to the accumulation of rubbish and litter on the shorelines. In the spring of 1997, he set out to make a difference, one river at a time, one piece of garbage at a time.

Chad's first thought was to try and get government agencies to do something about the situation. However, they failed to step up. At 23, he founded his own organization to do the job. Since 1997, Living Lands & Waters has succeeded in removing 6 million pounds of trash from some of America's greatest rivers. With the help of more than 60,000 volunteers and **advocates**, including a number of corporations, Chad's organization has helped clean up the Mississippi, Illinois, Ohio, Missouri, and Potomac Rivers.

Small Houses, Big Message

Except for a temporary dip in the 1980s when the economy was in recession, the trend in new American homes has been big, bigger, and bigger still. Small was an unfamiliar concept.

251

Smaller houses are becoming more and more popular.

That may be changing, however, since the size of new houses has been declining rather than increasing since 2007. The economy once again plays a big role. But there are other factors as well, including concern for the environment.

A bigger house means not only more wood and other materials for construction and **insulation**. It also means more energy to manufacture and transport the materials. More plumbing, wiring, paint, and woodwork increases maintenance costs, and more and bigger rooms means additional energy is needed for heating, cooling, and lighting.

The overall change in house size has not been huge. In 2006, the median size of new single-family homes under construction peaked at 2,268 square feet. By 2009 it was down to 2,100 square feet. But for some, 2,100 square feet is still **irrational** and way too big. A new movement claims than an **optimal** size for a house is not just smaller, but tiny. Houses under 1,000 square feet, and even under 100 square feet, are becoming more **commonplace**. Costs are much lower, beginning with construction and extending to maintenance, taxes,

and energy use. The growing group of people who reject the "bigger is better" concept want to take positive steps to minimize and reduce their negative and **invasive** impact on the planet.

Students Get an Environmental Education

In 2007, students at the Boston Latin School (BLS) in Boston, Massachusetts, founded Youth CAN, the Youth Climate Action Network. Youth CAN is committed to doing something about climate change. The network includes dedicated member groups from other schools. It also has enthusiastic partner organizations. These include the National Wildlife Federation and the New England Aquarium.

The group has developed a web page with links to resources for educators. It also holds a Global Climate Change Summit every year. The summit features speakers, workshops, and films. It is developing a statewide plan for educating students about sustainability. According to the U.S. Environmental Protection Agency, "Sustainability creates and maintains the conditions under which humans and nature can exist in productive harmony."

How to Start a Recycling Program at School

A recycling program is one of the simplest ways a school can "go green," and students can take the lead in creating one.

Many people are "going green" with recycling programs.

Step 1:

Build a team. **Designate** someone to act as a leader

Step 2:

Figure out how to pay for the program, from the school budget or another source.

Step 3:

Let people know about the program.

Step 4:

Choose bins and containers and label them clearly.

Step 5:

Place bins and containers where they will be easy to use.

Step 6:

Set goals and keep records of how much is recycled.

Step 7:

Celebrate success!

Respond to Reading

1. Identify the text features that help you identify "Stewards of the Environment" as an informational article. **GENRE**

2. Use key details from the text to identify the main idea of this article. **MAIN IDEA AND KEY DETAILS**

3. What is the meaning of *minimize* on page 252? Use a synonym for the word in the paragraph to help you. **SYNONYMS AND ANTONYMS**

4. How can the actions of someone like Chad Pregracke inspire other people? **TEXT TO WORLD**

Tetra Images/Corbis

Compare Texts

Read how improvements to mass transit in the ancient city of Athens, Greece paid off in more than one way.

Modern Transit for an ANCIENT CITY

A subway train pulls into a station in Athens, Greece.

In September 1997, the city of Athens, Greece, won the honor of hosting the 2004 summer Olympic Games. A key factor in the decision was the city's promise to have a modern metro (subway) system ready to serve people who came to the games. Most people who live in cities around the world are **advocates** of mass transit. Busses and trains move large numbers of people while minimizing the use of fossil fuels. Even a city as ancient as Athens can and should have a "green" mass transit system, Olympics or no Olympics.

Greece has a population of over 10.5 million people. Nearly half of them are crowded into the city of Athens. Before 1994, polluting emissions from cars and other vehicles were completely unregulated. Athens was frequently shrouded in smog. The dirty air was unhealthy for people, and it was damaging the ancient cultural treasures of Greece, including the Parthenon and other monuments.

Molly Evans/Alamy

At the Syntagma Station, metro riders can view remains of a sculpture foundry, a cemetery, a baths complex, an aqueduct, and a road.

That's why the expansion and upgrading of the subway system in Athens was so important. Officials estimated that the two new metro lines would reduce automobile trips to the center of Athens by 250,000 daily. Measures were taken to make all forms of mass transit more attractive, including upgrading bus service and banning private cars in the commercial district.

After Athens was awarded the 2004 Olympics, the initial celebration gave way to action. Public-sector agencies and private business had to work together to complete construction of the two new metro lines in an **optimal** amount of time. In the process, they met the special challenges that only a city with ancient antiquities faces. Their response was to turn subway stations into stunning archaeological showcases for Greece's past glory.

What the Archaeologists and Engineers Found

Under the streets of modern Athens lay priceless artifacts and structures from as far back as the Late Bronze Age. Engineers planned to dig the subway very deep, tunneling under the archaeological treasures. Still, it wasn't possible to avoid them all, and this led some people to feel that the subway should not have been built.

Construction revealed buildings, jewelry, and pottery from the ancient past. Sometimes the historical items were moved to new locations to be preserved. In other cases, work went on around them. Some Metro stations were designed to become mini-museums. As it turned out, updating the city of Athens for the future revealed the glories of its past. How cool is that?

POINT COUNTERPOINT

Make Connections

In what ways does mass transit promote a healthier environment?
ESSENTIAL QUESTION

How do each of the steps people have taken—recycling, promoting mass transit, cleaning up waterways and fighting global warming—work together to promote a healthier environment? **TEXT TO TEXT**

Albert Moldvay/National Geographic/Getty Images

255

Essential Question

How do people meet environmental challenges?

Read about a disaster that created rolling walls of dust throughout the Great Plains of the United States.

 Go Digital!

256

YEARS OF DUST

THE STORY OF THE DUST BOWL

BY ALBERT MARRIN

In the early 1930s, rolling walls of dust began to sweep across the Great Plains, burying crops, automobiles, even buildings. Families battled to survive as howling winds brought new storms year after year throughout the 1930s. What caused these storms? And more important, how could they be stopped?

TEXT: From YEARS OF DUST: THE STORY OF THE DUST BOWL by Albert Marrin, text. Used by permission of Viking Children's Books, A Division of Penguin Young Readers Group. A Member of Penguin Group (USA) Inc., 345 Hudson Street, New York, NY 10014. All rights reserved.; Franklin D. Roosevelt Library

THE GREAT PLAINS WORLD

There is no way to understand the Dust Bowl tragedy without first understanding the ecology of the Great Plains. Ecology is the branch of science that deals with the relationships between living beings and their physical environment. Mountains, rivers, lakes, deserts, jungles, and Arctic regions—to name a few—are all special environments. Each has unique life-forms that interact with each other and depend on each other to survive. So does the Great Plains.

A region of seemingly boundless open spaces, the plains lie at the heart of North America. Reaching southward from the Canadian provinces of Alberta, Saskatchewan, and Manitoba, they extend into northern Mexico. The plains also stretch eastward from the bases of the Rocky Mountains to the banks of the Mississippi and Missouri rivers.

Except for the Llano Estacado (Spanish for "Staked Plains") of Texas, the plains are not pancake-flat. They are wavelike, gently sloping downward from the Rockies toward the east. The plains have not always been dry land. Fossil seashells and fish show that they once formed the bed of a shallow inland sea. They owe their slope to the buildup of soil and stones washed down from the Rockies. Trees, mostly cottonwoods, grow along the banks of plains rivers. Otherwise, the region is treeless. In a few places, like the Black Hills of South Dakota, hills rise sharply from the surrounding countryside. Millions of years ago, when dinosaurs roamed the land, molten rock from the earth's core forced its way to the surface and solidified, forming the hills we see today.

The Great Plains is a place of extreme, violent weather. Weather can change suddenly from heavenly to horrid. With no trees to block it, the wind blows constantly. Often the wind reaches speeds seen nowhere else but at the seashore, blowing over one hundred miles an hour. Its moaning, whistling, and howling often tormented the first white settlers, people unused to such sounds. "A high wind is an awful thing," a woman wrote, "it wears you down, it nags at you day after day, it sounds like an invisible army, it fills you with terror as something invisible does."*

After the blizzard. A street scene in a Great Plains town. The group of men hold signs advertising local businesses. Photograph taken in Milton, North Dakota, April 13, 1893.

Winter on the Plains

Arctic winds lash the Great Plains in fall and winter. Called "northers," because they come out of the north, the fierce winds can make the thermometer drop fifty degrees in just a few minutes. Northers often bring blizzards. Even today, windows and doors must fit snugly to keep the fine wind-driven snow out of a house. In *The Plains of the Great West* (1877), army veteran Colonel Richard Irving Dodge wrote: "For a week each day will be clear [and] calm . . . No overcoat is needed, and the presence of winter is scarcely recognized. Then comes a storm; the icy wind cuts like a knife, no clothing seems to keep it from the person, and penetrating to every part it drags out every particle of vital heat, leaving but a stiffened corpse of him who is so unfortunate as to be exposed to it."

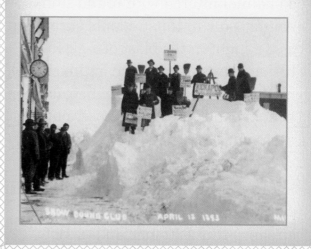

NDSU; *T.H. Watkins, *The Hungry Years: A Narrative History of the Great Depression in America* (New York: Henry Holt Co., 1999), 424.

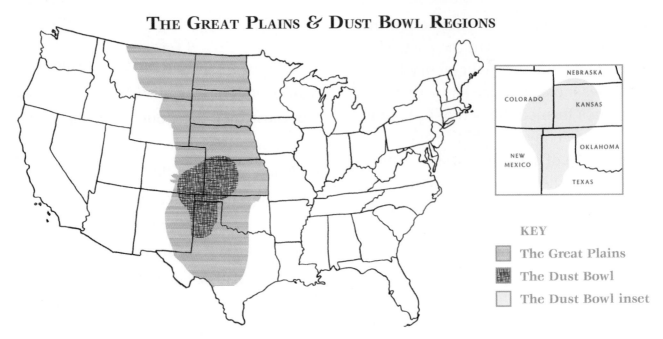

THE GREAT PLAINS & DUST BOWL REGIONS

KEY

[grid pattern] The Great Plains

[crosshatch pattern] The Dust Bowl

[light gray] The Dust Bowl inset

An immense area of 1.25 million square miles, the Great Plains cover about a third of the continental United States, and includes parts of ten Western states: Montana, North Dakota, South Dakota, Wyoming, Nebraska, Colorado, Kansas, New Mexico, Oklahoma, and Texas.

Depending on the season, the wind brings scorching heat and numbing cold. Summer winds whip out of the Mexican deserts. Plains temperatures soar past one hundred degrees in the shade, and stay there for weeks, with no relief even at night. The dry heat is a killer. Streams vanish, leaving only a channel littered with round stones. Animals die of thirst. Plants shrivel up, as if caught in the blast of a gigantic furnace. In summertime, railroads might have to stop service because the heat expands the steel tracks, putting them out of **alignment**.

Even today, wildfires ignited by lightning and driven by wind may burn until they run out of fuel or reach a stream. "It is a strange and terrible sight to see," wrote one settler, "all the fields a sea of fire. Quite often the scorching flames sweep everything along in their path—people, cattle, hay, fences. In dry weather with a strong wind the fire will race faster than the speediest horse."* To survive a plains fire, every creature in its path must run or fly, dig—or die. Yet the plains need periodic fires to stay healthy. Fire clears dead vegetation. The remaining ashes return as minerals to the soil, increasing its fertility.

Rainfall decides what, if anything, will grow. The Great Plains have what scientists call a semiarid climate, that is, a climate with light rainfall. Normally, the Great Plains region gets ten to twenty inches of rain a year,

* Jon E. Lewis, The West: The Making of the American West (New York: Carroll & Graf, 2001), 463.

Cattle in a blizzard on the plains. This wood engraving was created in 1886 and published as a print in *Harper's Weekly*.

compared to twenty to forty inches in the Mississippi Valley and seventy-five inches in the Pacific Northwest. This is due in part to the Rocky Mountains. Their towering peaks form a wall, allowing few moisture-bearing clouds to drift eastward from the Pacific Ocean. Most moisture reaches the plains thanks to a low-level jet stream, a fast-moving current of winds that moves close to the earth's surface. This wind current goes from east to west across the Atlantic Ocean. It curves northward as it crosses the Gulf of Mexico, drawing in tropical moisture. Naturally, the farther north the low-level jet stream goes, the less moisture it bears, because it has already fallen as rain. For this reason, the northern plains are generally drier than the southern plains.

From a 1901 painting by Charles Schreyvogel titled *Doomed*. Native American hunters often killed their prey by plunging a lance into their bodies.

The Buffalo and the Indian

Plains Indian tribes like the Lakota (Sioux) and Cheyenne said everything they needed, except water for drinking and cooking, and wood for tepee poles, came from the buffalo. These hunters ate buffalo meat at every meal, several pounds at a time. Tanned buffalo hide became robes, blankets, caps, mittens, moccasins, leggings, shields, saddlebags, drums, and tepee walls. Their hair became rope, their tails flyswatters, their horns spoons, cups, and storage containers. Bones were shaped into needles, knife blades, spear points, war clubs, and awls to punch holes in leather. Boiled hooves made excellent glue, used to fasten arrowheads to their shafts. When it rained, buffalo dung stayed dry on the inside, making an all-weather fuel to warm a tepee or cook a meal.

Prairie Dog Town

Prairie dogs, a type of ground squirrel, live in vast underground "towns," or tunnels that extend for miles in all directions. A prairie dog town in Texas once took up 25,000 square miles and held an estimated 400 million animals—and there were hundreds like it. In all, scientists believe that as many as 25 billion prairie dogs once inhabited the plains. Soldiers on long patrols and pioneers sometimes ate prairie dogs. "He is not excellent eating," wrote Colonel Richard Irving Dodge, "but the young are as good as the common squirrel, and, when other meat is not to be had, they made no unwelcome addition to the bill of fare."

The Mississippi River is a natural dividing line for different types of plants, notably grasses. Since tall grasses such as big bluestem need more water, they grow east of the river. Because they need little water, short grasses grow west of the river. When white farmers first settled west of the river on the Great Plains, blue grama and buffalo grass were the chief short grasses. Called perennials, because they live for many years, these short grasses anchored themselves in the soil by a shallow network of tangled roots. This tough root mat, called "sod," easily absorbed rainwater. Equally important, sod held the soil in place, preventing it from washing or blowing away. Though fire burned the plains grasses, it could not reach their roots. Soon after the fire passed, fresh blades of grass would appear.

Animals, and people, depend on plants that chemically change the sun's radiant or light energy into food. The plains once teemed with plant-eating animals. Some, like jackrabbits, mice, and prairie dogs, were small. There were many larger animals, too. Scientists estimate that, before the arrival of white settlers, 25 million pronghorn antelopes bounded across the sea of grass. Nature designed the pronghorn for speed and endurance. With long, muscular legs, a large heart, and oversize lungs, it could travel for hours at thirty miles an hour.

The lord of the Great Plains was the American bison, or buffalo. When the first Europeans reached the New World, some 40 to 60 million buffalo roamed the region in their endless search for pasture. The buffalo was what ecologists call a keystone animal. In architecture, the keystone of an arch keeps the other stones in place.

A keystone animal is one that other life-forms need to survive. For example, the hooves of grazing buffalo pushed seeds into the ground, where they sprouted and grew, becoming food for other herbivores. Another example is the prairie dog, which cannot live in tall grass. By grazing, buffalo kept the grass to the small creature's liking. This is important, for in digging their burrows, prairie dogs bring mineral-rich soil to the surface. In return, buffalo get needed salts by licking up dried urine around prairie dog holes. Buffalo dung—lumps of digested grass—served as breeding grounds for necessary insects and molds. Finally, after death, the buffalo's decaying body fertilized the soil and provided a feast for buzzards and bugs, coyotes and worms.

Carnivores (meat-eaters) thrived in the Great Plains environment. Golden eagles glided overhead, their keen eyes searching the ground for prey. Grizzly bears fed on living and dead animals of all sizes; a white traveler once counted 220 grizzlies in a day. Wolves ran in packs of fifty members or more. Seen from a distance, travelers said their light coats made them resemble flocks of sheep. Coyotes, rattlesnakes, and bobcats also had good hunting.

For sheer numbers, though, no plains creature equaled the grasshopper. Historical records describe what grasshopper outbreaks on the Great Plains were once like. Sometimes "hoppers" came in miles-wide clouds, billions upon billions of them, streaming across the sky. In her novel, *On the Banks of Plum Creek,* Laura Ingalls Wilder describes a grasshopper swarm in the mid-1880s:

Hunters stampeding a buffalo herd, January 2, 1917.

STOP AND CHECK

Reread In what ways did animals depend on one another in the Great Plains environment? Reread to check your understanding.

The Lord of the Plains

An adult buffalo eats up to thirty pounds of grass a day. The largest land animal in North America, a full-grown bull can stand six feet six inches tall at the shoulders, be ten feet from snout to rump, and weigh two thousand pounds. Adult cows are smaller, weighing just twelve hundred pounds. Buffalo once grazed in herds so large we can scarcely imagine them today. Easily excited, their stampedes shook the earth; their bellowing made it hard to get a night's sleep. Sometimes herds drank small rivers dry. As late as 1871, U.S. Army patrols found their way blocked by moving herds. Once, an officer reported, a herd took five days to pass and was fifty miles deep by ten miles wide. This herd was nothing special, just one of countless others that roamed the plains.

. . . A cloud was over the sun. It was not like any cloud they had ever seen before. It was a cloud of something like snowflakes, and thin and glittering. Light shone through each flickering particle.

There was no wind. The grasses were still and the hot air did not stir, but the edge of the cloud came across the sky faster than the wind. The hair stood up on [our dog] Jack's neck. All at once he made a frightful sound up at that cloud, a growl and a whine.

Plunk! Something hit Laura's head and fell to the ground. She looked down and saw the biggest grasshopper she had ever seen. . . .

The cloud was hailing grasshoppers. The cloud was grasshoppers. Their bodies hid the sun and made darkness. . . . The rasping whirring of their wings filled the whole air and they hit the ground and the house with the noise of a hailstorm.*

Whenever a grasshopper cloud set down, it cleared the ground of plant life. All you could hear was the sound of countless jaws *CHOMP, CHOMP, CHOMPING* until nothing remained to eat. Young children, caught outdoors, screamed in terror as the insects' claws caught in their hair and bodies wriggled into their clothing. On railroad tracks slippery with crushed grasshoppers, trains could not start or, worse, stop. Yet, since grasshopper jaws could not get at their roots, the native prairie grasses always grew back.

The Great Plains, then, was (and is) a harsh land. Despite the hardships, Americans still saw the plains as a place of opportunity. A place where, through hard work and good luck, they could build a better future. And so, in the nineteenth and early twentieth centuries, settlers flocked to the rolling grasslands west of the Mississippi.

A plague of locusts fill the sky. Locust plagues have been recorded in different places throughout the world since ancient times.

Grasshoppers: A Plains Plague

The word "locust" refers to the swarming phase of a short-horned grasshopper. Government scientists estimated that one particularly large swarm of grasshoppers was over one hundred miles long by one hundred miles wide. Creatures of summer, these insects thrive in hot, dry weather. Heat checks their natural enemies, which include bacteria, birds, and rodents. These insects also favor dry weather because abundant rain allows a certain type of fungus to grow which kills grasshoppers by releasing poisons into their bodies.

Plains grasshoppers can reach a length of four inches.

A farmer and his sons in a dust storm in Cimarron County, Oklahoma, 1936.

Library of Congress, Prints & Photographs Division [LC-DIG-ppmsc-00241]; *"Hugh Hammond Bennett" in "The American Experience: Surviving the Dust Bowl," www.pbs.org/wgbh/pages/amex/dustbowl.

Dust Bowl Days

To those who spent their days behind desks in the nation's capital, it seemed that the fertility of the soil was boundless. Said an official report of the U.S. Department of Agriculture, "The soil is the one . . . resource that cannot be exhausted; that cannot be used up."* This statement had more to do with ignorance and wishful thinking than science.

A drought that began in 1930 became the worst in the nation's history, affecting more than three-quarters of the country. Throughout the East, crops withered in the fields and bank foreclosures increased. The next year, the center of the drought shifted westward, to the Great Plains.

As usual, heat went along with drought. Out on the plains, the early 1930s saw record-breaking heat waves. In some states, like Nebraska, the temperature soared to 118 degrees, and stayed there for days without letup or relief. It was so hot that a cook in Grafton, South Dakota, made a melted cheese sandwich by putting it on the sidewalk outside her restaurant. Thousands of people suffered heatstroke, a sudden collapse brought on by extreme heat. Hundreds died. There was no air-conditioning back then, even in town homes with electricity. Residents might have electric fans, but these merely circulated the hot air, so that it felt like a hot hand held over the face. Few farm homes had electricity, and thus most had no electric fans.

Periodic dust storms are normal on the Great Plains. People expected them. Since nothing could be done about the storms, you accepted the **inconvenience** and waited until they passed. Yet the dust storms of the 1930s were different. They were not "natural disasters," like hurricanes, tornadoes, and earthquakes, over which humans have no control. Humans can neither make such natural disasters, nor prevent them. Although dust storms would have occurred anyhow, human actions made the storms of the 1930s much worse than they would have been. The result was an ecological catastrophe.

Electrical Storms

Trillions of dust particles striking against each other **generated** static electricity. Sometimes there was so much electricity in the air that it knocked people down if they shook hands. Static electricity made the barbs on barbed wire fences glow. Animals blown into wire fences could be seriously injured by the electrical charge. To avoid shocks, housewives covered door handles with cloth. Motorists had to outfit cars with chains to drag for grounding, or risk having their engines short out in a storm.*

Photo courtesy of USDA Natural Resources Conservation Service; *Timothy Egan, *The Worst Hard Time: The Untold Story of Those Who Survived the Great American Dust Bowl.* (Boston: Houghton Mifflin, 2005), 153, 172.

This catastrophe has a simple explanation. A Texas sheepherder explained a basic fact: "Grass is what counts. It's what saves us all—far as we get saved. . . . Grass is what holds the earth together."* Plowing up millions of acres of drought-resistant native grasses removed the very thing that had held the plains soil in place for countless centuries. Replacing these grasses with cash crops like wheat and corn added to the problem. Unlike native grasses, which continue to grow year after year, these crops are annuals; that is, they die after a single growing season. Because the crops live for only one season and have shallow root systems, they do not survive **prolonged** heat and dry spells.

Thus, all the elements for disaster came together in the 1930s: drought, heat, sod-destroying farming methods, annual cash crops. When the winds came, the ground cracked and the dust became airborne. And so, the dust-storm catastrophe of the 1930s was no natural disaster. It was manmade.

For people already reeling under the hardships of the Great Depression, life in the Dust Bowl became the supreme test of the human spirit. What was it like for them?

Mammoth dust storms gave the era its nickname, the "dirty thirties." The storms began in 1933, on the northern plains. At first, they were not particularly alarming. Plains people were used to dust storms and expected them to end quickly. Instead, the storms grew in number, lasted longer, and were more severe than any in living memory.

A farmer described the 1934 dust storms as "lollapaloosas," slang for unimaginably large. On May 9, cool Canadian winds whipped up an immense dust cloud over Montana and Wyoming. Government scientists

Street view of a dust storm in Scott City, Kansas, 1935.

estimated that this storm alone carried away 350 million tons of topsoil. For the next two days, dust clouds raced south and east. Airline pilots climbed up to fifteen thousand feet to reach clear air; the dust would have clogged their engines, causing them to burn out. Some 12 million tons of dust enveloped Chicago in a gritty haze—four pounds for every man, woman, and child in the Windy City. On May 12, the *New York Times* reported, "a cloud of dust thousands of feet high . . . filtered the rays of the sun for five hours yesterday. New York was obscured in a half-light similar to the light cast by the sun in a partial **eclipse**." Three hundred miles out at sea, sailors wrote their names in the dust that settled on ships' decks.

The storm that farmers called "the granddaddy of 'em all" burst out of South Dakota on April 14, 1935—"Black Sunday." Gathering force while growing in size, this monster was over one thousand miles wide. It traveled fifteen hundred miles before breaking up over the Gulf of Mexico. People who saw the cloud from different angles said it ranged from two miles to only several hundred feet in height.

STOP AND CHECK

Reread What factors created the Dust Bowl, and what could have been done to prevent it? Reread to check your understanding.

In nearby Pampa, Texas, the day began gloriously. The air was so clear you could see to the horizon in all directions. Texan A. D. Kirk had just parked his car when he saw something strange.

I noticed a low dark line of what I first thought was a cloud along the northern horizon. It made no sense. There was not a cloud in the sky. As I watched, it got taller and spread from the west to the east horizon. The black mass was coming on fast. . . . The front of the cloud was a rolling, tumbling, boiling mass of dust and dirt about two hundred feet high, almost vertical, and as black as an Angus bull. There was no dust in the air above it or in front of it. It came across the prairie like a two-hundred-foot-high tidal wave, pushed along by a sixty-mile-per-hour wind. When it got to a house or power pole or any other object, the house or whatever disappeared. It was weird. After the front passed, the darkness rivaled the darkness inside a whale resting on the bottom of the ocean at midnight. . . .*

For Want of Oxygen

When a dust storm struck, family members quickly sealed windows and doors with gummed tape, felt strips, or rags. This cut air circulation to such a degree that lamps flickered for lack of oxygen and breathing became difficult. When someone felt as if they might pass out, a window was opened just a bit, letting in a swirling dust-deluge. Yet even with every opening sealed, the dust, fine as talcum powder, got in through invisible cracks.

The kitchen of a house in Williams County, North Dakota, 1937. Notice the windowpane stuffed with rags in a vain attempt to keep the dust out.

While many thought Black Sunday heralded doomsday, others saw a chance to make a fast profit. Collecting dust in old soda bottles, they offered it for sale as "Genuine 1935 Rolling Duster Dust—25 cents."** Sales could not have been very good. Most who had lived through Black Sunday wanted to forget it. But nature would not let them forget.

Although nothing equaled the Black Sunday blizzard of 1935, for the next four years scores of dust storms swept across the Great Plains. While different places fared better or worse in any given year, the true Dust Bowl, the hardest-hit region, centered in the five states of the southern plains. This region, stretching roughly five hundred miles by three hundred miles, included the western third of Kansas, southeastern Colorado, the Oklahoma Panhandle, the northern two-thirds of the Texas Panhandle, and northeastern New Mexico. "If you would like to have your heart broken, just come out here," wrote Ernie Pyle, among the era's finest reporters. "This is the dust-storm country. It is the saddest land I have ever seen."***

Library of Congress, Prints & Photographs Division [LC-USF347-003801-ZE]; **Franklin L. Stallings, Jr. Black Sunday: The Great Dust Storm of April 14, 1935 (Austin, TX: Eakin Press, 2001), 136.***"The Drought," www.pbs.org/wgbh/amex/dustbowl.

STOP AND CHECK

Ask and Answer Questions As a reporter, what questions would you have wanted to ask someone who experienced "Black Sunday" in 1935?

About the Author

Albert Marrin

has always been fascinated by history. He spent nine years as a history teacher in a New York City junior high school before becoming a university professor of history and then a full-time writer. In award-winning books such as *1812: The War Nobody Won* and *The Great Adventure: Theodore Roosevelt and the Rise of Modern America,* Albert created an overview of United States history by focusing on dramatic moments and famous personalities. In 2008, Albert won the National Endowment for the Humanities Medal. It was presented to him at a White House ceremony, where he was praised for "opening young minds to the glorious pageant of history."

Author's Purpose

The author uses photos, captions, a map, and sidebars in this selection. How do these text features help you to understand the topic?

Respond to Reading

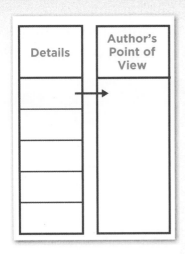

Details	Author's Point of View

Summarize

Use details from *Years of Dust* to summarize what you have learned about conditions on the Great Plains during the Dust Bowl era. Information from your Author's Point of View Chart may help you.

Text Evidence

1. Identify at least two text features that help you identify the selection *Years of Dust: The Story of the Dust Bowl* as an example of an expository text. **GENRE**

2. What is the author's point of view, or attitude toward, the Dust Bowl and the people who had to live through it? How is this point of view conveyed, or shown, in the text? **AUTHOR'S POINT OF VIEW**

3. What does the word *boundless* mean in the first paragraph on page 266? Use context clues in the surrounding sentences to help you figure out the meaning of the word. **PARAGRAPH CLUES**

4. Write about how the author uses eyewitness accounts to convince readers that the Dust Bowl was an ecological catastrophe. **WRITE ABOUT READING**

Make Connections

How did people view the environmental challenge of the Dust Bowl? **ESSENTIAL QUESTION**

Identify the cause or feature of the Dust Bowl that you feel was the most interesting fact you learned about this disaster. What can we learn about preventing future dust bowls from reading this selection? **TEXT TO WORLD**

Compare Texts

Read about how one teenager organized her community to meet an environmental challenge.

ERICA Fernandez
ENVIRONMENTAL ACTIVIST

Anyone who doesn't believe that young people can fight for change and succeed hasn't met Erica Fernandez.

Erica was barely into her teens when she arrived in California from Mexico with her parents. Not long afterward, Erica found out that a liquefied natural gas facility was being planned for the coast of Oxnard and Malibu. It would include a three-foot wide pipeline that would run through low-income neighborhoods.

The result, Erica learned, would be a **calamity** for the area. Some people estimated that the facility would spew hundreds of tons of pollutants into the air and waters of nearby coastal towns each year.

Erica was outraged, and she soon began to educate others about the issue. She wanted to mobilize youth, kids her own age and older, because she knew the pipeline would affect their future. Soon over 300 students from neighboring schools were knocking on doors and handing out flyers.

By the time two different state commissions met to discuss the project, other large environmental organizations had joined the fight. Next, Erica helped launch a mail and phone call campaign to the governor. After receiving thousands of postcards and phone calls, the governor declared that there would be no pipeline in Oxnard or Malibu.

In 2007, Erica's passion and **tenacity** was rewarded when she was selected as one of six young people to receive the Brower Youth Award. Each year this award is given to students in recognition for their work on behalf of the environment. Young people between the ages of 13 and 22 are eligible for the award.

I want you to close your eyes. Imagine yourself one day waking up in the morning and not being able to breathe. What would you do? Who would you blame?

My inspiration is my dad who is in front of me right now. He suffers from respiratory problems. Knowing that he was close to death many times, I wasn't going to let a multi-billion dollar company bring more pollution to Mother Earth.

I wanted to be the voice for those who thought they did not have one.… I wanted to be the inspiration for those who believed that a person can make a difference. I wanted to be heard and I was heard. For that I thank my community for teaching me a life lesson—that a united community is more powerful than money.…

Now I would like to finish with the words of my role model César Chávez: Once social change begins, it cannot be reversed. You cannot uneducate the people who have learned to read. You cannot humiliate the people who feel pride. You cannot oppress people who are not afraid anymore.

Postscript

Soon after receiving her award, Erica Fernandez became a freshman at Stanford University.

Make Connections

Why is it useful for people to work together when meeting a challenge? **ESSENTIAL QUESTION**

How have other people you've read about met environmental challenges? **TEXT TO TEXT**

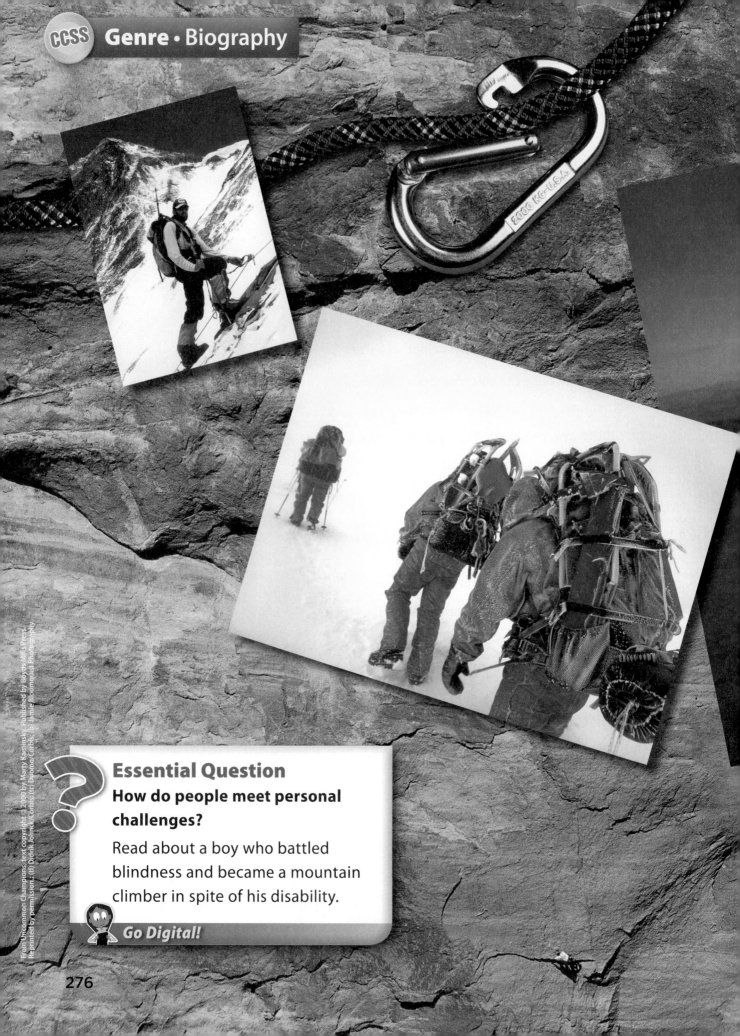

Essential Question

How do people meet personal challenges?

Read about a boy who battled blindness and became a mountain climber in spite of his disability.

Go Digital!

Seeing Things His Own Way

by Marty Kaminsky

Erik Weihenmayer thrust his ice ax into the deep snow, hoping to grip a hold long enough to catch his breath. The howling winds, gusting up to 100 miles per hour, roared like a fleet of jet planes. To communicate with his climbing partners, Erik had to scream to be heard. It was only 3,000 more feet to the **summit**, but Erik's team was hopelessly trapped for five days in a blizzard on the high slopes of Mt. McKinley.

At 20,320 feet, Alaska's Mt. McKinley is the highest peak in North America. Freezing temperatures, sudden avalanches, and **devastating** storms make it one of the most difficult mountains in the world to climb. Nearly one hundred climbers have lost their lives there after falling into deep crevasses or being blown off the face by gale-force winds. For even the most experienced mountaineers and rugged explorers, climbing McKinley is the challenge of a lifetime.

Imagine climbing such a treacherous peak without being able to see a single step. That is the task that Erik Weihenmayer faced in June 1995. Erik is completely blind, having lost his vision at age thirteen due to a condition he was born with called retinoschisis. But blindness has never stopped him from living an exciting life and pursuing adventures most of us only dream about.

"I am not a daredevil," Erik explains. "I have a healthy fear and respect of the mountains, but I believe with proper training and skill a blind person can tackle some awesome challenges."

From a young age, life itself proved to be a challenge for Erik. When he was a three-month-old baby, Erik's eyes began to quiver and shake. His parents were alarmed and brought him to teams of specialists over a year and a half. The doctors diagnosed his problem as retinoschisis, a rare condition that causes pressure to build in the retina until it disintegrates, eventually leading to blindness. To view something directly in front of him Erik would have to look up, down, or sideways. He relied on his **peripheral** (side) vision to navigate his neighborhood and to do daily chores and tasks.

Erik at a base camp on Mt. McKinley. ▶

But Erik hated to be treated differently, so he learned to **compensate** for his poor vision. When he played basketball with friends, they helped him cover the court by playing zone defenses. They also learned to feed him the ball with a bounce pass. "Erik would hear a bounce pass," his father, Ed Weihenmayer, explains. "But lots of passes hit him in the face anyway. After most games Erik had a bloody nose and looked as if he was playing football, not basketball."

With the help of family and friends, Erik was encouraged to find creative ways to participate in everyday activities. When his brothers raced their mountain bikes over a ramp, Erik joined in, but sometimes he rode off the edge, picking up scraped knees for his efforts. Though he rarely complained or showed his frustration, Erik's family was aware of his struggles. His father solved the bike problem by painting the ramp bright orange. After two more months of bike stunts on the ramp, however, Erik's eyesight had **deteriorated** to the point that the ramp became an orange blur. He rode off his driveway one day and broke his arm.

Despite his failing vision Erik continued his attempts to blend in and be like everyone else. Frequently he walked into trees or doors, and he had constant bruises and black-and-blue shins. "I guess it was a lack of maturity on my part," Erik admits. "It was a sense of denial. I refused to learn to read Braille or to use a cane, even though I needed one for my own safety."

By the time he was thirteen, Erik's eyesight was completely gone. At first he tried to function without the use of canes or visual aids, but that proved dangerous. While visiting his grandparents, he stepped off a dock and fell eight feet into a boat. Though unharmed by the incident, it shook him up. Out of sheer desperation, Erik came to accept his blindness.

"I realized that if I got good at using the systems for the blind I would blend in better and be more like everyone else," he says. "If I didn't use my cane I would be stumbling about, and that would make me stand out more."

STOP AND CHECK

Reread How did Erik and his family compensate for his failing eyesight? Reread to check your understanding.

Erik and his dog, Wizard

Machu Picchu

At fifteen Erik joined his high school's wrestling team. Because the sport depends on physical contact, strength, and instinct, Erik found he could compete on even terms with his opponents. He did not win a match as a freshman, but by his senior year he was chosen team captain and sported a 30-3-3 record. He was selected to represent Connecticut in the National Freestyle Wrestling Championships and went on to wrestle at Boston College.

Just as Erik was beginning to accept his blindness and learning to function in a sightless world, tragedy struck hard. While he was away at summer wrestling camp, Erik's mother was killed in an automobile accident. The loss was devastating, but Erik's father exerted extra efforts to spend more time with his children. As a way to bring the family closer, Ed Weihenmayer brought his children together for adventurous treks around the world. Among many other journeys, they visited the Batura Glacier in Pakistan and the Inca ruins at Machu Picchu in Peru.

"Facing his mother's death and blindness so close together was difficult," Ed recalls. "But Erik never used them as an excuse for not measuring up and going for it." Rock-climbing trips to New Hampshire and other travels with his family whet Erik's appetite for adventure. He soon became a skillful rock climber, scuba diver, and sky diver.

Erik with students

After getting his master's degree from Lesley College in Massachusetts, Erik was hired to teach at an elementary school in Phoenix, Arizona. Managing a class of lively fifth graders was a challenge equal to any Erik had undertaken, but he loved his work and handled it well. "My dad worked on Wall Street for thirty years," he says. "He struggled to find meaning in his work. I don't have that struggle as a teacher." The students in his classes quickly realize that Erik needs their help to make learning work for them. With his guidance they devise systems to communicate and get things done. Students pitch in taking turns writing on the board, hanging posters, and passing out papers. Although the class could take advantage of their sightless teacher, they rarely do. In fact, they fall over each other to be the first to fill his dog's water bowl.

As he settled into his teaching job, Erik and a buddy filled their weekends with climbing trips to the rock faces and mountains of Arizona. On the higher slopes Erik and his partners devised a climbing language that the lead climber would call out. If a teammate shouted, "Iceberg ahead," for example, Erik understood that a pointy rock sticking out of the ground was in his path. A cry of "ankle breaker" meant that little loose rocks lay ahead. By learning to follow in the footsteps of his partners and to rely on his other senses, Erik took on the tallest peaks in Africa and North and South America with his climbing friends.

Erik rock climbing at the Phoenix, Arizona, Bouldering Competition

"Feeling the rock under my hand, feeling the wind and sensing I am hundreds of feet above tree line is an incredible experience," Erik says. "It's exciting to work on a team for a common goal." So great is his love of the mountains that Erik and his wife, Ellen, were wed at a rock altar 13,000 feet up the slopes of Mt. Kilimanjaro in Tanzania.

But pulling yourself up a sheer rock wall, balancing on an icy ridge, and handling sub-zero temperatures can prove frustrating for any mountaineer, particularly one who is blind. While climbing Mt. Rainier in 1985 Erik discovered he could not set up his tent in the freezing weather with his bulky gloves covering his hands. In typical fashion he refused to admit failure. "I was so embarrassed that I resolved never to let that happen again," he says. "When I returned to Phoenix I practiced setting up a tent in the one-hundred-degree heat with gloves on over and over. It is no longer a problem for me."

Careful planning and practice have always helped Erik work around the problems caused by his lack of vision. To prepare for the risky climb up Mt. McKinley, Erik's team practiced on Mt. Rainier in Washington and Long's Peak in Colorado. Back in Phoenix, Erik and a teammate strapped on fifty-pound packs and raced up and down the stairs of a forty-story skyscraper to build strength and endurance.

Before the McKinley trip Erik's climbing group, which called itself Team High Sights, secured the sponsorship of the American Foundation for the Blind. "I was hopeful that my climb would make a statement," Erik says.

STOP AND CHECK

Reread How did both planning and practice help Erik to work out the problems his lack of vision caused while mountain climbing? Reread to check your understanding.

Erik(right) in an igloo on Mt. McKinley at 17,000 feet. ▶

Huddling in their ice-coated tents at 17,000 feet, Team High Sights was forced to wait out a five-day storm on Mt. McKinley. Their food supply was dwindling and all that could be seen of the summit was a plume of snow blowing hundreds of feet into the air. Unless the storm let up, all hope of reaching the summit would have to be abandoned. On the sixth day they heard on their weather radio the news they'd been waiting for: There would be a twelve-hour period of clear weather in which to reach the summit and return before the next storm system closed off the mountain.

Strapping on their ice shoes and insulated gear, the climbers tied themselves together with sturdy rope. Pushing through thigh-deep snow was exhausting work, but Team High Sights carefully moved up the mountain. For Erik, the climb to the summit seemed endless. At the top of a knife-edge ridge his ski pole slipped and all he could feel was air. "I was concentrating very hard with each step," he explains. "Finally I took a step and my friend Stacey said, 'Congratulations, you're on the top of North America.'"

With tears in their eyes, the climbers embraced and snapped photographs of each other. Erik held aloft a pair of banners— one designed by a girl at his school, and one for the American Foundation for the Blind. After fifteen minutes at the peak, the team headed down, safely making their way back to a lower camp.

The climb to the top of Mt. McKinley was a proud accomplishment for Erik, and one that he hopes provides inspiration for others. "Before McKinley I never thought I was extremely tough," Erik says. "I always felt I had the **potential** to do much more. I hope my climb proves that we can all push beyond what we think we can do."

Having climbed McKinley, the highest mountain in North America, Erik is well on the way to meeting one of his climbing goals. In the next few years he plans to summit the highest peak on each continent, including Mt. Everest in Asia. He has learned to step around every obstacle in his path, and though it will be a difficult task, Erik knows there is no reason a blind man cannot sit atop the tallest mountain in the world.

Erik recently reached his goal of climbing Mt. Everest.

About the Author

Marty Kaminsky

believes strongly that "we have an obligation to leave the world a better place." One way that Marty tries to accomplish this is through his volunteer work. Inspired by his father's efforts to help others, Marty started a volunteer tutoring group of his own. It was an appropriate choice because Marty is a retired teacher.

Since he left teaching, Marty has also published numerous articles in children's magazines. "Seeing Things His Own Way" is a chapter from a collection of biographies about athletes who have overcome personal challenges and inspired others through their courage.

Author's Purpose

How are the events Marty Kaminsky describes in "Seeing Things His Own Way" likely to inspire readers?

Respond to Reading

Summarize

Use important details from "Seeing Things His Own Way" to summarize how Erik met his own personal challenge. Information from your Author's Point of View chart may help you.

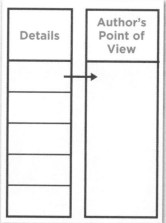

Details	Author's Point of View

Text Evidence

1. How do you know that "Seeing Things His Own Way" is an example of a biography? Use evidence from the text to support your answer. **GENRE**

2. What is the author's point of view toward Erik and his achievements, and how is it conveyed, or shown, in the text? Cite examples from the selection in your answer. **AUTHOR'S POINT OF VIEW**

3. What is the meaning of the phrase "push beyond what we think we can do" on page 287? Use context clues in the surrounding sentences to help you figure out the meaning. **IDIOMS**

4. Write about the author's use of persuasive language and how he uses it to convince readers that Erik should be seen as a role model. **WRITE ABOUT READING**

Make Connections

What did Erik prove to himself and others by testing his limits as he did? **ESSENTIAL QUESTION**

What other kinds of challenges have you read about that have inspired you to act or think in a new way? What did you learn from the example? **TEXT TO WORLD**

Compare Texts
Read about how you can meet the
challenge of getting–and staying–fit.

get FIT for FUN!

What Is Fitness?

Do you consider yourself fit? Being fit doesn't mean
you need to spend every day running mile after mile.
You don't need to be on any special diet, either. But nearly
everyone can get into better shape with very little effort.

There are three main things you should do to be fit.
First, it's important to be physically active. Second,
eat a healthful diet. And third, maintain a healthy
weight for your age and body type. It doesn't matter
what your friends weigh!

As any athlete will tell you, there are degrees of fitness.
You can probably walk a mile without getting winded,
but could you run a mile? Can you climb several
flights of stairs without stopping to catch your breath?
Do you think you might eat too much junk food, such as
chips, candy, or sugary sodas? Professional athletes must
pay attention to diet and exercise to perform at their best,
but nearly everybody can increase their regular physical
activity and eat a balanced diet.

The Benefits of Exercise

Before you begin any type of exercise program, remember to check with your doctor first. Your routine may include both strength training and aerobic training. Strength training helps you build muscles and of course makes you stronger. Try push-ups, sit-ups, and other exercises that make you use your own body for resistance. That means moving your own weight to build muscle. Ask a physical education teacher for pointers.

Aerobic exercise gets your heart and lungs working harder; you breathe deeply and move oxygen around your body. Your brain needs oxygen to stay alert! Your cells need oxygen too, so they can grow more cells and turn food into energy. Walking, swimming, jumping rope, and dancing are some great ways to build muscle and get your heart pumping.

Before you begin either strength or aerobic training it's best to start your workout with gentle stretching. Stretching keeps you flexible and helps you avoid injuring yourself. Did you ever watch cats stretch? They know how good it feels! Stretching after you exercise is also a good idea.

What Not to Do

Are you ready to **implement** an exercise program and get fit? As you work to increase your overall fitness, keep in mind there are also some things you should avoid. People your age are not supposed to have big bulging muscles and should not lift heavy weights. Heavy weights can put stress on your growing joints and tendons, the tissues that connect your muscles to your bones. This can lead to permanent damage. Another thing to keep in mind is that you should start exercising gradually.

Eating a Balanced Diet

Experts help professional athletes eat for peak performance, but kids must rely on families and their own judgment. One good plan is to follow the recommendations of nutritionists and choose a diet based on the major food groups.

Instead of too much pizza or too many burgers, fruits and vegetables should play a big role in your diet. These foods are important both for growing young people and adults. Several fruits and vegetables, such as bananas and avocados, are rich in potassium, a mineral that can lower your blood pressure. High blood pressure means that your heart is working overtime. Potassium also helps build muscle.

Grains such as cereals, bread, rice, and pasta form another food group you should eat daily. You should try to eat mostly whole grains, which still have their outer layers. These are the healthiest parts of the grain.

Grains that are refined, or milled, have their two outer layers scraped away. These outer layers contain the most nutrients. When grains are milled, they lose important nutrients such as B vitamins and iron. The B vitamins help your nerves function, and iron carries oxygen to your cells, so you have more energy. A lack of iron can leave you feeling both tired and weak. Eating whole grains can also cut down on your risk of heart disease.

You need dairy products such as milk, yogurt, and cheese for calcium to build strong teeth and bones. Most of the foods you eat in this group should have no fat or low fat. That means cutting back on foods such as ice cream.

Proteins form the building blocks for your blood, muscles, skin, and bones. Protein sources include meats, fish,

chicken, eggs, and nuts. These nutrients build blood cells and give you energy. Dried beans and peas are an important source of protein if you don't eat meat.

Most junk foods and sweetened drinks add fat, salt, sugar, or calories without giving you important nutrients. If you eat the right amounts of the major food groups, you'll be at a healthier weight naturally.

Your Need for Water

Is all this talk of exercise making you thirsty? That's a good thing. In addition to a balanced diet, your body needs water to work properly. You use water to digest your food, to carry nutrients through your blood, to remove waste products, and to cool you through sweating.

Getting Started

It's easy to implement a fitness routine. Step away from the remote. Click off the computer. Get off the couch and get moving. Find an exercise buddy. And think about what to eat before you eat it.

How can you **assess** whether you're on the road to fitness? You'll have more energy and feel better.

Make Connections

What simple steps can kids your age take to meet the challenge of staying fit? **ESSENTIAL QUESTION**

Why is it important for athletes to follow the rules of good nutrition? **TEXT TO TEXT**

TIPS FOR GETTING FIT

1 Get moving. Sitting for long periods of time is one of the most unhealthy things you can do.

2 Eat a balanced diet.

3 Drink plenty of water and low fat or skim milk.

4 Pay attention to your body. Stop eating when you feel full and rest when you are tired.

BananaStock/Jupiter Images

Essential Question

When are decisions hard to make?

Read how a young detective has to make some hard decisions when he is asked to solve a mystery at the school he attends.

Go Digital!

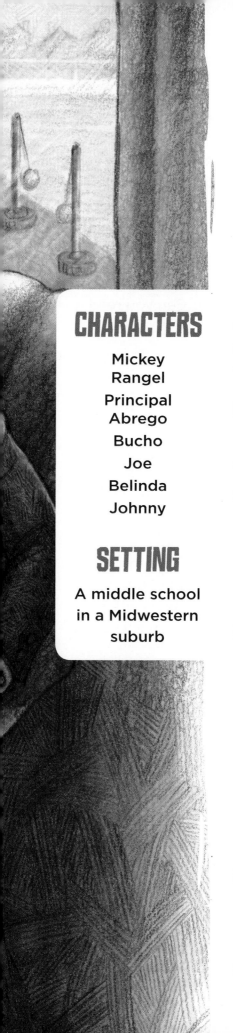

THE CASE OF THE MAGIC MARKER MISCHIEF MAKER

A MICKEY RANGEL MYSTERY

A Play in Three Acts by René Saldaña, Jr.
Illustrated by Manelle Oliphant

CHARACTERS

Mickey Rangel

Principal Abrego

Bucho

Joe

Belinda

Johnny

SETTING

A middle school in a Midwestern suburb

ACT ONE: PRINCIPAL ABREGO's office. The principal is sitting at a large wooden desk. Sunlight streams in from two large windows to her right.

PRINCIPAL ABREGO *(buzzes phone)*: Angie, can you please send Mickey in now?

(door opens, MICKEY RANGEL reluctantly walks in)

PRINCIPAL ABREGO *(shuffling papers, and without looking at MICKEY)*: Won't you have a seat, Mr. Rangel? I'll be just a moment. *(continues shuffling papers for a couple more seconds, then sets them in order and places them on the desk)* So, *(looks up at MICKEY finally)* you must be wondering why I've called you to my office?

MICKEY *(leg shaking, swallows hard)*: Sort of. I've been going over in my head what I could have possibly done to merit being summoned to the principal's office, and though there is that spitball incident from this morning on the bus, it was only this morning and mostly between my brother Ricky and me, so word couldn't have gotten to you this quickly, and even if it had, my actions weren't so bad that . . . *(MICKEY notices PRINCIPAL ABREGO has reached for a pen to begin taking notes, and that she also has the traces of a smile on her face.)* I mean, yes, ma'am, I am wondering why you would call me here.

PRINCIPAL ABREGO: Well . . . never mind about the, uh, spitball episode, at least for now. *(raises an eyebrow, then smiles)* As to why I've asked you to my office this morning, Mr. Rangel—may I call you Mickey?

MICKEY: Certainly, ma'am.

295

PRINCIPAL ABREGO: I'm sure you've seen the graffiti marring our walls lately. The substance of the messages, mostly aimed at me, is fairly harmless. I'm a principal, so I've had to grow a thick skin over the years. What is bothersome beyond belief, though, is that someone thinks so very little of our school that they would show such disrespect. *(shakes her head)*

MICKEY: Mrs. Abrego, you don't think that I . . . ?

PRINCIPAL ABREGO: Oh, goodness no, Mickey. I'm sorry I haven't made myself clear. No, I don't think for a second you have anything to do with this.

MICKEY *(sighs in relief)***:** So then why am I here, if you don't mind me asking?

PRINCIPAL ABREGO: Am I right in saying you're sort of a detective, young though you are?

MICKEY: Actually, Mrs. Abrego, I'm the real deal. I took the required online courses to earn my degree. I've got a framed diploma at home to prove it. *(pulls wallet from back pocket, rifles through it as though in search of something)* I also carry my official P.I. ID card. P.I.—that stands for private investigator. You want to see it? *(finds it and offers it to PRINCIPAL ABREGO)*

PRINCIPAL ABREGO *(takes it from MICKEY and studies it briefly, then returns it)***:** That's very impressive, Mickey.

MICKEY: Thank you, ma'am. But I still don't understand why I'm here.

PRINCIPAL ABREGO: Mickey, I'll be frank with you: I'm in a bit of a sticky situation. *(pushes aside a few papers on her desk, stands, and walks to the window overlooking the playground)* Take a look out the window with me and tell me what you see.

MICKEY: Yes, ma'am. *(rises, makes his way around the desk, and walks over to the window)*

PRINCIPAL ABREGO: Can you read it from here?

MICKEY *(reads aloud)***:** "Our Principle's no pal of nobodies!" Interesting spelling and punctuation choices this Magic Marker Mischief Maker has made.

PRINCIPAL ABREGO: You noticed? Good. Yes, it should read "principal," ending in "PAL," not "PLE." Major difference.

MICKEY: Yes, and "nobody" is spelled as though it were plural, ending in "-dies," though it should not be a plural. And is that a small letter "B" at the bottom right corner, like a signature?

PRINCIPAL ABREGO: You caught that too? Most impressive Mickey.

MICKEY (*smiles*): Thanks, ma'am.

PRINCIPAL ABREGO: I also got this anonymous email this morning right as I turned on my computer. The author claims to be an eye-witness to the wrongdoing. What do you make of it? (*hands MICKEY the sheet of paper*)

MICKEY (*reads the email*): Hmmmm. Incriminating, to say the least. So the letter "B" on the wall would make sense. Based on these two clues, all fingers point to Bucho being our mischief maker.

PRINCIPAL ABREGO: Yes, that's what I thought. But here's the thing, Mickey. I confronted him with this evidence, and he denies having anything to do with marking up our walls. Believe it or not, tough though he comes across, he was nearly in tears.

MICKEY: Ma'am, I'm not so sure you should be telling me this. Isn't there some kind of student-principal privilege?

PRINCIPAL ABREGO: Normally, yes, but he gave me permission to discuss this whole matter with you, every bit of it.

MICKEY: Wait—what? You mean he told you it was okay to talk to me about this? Why would he do that?

PRINCIPAL ABREGO: Mickey, Bucho was so adamant that he wasn't the culprit that he recommended I bring you in on the case. He's the one who told me you were a detective.

MICKEY: He said that?

PRINCIPAL ABREGO: Are you surprised?

MICKEY: Yes, ma'am. You might not know this about us, but he and I are not the best of friends. To be honest, Mrs. Abrego, he's a bit of a bully.

PRINCIPAL ABREGO: That he is. But he and I have been trying to work on that part of his life. In the last few months he's made some great strides, and so when I got this email and put it together with the so-called signature, it was easy to jump to conclusions. And this is where you come in, Mickey. I was filled with **indecision** about what I should do about this, but now I think I've found an answer. I need you to find out who is to blame for the graffiti. Can you help me?

MICKEY: You can count on me. Mickey Rangel is on the case.

PRINCIPAL ABREGO: Good. Whatever you need, please don't hesitate to ask. In fact, think of me as your **benefactor**.

LIGHTS OUT

STOP AND CHECK

Summarize Reread and summarize the events that led Principal Abrego to call Mickey into her office and ask him to solve the mystery of the magic marker mischief maker.

ACT TWO, SCENE 1: First lunch period. MICKEY is eating at a table in the school cafeteria; with him are his friends BELINDA and JOHNNY. JOE, another student, is sitting alone at a nearby table, eavesdropping on MICKEY and friends.

BELINDA: You know, Mickey, I'm not the only one who thinks this school would be a better place without that bully, Bucho. I can't even count the **multitude** of times he's knocked my book bag off my shoulder, as if that were some kind of big joke. (*BELINDA looks reflective for a moment.*) Come to think of it, though, he's walked past me a couple of times the past few weeks and nothing's happened.

JOHNNY: Well, all I can say is, I thought it was just a myth about the school bully taking your lunch, but it's true. He hasn't done it for awhile, but I still bring rice cakes and celery sticks for lunch because it's the only stuff he won't try and steal from me.

MICKEY: Yeah, but what kind of a detective would I be if I'm presuming a kid is guilty instead of presuming he's innocent? Not a very good one. And Principal Abrego has been having talks with him, and she claims he's really trying hard to be less of a bully lately.

JOHNNY: You might be right about that, but I'd be able to bring a sandwich for lunch again if you did assume he's guilty and found the proof of it. I mean, it's Bucho we're talking about here.

(*JOE looks over his shoulder at MICKEY and friends, smiles to himself and rubs his hands as if he's won a game of chess; he coughs into his fist: "Bucho's a loser!"*)

MICKEY: (*turns to JOE*) I'm sorry; did you say something, Joe?

JOE: Who, me? Nope. You must be hearing things.

MICKEY: Maybe, Joe. But I thought I heard you say, "Bucho's a loser."

JOE: I said no such thing. Like I told you, Mickey, you must be hearing things. Get your ears checked.

MICKEY: You're probably right. *(turns back to his friends, thinks for a split second, then turns back to JOE)* Say, Joe, why are you eating all alone? Don't you normally eat lunch with Bucho? He is your best friend, isn't he?

JOE: Yeah, well . . . *(JOE scans the room as if looking for somebody)* Maybe he is and maybe he isn't. Anyway, I'll bet he's probably out marking up a wall somewhere. And I think your pals here are right: Bucho's your man. What is it they say about leopards and their dots?

MICKEY: Spots, Joe, you mean "spots."

JOE: Yeah, whatever. But like I'm saying, he's so dumb he's even signing his tags with a "B" right? *(JOE stands up and takes his tray off the table.)*

MICKEY: Funny way to talk about your best friend. *(JOE gives MICKEY a hard look and then departs without saying anything.)*

MICKEY *(turns back to his friends,* *thinks for a couple short beats)*: Anyhow, I'd like to see Bucho gone, too, but I made a promise, Johnny. It's not so simple for me. I've got to do the job right, even if it means going against my gut instinct.

BELINDA: So what are you saying, Mickey? You think he's innocent? If you ask a hundred kids who they think is leaving those messages around the school, a hundred of them will say it's got to be Bucho. Who else would it be? He's probably not bullying people as much now because he has a new **endeavor**— writing graffiti.

MICKEY: But a survey isn't evidence.

JOHNNY: But you do have evidence, don't you? You said the principal showed you the email in which someone claimed to have seen Bucho in action, writing on the wall.

MICKEY: That's circumstantial. Not in the least incriminating without anything else of substance.

BELINDA: So, what about the letter "B" the culprit has left behind as a kind of signature—is Joe lying about that?

MICKEY: Also circumstantial. I mean, if a "B" is all we've got, who's to say it doesn't stand for "Belinda"? *(BELINDA looks as though she's been accused)* Don't get me wrong—I'm not saying it is you, I'm saying a "B" is not enough to prove a guy's guilt.

BELINDA: Are you saying you're not willing to stand with me—*(looks at JOHNNY)* with us—and instead you're going to side with Bucho?

MICKEY: That's not it at all. What I'm saying is that I've got to do this the right way. I would think you'd understand that my work and doing it right are important to me.

BELINDA: No, Mickey. There's nothing "right" about Bucho's ugly behavior all these years. Do you really think a few weeks of acting nice can erase years of mean behavior? Whatever! It's up to you to do the right thing. *(BELINDA stands suddenly and walks away.)*

MICKEY: Belinda just doesn't get it, Johnny. I'm a detective; I took an oath to dig and dig until I find the truth, even if I don't like the outcome. I'm not saying it's not Bucho, it's just that I need **extensive** evidence to prove that it is him. *(he pauses, then looks at JOHNNY)* Besides, putting the blame on Bucho without evidence is just another form of bullying, isn't it? Only this time, we'd be the bullies. *(JOHNNY looks thoughtful and walks away.)*

ACT TWO, SCENE 2: Second lunch period. MICKEY is sitting alone, deep in thought, unaware that the bell has rung. Suddenly, BUCHO looms in front of MICKEY.)

BUCHO: Hey, Mickey . . . I imagine Mrs. A told you the story. Somebody's trying to frame me for all this graffiti, and I bet you won't believe me, but it wasn't me. And you're the only one I trust to uncover the truth.

MICKEY: I told Mrs. A I would, so I'm going to help any way I can.

BUCHO: OK, bro. Say, you going to eat that? *(Before MICKEY can answer, BUCHO reaches for MICKEY'S brownie and swallows it in one bite; then he walks away from the table with his own tray in hand.)*

MICKEY: Hey, Bucho. *(BUCHO turns)* How do you spell "principal"? As in Mrs. Abrego, the school's big cheese?

BUCHO: First, are you kidding? What other kind of principal is there? Second, are you making fun of me? Because if you are . . . *(BUCHO shakes a fist at MICKEY, but then he thinks better of it and puts his hand down.)*

MICKEY: So spell it.

BUCHO *(scowling, exaggerating his pronunciation)*: P-R-I-N-C-I-P-A-L. As in, Mrs. Abrego is our PAL. Satisfied?

MICKEY: Yup. *(BUCHO walks away, this time for good.)*

 LIGHTS OUT

STOP AND CHECK

Summarize Reread and summarize the evidence Mickey has gathered so far. Then use your summary to help you predict who the "mischief maker" might be.

ACT THREE: Outside, the school playground, where PRINCIPAL ABREGO, BUCHO, and OTHERS have gathered in front of the site of the latest graffiti. MICKEY enters from stage right.

PRINCIPAL ABREGO: There you are, Mickey. As you can see, I've asked Bucho to join us, as you requested. Can we get started now? *(Beyond PRINCIPAL ABREGO and BUCHO are a multitude of kids playing different games. Among them are JOE, who is noticeably nervous and keeping a careful eye on the developments from a safe distance, and BELINDA, who is standing against a wall nearby.)*

MICKEY: Sure thing. First of all, you were right. In the case of The Magic Marker Mischief Maker, someone other than Bucho is responsible for this graffiti. My first clue was the curious spelling. Only two weeks ago in English we were studying homophones. One set of words we

were asked to learn included the "principal/principle" set.

BUCHO: Yeah, that's right. Miss Garza gave us a trick to remember how to spell it: "Mrs. Abrego, the principal, is our pal." *(BUCHO looks at MICKEY.)* Like I told you at lunch.

MICKEY: Exactly, but at lunch you also said, "What other kind of 'principal' is there?" when in fact there are two. You had no clue about the other spelling: P-R-I-N-C-I-P-L-E, which means "a high standard that guides one's actions and reactions." You must've been looking at the insides of your eyelids when Miss Garza was going over that one.

BUCHO: Watch yourself.

PRINCIPAL ABREGO: No, watch yourself, Bernard. Mickey's trying to help, so help yourself by minding your temper.

BUCHO: Yes, ma'am.

MICKEY: *Bernard?* Really?

*(BUCHO scowls and **tentatively** takes a step in MICKEY's direction, but then he steps back.)*

MICKEY: Allow me to go on. If you don't know how to spell both words, much less that there are two variations, then you couldn't have written this graffiti. *(waves a hand at the wall)* This tells me that our culprit is also studying vocabulary in Miss Garza's class, though it's obvious he's not learning.

BUCHO: Well, spit it out: if it wasn't me, then who?

MICKEY: Hey, Joe, can you come here?

JOE *(walks over)*: What's up, man? *(He refuses to acknowledge BUCHO.)*

MICKEY: Can you spell the word "principal" for us, as in Mrs. Abrego, our school's principal? You know, like we were supposed to have learned in Miss Garza's class.

JOE: Are you kidding me?

PRINCIPAL ABREGO: Mickey?

MICKEY: Ma'am? *(motions as though for support from MRS. ABREGO)*

PRINCIPAL ABREGO: Okay then. Go on, Joe, do as he says.

JOE *(puffs his chest out proudly)*: P-R-I-N-C-I-P-L-E, "principle," as in "The last thing I want is to be sent to the principle's office." Satisfied?

MICKEY: Quite.

PRINCIPAL ABREGO: Quite indeed. *(speaking to JOE)* Young man, though it's the last thing you want

STOP AND CHECK

Ask and Answer Questions Explain whether you think Mickey and Bucho will be friends in the future. Cite evidence in the play to help support your answer.

to do, you will follow me to my office. *(the two leave, though MRS. ABREGO does put an arm around JOE's shoulders indicating she will want to "work with" him in the same way she's been working with BUCHO)*

BUCHO: Mickey, you did it! You proved my innocence!

MICKEY: I also proved you need to pay more attention in class.

BUCHO *(looks to make sure MRS. ABREGO is out of sight before taking a menacing step toward MICKEY)*: Why, I oughta . . .

LIGHTS OUT

303

ABOUT THE AUTHOR

RENÉ SALDAÑA, JR.

grew up in Nuevo Peñitas, a small town in southern Texas. After graduating from college, he returned to his own Texas high school to teach writing, where he began to use his own stories as writing examples for his students. "I wanted to show them how to write from personal experience," René says now. Many of these same stories became part of his first novel, *The Jumping Tree.* In 2009, René published his first Mickey Rangel mystery, *The Case of the Pen Gone Missing,* which has now become a series.

Today, Saldaña lives in Lubbock, Texas, where he continues writing and teaching at the College of Education at Texas Tech University. "I can't think of any job other than writing that I'd rather be doing, with the possible exception of teaching," René says. "The writing is cool, the revision is better, and meeting face-to-face with my readers, that's the cherry on top."

AUTHOR'S PURPOSE

The author uses realistic dialogue in the play. How does the dialogue, as well as the characters' actions, draw you into the mystery?

CERTIFIED PRIVATE INVESTIGATOR

SIGN Mickey Rangel

RESPOND TO READING

SUMMARIZE

Use important details from *The Case of the Magic Marker Mischief Maker* to summarize the play and what you learned about decisions and why they are sometimes hard to make. Information from your Theme Chart may help you.

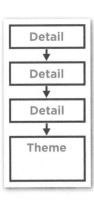

Detail
↓
Detail
↓
Detail
↓
Theme

TEXT EVIDENCE

1. Identify at least two features from the text that help you to identify *The Case of the Magic Marker Mischief Maker* as a play. **GENRE**

2. What is the theme of the play? Give two details to support your answer. **THEME**

3. What is a homophone for the word *seen* on page 300? What is the meaning of each homophone? Context clues in the story may help you. **HOMOPHONES**

4. In the play, it is clear that Mickey tries to be fair to Bucho, even though Bucho has been a bully. Write about how the story would have been different if Mickey and Principal Abrego had acted on their first suspicions. **WRITE ABOUT READING**

Make Connections

How did Mickey defend the decisions he had to make in order to solve the mystery? **ESSENTIAL QUESTION**

In the play, Mickey has to make a hard decision and risks upsetting his friends. Why is it important to do what you believe to be right, even though it may upset others? **TEXT TO WORLD**

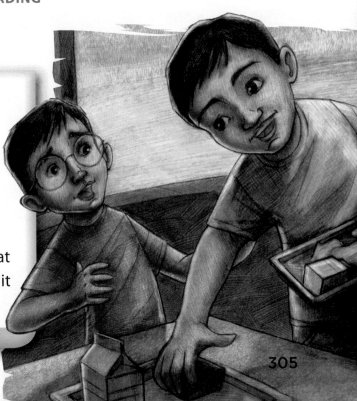

Compare Texts

Read how drama has explored the difficult decisions people have had to make for thousands of years.

DRAMATIC DECISIONS

THEATER THROUGH THE AGES

A hush falls over the darkened room. The crowd is alert with anticipation, their eyes focused on the stage. As an actor's voice fills the air, the audience relaxes, settling back in their seats and ready to be entertained.

This scene could be taking place in any number of theaters throughout the world today—or it might be describing a scene that took place thousands of years ago. People have enjoyed watching theatrical performances since the dawn of civilization, and perhaps even before. The word *theater* means "a place for seeing." Through plays, we see and experience how people face and solve dilemmas in their lives. And through

No one knows when the first performances were given. Wall paintings and other artifacts tell us that people have been dramatizing important events since they began living in communities. Some archeologists believe that the ceremonies that marked key occasions in the lives of prehistoric people were the first "plays." After a successful hunt, for example, the hunters may have reenacted the choices they made as they pursued and captured their prey, showing how they found and approached a herd of animals and then

Ancient Greek and Roman Theater

While the details and origins of the earliest dramas are a mystery, we know much more about theater in ancient Greece. Festivals that took place there 2,500 years ago included competitive performances that were designed to honor and welcome gods. Over time, these festivals became major competitions. Great plays were written and performed in the city of Athens and are still staged today.

During this Golden Age of drama, Greeks performed plays in open-air amphitheaters. Circular stages were built at the bottom of hills. Seats rose up in a semicircle along the hillsides, but instead of the seats we have in today's theaters, audiences as large as 15,000 people sat on stone slabs. Men played all of the parts in these plays, and no scenery or props were used. Actors wore robes and tall masks that could be seen by audience members sitting in the uppermost seats and a chorus of players spoke in unison to accompany the actors. These ancient plays were about famous people in mythology or told stories about the Greek gods.

One of the greatest plays from that period is *Antigone*, by Sophocles. It is about what happens after a civil war in Thebes, a Greek city-state. Two brothers of a woman named Antigone were on opposite sides in the war, and both died fighting. The new king of Thebes, Creon, threatened to kill anyone who buried the brother whose side lost in the war, but Antigone buried her brother in defiance of the king. The play explores her difficult decision and the consequences that followed. The audience identifies with Antigone's dilemma and feels **empathy** for her.

Such tragedies were popular in Greece, but ancient Romans preferred comedies. They performed them in buildings that were different from the Greek amphitheaters. As in Greece, ancient Roman theaters had no roof, but they had a backstage area, a raised stage, and a curtain. They also had a decorated background for scenery.

An amphitheater has seats that rise up in a semicircle around a central open space.

Mimmo Jodice/Corbis

The Globe Theatre in London is best known for its productions of Shakespeare's plays.

Renaissance Theater

The next major changes in theater design didn't occur until about 1,000 years later, during a period in Europe called the Renaissance, which lasted from the 1300s through the 1600s. One of those innovations was the proscenium arch. It was developed in Italy in the fifteenth century. This arch frames and surrounds the stage and separates the stage from the audience. Today, when you see a curtain rise at the beginning of a play, it is inside the proscenium arch.

These ideas from Italy soon spread across Europe. In England, theaters had thrust stages that extended into the audience so that people surrounded them on three sides. In addition, a small house in the back of the theater allowed actors to change costumes and wait to enter the stage through two or three small doors.

Queen Elizabeth I of England, who reigned from 1558 to 1603, was a strong supporter of the theater. She often attended performances. It was during Elizabeth's reign that one of the best-known playwrights in history, William Shakespeare, wrote some of his greatest plays. Shakespeare's play *Romeo and Juliet,* first published in 1597, revolves around the title characters and their love for one another. The teenagers want to be together but their families forbid it because they are ancient enemies. Finally, Romeo and Juliet come up with a way to be together forever. But this decision leads to a series of other bad decisions and miscommunications, and the story ends tragically.

Kabuki Theater

On the other side of the world at about the same time, another new theatrical style was developing in Japan. Called "kabuki," it began in the early 1600s with female casts. Soon, however, the actors were all males. Kabuki performances **entail** extravagant makeup and costumes and include dancing and singing.

One of the greatest kabuki playwrights is Chikamatsu Monzaemon. His play *Sonezaki Shinju,* which was published in 1720, has a plot that is similar to *Romeo and Juliet*. In it two young people are in love, but circumstances prevent them from being together. Audiences identify with them as they unsuccessfully try to follow their hearts and make a desperate decision to escape together.

Actors perform in kabuki (left) and in an American play (right).

(l) Bruno Vincent/Getty Images News/Getty Images; (r) Tristram Kenton/Lebrecht Music & Arts

Modern American Theater

In 1736, the Dock Street Theatre in Charles-Towne, South Carolina—now called Charleston—was built. It was the first building in the North American colonies erected solely to be a theater. Today, actors perform in theaters everywhere across the country, from the great stages of New York to small community theaters. But some aspects of the experience have never changed, including the popularity of plays in which characters are faced with difficult decisions to make.

One very popular modern American play is *A Raisin in the Sun* by Lorraine Hansberry. The play centers around the Youngers, an African-American family on the South Side of Chicago. Set in the 1950s, the story dramatizes the difficult choice faced by the family, which is about to receive a large sum of money. The adult Youngers have different ideas about what to do with the money. Each person's idea is valid, but each has a different goal—and it excludes the others. In the end, decisions are made and problems are resolved as the characters hoped they would be.

From the open amphitheaters of ancient Greece to the thrust stages of Shakespeare's time to modern dramas, theater has changed over the centuries. But the element that has remained the same for more than 2,500 years is the desire of an audience to be entertained, moved, and informed. Seeing how the characters respond to their circumstances appeals to audiences. We don't see only the actors on the stage. We see our own experiences.

Make Connections

Why have plays in which characters have had to make difficult decisions appealed to audiences over thousands of years? **ESSENTIAL QUESTION**

How do the decisions and problems faced by some of the characters described in this selection compare to others in plays you have read? **TEXT TO TEXT**

HOME OF THE BRAVE

? Essential Question

How do people uncover what they have in common?

Read what happens when a young immigrant from Africa meets his new classmates on his first day of school in the United States.

by Katherine Applegate
illustrated by Marcos Calo

Go Digital!

Eleven-year-old Kek comes from a country in Africa that has been torn apart by civil war. He was part of a **nomadic** herding culture. Kek lived with his father, mother, and brother. Now only Kek and his mother have survived, and she is missing.

Arriving in America in early February, Kek sees snow and ice for the first time and is amazed by all the leafless trees. And he meets Dave, who works for the Refugee Resettlement Center. Dave **reunites** Kek with his aunt and cousin, who entered America months earlier. It doesn't take Kek long to settle in. Soon he is learning to make snowballs with a girl named Hannah who lives in his building.

Then, one day, Dave takes Kek to school. Will Kek find it hard to make an **adjustment** to a whole new way of learning?

NEW DESK

Dave takes me to school.
When I see it, I use the words
I learned from the TV machine:
No way!
It's big enough to graze
a herd of cattle in,
made of fine, red square stones
and surrounded by many
tall not-dead trees.
It's a place for
a leader of men to work in,
not a place for small children
to learn their numbers.

Dave sees my falling-open mouth.
Don't be scared, Kek, he says.
But I'm not scared,
not like that.
Scared is for men with guns
and maybe just a little
for a flying boat
finding its way
back to earth.

Inside my school
the floor shines like ice.
I walk carefully.
Thin metal doors with silver handles
line the walls.
Those are called lockers, Dave says.
C'mon. We're early,
but the teacher wants to meet you.

Waiting in a big-windowed room
is a woman with black hair that dances
and **sturdy** arms
and eyes that tell jokes.
You must be Kek, she says,
and then she uses my word
for hello.

I'm ready to begin
my learning, I say,
and she tosses out a loud laugh
like a ball into the air.

I can see you mean business, she says.
A man comes in,
young and short
with skin the color of rich earth,
just like mine.
He says he is Mr. Franklin
and he helps sometimes in class
when Ms. Hernandez needs
to do her deep breathing.
Everyone laughs,
so I laugh too,
because it's always
good to be polite.

This will be your desk,
   Ms. Hernandez says.
Have a seat.
She points to a shiny chair
and little table.

A chair of my own
and a table, too?
I smother the thought
like an **ember** near dry grass.

I'm very sorry, but I can't,
I say softly. I don't have the cattle
for such a fine desk as this.

Oh, she says,
you don't have to pay for this
   desk, Kek.
School's free here.
You just bring your mind
and your smile
every day, OK?

Carefully I sit.
I like very much this new desk
with its cool, smooth top.

My mouth will not stop smiling.

READY

You're not going to understand
a lot of what we say at first,
   Ms. Hernandez says.
This is called an ESL class.
You and your classmates
will be learning English together.
It means they won't always
understand you.
And you won't always
understand them.

I'm used to not understanding, I say.
It's like playing a game
with no rules.

STOP AND CHECK

Summarize Summarize the important events that took place in Kek's life before his first day in Ms. Hernandez's ESL class.

She nods.
That's exactly what it's like.
I know, because when I came
to the U.S. from Mexico,
I couldn't speak a word of English.

This is a surprise.
A teacher who did not know
all things?
Did you not know things also?
I ask Mr. Franklin.

Me? I'm from Baton Rouge, he says.
That's kinda like another country.
I couldn't understand
these crazy northern folks
for the longest time.

Some of his words get lost
on their way to my ears.
But I can see from his face
that his meaning is kind.

When you have a question,
Mr. Franklin and I will be
here to help, says Ms. Hernandez.
She points to the sky.
You just raise your hand
like this, OK?

I nod. I say OK,
just like her.
I raise my hand.

Yes? she says, smiling big.

I ask,
When will the learning begin?

CATTLE

In my class,
my long-name class
called English-as-a-Second-Language,
we are sixteen.
Sixteen people
with twelve ways of talking.
When we talk at once
we sound like the music class
I can hear down the hall,
hoots and squeaks and thuds,
but no songs you can sing.

I look at our faces
and see all the colors of the earth—
brown and pink and yellow and white and black—
and yet we are all sitting at the same desks,
wanting to learn the same things.

Ms. Hernandez
tells everyone my name
and my old home.
Then she asks us
to draw a picture
on the black wall
to show where we come from.

One boy,
Jaime from Guatemala,
draws a mountain with a hole
called a volcano.
Sahar from Afghanistan
draws a camel,
though to be truthful
it looks like a lumpy dog.

I draw a bull with great curving horns,
like the finest in my father's herd.
I even give him a smile.
But it takes me a while
to decide on his coat.
In my words
we have ten different names
for the color of cattle.
But the writing chalk is only white.

I am working on the tail
when someone in the back
    of the room says,
Moo.
Then more say it,
and more,
and soon we are
a class of cattle.

At least we can all
understand each other.

I think maybe some of the
students are laughing at me.
But I don't mind so much.

To hear the cattle again
is good music.

STOP AND CHECK

Summarize Summarize the different backgrounds and experiences of the students in Ms. Hernandez's class.

LUNCH

After much schooling,
a sound comes
like a great bee buzzing.
The bell means lunch,
Mr. Franklin explains.
He gives me a small piece
of blue paper.
This is for your food.

Thank you very much,
I say in my most polite English words,
but I don't understand how the
paper can help my noisy belly.

You give the paper
to the cooking people
and they will give you food,
    Mr. Franklin explains.
Tastes much better than paper.
He laughs. Well, usually, anyway.

The eating room is grand
with long tables
and strange and wonderful smells
and many students **chattering**.
I stand in a line
and soon kind, white-hatted people
fill my plate high with food.

317

Ahead of me
I see the snowball girl named Hannah
from my building.
She says, Don't eat the mystery meat
if you value your life.
Then she points to a brown wet pile
on my plate and makes a face that says
bad taste.

When my tray is heavy
with the gifts of food,
I stand still in the
stream of students.
I don't know where to go
to enjoy my feast.

Hannah waves.
Follow me, she says.
I'll tell you what's
safe to eat.

But it's all so fine! I say.

She shakes her head.
Kid, you got
a lot to learn.

FRIES

We sit at one of the long tables.
Nearby are two students
from my class:
Jaime, the boy from Guatemala
and Nishan, the girl from Ethiopia.
Hey, Jaime says.

Hey, I say back,
but I can't talk anymore
because my mouth is already
full of new tastes.

Excuse me, I say when
I have swallowed at last,
but what is this amazing food?
I hold up a brown stick.

Fry, Hannah says.
One of the five major food groups.

This fry,
it grows in your
America ground? I ask.

Hannah laughs,
a sound like bells
on a windy day.
I suppose you could say that.
You're Kek, right?
I know because
I asked your cousin.

Hannah passes me a paper cup
filled with strange and beautiful red food.
Ketchup, she says.
You dip your fries in it.

I do what she says,
then eat.
You're a fine cook, I say.
Hannah and Jaime and Nishan laugh.
I feel glad I found enough words
to make people happy.
When a friend laughs,
it's always a good surprise.

STOP AND CHECK

Ask and Answer Questions Is this the first day of school for Jaime and Nishan, as it is for Kek? What evidence in the text can help you answer this question?

319

ABOUT THE AUTHOR

KATHERINE APPLEGATE

has written more than 100 books. She was born in Michigan but has lived in six different states and even moved to Italy before finally settling in Southern California. Some of Katherine's most popular books are science fiction, fantasy and adventure novels, and she has co-authored several books with her husband, Michael Grant.

Home of the Brave won the 2008 Golden Kite Award for Best Fiction. When people read it, Katherine says she hopes they will "see the neighbor child with a strange accent, the new kid in class from some faraway land, the child in odd clothes who doesn't belong. I hope they will see themselves."

AUTHOR'S PURPOSE

Katherine Applegate uses similes throughout *Home of the Brave,* such as *She tosses out a loud laugh like a ball into the air.* How does this help the reader understand Kek's story? Use examples from the text in your answer.

RESPOND TO READING

SUMMARIZE

Use important details from *Home of the Brave* to summarize how the characters uncovered the things they have in common. Information from your Theme Chart may help you.

Detail
↓
Detail
↓
Detail
↓
Theme

TEXT EVIDENCE

1. What details in the text help you to recognize *Home of the Brave* as free verse realistic fiction? Identify at least two features from the selection to support your answer. **GENRE**

2. What is the theme of *Home of the Brave*? Give two details to support your answer. **THEME**

3. Homographs are words that are spelled the same but have different meanings and may be pronounced differently. The homograph *graze* can mean "eat grass" or "touch or rub lightly when passing." What is the meaning of *graze* in the first stanza on page 311? How do you know? **HOMOGRAPHS**

4. The author describes Kek's expression when he sees his new school, and Dave misinterprets it as fear. Write about how Dave and Kek see fear differently, and how these feelings help reveal the theme of the selection. **WRITE ABOUT READING**

> ### Make Connections
>
> How did the students in Kek's class find a way to discover what they have in common? **ESSENTIAL QUESTION**
>
> How can discovering what people have in common lead to friendship? What are some other ways people can make friends? **TEXT TO WORLD**

CCSS **Genre • Realistic Fiction**

Compare Texts

Read how one teenager found a way to communicate with other students when no one could understand her language.

Aminata's Tale

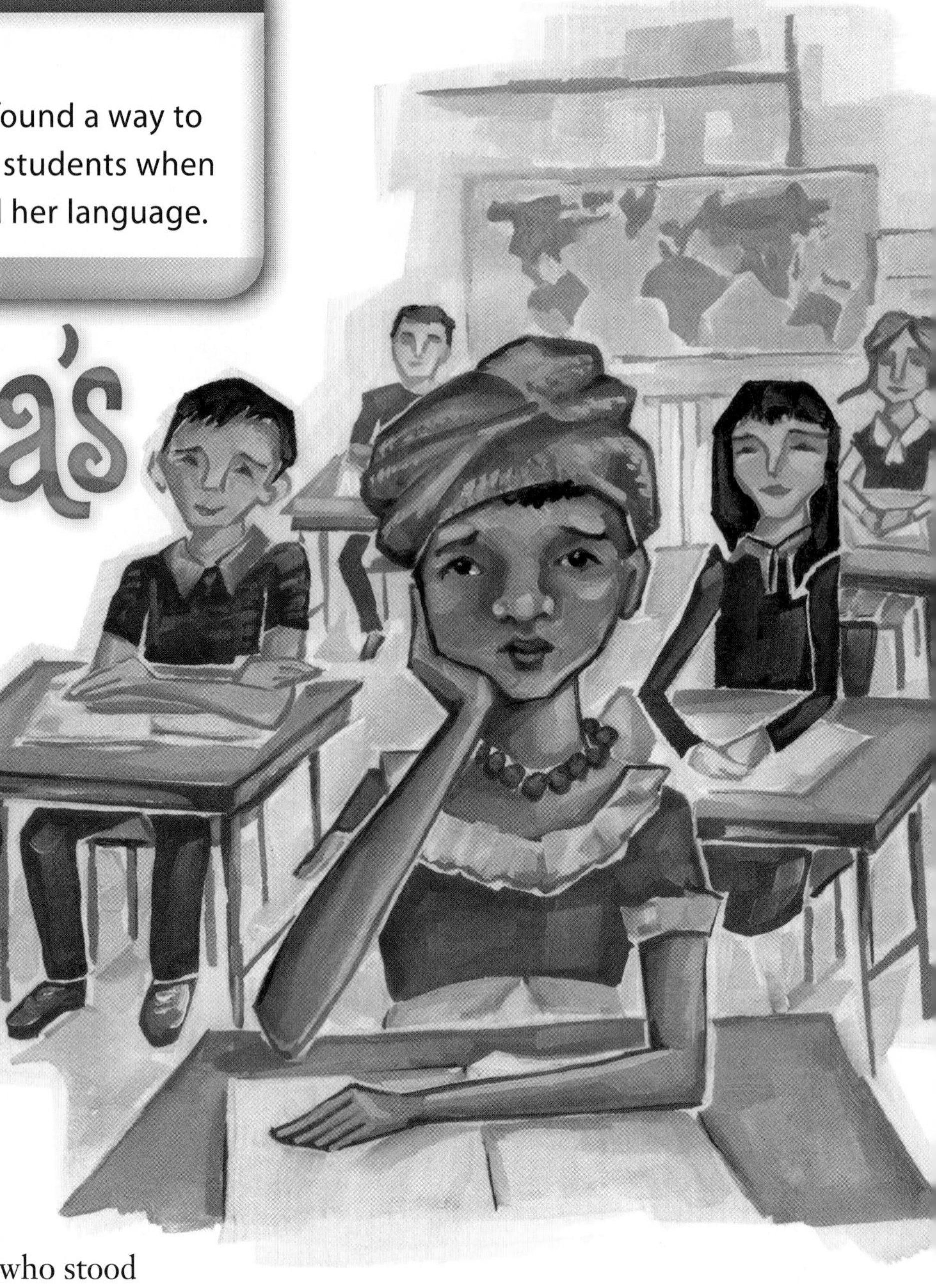

Aminata watched the girl who stood in front of the classroom carefully. Her flowing, long black hair swung from side to side as she drew a map on the big white board with a fat purple pen. In neat letters, she wrote "Vietnam" on the map, and then she drew a boat next to it.

"*Je suis très confus*!" Aminata blurted out when the girl finished—because she was confused. All morning, students had taken turns making presentations in front of her new American classroom. Some motioned with their hands and moved their bodies. Others wrote on the board. All of them spoke in languages Aminata couldn't comprehend. Some sounded sharp, some smooth, some like singing. But none was French, the language spoken in Senegal, where she comes from. Aminata also spoke Mandinka, but since that was unusual even in Africa, she doubted anyone knew it.

Erin Bennett Banks

Aminata's teacher, Ms. Simpson, typed something on her computer and rushed to her side. "*Dites-nous comment vous est venu aux Etats-Unis*," she said in a kind voice.

"*Moi?*" Aminata asked, pointing to herself. Did Ms. Simpson really expect her to stand up in front of the class and tell them how she had come to this country?

When Ms. Simpson nodded, a rush of hot terror burned in Aminata's stomach and seemed to dash down to her toes, paralyzing her on the spot. She had been in the United States only a short time and barely knew any words in English. How could she possibly tell the story of her trip from Africa? After all, she was in this English Language Learners classroom along with all of the other students to learn a new language. Until that happened Aminata felt she couldn't possibly tell anyone else what she needed to say. She shook her head and Ms. Simpson asked a boy to go up in her place.

The boy was named Rodolfo. He drew a picture of a flag. "This is Brazil," he said, stopping between the words. Aminata was shocked to discover she recognized what he was saying. *He knows English!* she thought—and so do I! Her delighted surprise disappeared, however, as the boy continued in what sounded like English to her, only she could no longer understand what he was saying.

Aminata's heart pounded. She was horrified that when Ms. Simpson called on her, she would make an utter fool of herself.

Brrrrrng! A bell on the wall signaled the beginning of lunch. Aminata felt as though her legs would turn to water with relief when the class ended.

In the hallway, laughing, rushing, shouting students jostled her. She longed to be one of them—but how, when she understood none of their jokes or conversation?

Desperately hoping to escape, Aminata ducked into the library. As she walked through the big, cool room, a small display table filled with books caught her eye. The books were about Africa. Aminata could not read many of the words on the covers, but one book stood out. On the dust jacket was a picture of several baobab trees, which grew all around her old home. She flipped through it and was flooded with memories.

Aminata recalled the lush green of the hills near her village and Niokolo-Koba National Park. Her homesickness was like a weight resting on the back of her shoulders, and for a moment, she was afraid she would begin to sob right there.

Then a photograph of a man holding a kora shook away Aminata's sadness. The man's right hand touched one of the kora's 21 strings, and the other cradled the body of the instrument, which was carved out of a vegetable gourd called a calabash. The image transported Aminata back to her village, and in her mind she heard the griotte, Nyima, the keeper of the history of the Mandinka.

Nyima's stories and songs recounted the feats of many generations of the Mandinka people. She had learned her skill through years of study with her father, who had been the clan's griot before her. Just as his father had been griot before him, and his father before him, going back hundreds of years.

Aminata closed her eyes and imagined Nyima telling one of her favorite stories, an epic that took almost a week to sing, two hours at a time. It was the tale of how so many men and women from Aminata's clan were captured hundreds of years ago and taken to Goree Island, where they were held in an infamous prison, the House of Slaves. Nyima's song told of how the Mandinka went through the "Door of No Return" and boarded ships to cross the Atlantic ocean.

Nyima had strummed the kora, sometimes singing, sometimes speaking, swaying in dance and pinning her arms as she showed how people were shackled and led onto the boats. Her voice and body rolled with the waves as they crossed the endless waters of the ocean, her arms spreading wide as she told how the Mandinka never forgot the

lost ones. It was a tragic but proud story that reminded all the people of Aminata's village that they have distant relatives in the land across the sea.

A bell rang, and Aminata opened her eyes, suddenly remembering that the next day she would have to find some way to tell her story to her classmates. As she closed the book, Aminata realized the answer was in its pages. Nyima would be her **mentor**, and Aminata could be a griotte like her. Everyone had understood what Nyima was saying—especially when she wasn't speaking.

The next day Aminata walked to the front of the class and looked around, meeting the eyes of the other students. They were young people just like her, trying to adjust to a new country, trying to learn English. They all had the same challenges to face.

Aminata took a deep breath, smiled, and then she began to dance. She spoke, too, in Mandinka and French, and she could see in the faces of her classmates that they had a sudden **rapport**. Although they couldn't understand Aminata's words, they understood her movements.

Cupping her hands, Aminata created the hills around her village. She hugged the space in front of her to show how she and her mother said good-bye to their relatives. She bounced up and down to mimic the bumpy bus ride to Dakar. Then Aminata pantomimed putting on a seat belt, and when she spread her arms and *whooshed* away as an airplane, the others in the classroom laughed and clapped.

Aminata nearly cried when she acted out the reunion with her father at the airport in the United States. Her classmates nodded as if they understood exactly how she had felt when she first arrived here.

When she finished, Aminata spoke in all the languages she knew: "*Abaraka bake. Merçi beaucoup.* Thank you very much." And then she told everyone something from her heart, in the language of her people. "*Dankutoo le be n´ teemaa,*" Aminata said, telling them that they have a bond between them. Aminata held her hands together in front of her chest and smiled, and everyone in the class understood. They nodded back. Aminata added, in halting English, *It is so good to be friends.*

Make Connections

How was Aminata able to uncover what she and her classmates in their new school have in common? ESSENTIAL QUESTION

What are some of the different methods the characters you have read about use to reach out to one another? TEXT TO TEXT

This Is Just to Say

I have eaten
the plums
that were in
the icebox

and which
you were probably
saving
for breakfast

Forgive me
they were delicious
so sweet
and so cold

— William Carlos Williams

Essential Question

How can we take responsibility?

Read how poets reflect on personal responsibility and what it means to them.

 *Go Digital!*

to Mrs. Garcia, in the office
This Is Just to Say

I have stolen
the jelly doughnuts
that were in
the teachers' lounge

and which
you were probably
saving
for teachers

Forgive me
they were delicious
so sweet
and so gloppy

too bad
the powdered sugar
spilled all over my shirt
and gave me
away

by Thomas

— Joyce Sidman

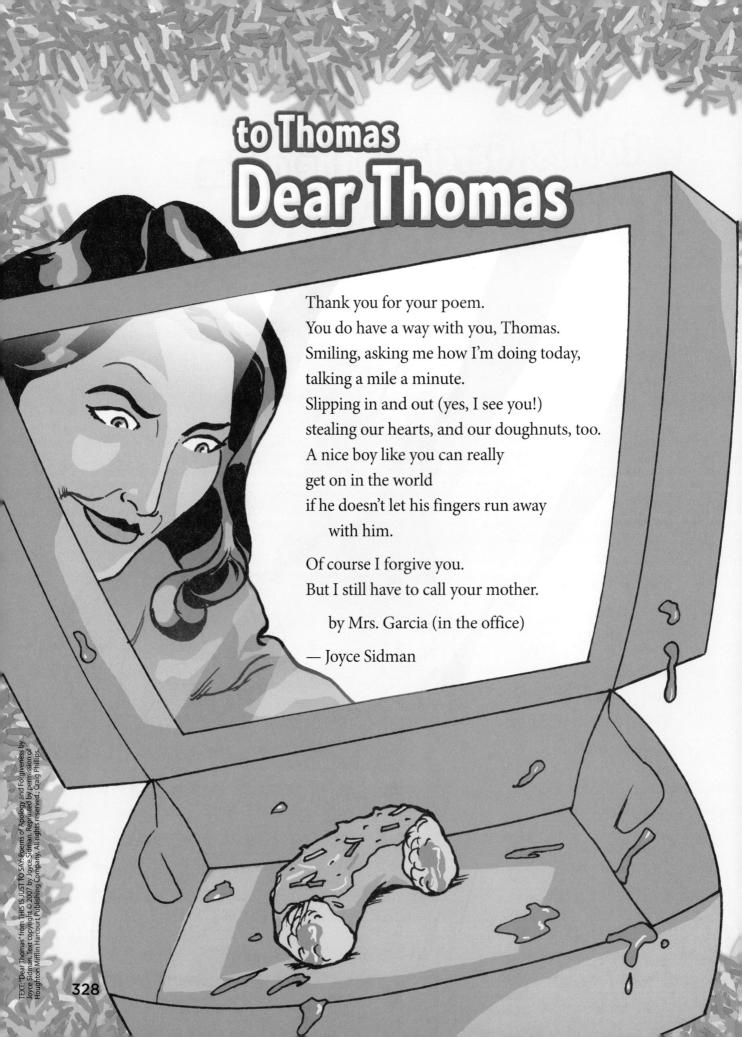

to Thomas
Dear Thomas

Thank you for your poem.
You do have a way with you, Thomas.
Smiling, asking me how I'm doing today,
talking a mile a minute.
Slipping in and out (yes, I see you!)
stealing our hearts, and our doughnuts, too.
A nice boy like you can really
get on in the world
if he doesn't let his fingers run away
    with him.

Of course I forgive you.
But I still have to call your mother.

   by Mrs. Garcia (in the office)

— Joyce Sidman

Respond to Reading

Summarize

Use important details from "This Is Just to Say" to summarize the poem. Information from your Point of View Chart may help you.

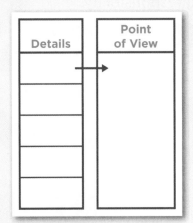

Details	Point of View

Text Evidence

1. Is the free verse poem "This Is Just to Say" an example of a narrative poem? Explain your answer. **GENRE**

2. Find an example of both alliteration and assonance in the poem "to Mrs. Garcia, in the office." **LITERARY ELEMENTS**

3. Identify an idiomatic expression the author uses in the poem "to Thomas" and explain its meaning. **IDIOMS**

4. Reread "This Is Just to Say" and "to Mrs. Garcia, in the office." Write about the point of view the poet uses in each poem and why it is effective.
WRITE ABOUT READING

 Make Connections
Think about each speaker's claim in proportion to his or her action. Why is it important to admit responsibility for your actions?
TEXT TO WORLD

CCSS

Genre • Poetry

Compare Texts

Read how two poets write about obligation and taking responsibility.

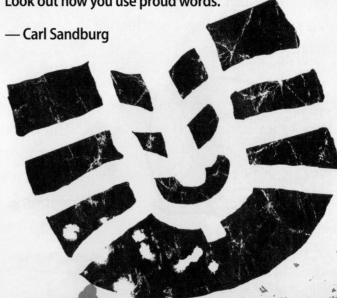

PRIMER LESSON

Look out how you use proud words.
When you let proud words go, it is
     not easy to call them back.
They wear long boots, hard boots; they
     walk off proud; they can't hear you
     calling—
Look out how you use proud words.

— Carl Sandburg

If I can stop one Heart from breaking

If I can stop one Heart from breaking
I shall not live in vain
If I can ease one Life the Aching
Or cool one Pain

Or help one fainting Robin
Unto his Nest again
I shall not live in Vain.

— Emily Dickinson

Make Connections

What are the poets in these two poems saying about taking responsibility? Use details from the poems in your answer.
ESSENTIAL QUESTION

How are these poems similar to others you have read about being answerable for your actions? **TEXT TO TEXT**

The HERO and the MINOTAUR

The Fantastic Adventures of Theseus

BY ROBERT BYRD

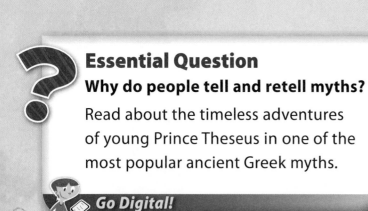

? **Essential Question**

Why do people tell and retell myths?

Read about the timeless adventures of young Prince Theseus in one of the most popular ancient Greek myths.

Go Digital!

Ages ago, in the days of gods and monsters, mighty Poseidon ruled the seas. This fearsome god rode over the waters in a golden chariot, forming earthquakes, furious storms, and thunderous waves in his wake. Yet he also drove the joyful dolphins, brought calm winds for smooth sailing, and created all of the delights of the sparkling ocean. Poseidon's brother was Zeus, king of all the gods.

In those days the gods mixed freely in the affairs of humankind. They even let themselves feel human emotions—jealousy, anger, envy, and love—for men and women on Earth. Poseidon loved a woman, the beautiful Princess Aethra of Troezen, and watched over her tenderly. When Aethra fell in love with a human king and gave birth to a son, Theseus, Poseidon protected him . . . but that is getting ahead of the story.

Poseidon was called the earth-shaker, for once long ago he shook
his mighty trident, and the oceans churned and roared before him. The
goddess of the moon, the god of the sun, and all the ancient spirits looked
on in awe as earth rose up from the bottom of the sea and the glorious
lands of Greece were born. The most beautiful countryside was filled with
craggy mountains and green olive groves, watered by clear streams and
warmed by a bright sun. King Aegeus ruled there from the city of Athens.
Aegeus was a good king, but there were many who were jealous of his
power and threatened him. So when the king traveled to Troezen, met
Princess Aethra, and had a son with her, the mother and baby stayed safely
in that town, while he returned to Athens.

In Troezen, inspired by his mother's tales of great heroes and warriors,
Theseus grew to be strong and brave. When he was only seven, Heracles,
the greatest hero of Greece, walked into the city wearing the skin of a lion.
Theseus' friends mistook Heracles for a lion walking on its hind legs and
fled in terror. But Theseus grabbed an ax and advanced, determined to
slay the beast. The boy's bravery delighted Heracles, and the two became

friends. Theseus soon vowed to become a hero like Heracles. While Heracles relied on his awesome strength, Theseus was clever, quick, and developed his wrestling skills.

Theseus often questioned his mother about his father. "Who is he? When can I go to him?" he would ask. His mother always answered that she would tell him when the time was right.

One morning, in a part of the forest where the trees grew thickly on either side of the path, Theseus came upon an enormous boulder blocking his way. He strained against it with all his might, and slowly it began to move. Beneath it Theseus found a pair of golden sandals and a shining golden sword.

STOP AND CHECK

Make, Revise, Confirm Predictions
Who do you think may have left the golden sandals and shining sword under the boulder? Use evidence from the text to support your prediction.

Aethra recognized what Theseus had found and said to him, "Your father, King Aegeus, left these treasures here for you. 'When our son is strong enough to turn the rock,' he told me, 'he must put on the sandals, take up the sword, and come to me in Athens. I shall recognize him by these things.'" Theseus was overjoyed to learn about his father. He wondered what it would be like to meet the great king.

Aethra helped Theseus prepare for his journey, though she was sad to see him leave Troezen and anxious for his safety. "You must take the sea route to Athens," she said, "for the road is filled with robbers and monsters."

But talk of danger only filled Theseus with excitement. Hoping to prove his courage, he decided to travel by land in spite of his mother's warning. So he set off along the road for Athens, his father's sandals on his feet and the golden sword strapped to his side.

Though the rocky path wound among **desolate** green hills and through rugged, lonely forests, Theseus felt only the thrill of adventure as he made his way to meet his father. After walking for some hours, he came upon a massive strongman named Cercyon, who liked to challenge travelers to a wrestling match and crush them to death. "Come, boy," Cercyon bellowed. "See if you can best me!" When Cercyon tried to grab him, Theseus was too clever for his tricks, and he nimbly stepped aside, causing Cercyon to stumble and lose his balance. Then Theseus, an accomplished wrestler, pressed the advantage and flipped the robber upside down. The evil grappler landed on his head and perished.

Next Theseus met Sinis the pine-bender, who was so tough he could bend pine trees down to the earth. Sinis would make travelers take hold of the treetop and then, letting go the tree, fling his victims to their doom. But Theseus proved too smart to be caught in that trap, and he made sure the pine-bender came to the very same end that he had brought to so many others.

As Poseidon watched from the sea, Theseus followed the road up and up along steep cliffs rising from the ocean below. At the top stood an enormous ogre called Sciron, who ordered all who passed to wash his feet. When they bent to the task, the ogre would kick the travelers into the sea, where a monstrous turtle waited to devour them. "I will wash your feet, sir, but first I must clean the water," Theseus called out to the ogre. "See how dirty it is?" When Sciron leaned down to look, Theseus quickly crashed the bowl over the giant's head and kicked him over the cliff. Then the frightful turtle came gleefully up to the rocky beach and made a meal of the hapless ogre.

Word of Theseus' adventures soon reached Athens. As Theseus approached the city, crowds came out to greet him.

"Who performs these daring deeds?" Aegeus asked. "Let me meet the **valiant** champion." Aegeus decided to honor the stranger's bravery with a magnificent banquet in the Temple of Dolphins. When the prince stepped forward to present himself, the old king recognized the sandals and the golden sword, and he knew the youth before him was his son. He welcomed Theseus with a cry of wonder and a loving embrace. The sight of their happy reunion filled everyone with joy, and the people feasted, danced, and lit altars in every temple in Athens.

STOP AND CHECK

Confirm or Revise Predictions
Was your prediction correct? Confirm or revise your prediction based on evidence in the text.

One morning shortly after the festivities ended, Theseus sensed a terrible sadness throughout the city. He also saw that his father's brow was creased with sorrow.

"Across the sea, a powerful king named Minos rules the island of Crete," Aegeus explained. "He keeps a beast called the Minotaur, a monster that is half-man, half-bull and feeds on human flesh. Many years ago, Minos' son visited our city and was killed here by a bull. In his rage, Minos made war on us and threatened to destroy Athens unless we sent him a tribute of seven young men and seven young women every year to sacrifice to the Minotaur. The time has come again to pay tribute," he finished bitterly, "and though I am their king, I can do nothing to protect the fourteen who will draw unlucky lots and be sent to Crete, never to return."

Theseus, angered by King Minos' cruelty, replied, "Let me go with those to be sacrificed. I will slay the Minotaur and end the curse that hangs over our city." Aegeus pleaded with him to stay in Athens, but Theseus remained **steadfast** and prepared for the voyage to Crete.

The next morning, the old king was forced to bid his son farewell.

"In mourning for those to be sacrificed," said Aegeus, "your ship has a black sail. If the gods grant you the power to kill the Minotaur, hoist this white sail on your return. I will see it far out on the horizon and rejoice that you are safe." Theseus promised his father he would remember, then eagerly boarded the vessel. Many around him wept at the sad departure, but Theseus could think only of the thrilling adventure before him.

The ship sailed south and soon approached the shores of Crete. A towering figure ran back and forth across the harbor entrance.

"What is this marvel?" cried Theseus in wonder.

"That is Talus," replied the captain. "A senseless giant made of bronze. It moves as though it were alive and guards the harbor against King Minos' enemies. He would smash us to bits if it were not for our black sail, which even he can recognize." The mechanical man allowed the Athenians to pass him as they approached the king's immense palace, where Minos and the Minotaur were waiting for them.

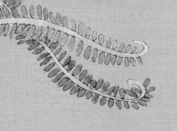
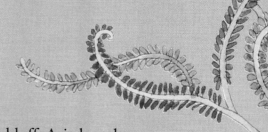

Not only Talus watched the ship arrive. From a bluff, Ariadne, the daughter of King Minos, stood with her friend Icarus and gazed down at the **somber** ship. Icarus was the son of Daedalus, a famous inventor. Long ago, at the king's command, it was Daedalus who built a labyrinth beneath the palace as a cage to hold the Minotaur.

"Who is that, who stands so tall and unafraid on the Athenian ship?" Ariadne asked. She was impressed by the stranger's confidence.

"That must be Theseus, son of Aegeus," Icarus replied. He was pleased to be able to show off his knowledge to the beautiful princess, but he wondered at her admiration of Theseus. "I have heard he freely chose to come here and face the Minotaur."

Ariadne knew very well that no one had ever escaped the circling passages and corridors of her father's enormous stone maze. Gazing at the prince, she made up her mind to save him from the king's rash cruelty. "We must go to your father and ask for his advice," she said to Icarus. "If anyone knows the secrets of the maze and can help us rescue Theseus, it is Daedalus." The bold princess was right, for the brilliant inventor revealed to her a clever plan.

That night, while the others slept, Ariadne secretly entered the king's chamber, gathered up the palace keys and Theseus' sword, and crept down to the prisoner's cell.

"Theseus," she whispered to him, "I am Ariadne. I have heard tales of your many good deeds. I can show you how to escape the labyrinth, but in return I ask that you help me to escape this island and my father, King Minos, who has grown wicked and pitiless."

Theseus agreed to help her, and so Ariadne explained Daedalus' secret. "You must secure one end of this ball of thread to the entrance of the labyrinth," she said, "and keep hold of the rest of the ball as the string unravels behind you. If you defeat the Minotaur, the thread's path will lead you back out of the labyrinth." Praying that the gods would help him, she led Theseus to the maze and watched as he descended the heavy stone steps. Then she returned to the prison hold to free the other captives.

In the corridors of the labyrinth, the odor was foul, the light dim. Theseus gripped his father's sword in one hand, and in the other he held the unraveling thread. The passages twisted and turned, leading him first one way and then another, winding around and around. Down, down he went, searching for the beast hidden deep in the black abyss.

Finally he came to an open space where the Minotaur lay sleeping on the rough stone floor. Its hot breath shook the cavern walls. The creature had the chest and arms of a powerful man, but the rest of its body had the shape of a bull, and two great horns grew out of its head.

Then the Minotaur opened one glowing red eye and fixed it on Theseus. Its snore died away, and the chamber grew deathly still.

With a thunderous bellow, the Minotaur rose to its feet and charged. Theseus leapt aside, but the deadly horns grazed his tunic. The Minotaur spun around, furious, and charged again. As the beast descended upon him, Theseus steadied himself, raised his golden sword, and with a great heave drove the blade through the Minotaur's heart. The monster dropped to the cold stone floor, silenced forever.

Shaken by the fury of the struggle, Theseus had dropped the ball of thread. Anxious to escape the gloomy maze, he picked it up again and followed the thread out of the labyrinth and into the cool night air.

Ariadne and Icarus were waiting for him. The princess cried out with delight to see Theseus unharmed.

"Let us waste no time in leaving. The king is sure to come after us," urged Ariadne. Theseus and the freed Athenians boarded the ship, but Icarus stepped back.

"Minos will blame Daedalus for your escape. I cannot abandon my father to the king's wrath," he explained, though it pained Icarus to see Theseus leave with Ariadne. "Daedalus and I will flee Minos together," he vowed. "Then we will join you in Athens."

Icarus watched from the bluffs as the ship set a course for Athens, but he was not the only one who followed the black sail in the breaking dawn. At the harbor entrance Talus spied the ship and raised his heavy club high to strike the boat. Theseus stepped forward with his sword, prepared to fight. But Poseidon, ever watchful, sent a massive wave smashing into the bronze giant. The Athenians watched in awe as the shining colossus, crushed into a heap of broken metal, sank to the bottom of the sea.

When King Minos woke and discovered all that had happened, he was enraged. Minos knew Daedalus was to blame for Theseus' success—for who else was clever enough to show the hero a way out of the labyrinth? To punish the inventor for his **deception**, the king locked both Daedalus and Icarus high up in a tower.

From a window in the tower, Icarus watched the birds and looked out to sea, imagining the fast ship that carried Ariadne and the Athenians to safety. He pictured the hero's welcome that Theseus would receive and longed for his own freedom and glory.

"Look how easily the birds move about!" he sighed to Daedalus. "It is their wings that make them free."

Now, Daedalus had a mind so wondrously quick that no one could keep it locked up. He devised a plan for escape and cunningly asked Minos for his tools and materials. The king agreed, wondering greedily what new marvel the inventor would make for him.

Then Daedalus had Icarus gather feathers from the birds that rested on the window ledge. When Icarus had piled up two great mounds of feathers, Daedalus went to work fashioning two marvelous pairs of wings held together by threads and wax. One day Icarus and his father attached the wings to their arms and shoulders and climbed into the tower windows. As they prepared to make their daring escape, Daedalus cautioned his son.

"Take a middle course, Icarus," he warned. "If you fly too low, the sea will soak the feathers. If you fly too high, the sun will melt the wax."

Off the window ledge they launched themselves, soaring into the sunlit sky like two grand eagles.

Icarus flew up high and dove down low, skimming the waves with delight. Then he climbed back up, higher and higher, spiraling toward the sun.

"Icarus!" called his father. "Remember my warning!" But Icarus did not want to take the middle course. Reveling in his freedom, he pumped the fantastic wings through the air and watched the ocean spread beneath him like a shining jewel. The higher he flew, the more powerful he felt. He vowed he would never again be caged.

STOP AND CHECK

Ask and Answer Questions
Do you think that Icarus is jealous of Theseus and his abilities? How might this affect his actions? Support your answer with evidence from the text.

Icarus flew closer and closer to the sun. Its warmth slowly melted the wax, and feathers began to fall from his wings. Suddenly Icarus, too, was falling. "Father! Father!" he cried. But Daedalus could only watch in horror as his son plunged into the water and drowned beneath the waves.

The grieving father buried his son on an island nearby, which came to be called Icaria. Then, his heart heavy with sorrow, Daedalus flew on to the island of Sicily, where he was welcomed with honor. In spite of his sadness, the great inventor lived to create many more wonderful things. But he destroyed the fateful wings and never flew again.

Oblivious to the terrible fate of Icarus, Ariadne and Theseus stopped their ship to rest on the isle of Naxos, unaware that the god Dionysus was following them. Dionysus was the god of all feasting and revelry. He had fallen in love with Ariadne, and while the Athenians slept he appeared to Theseus in a dream. "You cannot take the princess with you to Athens," Dionysus declared, "for I wish to make her my wife." Now Theseus had no choice but to leave, for he knew it would be foolish to challenge so mighty a god.

When Ariadne woke and found herself alone, she felt bitterly betrayed. But Dionysus was true to his word and married Ariadne. Over time she grew to love him in return and also became a great queen. When she died, Dionysus placed her jeweled crown in the sky, forming the constellation Corona Borealis. In the night sky, you can still see its diamonds shining like distant stars.

In Athens, King Aegeus watched for his son's return. Theseus was so exhausted from his journey and troubled by his loss of Ariadne that he forgot to put up the white sail his father had given him. When Aegeus saw the ship with the black sail on the horizon, he believed Theseus was dead. Without his son, all the old king's power and his beautiful city seemed meaningless to him. Overcome with despair, Aegeus threw himself off the cliffs and perished on the rocky shore below.

When the Athenians recognized the ship entering the harbor, they raised Theseus up as their greatest hero and new king. Though Theseus had saved many victims from the Minotaur and was glorious in the eyes of his city, he despaired at his own carelessness and wept for King Aegeus' tragic death.

Theseus named the blue sea around Athens the Aegean Sea in his father's honor. He brought his mother, Aethra, to the court, and with her advice, the young king who had been a valiant but reckless champion ruled Athens with wisdom and justice.

As Poseidon looked on, the city and its people grew in fame and influence through the ages. Its storytellers never tired of weaving tales about the adventures of Theseus, Ariadne, Icarus, and all of the famous heroes and heroines, gods and goddesses, and fabulous creatures of ancient Greece.

About Robert Byrd

Robert Byrd

studied art at the Philadelphia College of Art. He knew from the time he began his studies that he wanted to work as an illustrator one day. He has written and illustrated several children's books that focus on folktales or legends, such as *Finn MacCoul and his Fearless Wife*, a retelling of an amusing Celtic myth.

In 2003, Byrd won the Golden Kite Award from the Society of Children's Book Writers and Illustrators for his nonfiction picture book about Leonardo da Vinci, called *Leonardo: Beautiful Dreamer*. Today, Byrd teaches others how to illustrate children's books at Moore College of Art and Design and the University of the Arts in Philadelphia.

Author's Purpose

The author drew his own illustrations for this selection. How do they help to suggest the movement and action in the story?

Respond to Reading

Summarize

Use details from *The Hero and the Minotaur* to summarize the most important events in the plot. Information from your Character, Setting, and Plot Chart can help you.

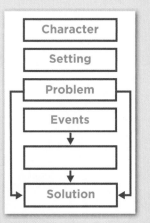

Character
Setting
Problem
Events
Solution

Text Evidence

1. What features in the selection *The Hero and the Minotaur* help you recognize that it is a myth? Name at least two of these features to support your answer. **GENRE**

2. What is the main problem the characters face in this myth, and how is it solved? Support your answer with details from the story. **PROBLEM AND SOLUTION**

3. The word *trident* at the top of page 334 contains the Latin root *dent,* which means "tooth," and the Latin prefix *tri-,* which means "three." How does knowing the Latin origins of *trident* help you to figure out what it means? **WORD ORIGINS**

4. Myths were often written to explain what a culture considered to be important. Write about the character of Theseus, and how he represented character traits the Greeks felt were valuable. **WRITE ABOUT READING**

Make Connections

Why would people tell and retell the story of Theseus and the Minotaur? **ESSENTIAL QUESTION**

How does Theseus as a hero compare to present-day heroes in fiction and movies? **TEXT TO WORLD**

Compare Texts

Read how the ancient Greek hero Theseus battles monsters with the ultimate weapon—a breakfast sandwich.

The A-MAZE-ing Tale of Theseus and the Minotaur

Sergey Kostik

Meet Our Hero

According to the ancient Greeks, Poseidon was this humongous water god who fell in love with a pretty princess named Aethra. She was obviously popular because a king named Aegeus also loved her, and the king married her. They had a son named Theseus.

Things were going great until the king decided to go back to his kingdom. But he didn't completely forget Aethra and Theseus, and before he departed, the king hid some gold sandals and a sword under a big rock, telling his wife that when their son was big and strong enough to move the rock, she should send him on over to his kingdom.

The Quest Begins

So Theseus grew bigger (but not that big) and stronger (but not that strong). He was always speculating who his father might be, but Aethra never told, for she wanted it to be a big surprise. Then one morning they went for a walk and came to a massive boulder.

"Look, Theseus! Why don't you try to push this immense rock?" his mother asked, knowing that this was the rock where the king had concealed the sandals and sword.

Even though Theseus thought it was a weird request, and that it was really much too hot to engage in this kind of physical exertion, he did what his mother asked. When he tried to push the rock, however, it wouldn't budge. Growing impatient, Aethra told him to try again, but Theseus still couldn't move the enormous stone.

"Oh, for goodness sake!" Aethra said. Then she leaned on the rock. When she did it went flying down the path and Theseus saw the sword and the sandals.

"Cool! Fancy sandals!" Theseus exclaimed and began to slip them on, even though the sandals were a bit crushed after lying out of sight under a rock for 14 years.

"Look, Theseus, there's a sword, too," his mother pointed out. Theseus told her she should take it, adding that she could use it to chop lettuce and tomatoes. But Aethra insisted that Theseus would need it more than she would and told him that now he could visit his father, the king.

"My father's a king?" said Theseus, impressed. "Wow. But I don't have to go yet, right, Ma? There's a new play opening tonight and I . . ."

"Yes, you really should get going right away," Aethra said, cutting him off. She made sure Theseus had his sword and she sent him off with a nice breakfast sandwich—cheese and olives.

So Theseus trudged along toward Athens. He was feeling pretty down because he had never left home before— not even for a sleepover. Soon enough, he saw this terrifying giant who yelled, "Hey, ya wanna fight?"

"Um, no, not really," said Theseus.

"But that's what I do!" yelled the giant. "I fight whomever comes by and then I consume them!" He smiled hungrily.

Gee, thought Theseus, I guess everyone needs a hobby, but really. As the giant approached him, however, he knew he had to think fast. "Wouldn't you rather eat a nice breakfast sandwich?" Theseus asked, "because my mom makes the best breakfast sandwiches ever." The giant, who loved olives, especially the kind his own mother bought at the market in Athens, decided to split the sandwich with Theseus.

In the next town, people soon heard about this amazing event. "What **audacity**!" they cried.

"Yeah, you should have seen me," Theseus bragged, "'cause I was really awesome."

An Athenian Welcome

Theseus saw a few other monsters, but he got very good at hiding behind rocks and waiting until the beasts wandered off. So it took him a long time to get to Athens, and when he did, people were astonished. "We thought you were dead!" they exclaimed.

"Nope, here I am," Theseus said. The king, recognizing Theseus' sword and gold sandals, shouted, "Son, we heard about how you beat all those monsters!"

"Dad?" Theseus said, a little nervous.

"Why don't you just call me 'King Aegeus'?" said his father. "We've got one more monster for you to tackle," he continued. "There's this king—King Minos of Crete—who's got a Minotaur stuck in a maze. Every year I have to send over seven boys and seven girls for the Minotaur's supper. It's a long story, but you've come just in time to help!"

"By 'help,' do you mean I'll have to carry your luggage?" Theseus asked.

The king laughed at what he thought was a joke. "Of course, a brave and strong boy like you will slay the Minotaur for us and become a great hero!"

"I don't have to go yet, right?" Theseus said. "I heard there's a discus-throwing contest tonight and I . . ."

"Yes, you have to go tonight," said his father. "Now scoot, time's a-wasting."

The king pushed his son onto a big boat, and in minutes, Theseus and the fourteen Athenian teenagers were sailing away to Crete. Theseus was pretty sure his luck had run out since he didn't have any more breakfast sandwiches on him.

"Ooh, it's that handsome Theseus whose **exploits** are known throughout the seven seas!" swooned Ariadne, Princess of Crete, when she saw Theseus hanging over the railing of the ship. He was a tiny bit seasick.

The Maze and the Minotaur

That night, Ariadne went to Theseus, who was reclining in one of the ship's deck chairs. "Theseus, wake up!" she whispered.

"Oh, I'm awake," Theseus said. "Would you be able to sleep if you knew you had to kill a Minotaur in the morning?"

"You can do it!" said Ariadne. "Here, I knitted this sweater for you because it's cold in that maze! When you get out, come for me. My father is so mean, and I know I could be happy with you."

Ariadne seemed very nice, and Theseus thought he could be happy with her, too, as long as she could make a

breakfast sandwich that was as tasty as the ones his mother made. "Okay, just one favor," he said. "Could you fix me a nice breakfast sandwich in the morning? I'll need my strength in the maze."

"With pleasure," said Ariadne.

In the morning, Ariadne sneaked Theseus a bag that held a nice breakfast sandwich, which he took in one hand while he carried his sword in the other. "I don't have to go just yet, right guys?" he asked the guards. "I . . ." But the guards pushed Theseus toward the maze.

At the entrance, a piece of yarn from the sweater Theseus was wearing snagged on the gate, and as he went into the maze the sweater unraveled, leaving a trail of yarn. After wandering around for what seemed like weeks, Theseus decided to take the breakfast sandwich out of the bag and eat it, but as he did so, he turned a corner and saw the fearsome face of the Minotaur.

"AAARRRHHHH!" said the Minotaur.

Theseus noticed that the monster could not take his eyes off of the breakfast sandwich. "Darn!" Theseus said to himself, but knowing it might be his only escape he slowly held up the sandwich and offered it to the Minotaur.

"Are you hungry?" Theseus asked.

"You'd be hungry too if you only ate once a year," replied the Minotaur, and then for good effect he roared again.

"Here," said Theseus, thrusting the breakfast sandwich toward the fearsome beast. "It was made with loving hands by the king's own daughter."

"Mmmm!" said the Minotaur. "This is much tastier than the teenagers I usually get. Can I get more of these?"

"You bet!" said Theseus, and together they followed the unraveled strand of yarn to exit the maze. Then Theseus took the Minotaur over to the royal kitchen. People screamed as they passed by, but the Minotaur was getting more gentle with every step. Theseus ran ahead and got the Minotaur fourteen breakfast sandwiches; finally Theseus, the Minotaur, Ariadne, and the fourteen lucky teenagers raced to the boat before mean King Minos could stop them.

Make Connections

Why are myths sometimes retold as parodies? **ESSENTIAL QUESTION**

In what ways is this parody different from the original myth? **TEXT TO TEXT**

Elijah of Buxton

By Christopher Paul Curtis
Illustrated by Chris Wormel

Essential Question
How do people show inner strength?

Read what happens when a dramatic event forces a young boy to discover his own inner strength.

Go Digital!

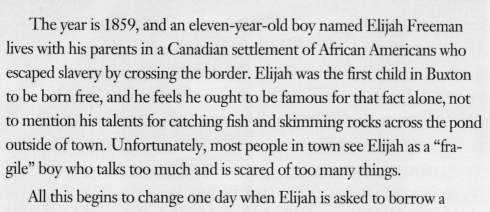

The year is 1859, and an eleven-year-old boy named Elijah Freeman lives with his parents in a Canadian settlement of African Americans who escaped slavery by crossing the border. Elijah was the first child in Buxton to be born free, and he feels he ought to be famous for that fact alone, not to mention his talents for catching fish and skimming rocks across the pond outside of town. Unfortunately, most people in town see Elijah as a "fragile" boy who talks too much and is scared of too many things.

All this begins to change one day when Elijah is asked to borrow a horse named Jingle Boy at the town stable, saddle up, and pick up the mail in nearby Chatham. There he discovers a letter from America addressed to his mother's friend, Emeline Holton. Elijah figures it must be bad news, and when his mother asks him to read the letter to Mrs. Holton, he finds a kind of strength he didn't know he had.

When me and Jingle Boy got to Chatham we went right to their post office. I tied the horse out front, waited for my insides to quit shaking, then stepped onto the **stoop**. I pulled on the doorknob and near 'bout jerked my shoulder out. The door was locked, which was mighty peculiar 'cause it couldn't've been much past four o'clock. It waren't till then that I saw the sign someone stuck up in the window:

CLOSED UNTIL THE FIFTH. ANY ENQUIRERYS
SEE GEORGE AT THE DRY GOODS STORE.

I went next door to MacMahon's Dry Goods.

The place had a great smell. It was fresh-cured leather and new material mixed up with fancy powder and soap. When you opened the screen door a bell runged to let people know you were there. It runged again when you left so's folks knowed you were gone.

The white man that was folding up sheets of cloth for women's dresses behind a counter looked up at me.

"Why, hello, Elijah. How're you?"

"Fine, thank you, Mr. MacMahon."

"And what can I do for you today, laddy?"

I'd learnt a long time ago that Mr. MacMahon didn't mean nothing bad when he called you laddy. It sure sounded like he was mispronouncing *lady* but we'd got told to ignore it.

"I'm here 'bout our mail, sir. The sign said come talk to you."

Leastways, that's what I hoped it said. *Enquirerys* was one n'em words that I ain't got notion the first about.

"Oh. I was wondering when someone from Buxton would come. Then you haven't heard what happened?"

"No, sir."

"Well, laddy, we've had to find a new postman. Larry Butler had an absolutely terrible accident."

When Mr. MacMahon said words like *terrible* he made it sound like they had seven or eight Rs in 'em 'stead of just one.

"What happened, sir?"

"As near as we can figure, his horse threw him and trampled him. Hoof caught him right in the head."

This was more proof that a mule is way better than a horse. If Mr. Butler had been riding Old Flapjack, he'd still be delivering mail.

Mr. MacMahon said, "Give me one more minute, Elijah. I know there's a package in the post office and perhaps a letter or two. Not much."

"Yes, sir."

He finished folding the cloth and picked up his crutches to take me back to the post office.

A long time ago Mr. MacMahon had a bad run-in with a horse hisself. That's why his right leg ended at his knee 'stead of at his foot.

When he was on his crutches he moved real graceful and smooth. He'd been without that leg for so long that it looked like the crutches were a part of his body. It almost looked like he was dancing when he walked.

When we got inside the post office Mr. MacMahon hefted a box onto the shelf then looked in a mailbag that had BUXTON writ 'cross the front.

"Hmm, seems to be only one package and one letter, Elijah. I could have swore there was more."

He handed me the letter.

"Thank you, sir."

"Someone's going to have to come pick up the mail until the fifth. The new man should be up and running by then."

"Yes, sir. Tell Mr. Butler I'm sorry 'bout his accident."

"Thanks for the kind words, laddy. Wouldn't matter much what we told him, his mind isn't amongst us anymore."

Mr. MacMahon danced to the door then locked up behind us. He went over to Jingle Boy and patted him on the neck. "Most beautiful horse I've ever seen, Elijah. Hard to believe he's so fast."

"He is, sir."

I lifted the box onto the saddle then jumped up myself.

What with seeing all the damage horses had done in Chatham and being natural nervous 'bout being up this high, I didn't look to see who the letter was to until we were halfway back to Buxton.

My heart sunked when I saw what was writ 'cross the front in proper letters: MRS. EMELINE HOLTON, NEGRO SETTLEMENT AT RALEIGH, CANADA WEST.

On the back, above the red wax seal, it said: APPLEWOOD, FAIRFAX COUNTY, VIRGINIA, UNITED STATES.

This was trouble. Didn't nothing good ever come out of one of these letters from America. If the words on the envelope were writ in regular old plain letters that looked like someone had fought hard and long to get the writing down, most times it meant that some person who was a slave had snucked it out and it was full of rotten news. It was gonna tell 'bout a father getting sick or a brother getting whupped bad or a mother's children getting sold away. If the letter was writ fancy, like this one was, with swirlingness and curlycues and such nonsense it only meant one thing: A friendly white person was writing to let you know somebody was dead.

Since this letter was addressed to Mrs. Holton, it probably had some bad news 'bout her husband.

My ride back from Chatham waren't a good one. It waren't that the road had gone bad or the skeeters were heavier than they were afore or that Jingle Boy was bouncing more than regular, but the fancy writ envelope in the pouch made the ride home long and sad.

STOP AND CHECK

Make, Confirm, Revise Predictions As the letter is addressed to Mrs. Emeline Holton, what news do you think it may contain? Support your prediction with evidence from the text.

I left Mr. Polite's package on his stoop then took Jingle Boy back to Mr. Segee. 'Stead of taking the letter di-rect to Mrs. Holton, I walked back home with it to see what Ma was gonna say.

I pulled my brogans off and went in through the front door.

"Ma?"

She waren't in the parlour.

"Ma?"

Nor upstairs in her bedroom.

"Ma?"

Nor my bedroom.

"Ma?"

Nor the kitchen.

There was one of her peach pies on the kitchen table cooling and I thought for a second 'bout lifting a piece of the crust and digging a couple peaches out of it with my finger. Then I thought better of it.

I pulled my socks off and went out the back door. Ma was squatted down tending to her truck patch.

She saw me and smiled and was just 'bout to say hello.

Mas are some amazing and scary people. Seems like they got ways of seeing things that ain't showing, and hearing things that ain't being said. I didn't even open my mouth but Ma knowed by some mystery way that something waren't right. She quick stood up and said, "'Lijah? What's wrong?"

The trowel she'd been using and a fistful of weeds fell out of her hand.

"What happened?"

She ran up to me and I showed her the letter from America.

She wiped her hands on her coveralls and said, "You see I ain't got my spectacles on. Who it to, who it from?"

All the growned folks that hadn't never learnt to read nor write whilst they were 'slaved in America had to take lessons at the schoolhouse at night. Between cooking and cleaning and gardening and sewing and knitting and working the fields at harvesttime and helping out at the chopping bees and the raising bees and tending to her sheep and shearing 'em and gathering wool and carding it and spinning it, Ma had been lazy and was slacking off on her school lessons and they waren't sticking particular good.

I told her what was writ on the envelope and she said, "Awww, no. No, no, no. Don't it never end?"

Ma didn't waste no time, she said, "Go get your Sunday clothes on, 'Lijah. We gunn go together to tell her."

I knowed I was gonna have to read the letter out loud to Mrs. Holton too. She was taking lessons with Ma, and I don't mean no disrespect to Mr. Travis, but it 'peared he was having a powerful bad time in making his lessons stick with any of the growned folks.

I changed to my Sabbath school clothes and walked into the parlour. Ma had already put on her Sunday dress and was carrying that pie she'd baked.

She said, "Good thing I baked this here pie. I hate to go for something like this barehand."

She set the pie down and opened her arms.

I walked in and she kissed the top of my head and mashed her cheek there.

Her voice and the warmness from her face both spread 'cross the top of my head. "Now, 'Lijah, you know you most likely gunn be breaking some bad news to Mrs. Holton so don't forget, I'm-a need you to be strong. I'm-a need you not to rile her and n'em girls up none by crying and carrying on, sweetie. And I'm-a 'specially need you not to go tearing out of Mrs. Holton's home screaming if this here *is* bad news. Can you do it?"

I know it ain't a child's place to feel this way 'bout the person that raised you, but I was disappointed in Ma something awful. She hadn't took no notice that I'd been doing a lot of growing in the pass couple of weeks.

'Twaren't but the other day I was **eavesdropping** and heard her tell Pa that it's a miracle I waren't born in slavery 'cause I'm way too fra-gile to have survived even a minute of it. Maybe I use to be a little fra-gile, but I ain't been afeared of nonsense nor run off screaming 'bout the littlest things for the longest time. And besides, it just ain't right to be calling somebody fra-gile nohow.

"Can I count on you to be growned, 'Lijah?"

"Yes, ma'am." It was gonna be hard, though. Don't nothing seem to make you want to tear up and cry more than being told not to. I was even starting to feel something loosening up and slopping 'round in my nose.

Ma kissed the top of my head again and turned me a-loose.

We started out toward Mrs. Holton's place.

Miss Duncan-the-first and Miss Duncan-the-second were tending their flower garden out front of their home.

Miss Duncan-the-first saw us and stood up and called, "Sarah? What's wrong? What happened?"

Miss Duncan-the-second stood up too. She said, "Sarah?"

Ma told 'em, "'Lijah done pick up a letter for Mrs. Holton, it come from down home."

Both the women wiped their hands on their skirts, and Miss Duncan-the-second said, "Hold on, we's coming with you. That poor, poor thing."

By the time we got to Mrs. Holton's home, what started out with me and Ma and a letter had turned into a whole parade of people. There were twelve of us: me, three babies, and eight women that were all carrying something to eat. There were pies and corn bread and chicken livers and ham and dandelion greens and grits.

There waren't a whole lot of talking going on as we walked to Mrs. Holton's.

When we got there Ma pushed me forward onto the stoop to knock. There waren't nothing but a screen door to keep horseflies out. The main door was open and I could look right into the parlour.

I knocked and Penelope and Cicely, Mrs. Holton's girls, looked up at me from where they were playing on the floor. They smiled when they saw it was me.

Mrs. Holton got up out of her chair. She was holding the same reading primer that I'd studied from five years pass.

She smiled at me and said, "Why, 'lo, Elijah. Mr. Leroy ain't working yet. My goodness, how come you's in your Sunday . . ."

She opened the door and her breathing got stuck in her throat for a minute when she saw the bunch on her stoop. She said, "Oh! Oh."

The primer slipped from her fingers and landed on the stoop's wood floor. I handed it back to her.

She smiled at everyone and said, "Welcome. Y'all come on in."

We all pulled off our shoes and walked in.

She had her parlour set up just as nice as our'n. There was a table and a rocking chair and a bench and a big brick fireplace and maplewood floors and rugs.

She said, "I'm sorry there ain't enough chairs, but please make you'selves comforted best way y'all can."

She turned to her two children and told 'em, "Y'all go on in the garden and pick Mama some flowers. Make sure you bring me some them pretty purple and white ones."

The oldest girl said, "But, Ma, you said they ain't ready to be picked yet."

Mrs. Holton said, "I think they's ready now, Penelope."

Penelope said, "Good afternoon, y'all," then asked her mother, "Why're all these folks visiting us?"

Mrs. Holton said, "Ain't nothing to worry 'bout, darling. Now do as I say. Stay till I calls you, and don't leave the yard." She gave both of the girls a hug and a kiss.

Penelope held on to Cicely's hand and took her out through the front door.

"Can I offer y'all something?"

Ma said, "Thank you kindly, Sister Holton, but 'Lijah done pick up a letter for you in Chatham. It from down home."

Mrs Holton told me, "Elijah, could you read it for me?" She waved the primer she was studying from. "I ain't too far 'long in my lessons."

Miss Duncan-the-first put her hand on the rocking chair and said, "Why don't you get off your feet, Sister Holton?"

"I'm fine, Miss Duncan. Really I am, but thank you kindly. Elijah?"

I started opening the letter but afore I could get my finger in it and bust the wax seal open she said, "If you don't mind, Elijah, I wants to open it."

"I don't mind atall, ma'am."

She picked the wax off the envelope and put it in the front pocket of her apron. She pulled the letter out. She looked it over then handed it back to me.

I said, "It was writ 'bout a year ago, Mrs. Holton." I looked the letter over and knowed I was gonna have to sound some of the words out. I read:

My Dearest Emeline,

 *I'm hoping that this letter finds you and the children in good health. We hear many wonderful things about the Negro settlement there and are grateful that God in his **infinite** mercy and wisdom has seen fit to provide you and yours a refuge.*

Mrs. Holton stopped me. I was afeared she was upset 'cause I stumbled on some of the words, but that waren't it atall. She looked the envelope over and said, "I believe this here's Miss Poole's handwriting. She *do* like prettying up what she say. You gunn have to tell me what some them words is, Elijah. What *refuge* mean?"

I knowed that from Sabbath school.

I said, "*Refuge* means it's somewhere that's safe."

She nodded her head.

I started back up reading:

 However I'm afraid this missive is not one of glad tidings. I'm afraid I have some tragic news I must tell you.

I stopped to see if Mrs. Holton needed any more explaining but she didn't. I was glad 'cause I didn't have notion the first what *mis-sive* meant.

 *After a harsh forced journey to Applewood, John was brought back into servitude. Much to our horror, to set an example and in **retaliation** for the gold he claims John stole, Mr. Tillman exacted a punishment so severe that due to the **rigors** of the march home, John's body could not endure and he went to the loving arms of our Savior on the seventh day of the fifth month in the year of our Lord eighteen hundred and fifty-nine.*

 He is resting peacefully in the slave burial grounds and we made certain he had a Christian service and paid fifteen dollars for a marked grave.

 *I am sorry to have to burden you with such news. You and the children are in our prayers. If you are so **disposed** to remunerate me for this expense, please forward the money to me at Applewood.*

Sincerely,
Mrs. Jacob Poole

Mrs. Holton stood there. It didn't seem like none of those eight women looked di-rect in her face but I knowed they all were ready to jump in case she had a fainting spell or went fra-gile.

But Mrs. Holton didn't flinch or nothing. She said to me, "Read that part again, please, Elijah, that part 'bout John getting punished."

I cleared my throat and read, "'Mr. Tillman ex-act-ed a punishment so severe that due to the rig-ors of the march home, John's body could not endure.'"

She raised her hand. I got ready to tell her that I was middling good at reading words but lots of times I didn't know what they meant, but she shook her head back and forth and said, "'His body could not endure.' That sure 'nough is a gentle way of putting it when one man done killed another one with a whip."

STOP AND CHECK

Revise or Confirm Predictions Was your prediction correct? Confirm or revise your prediction based on evidence in the text.

Mrs. Holton smiled at the women and said, "Thank y'all kindly for your care, but I'm-a be all right. I knowed. I knowed already.

"I been left kind of hanging since we got here but now . . . All I hopes is that he felt we got through. Spite of what Miss Poole say, that'd be the only thing what would make John rest peaceful. I hope he felt the joy and love y'all done give us this pass year."

She gave a little snuffle and I thought for sure she was fixing to cry, but she just said, "I hope he knowed how beautiful his girls look when they free."

Mrs. Holton sat down in the rocker and said, "He wouldn't've wanted no heavy mourning and I love him 'nough to honor that, so I'm-a be all right."

The women started in with touching Mrs. Holton and saying a lot of "sorry" and "here to help" and "call on me."

Mrs. Holton touched each of their hands and said, "Y'all forgive me, y'all been kind enough to bring all this food and here I am acting like I ain't got no manners atall. Please, let's us eat."

She stood up and went to the kitchen.

She called her children in and we all started eating.

When it came time to go, me and Ma hung back till everyone else had left. Once they'd got to talking, Ma and Mrs. Holton found out they were both from the same state down in America and the plantations they were trapped on were a couple miles one from the 'nother. They could even call the names of some of the same people from back there. But it was all white people 'cause the people who were slaves waren't allowed to go from place to place.

We were on the front stoop and I was pulling my brogans on. Ma and Mrs. Holton hugged, and Ma said, "Sister Emeline, please, if you find you'self needing anything, come see me or send word through Eli or Leroy."

Mrs. Holton said, "Thank you, Sister Sarah. Small world, ain't it? It sure is comforting to know we's from the same place. I'm-a be all right. I's just relieved to know what happened, that's all. Ain't too much harder nor more wearying to keep up than false hopes, and I'm glad they gone. Only thing is, I caint get them words Miss Poole wrote out my head. 'His body could not endure.' It don't seem to be right. It don't seem like them should be the last words spoke 'bout John Holton."

Ma said, "Well, the body don't never endure, do it? But I hopes . . . naw, I *knows* that something inside all of us be so strong it *caint* be stopped. It fly on forever."

Mrs. Holton said, "Sister Sarah, your words been a big comfort to me, and you and all the other Buxton sisters been a big help. Thank you kindly. And thank you kindly, Elijah, for reading this letter. Me and your ma is gunn be doing that on our own 'fore too much longer."

Ma laughed and said, "You got more faith than me, Emeline. This reading and writing seem to be two them things what don't come easy once you's full growned. Ain't nothing to do but struggle on, though."

Whilst me and Ma were walking home I was 'bout to bust waiting on her to tell me how I did. You caint never be sure till you get the word from someone that's growned, but I was thinking what I just did was a pretty good sign that my days of being fra-gile were over! I hadn't cried nor let my voice get shake-ity nor even sniffled whilst I was reading the letter to Mrs. Holton.

I waren't gonna tell Ma, but I didn't think it was being growned that got me through it. Mostly I think I didn't bawl 'cause once Ma and them women bunched up 'round Mrs. Holton with their watching, waiting eyes and hands, it felt like a whole slew of soldiers was ringing that parlour with swords drawed and waren't no sorrow so powerful it could bust through.

Once them women bunched up like that in Mrs. Holton's parlour, it seemed like they'd built a wall of Jericho 'round us, and a hundred Joshuas and a thousand children couldn't've knocked the wall down if they'd blowed trumpets and shouted till their throats bust.

Once them women bunched up in that parlour 'round me and Mrs. Holton, I couldn't've cried even if I was fra-gile.

But I was hoping Ma would peg it on me being growned.

We were near 'bout home afore she wrapped her arm 'round my neck and pulled me in to her and said, "'Lijah Freeman, I knowed you could do it, baby! What you done was real growned, son! Wait till I tell your daddy!"

I felt so proud I was afeared I'd bust.

> **STOP AND CHECK**
>
> **Ask and Answer Questions** Why do you think Mrs. Holton felt *his body could not endure* should not be the last words spoken about her husband John?

About the Author

Christopher Paul Curtis

worked for over a decade in an auto factory after high school while also studying at the University of Michigan in Flint. He used his work breaks to study and write. Curtis took a year off from his job to write his first book, *The Watsons Go to Birmingham—1963*. The book went on to win many awards, including a Coretta Scott King Author Honor Award and the Newbery Honor.

Elijah of Buxton also won Newbery and King awards. About the character of Elijah, Curtis has said, "From the word 'go' Elijah and I became close friends. When I'd go to the library to write, it was as if he were anxiously waiting for me, waiting to tell about his life, his worries, his adventures." Today Christopher Paul Curtis still lives in Michigan, the setting of his acclaimed novel *Bud, Not Buddy*.

Author's Purpose

Elijah and his neighbors in Buxton speak in a dialect. What is dialect, and why does the author include it in this historical novel?

Respond to Reading

Summarize

Use important details from *Elijah of Buxton* to summarize how Elijah discovered his own inner strength. Information from your Cause and Effect Chart may help you.

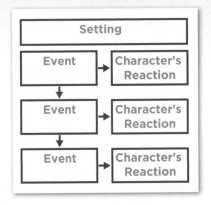

Setting

Event	→	Character's Reaction
Event	→	Character's Reaction
Event	→	Character's Reaction

Text Evidence

1. What details in the text help you to identify *Elijah of Buxton* as a work of historical fiction? Give at least two details from the story to support your answer. **GENRE**

2. Why are Elijah and his mother upset about the letter addressed to Mrs. Holton even before the letter has been opened? Give two details to support your answer. **CAUSE AND EFFECT**

3. On page 357 Elijah says, "This was more proof that a mule is way better than a horse." How does knowing the adage "It is better to ride on a mule that carries me than a horse that throws me" help you understand Elijah's statement? **ADAGES AND PROVERBS**

4. Elijah wants his mother to notice how grown up he has become. Write about how reading the letter changes how Elijah's mother sees him and how he feels about himself. **WRITE ABOUT READING**

Make Connections

What are some ways in which people show their inner strength in *Elijah of Buxton*? **ESSENTIAL QUESTION**

What other situations might cause people to draw on their inner strength? What can help people remain strong in the face of challenges? **TEXT TO WORLD**

Compare Texts

Read how some Africans regain a special power and soar to freedom after they are captured and sold into slavery.

Told by Virginia Hamilton
Illustrated by Leonard and Diane Dillon

The People *Could Fly*

What if people could escape their misery, simply by flying away? In this traditional black folktale, that's what some of the men and women who were brought to America as slaves decide to do. **Undaunted** by the Driver's whip, an old man named Toby gives the laboring slaves the **fortitude**—and the magic—to lift themselves off the ground and leave. And the ones who cannot fly remain to tell their story.

They say the people could fly. Say that long ago in Africa, some of the people knew magic. And they would walk up on the air like climbin up on a gate. And they flew like blackbirds over the fields. Black, shiny wings flappin against the blue up there.

Then, many of the people were captured for Slavery. The ones that could fly shed their wings. They couldn't take their wings across the water on the slave ships. Too crowded, don't you know.

The folks were full of misery, then. Got sick with the up and down of the sea. So they forgot about flyin when they could no longer breathe the sweet scent of Africa.

Say the people who could fly kept their power, although they shed their wings. They kept their secret magic in the land of slavery. They looked the same as the other people from Africa who had been coming over, who had dark skin. Say you couldn't tell anymore one who could fly from one who couldn't.

One such who could was an old man, call him Toby. And standin tall, yet afraid, was a young woman who once had wings. Call her Sarah. Now Sarah carried a babe tied to her back. She trembled to be so hard worked and scorned.

The slaves labored in the fields from sunup to sundown. The owner of the slaves callin himself their Master. Say he was a hard lump of clay. A hard, glinty coal. A hard rock pile, wouldn't be moved. His Overseer on horseback pointed out the slaves who were slowin down. So the one called Driver cracked his whip over the slow ones to make them move faster. That whip was a slice-open cut of pain. So they did move faster. Had to.

Sarah hoed and chopped the row as the babe on her back slept.

Say the child grew hungry. That babe started up bawling too loud. Sarah couldn't stop to feed it. Couldn't stop to soothe and quiet it down. She let it cry. She didn't want to. She had no heart to croon to it.

"Keep that thing quiet," called the Overseer. He pointed his finger at the babe. The woman scrunched low. The Driver cracked his whip across the babe anyhow. The babe hollered like any hurt child, and the woman fell to earth.

The old man that was there, Toby, came and helped her to her feet.

"I must go soon," she told him.

"Soon," he said.

Sarah couldn't stand up straight any longer. She was too weak. The sun burned her face. The babe cried and cried, "Pity me, oh, pity me," say it sounded like. Sarah was so sad and starvin, she sat down in a row.

"Get up, you black cow," called the Overseer. He pointed his hand, and the Driver's whip snarled around Sarah's legs. Her sack dress tore into rags. Her legs bled onto the earth. She couldn't get up.

Toby was there where there was no one to help her and the babe.

"Now, before it's too late," panted Sarah. "Now, Father!"

"Yes, Daughter, the time is come," Toby answered. "Go, as you know how to go!"

He raised his arms, holding them out to her. "*Kum . . . yali, kum buba tambe,*" and more magic words, said so quickly, they sounded like whispers and sighs.

The young woman lifted one foot on the air. Then the other. She flew clumsily at first, with the child now held tightly in her arms. Then she felt the magic, the African mystery. Say she rose just as free as a bird. As light as a feather.

The Overseer rode after her, hollerin. Sarah flew over the fences. She flew over the woods. Tall trees could not snag her. Nor could the Overseer. She flew like an eagle now, until she was gone from sight. No one dared speak about it. Couldn't believe it. But it was, because they that was there saw that it was.

Say the next day was dead hot in the fields. A young man slave fell from the heat. The Driver come and whipped him. Toby come over and spoke words to the fallen one. The words of ancient Africa once heard are never remembered completely. The young man forgot them as soon as he heard them. They went way inside him. He got up and rolled over on the air. He rode it awhile. And he flew away.

Another and another fell from the heat. Toby was there. He cried out to the fallen and reached his arms out to them. "*Kum kunka yali, kum . . . tambe!*" Whispers and sighs. And they too rose on the air. They rode the hot breezes. The ones flyin were black and shinin sticks, wheelin above the head of the Overseer. They crossed the rows, the fields, the fences, the streams, and were away.

"Seize the old man!" cried the Overseer. "I heard him say the magic *words*. Seize him!"

The one callin himself Master come runnin. The Driver got his whip ready to curl around old Toby and tie him up. The slaveowner took his hip gun from its place. He meant to kill old, black Toby.

But Toby just laughed. Say he threw back his head and said, "Hee, hee! Don't you know who I am? Don't you know some of us in this field?" He said it to their faces. "We are the ones who fly!"

And he sighed the ancient words that were a dark promise. He said them all around to the others in the field under the whip, ". . . *buba yali . . . buba tambe. . . .*"

There was a great outcryin. The bent backs straighted up. Old and young who were called slaves and could fly joined hands. Say like they would ring-sing.

374

But they didn't shuffle in a circle. They didn't sing. They rose on the air. They flew in a flock that was black against the heavenly blue. Black crows or black shadows. It didn't matter, they went so high. Way above the plantation, way over the slavery land. Say they flew away to *Free-dom.*

And the old man, old Toby, flew behind them, takin care of them. He wasn't cryin. He wasn't laughin. He was the seer. His gaze fell on the plantation where the slaves who could not fly waited.

"*Take us with you!*" Their looks spoke it but they were afraid to shout it. Toby couldn't take them with him. Hadn't the time to teach them to fly.

They must wait for a chance to run.

"Goodie-bye!" The old man called Toby spoke to them, poor souls! And he was flyin gone.

So they say. The Overseer told it. The one called Master said it was a lie, a trick of the light. The Driver kept his mouth shut.

The slaves who could not fly told about the people who could fly to their children. When they were free. When they sat close before the fire in the free land, they told it. They did so love firelight and *Free-dom,* and tellin.

They say that the children of the ones who could not fly told their children. And now, me, I have told it to you.

Make Connections

How do characters in *The People Could Fly* show their inner strength? **ESSENTIAL QUESTION**

What are some different ways people have called upon their inner strength in the selections you have read? **TEXT TO TEXT**

BEFORE COLUMBUS

THE AMERICAS OF 1491

BY CHARLES C. MANN

Reprinted with the permission of Atheneum Books for Young Readers, an imprint of Simon & Schuster Children's Publishing Division from BEFORE COLUMBUS: The Americas of 1491 by Charles C. Mann. Copyright © 2009 by Charles C. Mann and Downtown Bookworks Inc.

Essential Question

How do people benefit from innovation?

Read how people in present-day Mexico and Central America created corn more than 6,000 years ago.

 Go Digital!

What was life like in the Americas before Christopher Columbus made his now famous voyage in 1492, and contact was established between Europe and the "New World"? Author Charles C. Mann argues that Native Americans created societies that were older, larger, and more highly developed than we once believed. In this chapter from his book *Before Columbus: The Americas of 1491*, Mann examines the development of corn, an important and popular food source, and its beginnings in Mexico and Central America thousands of years ago.

I f you asked modern scientists to name the world's greatest achievements in genetic engineering, you might be surprised by one of their low-tech answers: maize.

Scientists know that maize, called "corn" in the United States, was created more than 6,000 years ago. Although exactly how this well-known plant was invented is still a mystery, they do know where it was invented—in the narrow "waist" of southern Mexico. This jumble of mountains, beaches, wet tropical forests, and dry plains is the most ecologically diverse part of Mesoamerica. Today, it is home to more than a dozen different Indian groups, but the human history of these hills and valleys stretches far into the past.

FROM HUNTING TO GATHERING TO FARMING

About 11,500 years ago a group of Paleoindians was living in caves in what is now the Mexican state of Puebla. These people were hunters, but they did not bring down mastodons and mammoths. Those huge species were already extinct. Instead, the hunters preyed on smaller game, such as deer and jackrabbits. Now and then they even feasted on giant turtles (which were probably a lot easier to catch than the fast-moving deer and rabbits.)

Over the next 2,000 years, though, game animals grew scarce. Maybe the people of the area had been too successful at hunting. Maybe, as the climate grew slowly hotter and drier, the grasslands where the animals lived shrank, and so the animal populations shrank, as well. Perhaps the situation was a combination of these two reasons. Whatever the explanation, hunters of Puebla and the neighboring state of Oaxaca turned to plants for more of their food.

Their lives—and their diets—were shaped by the rhythm of the seasons. For most of the year, individual families lived by themselves, moving from place to place. During the winter, they hunted. In spring and fall, they gathered seeds and fruits. By summer, one of their favorite foods—cactus leaves—was plentiful enough to feed larger groups. With enough food available, 25 or 30 people might gather in a band to spend the season together.

Opposite: Some of the many different varieties of maize still grown in southern Mexico.

Meanwhile, the people kept learning about their environment. They discovered that the thick-leaved, cactus-like agave plants could be eaten if they were first roasted over a fire. They found a way to make acorns into nutritious food: grind them into powder, then soak the powder in water and let it dry. Along the way, people might have noticed that seeds they threw into the garbage one year would sprout as new plants the next year. At some point, they started to intentionally scatter seeds, so that they would have food to gather during the next growing season. They were practicing agriculture.

This happened in many places across southern Mexico. People began to grow food crops that are still harvested across Mesoamerica today—squash, gourds, and peppers. Then came maize.

THE MYSTERY OF MAIZE

If when you think of corn, you see yellow kernels, Mexican maize might surprise you. It can be red, blue, yellow, orange, black, pink, purple, creamy white, and even multicolored. People in one valley may grow cobs the size of a baby's hand, with little red kernels no bigger than grains of rice that turn into tiny puffs when they are popped. In the next valley, maize plants produce two-foot-long cobs, with big fluffy kernels that people float in their soup.

Maize is a cereal, like wheat, rice, barley, and many other grains, but it looks and acts differently from the rest. Other cereals can reproduce themselves by scattering their grains. Maize kernels, which are a plant's seeds, are wrapped in a tough husk and don't scatter naturally. This means that maize can't reproduce on its own—it has to be planted by people. Other cereals grew wild before people began to farm them, and in many places they still grow wild today. No wild ancestor of maize has ever been found, however. So where did it come from?

No wild ancestor of maize has ever been found.

In the 1960s, an archaeological team combed the Tehuacán Valley in Puebla, Central Mexico, for signs of early agriculture. The archaeologists sifted through 49 caves before they found anything. In the fiftieth site, they found ancient maize cobs no bigger than a small toe.

All in all, the team found more than 23,000 whole or broken maize cobs in the valley. These little cobs became the ammunition in a debate about the origins of maize. One side thought that maize must have come from a wild ancestor plant that is now extinct. This vanished plant interbred long ago with wild grasses, and the result was maize.

The other side in the debate claimed maize was descended from its closest known relative, teosinte, a kind of wild mountain grass. Teosinte looks nothing like maize, though, and it is not a practical food source. Its hard, woody seeds are **sparse**. A whole ear of teosinte has less nutritional value than a single kernel of maize. Plant scientists couldn't explain how teosinte might have evolved naturally into maize.

On the left is a wild grass called teosinte, the cob of which is less than two inches long. On the right is a maize cob produced by crossing teosinte with a type of modern South American maize. It looks a lot like the oldest known maize cobs and may offer a clue as to how people created maize.

But some experts think maize came from a mutated form of teosinte. Mutations occur naturally in nature, when the genetic codes of parent plants or animals get slightly scrambled in their offspring. The Indians might have noticed that a **mutated** form of teosinte seemed a little more useful. They could have picked through strands of teosinte, looking for the plants with the useful qualities, then bred them with each other to create a new generation of plants. Experts think that skilled, determined plant breeders could have turned the right teosinte mutations into maize in just ten years.

Maybe teosinte is not the answer. Another idea about the origin of maize is that Indians came across a hybrid cereal plant that had come about by chance when two different kinds of wild grasses hybridized, or crossbred. The Indians realized that they could purposely mix two kinds of grasses by fertilizing one kind with pollen from the other kind. In this way, they could create something new: maize.

To historians, it doesn't really matter whether maize came from teosinte or from other grasses. The key thing is that maize was created by the Indians in a bold act of biological **manipulation**. The result was a hardy, nutritious new food source that would change agriculture—and society— in Mesoamerica and beyond.

MILPA

The Indians of Mesoamerica did more than invent maize. They also perfected the ideal way of growing it. They created the *milpa*, a system of agriculture that has been in use in Mesoamerica for thousands of years.

The word *milpa* means "maize field," but its true meaning is more complex. A *milpa* is a field in which farmers plant many different crops at the same time. In addition to maize, a *milpa* often contains several kinds of beans and squash, avocados, sweet potatoes, tomatoes, chili peppers, melons, and more.

In nature, wild beans can grow next to teosinte. When this happens, the beans benefit because they can use the tall teosinte stalks to climb toward the sun. The teosinte benefits because the beans' roots add **nutrients** to the soil. Indians either invented this arrangement on their own or adopted it after seeing it in the wild. They put corn and beans together in their *milpa* and added even more plants.

A *milpa* is the beginning of a well-balanced diet. A person who ate only maize would be unhealthy because maize doesn't have two amino acids that the human body needs. Those acids are found in beans, but beans lack another acid, called methionine, that maize just happens to have. Together, though, beans and maize make a complete meal. You could live for a pretty long time on just those two foods, but after a while, your body would miss the vitamins and healthy fats that come from other *milpa* crops, such as squash and avocados.

Below: Wheeled jaguar from Veracruz, Mexico

WHY NO WHEELS?

When the Europeans arrived in the Americas, the Indians had no wheeled vehicles. No carts, wagons, chariots, or wheelbarrows. They did not even have wheels for grinding grain or making pottery, as some other cultures did.

At several places in Mexico, though, archaeologists have found toy-sized figurines, such as dogs and jaguars, with wheels. If the Mesoamericans equipped their toys or models with wheels, why didn't they make bigger wheels and use them on wagons?

Maybe they did not have livestock to pull wagons. There were no domestic horses or cattle in the Americas until the Europeans introduced them. Even with animals, people in wet, heavily forested, and mountainous areas might not have had much use for wheels, because wagons could not travel easily over the ground.

A better reason is simply that even complex societies do not always invent every possible kind of complex technology. The lack of a particular piece of technology doesn't make a civilization inferior. Millions of Europeans, for example, plowed their fields with a painfully **inefficient** plow for centuries after the Chinese had come up with a much better design. One culture's achievement may be another culture's blind spot.

STOP AND CHECK

Reread In what ways does the *milpa* system of agriculture benefit both people and plants? Reread to check your understanding.

bpk, Berlin/Ethnologisches Museum/Waltraud Schneider-Schütz/Art Resource, NY

Growing different kinds of plants together is much better than growing a single crop.

The *milpa* has been called one of the most successful of all human inventions, and not just because it is nutritious. The *milpa* can also let people farm the land without wearing out the soil. Today, farmers in Europe and Asia usually plant just one crop in a field. This can drain the soil of nutrients, so the farmers have to add fertilizer, which may bring new problems. This method is expensive, and fertilizer that runs off fields in rainwater may end up in streams, rivers, or the ocean, where it causes an excess growth of the tiny plants known as algae, unbalancing the ecosystem.

Most crops drain the soil of nitrogen, which must be replaced with fertilizer. The *milpa's* beans, however, put nitrogen into the soil. In addition, by growing multiple crops at the same time, *milpa* farmers imitate the variety found in natural ecosystems. Growing different kinds of plants together is, from an environmental point of view, often much better than growing a single crop. It protects the soil from erosion and nourishes the helpful bacteria and other microorganisms in the soil. The *milpa* is the only known system of farming that has kept some fields productive for more than 4,000 years of constant use. By studying traditional *milpa* farming, agricultural scientists may learn techniques that will help modern **industrial** farmers preserve the health of their soils.

LANDSCAPES OF FOOD

Before people in the ancient Middle East began to farm wheat, they gathered the grain from wild wheat. Cereal grasses grew naturally across large stretches of the land. People knew what it was like to stand in a field of wheat stretching to the horizon. People in Mesoamerica had never encountered fields of wild grain, though. When the Mesoamericans invented maize, they also invented the grain field for themselves. This landscape of food was completely new in the Americas. This may be why maize played such an important role in many Native American religions. It was not something the Indians took for granted.

MAIZE AROUND THE WORLD

Maize, the product of Native American genetic engineering, was carried to other parts of the world by Europeans after the fifteenth century. Maize quickly became an important food in places where nothing like it had ever grown before.

People in many parts of Europe adopted maize as a staple grain. Unfortunately, they didn't know how to combine maize and beans in a nutritionally complete diet as the Mesoamericans did. Europeans in some regions ate so much maize that they suffered from pellagra. This disease is caused by a lack of niacin (vitamin B3). Maize has niacin, but it is bound up in compounds that the body can't digest unless it has been treated with a type of chemical called alkali. When Mesoamericans make tortillas, they soak the maize in lime, which makes the niacin in the maize useable by the body. Europeans, however, did not know how to make tortillas.

In Africa, maize became part of a complex web of interconnections. Europeans introduced American maize to Africa, and by the end of the sixteenth century, Africans were raising maize as well as other American foods, including peanuts and manioc. These new crops boosted Africa's food production, leading to a population boom just at the time the Europeans were taking millions of Africans as slaves for their mines and plantations in the Americas. In this way, maize, the foundation of Mesoamerican civilization, may have fed the terrible slave trade.

A Huichol farmer harvests maize in the Sierra Madre Occidental Mountains in Mexico.

385

Maize and the *milpa* slowly spread beyond their birthplaces in Mesoamerica. To the south, maize traveled all the way to Peru and Chile in South America. The people of these Andean lands had developed their own agriculture based on potatoes, but still they prized maize as a luxury item. (Maize didn't seem to catch on in the Amazon basin, though. Most researchers think that manioc, or cassava, as it is sometimes called, was already the staple food there.)

Maize traveled north, too. By the time the Pilgrims came to New England in the seventeenth century, the coast was lined with fields of mixed maize, beans, and squash. In some places, the fields stretched for miles inland from the coast.

A carving of the Maya corn god from AD 500.

First, though, maize conquered Mesoamerica. Archaeologists have found signs that people in southern Mexico were clearing large areas of land for *milpa* as long ago as 2000 to 1500 BC. Maize was part of a great explosion of creativity that took place in Mesoamerica at that time.

Great civilizations were about to rise in Mesoamerica. Maize would feed the growing populations that built big new urban centers. It would nourish workers, soldiers, and priests. In their monuments and artworks, the people of these civilizations would honor maize. Stone carvings would show ears of maize springing from the skulls of the gods and decorating the headdresses of kings.

STOP AND CHECK

Reread What did the Mesoamericans understand about maize that many Europeans did not? Reread to check your understanding.

Mesoamerica, 1000 BC–AD 1000

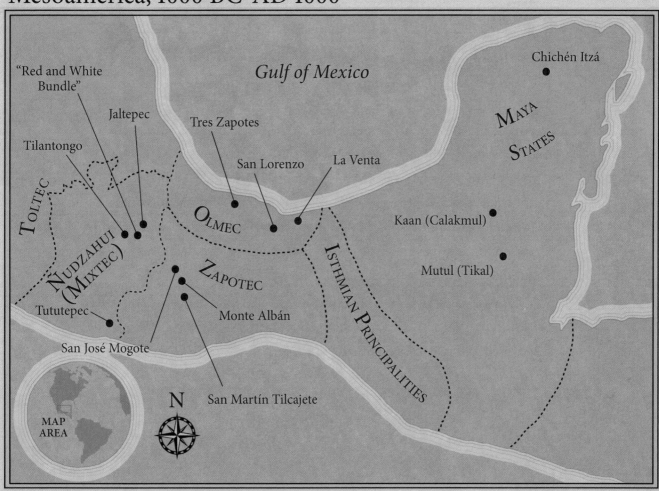

For thousands of years, Mesoamerica was a wellspring of cultural innovation and growth. This map shows some of the most important societies that lived there over a two-thousand-year span.

ABOUT THE AUTHOR

Charles C. Mann

has written many books and magazine articles about science and technology. *Before Columbus* is an adaptation of his book *1491*, which won a U.S. National Academy of Sciences' Keck award for best science book of the year.

Two events drew Mann to this subject matter. First, the summer before seventh grade, his family moved from Michigan to the Pacific Northwest, where the influence and presence of Native Americans were much more visible. Then, as an adult journalist, Mann travelled to the Yucatán Peninsula in Mexico. He realized that in 1492 Christopher Columbus and the explorers that followed him had stumbled across an entire hemisphere—nearly half of the world—full of people whose cultures had developed separately from cultures in Europe and Asia. This fact fascinated Mann and he decided to write about them.

Mann has also written a sequel to *Before Columbus* and *1491*. The book explores how civilization changed after the nations of Europe discovered and began to colonize both North and South America.

Author's Purpose

The author includes a map in the selection that shows the location of different cultures over a 2,000-year span. How does the map help you to understand where these cultures were located in relation to the United States?

RESPOND TO READING

Summarize

Use important details from *Before Columbus: The Americas of 1491* to summarize how advances in farming made by Native American people were of benefit to the entire world. Information from your Cause and Effect Chart may help you.

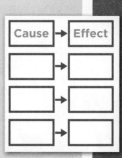

Cause	→	Effect
	→	
	→	
	→	

Text Evidence

1. How do you know that *Before Columbus* is an example of expository text? Identify at least two details from the text that support your answer. **GENRE**

2. What effect did the development of maize have on the diets of people around the world? Include three details in your answer. **CAUSE AND EFFECT**

3. What is the meaning of the word *benefit* on page 382? Use the cause-and-effect relationship in the text as a context clue to help you figure out the meaning. **CONTEXT CLUES**

4. Write about the advantages of *milpa* and how it changed farming forever. **WRITE ABOUT READING**

Make Connections

Talk about how people's lives have been helped by innovations in farming. **ESSENTIAL QUESTION**

Identify an interesting fact you learned about the development of maize. How has the development of corn affected your diet? **TEXT TO WORLD**

Compare Texts
Read how understanding ancient ways of treating illness can lead to innovations in medicine.

Looking Back to
Move Forward

A Roman ship lost beneath the sea over 2,000 years ago may hold clues about medicines used in ancient times.

Ancient Cures

Over two decades ago, two divers plunged into the murky depths of the Mediterranean Sea off the coast of Italy. Their mission was the exploration of a 50-foot long shipwreck. It had been lost beneath the waves over 2,000 years ago. As they trained their underwater lights across the vast hulk, they spotted amphorae—vases used for holding olive oil and other products. But a close inspection revealed something much more remarkable. Pulled from the wreck, the explorers found tin-lined wooden containers. They held tablets the size of small coins.

Scientists later found that these tablets were probably pills that the ship's sailors would have swallowed with water, perhaps when they felt seasick. This sort of medicine is nothing new to us today. At the time, however, they must have been something new, for they may be the oldest pills ever discovered.

tea made from the yarrow plant was believed to stop bleeding inside the body.

People long ago knew which plants were effective in treating illness but they didn't know why they were effective. Today, scientists have a much keener understanding of the medicinal value of plants. They recognize that some plants contain chemicals that help them to survive and defend themselves against disease or animals that might eat them. Sometimes, these chemicals are harmful to humans, making the plants poisonous if eaten. However, in a great many other cases, the chemicals that protect the plants are extremely effective in treating human ailments and disease as well.

Today's Medicines

The majority of today's most common medicines initially came from natural resources. Often they are still derived from the original herbal sources. In some cases, however, a natural resource used in making a medicine has become too expensive or too rare. Researchers have had to use innovative technologies to make a synthetic version of the natural compound. Sometimes these human made versions also involve a **modification** of the natural compound.

Aspirin is one of today's most commonly used medicines. It evolved from chemical compounds found in

This evidence confirms the notion that throughout history, people have looked for ways to treat and cure disease. Roots, herbs, and other plants were not just considered food. They often provided effective treatment for specific symptoms and illnesses.

A Chinese book, thousands of years old, lists 365 medicinal plants and their uses. The ancient Egyptians also used a wide variety of plant sources to treat sickness. They used the spice coriander to calm upset stomachs. Honey was spread on cuts and wounds. It proved ideal because bacteria cannot grow in honey. In Europe during the Middle Ages,

A Natural Remedy

The quinine tree can be found in South America.

Bark is taken from the quinine tree.

Shredded bark is turned into a powder.

The powder is used in pills and other medicine.

the leaves and bark of the willow tree. Quinine is a drug that is used to treat lupus, a disease that makes it hard to fight other illnesses. Quinine can now be made synthetically. But it originally came from the bark of a tree that grows in South America. Remarkably, the United States National Cancer Institute has identified approximately 3,000 plants from which, they believe, anti-cancer drugs are or can be made.

Biodiversity on Earth

Scientists estimate that there may be as many as a half-million plant species on Earth. The majority are found in the world's rainforests. Yet less than 1% of these plant species have been thoroughly investigated for their potential use as medicine.

Researchers don't view the remaining 99% as a **surplus** but rather an essential resource. But how can scientists ever identify and test so many plant species? Many scientists are turning for guidance to people around the world who still use traditional plant remedies.

Rainforest Remedies

The World Health Organization (WHO) estimates that patients who still use plant remedies make up about 80% of the world's population. The WHO suggests that some people seek these cures because certain medicines are too expensive and not readily available. And some use the plants simply because they work.

Remarkably, a study in the 1990s found that 86% of the plants used by native healers on the island of Samoa were effective in treating human ailments. Many researchers are eager to explore the biodiversity of the world's rainforests. But the rainforests themselves are shrinking. Trees and other plants have been cut down to make farms and grazing pasture. As forests are lost, the native groups who have lived in them are being displaced. Their knowledge of medicinal cures is being lost. As a result, many researchers have increased their efforts to study the plants that grow in the rainforests.

Many modern medicines come from natural sources.

Still others are working tirelessly to try to protect the rainforests and the people who inhabit them. In doing so, they hope to ensure the preservation of treatments and cures that have been handed down for generations.

Researchers also continue to look at the past in order to investigate cures that were used long ago. One such opportunity presented itself with the discovery of that ancient Roman shipwreck in the Mediterranean. Although the pills were discovered in 1989, recent advances in DNA research are now making it possible to better understand what chemical compounds these pills contained. This research will also help determine what illnesses the pills were used to treat. The hope is that advances in technology will build upon ancient wisdom.

Make Connections

How have plants provided medical treatments for people throughout history? **ESSENTIAL QUESTION**

How does investigating the use of plants for medicine as well as food help us to learn more about the innovative ways people have used them? **TEXT TO TEXT**

PLANET HUNTER

Geoff Marcy
and the Search for Other Earths

By Vicki Oransky Wittenstein

Essential Question

How does technology lead to discoveries?

Read about the methods a group of scientists are using to discover planets outside of our solar system.

 Go Digital!

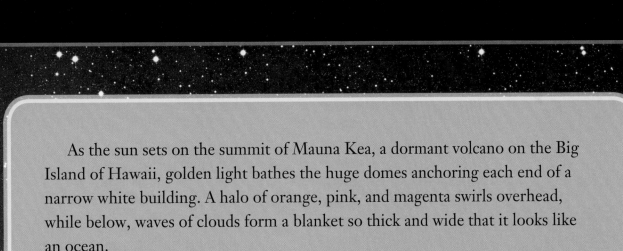

As the sun sets on the summit of Mauna Kea, a dormant volcano on the Big Island of Hawaii, golden light bathes the huge domes anchoring each end of a narrow white building. A halo of orange, pink, and magenta swirls overhead, while below, waves of clouds form a blanket so thick and wide that it looks like an ocean.

The weather on the shore is hot and humid. But here at almost fourteen thousand feet above sea level, temperatures rapidly drop below 20 degrees Fahrenheit, even in the summer. No trees or plants grow on the rounded hills. Coffee-colored lava and gray cinder cover the mountaintop and crunch underfoot as workers arrive. Except for the occasional howl of the wind, all is silent.

TEXT: *Planet Hunter* by Vicki Oransky Wittenstein. Copyright © 2010 by Vicki Oransky Wittenstein. Published by Boyds Mills Press. Reprinted by permission.

Gentle hills (in the background, at right) dot the remote summit of Mauna Kea. They are known as pu'u *in Hawaiian.*

When the sky begins to darken, a loud buzzer warns any technicians walking on the decks and catwalks inside the domes. A motor **drones** as the top and bottom shutters of one of the domes open. The dome rotates, rumbling like a train as its steel wheels roll along a track at the base. One of the twin telescopes at the W. M. Keck Observatory points to the stars. The night's viewing is about to begin.

Farther down the mountain, about two thousand feet above sea level, lies the W. M. Keck Observatory Headquarters. From there, astronomers can operate the telescope, using a real-time video connection between headquarters and the observatory. Tonight, Dr. Geoffrey W. Marcy, an astronomer who hunts for planets, is at headquarters. Jason McIlroy, an observing assistant, mans the telescope on the summit.

Mist hides the sky from headquarters, but Geoff Marcy isn't worried. He studies a computer screen that details the weather conditions at the summit. "Wow, the viewing is excellent, Jason," Marcy says into a microphone.

The Keck I telescope peers through the dome opening into the starry night. The Keck I and Keck II telescopes are the largest twin optical telescopes in the world. Marcy uses the Keck I.

Astronomers like Marcy no longer look directly through a telescope eyepiece. Instead, a device similar to a digital camera records the image in the telescope. The image is transmitted to computers for analysis.

The time is almost 7:00 P.M., the beginning of Marcy's block of time to use the telescope. A long night of planet hunting stretches ahead. He will finish at 5:30 in the morning. For the next three days, Marcy will sleep during the day, play tennis late in the afternoon, eat a quick dinner, and then go to the telescope control room at 7:00 P.M. He keeps his fingers crossed that the good weather will hold. Telescope time is costly, and the instrument is sensitive. When the weather is bad, the telescope shuts down for the night.

Tonight, Marcy is excited: maybe he will find another distant planet orbiting a star like our Sun. Maybe this time the planet will be similar to Earth—the kind of planet most likely to **sustain** life.

Since 1995, Marcy, Dr. Paul Butler, and their co-workers have discovered or helped to discover many planets found outside our solar system, which are known as extrasolar planets. Dr. Debra Fischer, a key member of the team, helps analyze the collected data. As the team develops more and more precise search techniques, Marcy comes closer to his dream of finding a small, rocky, Earth-like planet, one that might harbor life. In 2006, the team announced one of the smallest planets discovered so far. This planet, which orbits the star Gliese 876, is about six times more massive than Earth. The planet might seem large, but most of the known extrasolar planets are even bigger. They are about three hundred times more massive than Earth, which puts them in a class with Jupiter and Saturn.

More recent discoveries have been equally thrilling. In 2007, for the first time, astronomers determined the composition of an extrasolar planet by figuring out the planet's density. This planet, which orbits the star Gliese 436, is made of rock and water, similar to our Earth. Later that year, Marcy's team announced their finding of a fifth planet orbiting the star 55 Cancri,

This artist's interpretation of a planet forming around a distant star looks like Saturn might have looked when it formed in our own solar system.

Jason McIlroy operates the telescope at the summit. McIlroy and Marcy can see each other by video as they work. Marcy is shown in the monitor above McIlroy's desk.

the first time five extrasolar planets have been discovered orbiting one star. As of this writing, the structure of this planetary system is the closest we know of to our own solar system. And new planetary systems are being discovered all the time, by Marcy's team and by others.

"Is the Earth a one-in-a-thousand shot, a one-in-a-million shot?" Marcy wonders. He adjusts the controls on one of the fourteen computers that line the wall of the telescope control room. "Surely in this huge universe there are other planets that have conditions ripe for life. But are there ten in the Milky Way **galaxy**? A billion? Or is there only one, our Earth? And if there's a planet like Earth, how likely is it to have intelligent life?"

Stars and planets are continually forming in the universe. Marcy estimates that of the two hundred billion stars in our Milky Way galaxy, about 10 percent, or 20 billion, have planetary systems. About one quarter, or five billion, of these planetary systems probably have a rocky planet like Earth, ripe for life. That means there could be billions of Earth-like planets in our galaxy. Let's suppose, **conservatively**, that intelligent species live on only one Earth-like planet in a million. According to Marcy, the Milky Way then would have thousands of advanced civilizations.

Questions like these spurred Marcy to begin hunting for planets in 1985. At the time, some scientists thought other planets might lie outside our solar system, but no one had ever found one. Marcy wanted evidence. With Butler's help, Marcy refined and adapted a detection method, called Doppler spectroscopy. They worked for ten years to find their first planet.

Marcy doesn't detect extrasolar planets while he actually uses the telescope. The discovery occurs much later, after Marcy and his team have charted a star's movement and analyzed the data collected from years of observations.

"As a scientist, I want to be 100 percent certain before announcing a new planet," Marcy says. "For example, **colleagues** can say, 'How can you be absolutely sure there is a large planet like Jupiter out there?' Well, Jupiter takes twelve years to orbit the Sun. That means we have to chart a Jupiter-like planet for at least twelve years, plus some more, to verify that the planet is repeating its orbit." Despite the challenges of planet hunting, Marcy keeps searching. "**Ultimately**, you have to be passionate and really care about the planets," he says. "You are trying to do something that is part of you, as well as something great for the rest of the world."

STOP AND CHECK

Reread Why does it take Marcy and other astronomers such a long time to find evidence of an extrasolar planet? Reread to check your understanding.

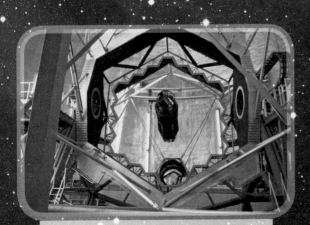

Each Keck telescope weighs roughly three hundred tons and is as tall as an eight-story building. The primary mirror in each is made up of thirty-six individual glass hexagons coated with a thin film of shiny aluminum. Above, the giant lens has been outlined in red.

Somewhere in the Milky Way galaxy, a rocky planet similar to Earth may be orbiting a Sun-like star. It may even harbor life.

Planet Hunter: Debra Fischer

Dr. Debra Fischer analyzed the data that revealed three Jupiter-sized planets orbiting the star Upsilon Andromedae. Her examination of star movements was crucial in the discovery of 55 Cancri f, the fifth planet orbiting the star 55 Cancri. Since then, she and her colleague Jeff Valenti have analyzed more than one thousand stars. They hope to learn more about how planets form.

The Upsilon Andromedae system held surprises. The first planet lies so close to the star that it completes an orbit in only four days. The second and third planets are about as far from their star as Venus and Mars are from the Sun. "I realized at a gut level that the process of forming planets must be easier than scientists had appreciated before," Fischer says. "How else could three Jupiter-size planets be crammed into the inner part of the Upsilon Andromedae system?"

Fischer is also hunting for Earth-like planets around the stars Alpha Centauri A and B, a double-star system and our closest neighbor. Says Fischer, "If you ever want to travel to another star system—too hard now!—this would be a likely destination."

In this artist's interpretation, a Jupiter-size planet is crossing in front of its parent star. So far, most of the planets detected have been the size of Jupiter or larger.

In the telescope control room at Keck Observatory's headquarters, Marcy checks the various computer screens. "Almost ready to start, Jason," he says into the microphone to McIlroy, the technician at the summit. Marcy watches McIlroy on the video screen mounted above the computers.

"Let's take a shot of the sky and see if it's dark enough," Marcy adds. He wants only pure starlight to enter the telescope.

"Right," McIlroy says. In the video screen, he nods.

Marcy settles into a swivel chair in front of the four main computers. "Anyone can have a telescope," he says, "but not everyone has a spectrometer."

A telescope alone, even one as powerful as the Keck I, cannot detect a planet outside our solar system. From Earth, a star's light is so bright that it washes out the light from a planet.

"Think of a searchlight on top of a lighthouse," Marcy explains. "If there were a little firefly sitting on that lighthouse, you'd never know."

So how does Marcy find a planet if he can't see it? He uses a Doppler spectrometer. If a planet is orbiting a star, the star will wobble as it is pulled by the gravity of the planet. Depending on where the planet lies in its orbit around the star, the star will be tugged either toward the Earth or away from it.

"A planet's like a frisky dog being walked by its owner, the star," Marcy says. "For a star and its planet, the leash is gravity. You can figure out how large the planet is—its mass—by how much the star wobbles. You can also figure out the planet's speed, or velocity. The bigger the planet, the faster the star gets yanked around."

A spectrometer reveals a star's wobble by recording the changes in its light waves. Light shining from a star, like all light, travels in waves. All white light, including starlight, is made up of the visible colors of light mixed together. The colors of a rainbow—red, orange, yellow, green, blue, indigo, and violet— are known as the visible spectrum, and they always appear in this order because of the lengths of their waves.

The longest visible wavelengths are red. The wavelengths of orange, yellow, and so on become increasingly shorter. Violet has the shortest visible wavelength. When scientists talk about the wavelengths of light, they often refer to the "blue end" and the "red end" of the spectrum.

Doppler Effect

The Doppler effect is named after Christian Doppler, an Austrian physicist. He noticed the change in light waves when a light source, such as a star, moves toward or away from an observer, such as an astronomer on Earth. Sound waves also produce Doppler shifts. Listen carefully the next time you hear an ambulance pass by. The *EEEEEEowww* of a siren is shrill as the ambulance zooms closer and the sound waves are compressed. The pitch lowers as the ambulance passes and the sound waves are stretched out.

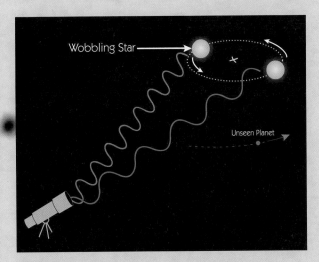

When starlight enters the telescope, the spectrum reveals a shift toward blue or red, depending on whether the star is moving toward earth (blue) or away from it (red). The blue waves of light are compressed. The red are stretched out.

NASA/Goddard Space Flight Center Scientific Visualization Studio

STOP AND CHECK

Reread If gravity can be seen as a leash, in what way is this similar to the movement of a star Marcy sees when a large planet is near it? Why would it be harder to see a small extrasolar planet than a large one? Reread and use evidence from the text in your answer.

The spectrometer is located to the right of the telescope, in the room with the door. The room is as big as a living room, about twenty by twenty feet, and is sealed to keep out dust and moisture.

Courtesy W. M. Keck Observatory

When light waves pass through something transparent, such as glass or water, the light slows down. When the speed decreases, the light bends, or refracts. If the light is bent sharply enough, as in a prism, the colors split apart from one another. Red light waves bend the least, followed by orange, then yellow, and so on. Violet light waves bend the most. When the waves bend and the colors split from one another, we see all the colors of the rainbow, or spectrum.

In a spectrometer, a device similar to a prism collects starlight through the telescope and separates it into a spectrum. Waves of starlight change depending on whether the star is moving away from or toward Earth. If the star is moving toward Earth, the waves are compressed and shift toward the blue end of the spectrum. Green light may look blue, for example, or orange light might look yellow. When the star moves away, the light waves are stretched out and shift toward the red end of the spectrum. Orange light may turn red, or blue light may look green. These changes in color are called Doppler shifts. Over time, a series of alternating redshifts and blueshifts indicate that a planet is causing a star to wobble.

Marcy uses a powerful spectrometer, known as the High Resolution Echelle Spectrometer (HIRES). It was built by a former member of the team, Dr. Steven Vogt, an astronomer at the University of California, Santa Cruz. Vogt continually improves and updates the spectrometer. The spectrometer at Keck is housed in a small room with steel walls, located next to the telescope's mirrors.

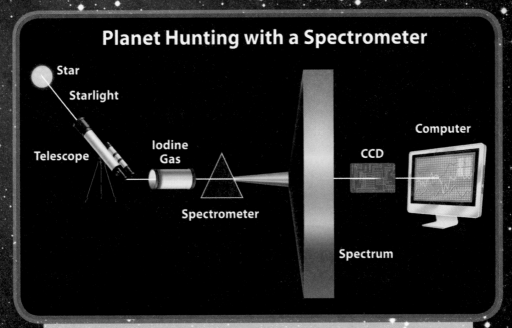

Planet Hunting with a Spectrometer

Star

Starlight

Telescope

Iodine Gas

Spectrometer

Computer

CCD

Spectrum

Starlight travels through the telescope and passes through a glass cylinder of iodine gas. The light continues through the spectrometer, which separates the light into a spectrum that shows patterns of both the gases around the star and the iodine in the cylinder. The spectrum is photographed by a device similar to a charge-coupled-device (CCD) light detector in a digital camera. A computer then stores and analyzes the image.

Debra Fischer observes a spectrum of starlight in the control room at Lick Observatory.

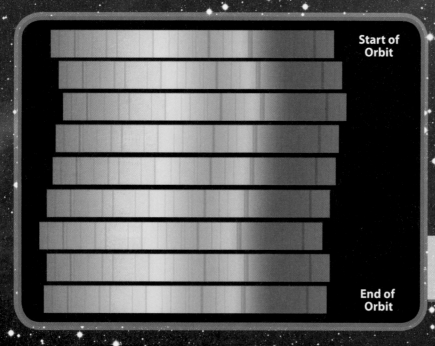

Start of Orbit

End of Orbit

These spectra of starlight show the small Doppler shifts that occur during one complete orbit of a star.

"The spectrometer works kind of like a digital camera," Marcy explains. "It takes a snapshot of the spectrum of light and records it."

Marcy points to a computer screen at the far left. "This computer controls the exposure time. It's like the control panel on a camera. Smaller stars, which give off less light, need longer exposure times than larger stars." He points to another screen just to the right. "And here's where all the spectrometer data is recorded. I'll take this back with me to the University of California, Berkeley, where we'll analyze it."

Marcy flips through a sheaf of papers stapled together. This is his script of the stars he'll observe tonight. "I've got the whole night planned out here, scene by scene," he says.

Marcy has spent hundred of hours selecting the stars. Currently, he is interested in about two thousand of them. Tonight, he will focus on eighty stars that he has been following for years. Although Marcy hunts for all kinds of extrasolar planets, he's most passionate about this group of stars—these are the ones he thinks are most likely to harbor Earth-like planets.

Over the next three nights, Marcy will page through his script, taking measurements of the same eighty stars. Perhaps after reviewing the new data, he will pare down his search to even fewer stars for his next visit. Maybe in this special group lies an Earth-like planet waiting to be discovered.

STOP AND CHECK

Ask and Answer Questions In what ways has the invention of the spectrometer made it easier to detect extra solar planets?

Beyond the Milky Way lie tens of billions of other galaxies, many similar to NGC 1232 (above), a large spiral galaxy that contains billions of stars and planets.

ABOUT THE AUTHOR

VICKI ORANSKY WITTENSTEIN

has been fascinated by stars and planets since she was a young girl growing up in New Jersey. Watching the stars one night while on a camping trip, she dreamed about other worlds that might be found beyond our solar system.

Wittenstein believes in pursuing all kinds of dreams. After graduating from college, she went to law school and then became an Assistant District Attorney. She switched careers to pursue her love of research and writing, and has written many magazine articles. When Wittenstein read about Geoff Marcy and his work attempting to find extrasolar planets, she wanted to know more. She was thrilled to be able to travel to Hawaii to interview Marcy and learn about the technology that makes his discoveries possible.

AUTHOR'S PURPOSE

The author uses photos, captions, and sidebars in this selection. How do these text features help you understand the topic?

RESPOND TO READING

SUMMARIZE

Use details from *Planet Hunter* to summarize what you have learned about the methods scientists use to discover extrasolar planets. Information from your Sequence Chart may help you.

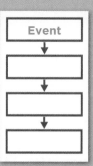

TEXT EVIDENCE

1. Identify two text features that help you to recognize *Planet Hunter* as an example of expository text. **GENRE**

2. What is Marcy's daily schedule when he is using the observatory telescope? Identify at least two words or phrases that signal a sequence of events. **SEQUENCE**

3. What is the meaning of the word *extrasolar* on page 398? Use context clues to help you figure out the meaning. **CONTEXT CLUES**

4. Write about the steps that scientists follow before they can announce the discovery of new planets. Describe them in order. **WRITE ABOUT READING**

Make Connections

How does technology, such as the Doppler Spectrometer, help Marcy and other scientists discover the existence of extrasolar planets? **ESSENTIAL QUESTION**

Identify the most interesting fact you learned about the scientists' discoveries. How could discoveries like this change people's perceptions of our world? **TEXT TO WORLD**

Compare Texts

Read how advanced technology in the year 2172 saves a colony on Mars from certain disaster.

EXCURSION TO MARS

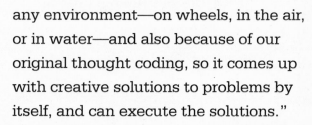

News from PERC

The eighth grade advanced teleportation class was working on some calculations when a hologram suddenly appeared in the front of the room. Everyone stopped talking and turned to look because the last time a hologram appeared in class it had bad news about a space disaster. Keisha bit her lip as she waited for the news.

"Congratulations, Keisha and Gene!" it said. "You have won the Planet Earth Robotics Competition for the year 2172!"

The class erupted in applause, and Keisha ran to hug the woman in the hologram that had made the announcement. Her arms just passed through the 3-D light image.

"I can't believe we won!" Keisha exclaimed as the hologram disappeared.

"Of course we won," said Gene, with his typical matter-of-fact tone, "and that's because our robot, Anisisbro, has the ability to navigate any environment—on wheels, in the air, or in water—and also because of our original thought coding, so it comes up with creative solutions to problems by itself, and can execute the solutions."

Keisha rolled her eyes and laughed. "I know all that, but you have to admit we had some serious competition. And think of the prize—a trip to the Mars Interplanetary-Life Research Colony with the best astronauts in the universe! No one in my family has ever been anywhere farther than the moon!"

"It's true that while I had anticipated this result, it certainly is satisfying to find ourselves the winners," Gene said with a slight smile.

Ralph Voltz

The Mission Begins

A week later, Keisha and Gene were in Houston, Texas, suiting up for the mission in sleek spacesuits that were made of a strong compression fabric, with built-in oxygen packs.

"Ready when you are," Keisha announced. Gene nodded, and the staff led them to the Daedalus 4000, a new kind of spacecraft that would take them to Mars.

Anisisbro rolled in front of Gene and Keisha onto the entry portal. Astronauts Clara Emmonds and Dominic Suiza gave a quick hello, barely taking their eyes off the instrument panel in front of them as they prepared for takeoff.

Before the teenagers knew it, they were lifting off and traveling through space. One whole wall of the spaceship served as a viewer that worked like a telescope to zoom in on other planets and moons in the solar system. The viewer was focused on Titan, Saturn's largest moon. "Wow! Look at that!" Keisha exclaimed. "A lake of liquid methane! I've never seen anything like that before."

"It's always intriguing to get a close-up view of other planets and moons," said Clara, stepping away from the controls now that they were safely in flight. "That's why Mars was chosen for the Interplanetary Life Research Colony. Over a hundred years ago, scientists discovered that Mars had some sort of water, and possibly bacteria, in underground streams, so that's why they built the colony there."

"Water has also been discovered on one of Saturn's other moons, right?" Keisha asked, and then she turned to Gene. "Didn't you tell me that we landed on Enceladus recently, or am I confusing that with another planet?"

"No, Enceladus, you're correct, but of course it was ice, not water," said Gene.

"Well, now that we have been on Mars for a number of years, we've been able to find water deep below the surface and the colony has running water," said Clara. "I'm sure you'll find the accommodations very comfortable."

"Can you imagine that first voyage to Mars?" said Dominic as he joined the group. "Now that we have warp speed, the whole trip only takes a few days. Back then, it took months!"

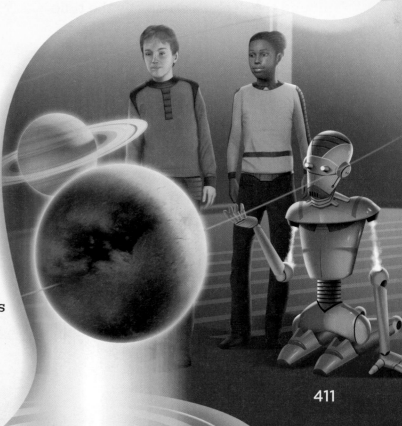

Alert, Alert!

That night, as Keisha and Gene were about to go to their tiny sleep cabins, a hologram arrived in the control room. "Alert! Alert! There is an illness spreading in the space colony on Mars, causing staff to exhibit extreme weakness as well as difficulty breathing."

"What is the cause?" Clara asked.

"A radioactive substance is contaminating the colony's air supply, but we don't know what it is," said the hologram. "Unfortunately, scientists are unable to **verify** the source of the contamination since even the strongest of them is very weak. Given the circumstances, you should return to your home planet." The hologram disappeared without further comment.

"We can't just leave them there to die!" exclaimed Dominic, as he paced around the deck. "Perhaps by the time we get there, the solution will be clearer."

"But is it right to take two fourteen-year-olds to a toxic environment?" asked Clara. "Of course, none of us wants to leave the colonists to die, but how can we go into the colony without risking all our lives?"

Keisha sat up suddenly and said, "Anisisbro may be able to help. It can go into the colony without being hurt."

"Keisha is correct," said Gene, "and if there is radiation, Anisisbro can pinpoint the exact location using the Geiger counter with which it is equipped. Then the robot's particle analyzer should prove invaluable in assessing what is causing the problem."

The robot, hearing its name, glided around the group, stopping next to Keisha. "The robot looks ready," said Gene, "and I think we should all prepare to fulfill our responsibilities, too."

A Colony on Mars

Keisha and Gene looked at each other nervously as the spaceship broke warp-speed and began to descend onto the surface of the red planet.

"Anisisbro, your moment has arrived," said Gene, as he directed the robot to the colony, which was enclosed under a clear dome and located about a mile away. Anisisbro zipped out of the spaceship and flew to the colony.

The team watched Anisisbro's progress through their visual receiver, and once it entered the colony, they winced as they saw people lying about in chairs in the research labs looking weak and exhausted. Anisisbro proceeded to a hot spot only it could discern and collected samples. Using its particle data analyzer, it then sent the data back to the spaceship.

"Anisisbro has made a fascinating **deduction**," Dominic said as he and Clara looked at the findings. "It seems the colonists have broken their own rules. Even though they all agreed to use natural pest control methods, someone brought in a pesticide that uses radioactivity to kill tiny organisms. Now it's leaked into the air supply, and that's a problem for both plant and animal life in the colony."

"Can it be removed from the air?" asked Keisha nervously.

"Yes, if Anisisbro is ready for another job," said Clara. "Do you think it can seal the source of the leak?"

"Certainly," sniffed Gene. "In fact, Anisisbro is already working on it."

The group watched as the robot quickly located and sealed a pierced barrel of pesticide. Within an hour, the colonists' symptoms began to subside.

"Nice work," said Clara to the two younger team members.

"Indeed, Anisisbro has performed admirably," said Gene. "Now I believe we have some scientists to meet!"

Make Connections

How does advanced robotic technology lead to discoveries in this story? **ESSENTIAL QUESTION**

How can science fiction sometimes predict what may become science fact in the future? **TEXT TO TEXT**

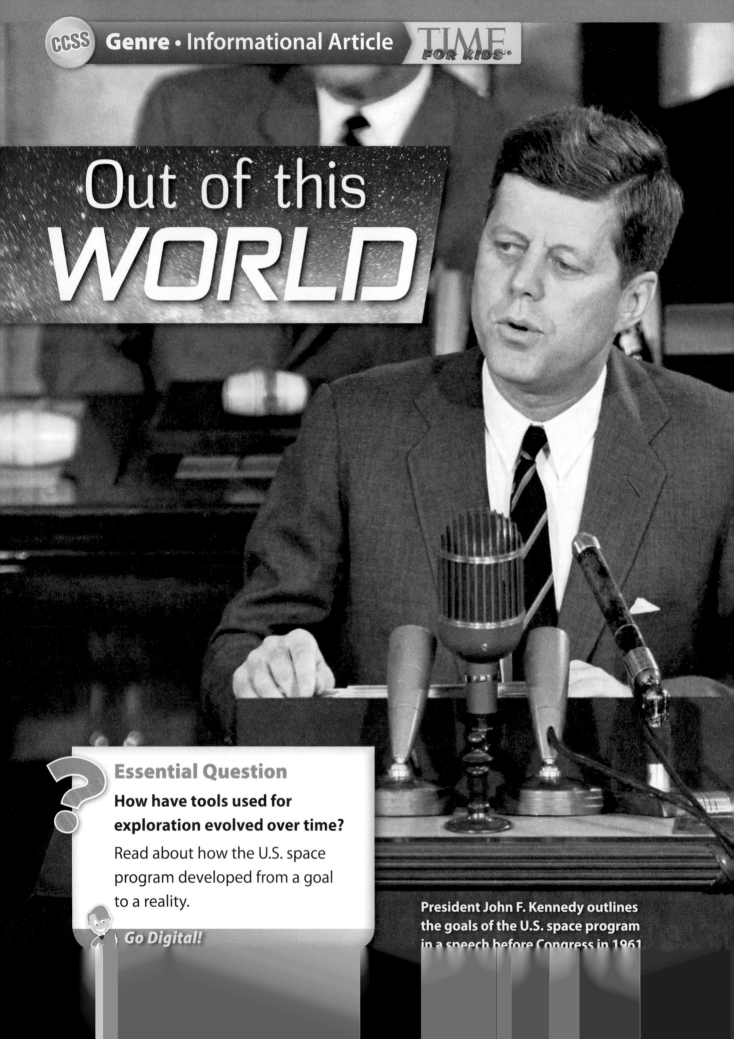

Out of this WORLD

Essential Question

How have tools used for exploration evolved over time?

Read about how the U.S. space program developed from a goal to a reality.

Go Digital!

President John F. Kennedy outlines the goals of the U.S. space program in a speech before Congress in 1961.

A space shuttle lands on a runway after a trip to space.

What tools have explorers used over the years to help them explore the wonders of outer space?

On May 25, 1961, President John F. Kennedy made a speech before a special session of Congress. In the speech he outlined the dramatic and ambitious goal of sending an American safely to the Moon before the end of the decade. A little more than eight years later, Kennedy's goal was achieved. On July 20, 1969, Apollo 11 commander Neil Armstrong stepped off the ladder of the Apollo Lunar Module and onto the Moon's surface.

And this was only the beginning.

Shuttling Through Space

The U.S. Space Shuttle program started in 1981 and lasted just over 30 years. The space shuttle was the world's first reusable spacecraft. It took off like a rocket, straight up into the sky, and landed like an airplane on a runway.

There were 134 combined missions flown by five of the fleet's six vehicles, as seen on the bar graph below. The *Enterprise* was used for training, and was never **deployed** on an actual mission.

The shuttles carried millions of pounds of construction materials into space for the International Space Station. This is a habitable, artificial satellite in orbit around the earth. On the space station, or ISS, crews conduct experiments in many fields including biology, astronomy, and meteorology. The shuttle missions also included research, mapping, and the launching and retrieving of satellites.

The shuttle program represented some of the best achievements of

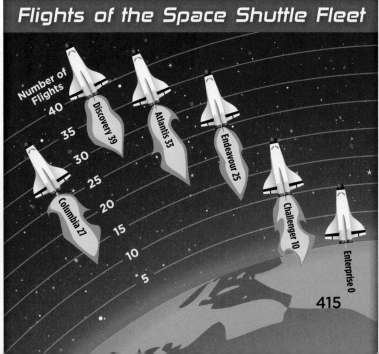

Flights of the Space Shuttle Fleet

Number of Flights

40
35
30
25
20
15
10
5

Discovery 39
Atlantis 33
Endeavour 25
Columbia 27
Challenger 10
Enterprise 0

415

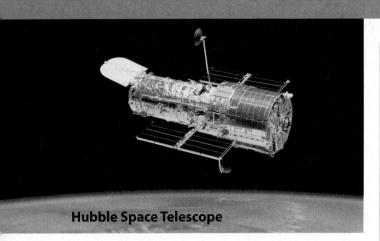

Hubble Space Telescope

science and technology. It will also be remembered for two of the worst accidents in the history of space exploration: the **catastrophic** loss of the *Challenger* and *Columbia* space shuttles. The *Challenger* exploded on takeoff in 1986. In 2003, the *Columbia* disintegrated while re-entering Earth's atmosphere. Even so, the shuttle program continued to ferry supplies and personnel to the ISS until the final mission in July of 2011.

The Hubble Space Telescope

The Hubble Space Telescope was launched by the space shuttle *Discovery* in April of 1990. Its purpose was to allow astronomers to look deeper into space than was possible with any earthbound telescope. Hubble's orbit is outside the distortion of Earth's atmosphere. This allows it to take extremely sharp images. Also, there is almost no background light as there is on Earth.

After it was launched, however, many of the images Hubble sent back were somewhat blurry. **Computations** by scientists who had worked on the project revealed that the main mirror in the telescope had been ground incorrectly. **Subsequently**, in 1993, a repair mission using the space shuttle *Endeavour* succeeded in fixing it.

The Hubble telescope has not made earthbound telescopes **obsolete**. But data and images from Hubble have succeeded in expanding and **elevating** the boundaries of our knowledge. Its spectacular images have helped us understand how stars and even galaxies are formed.

International Space Station

The first two components of the International Space Station (ISS) were delivered to space in 1998, and it was

HIGHLIGHTS OF SPACE EXPLORATION

1957	Soviet Union launches *Sputnik*, first satellite in space
1961	Russian cosmonaut, Yuri Gagarin, becomes first man in space
1962	John Glenn is first American to orbit Earth
1965	U.S. spacecraft *Mariner 4* sends back first pictures of Mars
1969	Neil Armstrong and Buzz Aldrin are the first humans on the Moon
1973	U.S. launches Skylab, its first space station
1981	First space shuttle, *Columbia*, is launched
1990	Hubble Telescope is deployed
1992	Mae Jemison is the first African-American woman in space
2000	First crew moves into the ISS
2003	Mars Rovers are launched
2011	Final space shuttle mission

"international" from the start. The first section was carried aboard a Russian rocket. The second was delivered by the U.S. space shuttle *Endeavour*. The partners in the ISS program are the space agencies of the United States, Russia, Europe, Japan, and Canada. By its tenth anniversary in 2008, the ISS had been built out to the size of a football field.

Mars Rovers

In the 1990s, NASA (National Aeronautics and Space Administration) developed two new methods for exploring space. These were the Mars Exploration Rovers *Spirit* and *Opportunity*, and in the summer of 2003, they were launched toward Mars. Each mechanical explorer weighed 384 pounds and was 5.2 feet long and 4.9 feet tall.

The rovers traveled on 10-inch aluminum wheels and were equipped with tools for taking pictures and analyzing rock and soil samples.

Both rovers continued to function far longer than the 90- to 180-day missions their designers had anticipated. *Spirit* sent data to Earth for more than six years and found evidence that Mars may once have had an environment suitable for life. And so the exciting discoveries, and the **application** of the information we find, continue.

EXPLORERS: Follow the Directions

Test your friends' skills at using a compass. Write directions for getting to a destination, such as a spot in the schoolyard, using only compass directions (N, S, E, W, NE, NW, SE, SW). For example:

1. Face due E.
2. Walk 20 paces and turn NE.
3. Walk 25 paces and turn N.
   ...and so on.

Practice uniform paces first. Place a note or other object at the destination for successful navigators to find. Remember, because of Earth's **magnetic** field, the needle of a compass always points north.

Respond to Reading

1. What text features help you recognize that *Out of this World* is an informational article? **GENRE**

2. What is the author's point of view toward the accomplishments of the U.S. space program? How is it shown in the text? **AUTHOR'S POINT OF VIEW**

3. The author describes some of the images captured by the Hubble telescope as "spectacular." What connotation does *spectacular* have that indicates how the author feels about the photographs? **CONNOTATIONS AND DENOTATIONS**

4. How did the development of technology help the U.S. space program reach its goals? **TEXT TO WORLD**

Compare Texts

Read what happens when NASA has to decide what to do with its retired space shuttles.

Roberto Gonzalez/Getty Images News/Getty Images

SPACE SHUTTLES on the MOVE

When NASA's space shuttle program ended in 2011, a decision had to be made. What should be done with some of the spaceships that had been taking off from Cape Canaveral in Florida since 1981? One newspaper made a few **computations** about the space shuttle *Discovery,* and made it sound as if NASA were selling a used car: "27 years old, 150 million miles traveled, somewhat damaged but well maintained. Price: $0. Dealer preparation and destination charges: $28.8 million."

Damaged or not, civic leaders, museum workers, and space buffs in 29 cities around the country eagerly awaited NASA's decision about where *Discovery* would end up. The space shuttles *Endeavour, Atlantis,* and *Enterprise* were also ending their careers in space, and their final destinations also had to be decided. In the end, the announcement brought joy for some, disappointment and even bitterness for others.

The space shuttle *Discovery* is now on its way to a new home at the Smithsonian National Air and Space Museum.

NASA's choices were finally announced on April 12, 2011. New York, New York, Chantilly, Virginia, Cape Canaveral, Florida, and Los Angeles, California all had reason to celebrate. *Enterprise* was headed to the Intrepid Sea, Air & Space Museum in New York. *Discovery* would land at the Smithsonian National Air & Space Museum in Chantilly. *Atlantis* would remain at its home base in Cape Canaveral. And *Endeavour* would touch down at the California Science Center in Los Angeles.

 When workers at the Johnson Space Center in Houston, Texas, realized it would not receive one of the shuttles, it made a bad situation worse. Employees at the Space Center were already stricken by the end of the shuttle program. Johnson Space Center had been the home of mission control for the program, and Houston was where the astronauts lived and worked when they weren't traveling in space. It seemed reasonable to predict that Houston might be home to one of the shuttles.

Elsewhere, four museums and cities prepared to welcome their new attractions. NASA also announced that hundreds of shuttle artifacts will be given to museums and education institutions around the country. Through the **application** of these artifacts and the discoveries made by the space shuttles, students and teachers will be able to meet new research needs.

Intrepid Sea, Air & Space Museum/AP Photo

Make Connections

How does the retirement of the space shuttles reflect one way that technology changes over time? **ESSENTIAL QUESTION**

How have changes in technology over thousands of years expanded our knowledge of both our world and the universe itself? **TEXT TO TEXT**

419

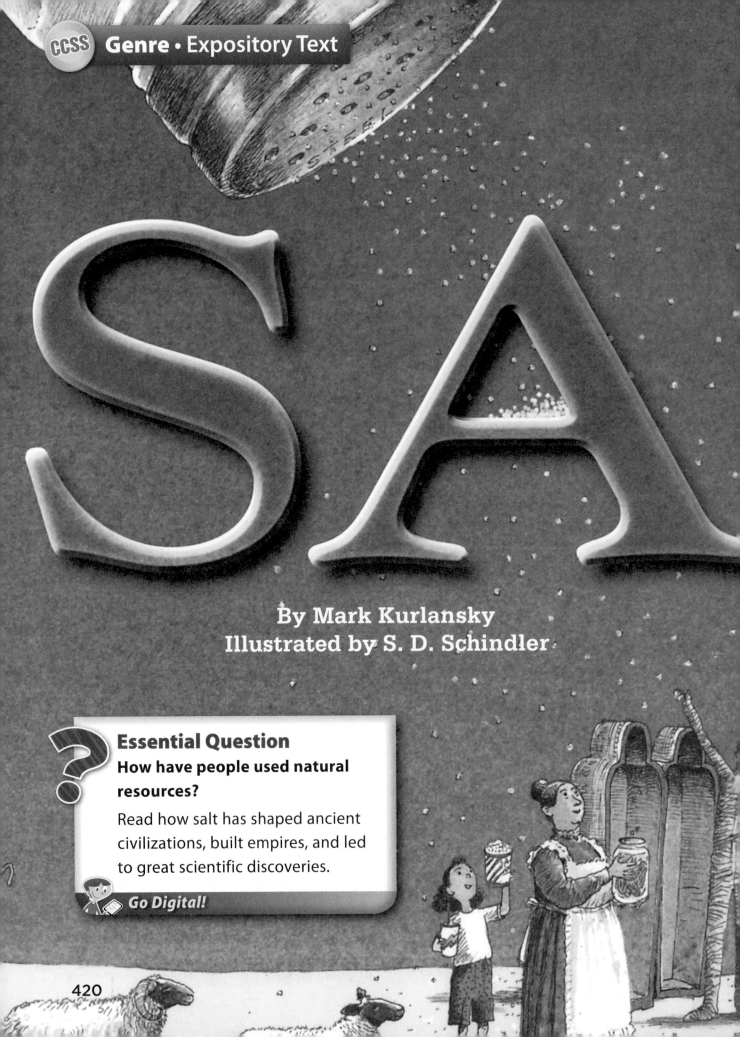

SA

By Mark Kurlansky
Illustrated by S. D. Schindler

? **Essential Question**

How have people used natural resources?

Read how salt has shaped ancient civilizations, built empires, and led to great scientific discoveries.

Go Digital!

The Story of

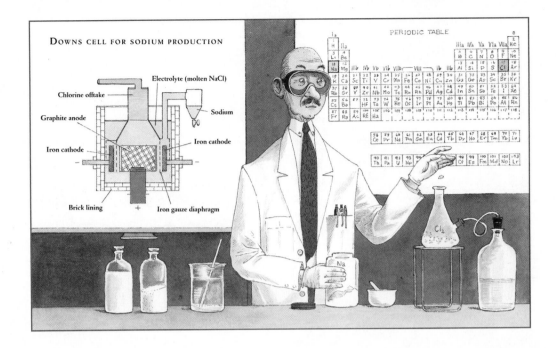

What Is Salt?

The earth is made up of ninety-two natural elements, which combine in nature to form compounds. Salt is a compound produced when sodium (Na^+), a metal so unstable that it easily bursts into flame, combines with chlorine (Cl^-), a deadly poisonous gas. This natural occurrence is known as a chemical reaction—think of it as two people who misbehave on their own but play well together. The two elements stabilize each other, and the resulting compound, sodium chloride, is neither explosive nor poisonous. This is what we call salt.

Salt is the only rock eaten by human beings. In fact, all mammals, including humans, need to eat sodium chloride in order to live.

Sodium chloride is needed for breathing and for digestion, and without salt, the body could not transport nourishment, oxygen, or nerve impulses, which means that the body would not function at all.

A healthy adult's body contains about 250 grams of salt, which would fill three large saltshakers. Our bodies continually lose salt through bodily functions and the supply needs to be constantly **replenished**.

422

How to Make Salt

The four most common ways to find salt in nature are on the ground in dry salt beds, in the oceans, in underground springs, and in rocks under the earth.

Humans first found salt on the surface of the land, where ancient salt lakes had dried up. Animals, who need even more salt than people, were usually the first to discover these places, sometimes called salt licks because animals would go lick the salty ground. When humans wanted to gather this salt, they simply scraped it up from the ground.

The most plentiful source of salt is the ocean. But seawater must be boiled for many hours before the water has evaporated and only salt is left. This is a very expensive way to produce salt because a great deal of fuel, such as wood or coal, must be burned up. The fuel may be more valuable than the salt.

One solution is to enclose the seawater in man-made ponds at the edge of the ocean and let it heat in the sun. This is a very slow process. The ponds can take more than a year to evaporate to salt crystals. But both the salt and the sunlight are free.

Another source of salt is rocks that are mined under the ground. There are large rock salt deposits in many parts of the United States, including Louisiana and Texas. Rock salt is still mined under Cleveland and Detroit today. Most rock salt is extremely pure.

Once miners turn on the lights, each salt mine looks unique. Some have black or gray walls, and others are so white, they look like a snowstorm just passed through. Some have white stripes while others, such as the mine in Cardona in northern Spain, have brightly colored stripes. Some mines have underground rivers and lakes that can be crossed by boat, and one mine in southern Poland even has **ornate** rooms carved out of salt!

STOP AND CHECK

Ask and Answer Questions What are some of the advantages and disadvantages of using the ocean as a source for salt? Do you think mining salt is more popular today? Why or why not?

Poland's Wieliczka salt mine in 1867.

Salting Civilization

Everywhere in the world, it has been found that early humans who survived by eating wild animals and gathering wild **edible** plants did not have to think about salt. Salt is in the blood and flesh of animals, so hunters got all the salt they needed.

But once people settled in one place and began farming to produce food, they had a great need for salt. Eating vegetables and grains supplies no sodium chloride, so salt has to be obtained from somewhere else. The animals that farmers raised, such as cattle, goats, sheep, and pigs, also needed to be fed salt. It is thought that wild animals were first tamed by farmers offering them salt. Soon these animals would pass their time near people in order to get the salt they needed.

Salt Preserves!

Once farmers formed communities, they began to trade and sell the things they produced. For many thousands of years, the most valued item of trade was food. But without refrigeration, food spoiled. It was discovered that salt preserved food by killing bacteria and drawing off moisture. Milk and cream could be cured with salt to become cheese. Cabbage could become sauerkraut. Cucumbers could be made into pickles. Meat could become ham or bacon, and fish could become salt fish.

Though it is unknown exactly when this was first discovered, it is one of the most **significant** changes in history. It meant that for the first time people could journey far from home, eating preserved food. In fact, food preserved in salt could be taken hundreds or thousands of miles away to be traded or sold.

Hence, when people had a good supply of salt, they could also have a thriving international trade, which in turn led to great power. On every continent, in every century, the **dominant** people were the ones who controlled the salt trade. Today, the largest producer of salt is the United States.

Salt Dynasties

The ancient Chinese built the first salt empire. The rulers understood the value of salt, so only the government was allowed to produce and sell it. The government could then raise the price of salt whenever they needed more money. During the Tang dynasty, which lasted from 618 to 907, half the money earned by the Chinese government came from salt.

Salt paid for the Great Wall of China, which is fifteen hundred miles long and is still standing today. It also paid for the Chinese army. But people did not like paying such high prices. Throughout Chinese history, rulers became unpopular by overcharging for salt.

Soy Sauce

Instead of sprinkling salt on their food, the Chinese made soy sauce to get the salt they needed. To make soy sauce, they would steam fresh whole soybeans to soften them, then spread them on large straw trays. Yeast was added, and the trays were put in a dark room until mold formed on the top. Next, the beans were mixed with salt and water and stored in crock jars to ferment for up to a year. Eventually the bean mush looked like mud. The mixture was filtered through pipes and sterilized with steam, resulting in a dark, salty syrup that could be mixed with water according to taste— soy sauce!

Meals and Mummies

The Egyptians were the first to produce salted food on a large scale. The Egyptian people depended on salted fish and meat to survive when a dry year prevented crops from growing along the green banks of the Nile River. They got their salt from the African desert out past the Nile. There they found dried lake beds covered with salt that could easily be scraped up.

The ancient Egyptians saved salted food for both the living and the dead. Egyptian tombs have been found that are filled with urns of preserved foods that were meant to help the dead on their journey to the underworld.

Dead bodies were also cleaned and salted to be preserved for eternity. Without salt, there would have been no mummies.

Across the Desert

Because salt is bulky, it is usually produced near ports or rivers to be transported by ships. But in the Sahara Desert, huge caravans of camels carried the salt. Large slabs or cone-shaped blocks of salt were wrapped in straw to travel hundreds of miles across the desert. In cities like Timbuktu, the salt would be traded for gold.

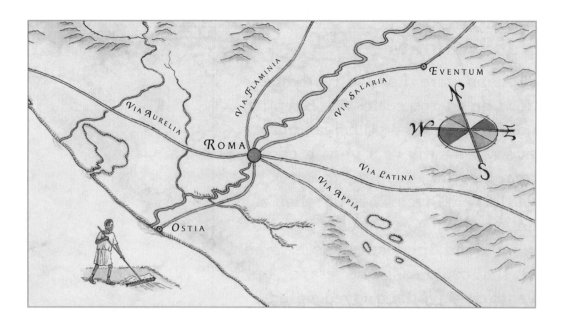

An Empire of Salt

For centuries, the Romans ruled the Western world. And from the beginning, salt was a key to their power. Roman cities were often founded near saltworks, and one of the great Roman roads—the Via Salaria, or "salt road"— was originally built to bring salt to Rome from the nearby saltworks at Ostia.

The Romans believed that everyone had a right to salt. "Common salt" was served in a simple seashell in most households or in an ornate silver bowl at a wealthy family's feast.

Unlike the Chinese emperors, the Roman rulers did not try to own all the salt but only to control the price. To make people happy, Roman leaders tried to keep prices low. Salt was occasionally taxed to raise money for armies, but sometimes Emperor Augustus distributed free salt when he wanted to gain public support for a war.

Words Salted by the Romans

Many English words are based on the Roman word for salt, *sal*—even the word "salt" itself. *Sal* is the root of the words "salary" and "soldier" because Roman soldiers were often paid in salt. This is also the origin of the expressions "worth his salt" and "to earn his salt." "Salad," too, comes from *insalata*, a salt word because Romans ate their greens with a dressing based on salt water.

STOP AND CHECK

Ask and Answer Questions How did salt lead to the rise and fall of empires throughout history?

North America's Shortcoming

Before the European colonists came, the Americas followed the same pattern as other continents. The Aztecs in Mexico, the Mayans in Central America, the Incas in Peru, and the Chibcha in Colombia were all dominant civilizations who controlled the salt trade. When they lost their power, they also lost control of salt.

When the British arrived in North America, they tried to control the salt trade, too. In 1607, Captain John Smith established the colony of Jamestown in Virginia and started a saltwork. In 1660, the Dutch started a saltwork for their colony of New Amsterdam by granting the right to make salt on a small island nearby—today known as Coney Island.

New Englanders were becoming wealthy trading cod and furs while Virginia's hams were becoming famous. However, most of the salt the colonists used was bought from other British colonies in the Caribbean or directly from England's main saltwork in Liverpool.

When America declared its independence from England, their salt supply was suddenly cut off. George Washington's army lacked salt to make gunpowder, to preserve food for marches, to maintain horses, or to heal wounds. Immediately, the Continental Congress had to start paying rewards to colonists to establish saltworks, and soon America had its own salt supply.

How Salt Lost Its Glitter

For centuries, geologists were fascinated by what were known as salt domes. While most underground salt is mined from large, shallow beds spread over a wide area, occasionally salt becomes compressed into columns that go several miles deep into the earth. The top of the dome then pushes right up to the surface, forming a slightly rounded hill with a thin layer of topsoil. Until the twentieth century, nobody knew how deep these domes went, because drills could not go very far into the earth.

In 1859, Edwin Drake was able to drill 69.5 feet on the edge of a salt dome in Titusville, Pennsylvania. Even more significantly, though geologists had said he would fail, Drake discovered oil in the dome.

Then, in 1901, Pattillo Higgins and Anthony Lucas again ignored the geologists and drilled into the edge of a salt dome in Texas known as Spindletop. A tall black fountain of oil erupted.

Scientists learned that the salt crystals in salt domes join together to form an **impenetrable**, glasslike wall. When other organic material gets trapped next to a dome, it slowly decomposes over millions of years and eventually turns into oil and gas.

After Spindletop, no one ever looked at salt domes or drilling the same way again. Drills and rigs became the tools of the oil industry. New drilling technology made it possible to understand what was really under the Earth's surface. And soon it was discovered that salt, far from being rare, is distributed in huge beds throughout the planet.

What were once thought to be isolated salt areas were actually part of enormous underground salt deposits that stretched for thousands of miles. In the United States, one bed covers the entire Great Lakes region. Another bed begins in eastern France and goes through Germany, Austria and southern Poland.

And so, today, when we put salt on our food, we barely give it a second thought. We live in a time when salt is taken for granted—it's common, inexpensive, and hardly worth fighting over.

But the next time you pick up a saltshaker, remember that not only do you need salt to live, you are holding rocks that shaped the history of the world!

STOP AND CHECK

Summarize Summarize the events leading to the realization that salt was hardly worth fighting over.

433

SALT
THROUGH
THE CENTURIES

9750 B.C.
The earliest known human cultivation of plants—peas, water chestnuts, and cucumbers—in Myanmar.

6000 B.C.
Lake Yuncheng in northern China is scraped for salt in the dry summer months.

2900 B.C.
The pyramid of Giza in Egypt contains salt-preserved mummies as well as food offerings.

2000 B.C.
Earliest records of Chinese preserving fish with salt.

1800 B.C.
The Chinese begin evaporating seawater.

1300 B.C.
The beginning of a Celtic salt-mining village in what is today Austria.

1000 B.C.
Mayans begin making salt in Central America.

640 B.C.
The Romans build their first saltwork, a seaside pond in Ostia.

1268
Austrian salt mines begin flooding shafts with water and pumping out brine rather than lifting rock salt from the mine.

1246
France's Louis IX establishes Aigues Mortes saltworks to raise money for the Crusades.

1207
King John of England grants permission to begin the port of Liverpool, which will become one of the world's biggest salt ports.

300
The first camel caravans cross the Sahara. Salt is one of the cargoes.

A.D. 100
Natural gas is used for the first time to boil down the salt water of Sichuan wells.

221 B.C.
China is unified for the first time and salt becomes a state monopoly.

264–146 B.C.
The Romans finance Punic Wars against Carthage with salt taxes.

1281
The Venetian government starts subsidizing salt shipments, making Venice the salt center of the Mediterranean.

1295
Venice merchant Marco Polo returns from China with stories of money made from salt and the Kublai Khan's wealth from salt trade.

1352
Ibn Batuta, an Arab explorer, finds a Saharan city made entirely of salt.

1380
Venice finally defeats Genoa to dominate Mediterranean salt trade.

1607
Captain John Smith establishes the colony of Jamestown with a saltwork.

1698
A French government official reports "salt smuggling is endless on the Loire River."

1807
Sir Humphrey Davy, a British chemist, isolates the element sodium, the seventh most common element on Earth, from salt, and three years later he isolates chloride. The salt-based chemical industry begins.

1789
The French Revolution begins, and the following year the salt taxes are abolished.

1787
Americans begin producing salt from underwater springs in Onondago, New York, buying the rights from the Onondago people for 150 bushels every year.

1776
The British take Long Island and New York, cutting off George Washington from his army's salt supply.

1775
The Second Continental Congress provides subsidies to American salt makers.

1812
The British go to war with the United States and attempt to cut off Cape Cod from supplying salt.

1817
Work begins on the Erie Canal, providing a water route for Onondago salt to the Great Lakes, the Midwest, the Hudson River, and New York Harbor.

1835
In Sichuan, China, the Shen Hai salt spring well is drilled 3,300 feet deep, the deepest well in the world until modern oil rigs.

1859
Edwin Drake drills almost 70 feet in a salt dome in Titusville, Pennsylvania, and finds oil.

1859
The richest vein of silver ever discovered in the U.S., the Comstock Lode, uses salt for separating ore and drives up California salt prices.

1861
Four days after the start of the Civil War, President Lincoln orders a naval blockade of the South, stopping shipments of British salt from Liverpool from supplying the Confederacy.

1947
India gains its independence from Britain and becomes a major salt producer.

1930
Gandhi leads a 240-mile march to the sea to make salt, defying the British ban.

1925
Clarence Birdseye moves to the fishing port of Gloucester and begins fast-freezing rather than salting cod, beginning the frozen-food industry.

1924
The Morton Salt Company, at the request of the Michigan medical association, adds iodine to its salt. Iodized salt has become the leading tool in fighting iodine deficiency around the world.

1901
Pattillo Higgins and Anthony Lucas drill the Spindletop salt dome in Texas and so much oil gushes out that the age of petroleum begins.

1863
The British ban the local production of salt in India, forcing Indians to buy British salt shipped from Liverpool.

About the Author and Illustrator

Mark Kurlansky

has been a playwright, a baker, a professional chef, a dockworker, and a commercial fisherman, among other things. As a baker and chef, Mark developed a long-standing interest in food and food history that is reflected in many of the magazine articles and books he has written, including *The Story of Salt.* For this book Mark traveled to such places as China, the Middle East, Africa, and Scandinavia to explore the history of salt and its effect on world culture.

S.D. Schindler

is the illustrator of many best-selling picture books, including *Big Pumpkin* and the Newbery Honor Book *Whittington.* He lives in Philadelphia, Pennsylvania.

Author's Purpose

Mark Kurlansky was interested in looking at the subject of salt from many different vantage points. What graphic device does he use in *The Story of Salt* to help readers understand this compound's role in many important events throughout history?

Lisa Klausner

436

Respond to Reading

Summarize

Use important details from *The Story of Salt* to summarize some of the ways that salt has had an impact on different civilizations throughout history. Information from your Main Idea and Key Details Chart may help you.

Main Idea
Detail
Detail
Detail

Text Evidence

1. Identify at least two details that help you recognize *The Story of Salt* as an example of expository text. **GENRE**

2. The discovery that salt preserved food and protected it against bacteria was, according to the author, one of the most significant changes in history. What three key details support this idea? **MAIN IDEA AND KEY DETAILS**

3. The Latin root *vapor* means "steam." How does this root help you figure out the meaning of the word *evaporated* on page 424? **LATIN ROOTS**

4. Identify three details and write about how they support the main idea in the section entitled "How Salt Lost Its Glitter" on pages 432-433. **WRITE ABOUT READING**

Make Connections

? Talk about how different civilizations have used salt as a resource. **ESSENTIAL QUESTION**

Identify the most interesting fact you discovered about salt. What can people learn about history from this type of selection? **TEXT TO WORLD**

Compare Texts

Read how one mythological character found out the hard way how the value of a natural resource can change.

THE NOT-SO-GOLDEN TOUCH

Satire is the use of humor and irony to pass judgment on or make fun of human faults.

Peter Malone

Long ago, a king named Midas ruled a large and peaceful kingdom. Midas loved to look at his paintings and his castle's fine furnishings, but most of all, he loved the large gold goblet and the golden statues that his staff polished every day. Midas knew he was a very lucky man to live surrounded by such beauty, but he also knew that the many golden objects in his possession made him a very rich man. Gold was a very rare and valuable **commodity**.

Midas was, however, not a terribly thoughtful man, and he tended to speak first and think later. One day Midas was riding in his carriage when he saw an old man sound asleep under a tree on the palace grounds. Midas was about to request that this trespasser be told to get off his property when one of Midas's minions spoke up, saying, "Surely, we can let him sleep here, your highness. He is an old man, after all."

King Midas thought about it and agreed, saying "Yes, let him sleep."

Soon after, the god Dionysus got word of Midas's kindness and came to thank him. "In appreciation of your hospitality to the poor man, I will make one wish come true, but please

438

think carefully about what you wish for, because sometimes people later discover the very unpleasant results of their wishes." Midas didn't need time to think, because he knew exactly what he wanted. How could he ever regret requesting that everything his fingers touched turn to gold?

Dionysus said, "Tomorrow, when you awake, your wish will be fulfilled."

Midas went to sleep a happy man, and as the sun rose, he remembered Dionysus's promise and his eyes snapped open. Midas raised one finger, tentatively reached over to touch the small table beside his bed, and miraculously it turned to gold!

Midas then slid out of bed, did a little dance, and raised the same finger, only this time he touched a chair, a book, and a rug. All of them turned to gold!

Moving from room to room, Midas walked over to his enormous bathtub, and with a single touch it became a golden basin. On his way out, he laid his hand on a bar of soap made out of honey from the royal beehive. Midas thought maybe he'd wash his hands but when he tried, he found he couldn't. He was frustrated, but the thought of turning more objects into gold beckoned him.

Then Midas's grumbling stomach interrupted his thoughts so he headed to the royal dining room, touching objects along the way, and walked over to a table covered with snacks. He popped a grape into his mouth. It was hard, and when he pulled it out, it looked golden and polished like a shiny river rock. Midas decided he could have someone feed him, for as long as he didn't touch the food with his own fingers, it did not turn to gold. It was a little awkward, but well worth it.

After lunch Midas called for his carriage; he wanted to ride through the countryside. When something caught his eye, he'd stop the carriage so that he could get out and soon trees, boulders, even houses had been transformed. There was so much gold everywhere that you had to squint to avoid the glare. For three days, Midas traveled throughout his kingdom where people seemed to be dazzled by the beauty of the golden objects around them. They were also thrilled because they thought that with so much gold, they must be rich, too.

At the end of the third day, however, Midas returned to the castle to find that his ministers wanted to speak with him. They told him that at first the idea of the golden touch had seemed a wonderful gift, but now they were concerned.

"Sire, because of your actions, gold is no longer valuable," one minister said.

"What?" said an astonished Midas. "How can that be?"

"Don't you see? Gold was valuable only when it was rare, but you have turned so many things into gold that it's now everywhere and it's as common as…as dirt!" said the minister. "Why this morning I passed a house that had gold garbage cans! We need something that is not in such wide **distribution** to use as money." But what?

Together Midas and his ministers talked into the night about what could possibly replace gold. Standing on the balcony, they watched as fireflies danced and glowed in the dark.

"Fireflies!" the king exclaimed, charmed by their golden glow, but his ministers tried to hide their chuckles.

"Your highness, fireflies live for only a few months," one said.

Peter Malone

440

So the discussion continued. What about rocks from the river? But there were too many rocks in the river and, as a result, they'd have little value. What about apples from the royal orchard? If they weren't eaten they would rot and anything used as money needed to last.

Then one of the ministers noticed a golden bowl on the snack table that held crystals of salt. That was it! Salt could be the new gold for it was important to people, it was valuable because it was mined from the earth, and there was only a modest amount of it available.

With that issue resolved, the king went to sleep happy, and the next morning he ordered a special breakfast. When it arrived, he picked up a silver fork, which immediately turned to gold. Then he took a bite of the steak and, following that, ate a forkful of egg, but somehow he felt disappointed. Something was missing, for this food didn't taste nearly as delicious as he remembered, and so the king immediately called for the cook.

Between Midas's outbursts, the cook tried patiently to explain that there was, in fact, something missing. Salt! Salt was now too valuable for anyone—even a king—to use as a seasoning on food.

The king sighed and picked at his bland food. He was beginning to realize what events he had set in motion and how, because of his greed, his food would never taste the same again.

Make Connections

How did easy access to gold change the kingdom's economy? **ESSENTIAL QUESTION**

What have you learned about resources from these selections? **TEXT TO TEXT**

Essential Question

How do we learn about historical events?

Read the first-hand accounts of people who escaped one of the greatest disasters in American history—the Great Chicago Fire of 1871.

Go Digital!

The Great Fire

by Jim Murphy

*O*n the evening of Sunday, October 8, 1871, a fire began in a poor neighborhood on the far west side of Chicago, Illinois. The wind, which had been strong all day, picked up the flames, and for over 31 hours drove them through the very heart of the city.

Panic and fear swept through Chicago as over 100,000 people were forced to flee what would later become known as the "Great Fire." Joseph Chamberlin, a reporter, covered the fire for the *Chicago Evening Post*. Many survivors later wrote about their experiences. Among them were Julia Lemos, a mother who had to save her children, and Alexander Frear, who rushed to rescue his relatives with help from their friend, Mr. Wood.

Believing that an ounce of prevention is worth a pound of cure, James Hildreth came up with a plan to save the city. He used explosives to blow up empty houses, clearing areas to help stop the fire's spread. Claire Innes, 12, was separated from her family by the flames. She later described being locked inside an alley, trapped, with the fire coming at her from all sides. . . .

From THE GREAT FIRE by Jim Murphy. Copyright © 1995 by Jim Murphy. Reprinted by permission of Scholastic Inc.; PHOTO: (l) John Thompson; (r) Wetzel & Company

Claire wasted little time in being frightened. Her first thought was to see if one or the other of the alley openings might be passable despite the billowing smoke. She got within thirty feet of the thick smoke only to be driven back. "The heat was like that of an oven. I tried to open the door to a building but found it bolted. Smoke was escaping from under the other doors, so I gave up hope of finding safety through them."

As the roofs and then the interiors of the surrounding structures were consumed by flames, a scorching wind swept around the alley. The rain of burning embers grew heavier and more unbearable. Claire retreated, seeking the safest, coolest place, and found herself back at the construction site.

"I cannot say that I actually decided to hide behind the bricks since I could not hear myself think in the terrible noise. I did not even look at the fire, but hid my face in the dirt and pulled my bundle, which I had retrieved, over my head."

For understandable reasons, Claire did not spend much time observing the burning buildings around her, so her description of what happened is limited. It can reasonably be assumed that she was surrounded by a frightening cacophony of sounds—wood igniting and burning wildly, the glass of windows exploding, stairways and ceilings collapsing. When the interior support framing of a building had been eaten through and weakened enough, parts of the exterior brick walls would fall with a ground-rumbling roar.

The pile of bricks Claire hid behind shielded her from the severest heat and most of the flying debris. But there is little doubt that she had a great deal of luck on her side as well. For one thing, it's likely that most of the building walls did not collapse to release a wave of fire and heat; those walls that did give way, fell far enough from her that she was not crushed. Other factors may have contributed to her survival. The buildings that ringed the construction site might have had few windows, thus containing the baking heat of their fires to some extent. Most important, a deadly convection column never

Crosby's Opera House burns while pedestrians scamper to safety. Just moments before this scene, a restaurant in the opera house was still serving customers. (*Harper's Weekly*, October 18, 1871)

established itself in the immediate area so a blanket of killing heat and fire did not cover her.

Exactly how long it took for the buildings to burn is not clear; Claire only says that it took "many minutes." It probably took much longer, an hour or more for the fires to completely gut the structures that lined the alley. During all of this time, "[I] kept my head hidden beneath the bundle and said my prayers."

STOP AND CHECK

Ask and Answer Questions Do you think the assumptions the author makes about Claire's situation are valid? Use text evidence to explain your answer.

Wetzel & Company; Chicago History Museum

Once the main force of the fires began to lessen, Claire peeked out. What she saw must have astonished her. Sturdy brick structures had been transformed into blackened skeletons whose insides continued to burn brightly. Still, Claire had more immediate concerns.

"My legs and arms and back [were] all burnt where my dress caught fire. . . . I put out the fire and made ready to leave which was not easy as the [alleyway] openings were blocked with brick and burning wood and smoke. I called [for help] again and again and at last a voice called back to me through the smoke. He told me to stand away from there as a wall of the building might fall on me, and that was all. This made me even more alarmed, but I did not want to stay in the alley alone, so I began climbing. The bricks were still

The streets of Chicago are jammed with frightened people trying to escape the flames. In this kind of confusion, it is easy to understand how Claire Innes was separated from her family.

Bettmann/Corbis; (bkgd) Wetzel/A Company

hot—very hot—but I found that if I did not stop [moving] my feet were not burnt so bad."

Claire scrambled over the **smoldering** pile of debris and made it to the street. She was by no means safe. Buildings up and down the block were burning and collapsing, punctuated every so often by the explosion of flammable liquids. Abandoned pieces of furniture on the street and sidewalk were fiery torches, while shadowy figures darted through the night seeking a safe escape. Claire made her way along the street with single-minded purpose. "Now," she said, sensing the enormity of the task facing her, "I had to find my family in all of this."

During the night, James Hildreth and his men were hard at work trying to prevent the fire from spreading south. After the first few blasts failed to bring down the structures, Hildreth figured out precisely how much powder was needed. Soon he and his helpers were blasting apart house after house along Harrison Street. By the time they had reached the Wabash Avenue Methodist Episcopal Church, they were capable of setting off a powerful charge every five minutes.

With the houses leveled, local residents grabbed buckets and kept the debris soaked until the threat of fire passed. Hildreth's methods appeared harsh to many people, especially those who saw their homes blown up while the fire was still blocks away. But there is little doubt that the firebreaks he created halted the southward creep of the fire and saved several blocks of homes from destruction.

While the fire was being contained in the south, to the north another story was unfolding. The width and speed of the fire made it impossible for weary firemen to work in an organized or coordinated way. Besides, they were now beyond exhaustion. Two nights of fire fighting and little rest or food had pushed many to the brink of collapse. Several had to be taken from the area in wagons. One tired fireman sat down on a street corner to catch his breath and promptly fell asleep despite the roar of the fire around him.

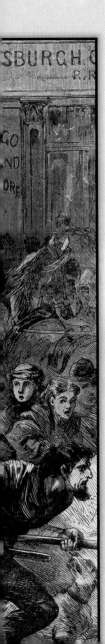

At six o'clock on Monday morning, the fire had been burning over nine hours, and seemed capable of continuing its march north unless more help could be found. Chicago's mayor, Robert B. Mason, had been up all night receiving reports about the spread of the fire and praying for a miracle. Finally, he gave up hope and sent urgent telegrams to the surrounding cities and towns. "CHICAGO IS IN FLAMES," read his message to the mayor of Milwaukee. "SEND YOUR WHOLE DEPARTMENT TO HELP US."

Aid came pouring in from Milwaukee, Cincinnati, Dayton, Louisville, Detroit, Port Huron, Bloomington, Springfield, Janesville, Allegheny, and Pittsburgh. Some cities sent steamers and ladder wagons, others sent badly needed hose and fresh firefighters. And many did so at great risk. Milwaukee put three steamers and their crews onboard a train, leaving that city with only one working engine.

The sun rose on Monday, and Chicago continued to burn. The fire went largely unchecked because the additional men and equipment took many hours to arrive.

After narrowly escaping the flames the night before, Joseph Chamberlin had gone to the North Division* to watch the fire there. Just before seven o'clock, he went back to the West Division. "Then a curious-looking crimson ball came out of the lake, which they said was the sun; but oh, how sickly and insignificant it looked! I had watched the greatest of the world's conflagrations from its beginning . . . and although the fire was still blazing all over the city with **undiminished** luster, I could not look at it. I was almost unable to walk with exhaustion and the effects of a long season of excitement, and sought my home for an hour's sleep."

Chamberlin went up Madison Street into an area untouched by the fire and was startled when he met "scores of working girls on their way 'down town' as usual, bearing their lunch-baskets, as if nothing had happened. They saw the fire and smoke before them, but could not believe that the city, with their means of livelihood, had been swept away during the night."

*Division Street is a major east-west street in Chicago. At one time it was used as a way to indicate certain areas of the city, as in "North Division."

Because telephones, radios, and televisions did not exist, people in the distant portions of Chicago did not know very much about the fire. Many people had seen the bright glow in the distance, but the true degree of disaster was not known until burned-out friends and relatives began knocking on their doors. Then, telegraph lines hummed with brief accounts of the tragedy, and these details were passed from city to city. Fuller accounts would follow. Before the end of Monday, the *Chicago Evening Journal* managed to get a one-page edition onto the streets. In searing headlines, it announced:

THE GREAT CALAMITY OF THE AGE!

Chicago in Ashes!!

Hundreds of Millions of Dollars' Worth of Property Destroyed

The South, the North and a Portion of the West Divisions of the City in Ruins.

All the Hotels, Banks, Public Buildings, Newspaper Offices and Great Business Blocks Swept Away.

The Conflagration Still in Progress.

Fury of the Flames.

Details, Etc., Etc.

Alexander Frear probably wished he could turn his back on the fire and find a cozy bed. Unfortunately, his adventures with the fire were far from over.

After fleeing across a burning bridge, Frear went directly to where his sister-in-law's house had been, his heart filled with grief. He had long ago decided that her three children had perished in the fire; now, on top of this, he had lost track of his sister-in-law, Mr. Wood, and another nephew in the chaos of the night. He **presumed** the worst.

He must have been pleasantly shocked not just to discover the house intact but to be greeted at the door by his nephew and Mr. Wood. What's more, they "informed me that Mrs. Frear had been taken to a private house in Huron Street, and was perfectly safe and well cared for."

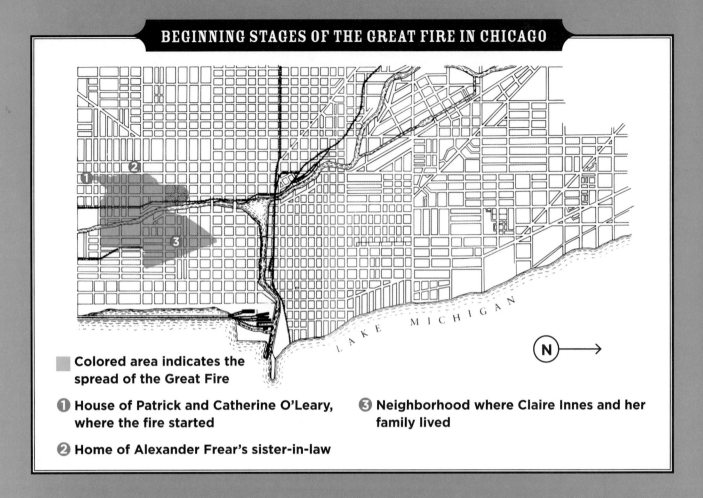

■ **Colored area indicates the spread of the Great Fire**

❶ **House of Patrick and Catherine O'Leary, where the fire started**

❷ **Home of Alexander Frear's sister-in-law**

❸ **Neighborhood where Claire Innes and her family lived**

N ⟶

At this point, Frear gave in to his physical exhaustion. "I was wet and scorched and bedraggled. My clothes were burnt full of holes on my arms and shoulders and back. . . . I fell down in the hallway and went to sleep."

Less than a half hour later, Frear was shaken awake and told that "Mrs. Frear must be moved again."

Mr. Wood knew exactly where she was on Huron Street and volunteered to lead Frear there. They went as quickly as possible up Des Plaines Street. For most of the way, houses blocked their view of the burnt and burning section of the city, but when they neared a bridge crossing to the North Division, the view opened up before them.

"It was about eight-thirty o'clock," Frear recalled. "We could see across the river at the cross streets that where yesterday was a **populous** city was now a mass of smoking ruins. All the way round we encountered thousands of people; but the excitement had given way to a terrible grief and desolation."

For the first time since the start of the fire, the light of day allowed everyone to see and feel the true extent of damage. Alfred Sewell noted the stunned emotions of the vast majority of citizens: "O, what a horrible scene was presented to the view of the spectator on that gloomy [morning]. . . . Heaps of ruins, and here and there a standing wall, as far as the eye could reach, and far beyond, for a stretch of four miles. . . . We walked through the streets, covered everywhere with heaps of debris and parts of walls, and could not help comparing ourselves to ghosts wandering through a vast grave-yard. 'Am I really awake, or am I having a horrible dream?' is a question we seriously asked ourselves many times. . . ."

People were stunned and overwhelmed, and probably feared the worst about relatives and friends who might have been in the path of the Great Fire. But Frear had to push aside his emotions and exhaustion—his sister-in-law was still somewhere near the burning fire, and he had to act if she was to be saved.

"Luckily Wood knew where to find Mrs. Frear, and [we] arrived at the house just in time to get her into a baker's wagon, which Wood and I pulled for half a mile."

His sister-in-law was still distraught over the loss of her children, and grew even more **agitated** when they passed a wagon loaded with frightened children. Frear and Wood hurried away as quickly as possible, weaving around the piles of personal property abandoned in the road.

Once back at his sister-in-law's home, Frear tried to make her comfortable, aided by the capable hands and kind words of neighbors. The shock of his experiences began to set in and he was overtaken by a pounding headache and fever. He had run the gauntlet of flames, risked his life several times in a **futile** effort to locate his young nieces and nephew, and barely managed to escape.

Imagine his feelings when, at four in the afternoon, the solemn, sad whispers in the house were replaced by loud, joyous shouts. A second later, Frear discovered that "word came from the Kimballs that the children were all safe out at Riverside." It was then that Frear could drag himself to a bedroom, climb into a bed, and pull a quilt over his head to shut out the fire.

As Frear slept, the fire went north with little opposition. House after house ignited and burned to the ground, leaving behind blackened foundations and charred heaps of wood. This area contained some of the city's largest, most stately homes, but the fire treated them with the same disdain it did the humblest wooden cottages on De Koven Street.

With the water supply gone, firemen could do very little unless they were near the river or lake and could draw water directly from those sources. Not even Hildreth's special talent with powder prevailed. After creating an effective firebreak in the south, Hildreth took his powder and scooted north to get in front of the fire. He took with him only two helpers, assuming that residents of the threatened blocks would eagerly volunteer. He tried to stop a number of men hurrying to escape, but none responded.

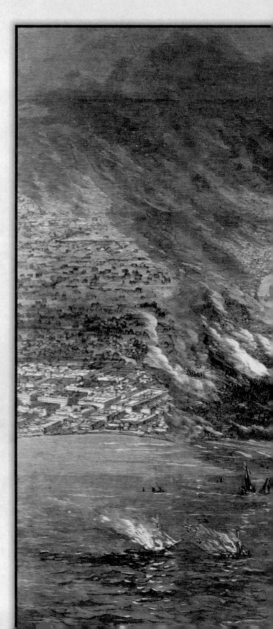

"I grabbed hold of them, took right hold of them with more force than if I'd been sheriff . . . but they would leave me, just as soon as I would take my hands off them, and cut. The word 'powder' was a terror to them."

Finally, Hildreth, frustrated and weary, admitted defeat and headed home.

The same chaos and flight took hold of the northern section of the city. Alfred Sewell remembered the panic in the North Division: "Like an immense drove of panic-stricken sheep, the terrified mass ran, and rushed, and scrambled, and screamed through the streets. . . ."

Men who wrote about the Great Fire generally portrayed women as passive and helpless, waiting for their husbands, brothers, or some other man to save them. This seemed to go doubly for women who were wealthier. But if we look beyond the condescending references, a remarkable picture of strong and active women emerges. Sewell might describe women as "weak and delicate [and] accustomed to no toil or trial" but they still managed to flee "with their arms full of treasures rescued from their doomed homes, and some even shouldered valises and trunks with the strength of strong men, and bore and dragged them through the crowd."

Chicago is blackened and burned, and several ships on Lake Michigan are in flames. The fire would continue to burn until it reached Fullerton Avenue, which is to the right almost two miles from the front wall of the fire shown here.

A slightly elevated view looking along Clark Street (to the left). Most of the buildings have collapsed or been completely consumed; those still standing in the distance have been gutted and will have to be leveled.

Or take the case of Julia Lemos. Lemos was a recent widow and the mother of five. In addition, she was taking care of her ailing mother and elderly father, all while holding down a job as an artist in a lithographer's shop. At the end of September, Lemos found the burden of caring for all of these dependents overwhelming, and, reluctantly and tearfully, she placed four of her children in the nearby Half-Orphan Asylum. She hoped that her mother would recover quickly so that the separation would be a very short one.

Lemos found the situation very hard emotionally. While the chores were a bit easier, she missed her children and worried about them constantly. On the weekend of the fire, Lemos went to the asylum to get her children back, but was told that it was against official policy to release them just then.

Monday morning, Lemos woke to discover that the fire was heading toward their block. Her first course of action was to march to the asylum to demand that her children be turned over to her without any official mumbo jumbo. With her children in tow, she hurried home to organize their flight.

Since Lemos had little money, she went next door to her landlord's house and asked for the twelve dollars she had given him for that month's rent. He refused to give back any money, but when she didn't leave, he offered a compromise: he would take a load of her possessions to the prairie for the rent money. Lemos agreed and got two large trunks packed and on the wagon, plus a mattress and a featherbed.

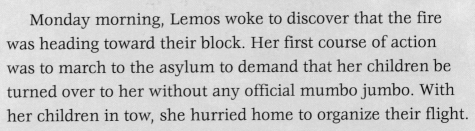

FINAL STAGES OF THE GREAT FIRE IN CHICAGO

LAKE MICHIGAN

N →

■ Colored area indicates the spread of the Great Fire

❶ House of Patrick and Catherine O'Leary, where the fire started

❷ Home of Alexander Frear's sister-in-law

❸ Neighborhood where Claire Innes and her family lived

❹ Approximate location of Julia Lemos's home

At this point, her aged father balked at leaving the house, insisting that the fire would change direction before it got to them. Lemos paced the house, baby in her arms and four children following closely, all the time trying to convince her father to leave. She was looking out the door as others fled up the street when a woman hurried by with three children behind her. "Madam," the woman yelled sharply, "ain't you going to save those children?"

This question jolted Lemos into action. After insisting her parents leave the house, she guided the group out of the city and into the empty prairie where their possessions had been left. Thirty minutes after settling down for the night, wind-driven debris from the fire ignited the dry grass nearby, forcing them to abandon their things and retreat farther north.

STOP AND CHECK

Ask and Answer Questions Why do you think Julia Lemos's father was so reluctant to leave the house when he knew about the fire?

In a building boom that lasted throughout the rest of the 19th century, Chicago quickly rose anew from the ashes of the Great Fire. With the rebuilding came better construction techniques and stricter fire codes in an effort to make sure that a disaster on this scale never happened again.

Lemos remembered feeling the heat of the flames on her back as she urged her parents and children along.

They stopped a mile from the first spot and formed a tight circle. Lemos cradled her baby in her arms while her nine-year-old son, Willy, slept with his head in her lap. Suddenly, he began to cry.

Lemos looked up. In the distance she could see the city on fire, the orange-red flames reaching toward the sky. She was about to say something comforting to Willy, when she saw a church steeple sag, then topple over into the dark smoke and flames. It certainly did seem like the Last Day, but she was sure of one thing: Despite all sorts of opposition, she had kept her family together and now they were truly safe.

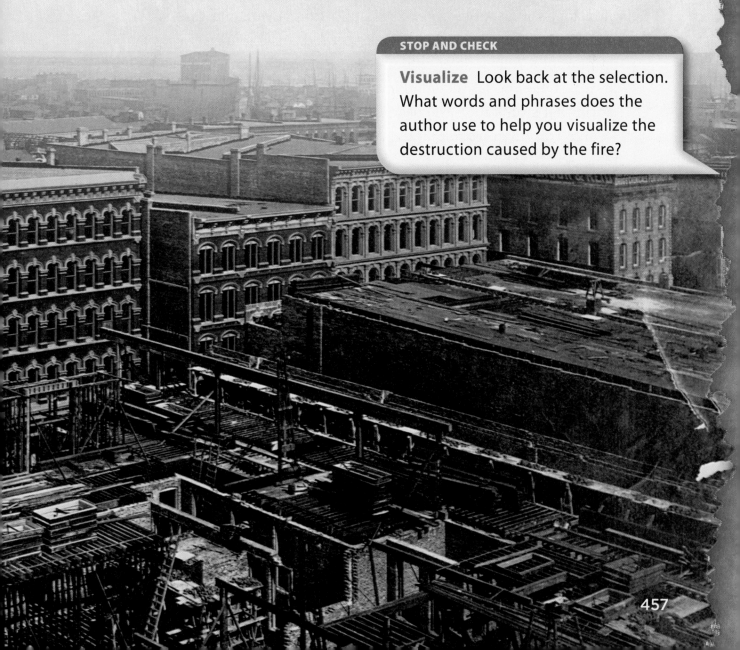

STOP AND CHECK

Visualize Look back at the selection. What words and phrases does the author use to help you visualize the destruction caused by the fire?

About the Author

Jim Murphy liked to write and illustrate his own comic books when he was growing up in New Jersey. Then, in seventh grade, he became interested in history when he had a teacher who made the subject sound like one exciting adventure after another. After graduating from college, he went to work as a children's book editor, and then began writing on his own. Ever since, Murphy has indulged his love of history with a series of books about historic events in America's past. Two of these books, *The Great Fire* and *An American Plague,* an account of a Yellow fever epidemic in 1793, have won Newbery Honor awards. Other books include *Blizzard!,* an account of the historic storm that struck the east coast in 1888, and *The Crossing,* the story of George Washington's role in the American Revolution.

"I love doing the research," Murphy says of his interest in historical topics. "It's like being a detective—hunting out what really took place, trying to find those odd, interesting and sometimes bizarre details I like to include in my books." Many of these details include the role kids played in historic events. "Kids—even very young kids— weren't just observers of the events that shaped our nation's history," Murphy says. "They often participated in an active, heroic way and then wrote movingly about their experiences. Unfortunately, many historians focus exclusively on the important adults involved—a president, general, scientist or other powerful individual—and never let us see who else was there."

Murphy does.

Author's Purpose

In writing *The Great Fire,* Jim Murphy wanted readers to experience the events of the Chicago Fire as if they were there themselves. What sources did he use to accomplish this?

Respond to Reading

Summarize

Use key details from *The Great Fire* to summarize the most important events in the selection as well as the effect the fire had on several Chicago citizens. Information from your Cause and Effect Chart may help you.

Cause	→	Effect
	→	
	→	
	→	

Text Evidence

1. Identify at least two text features that help you identify *The Great Fire* as an example of narrative nonfiction. **GENRE**

2. After Chicago's mayor sent urgent pleas for help, the fire continued to burn on Monday. Why did the fire go largely unchecked? **CAUSE AND EFFECT**

3. An adage or proverb is a traditional saying that uses figurative language to make statements about life. How does the adage "He who hesitates is lost" apply to many of the people the author describes in *The Great Fire*? **ADAGES AND PROVERBS**

4. A cause-and-effect text structure explains how or why something happens. Write about whether you think this was an effective way for the author to present information about events related to the Chicago Fire. **WRITE ABOUT READING**

Make Connections

How do primary sources help us to learn about historical events? **ESSENTIAL QUESTION**

Describe the most interesting fact you learned about the Great Fire. What can people learn from reading about this kind of catastrophic event? **TEXT TO WORLD**

CCSS **Genre • Magazine Article**

Compare Texts

Read one writer's comments on the Chicago Fire in this primary source from 1871.

AFTERMATH of a FIRE

An Excerpt from *The Nation*

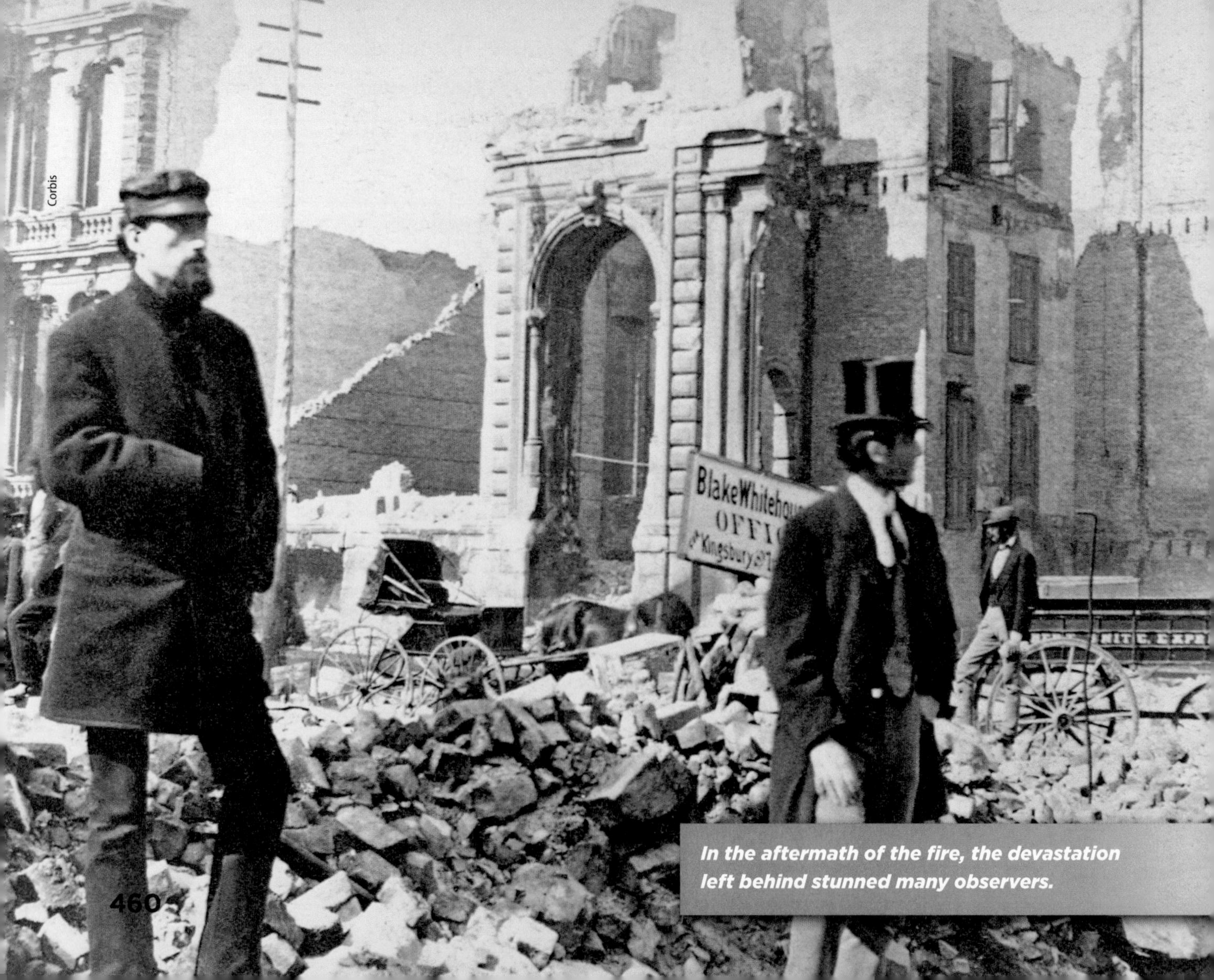

Corbis

In the aftermath of the fire, the devastation left behind stunned many observers.

Primary sources can bring historical events to life. This excerpt is from an article about the Chicago Fire that appeared in a magazine called *The Nation* on November 9, 1871. It was written by Frederick Law Olmsted, a journalist and landscape designer who helped create parks all across the country.

In this article, Olmsted addresses the problems posed with inferior building materials with some **urgency**.

Chicago has a weakness for "big things," and liked to think that it was outbuilding New York. It did a great deal of commercial advertising in its house-tops. The faults of construction as well as of art in its great showy buildings must have been numerous. Their walls were thin and were often overweighted with gross and coarse misornamentation. Some ostensibly stone fronts had huge overhanging wooden or sheet-metal cornices fastened directly to their roof timbers, with wooden parapets above them. Flat roofs covered with tarred felt and pebbles were common. In most cases, I am told by observers, the fire entered the great buildings by their roof timbers, even common sheet-metal seeming to offer but slight and very temporary protection to the wood on which it rested. Plain brick walls or walls of brick with solid stone quoins and window-dressings evidently resisted the fire much better than stone-faced walls with a thin backing of brick.

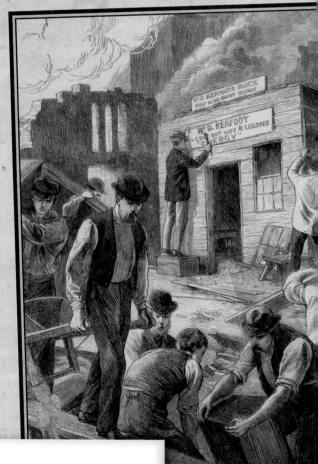

The rebuilding of Chicago begins. The job was so massive that twenty years after the fire there were still burned-out buildings in parts of the city.

Make Connections

In what ways does this article, written soon after the fire, help us understand the event and why certain building materials were **crucial** to the spread of the flames?
ESSENTIAL QUESTION

How did this description of Chicago's buildings clarify what Murphy describes in *The Great Fire?* **TEXT TO TEXT**

EXTREME SCIENTISTS

EXPLORING NATURE'S MYSTERIES FROM PERILOUS PLACES

BY DONNA M. JACKSON

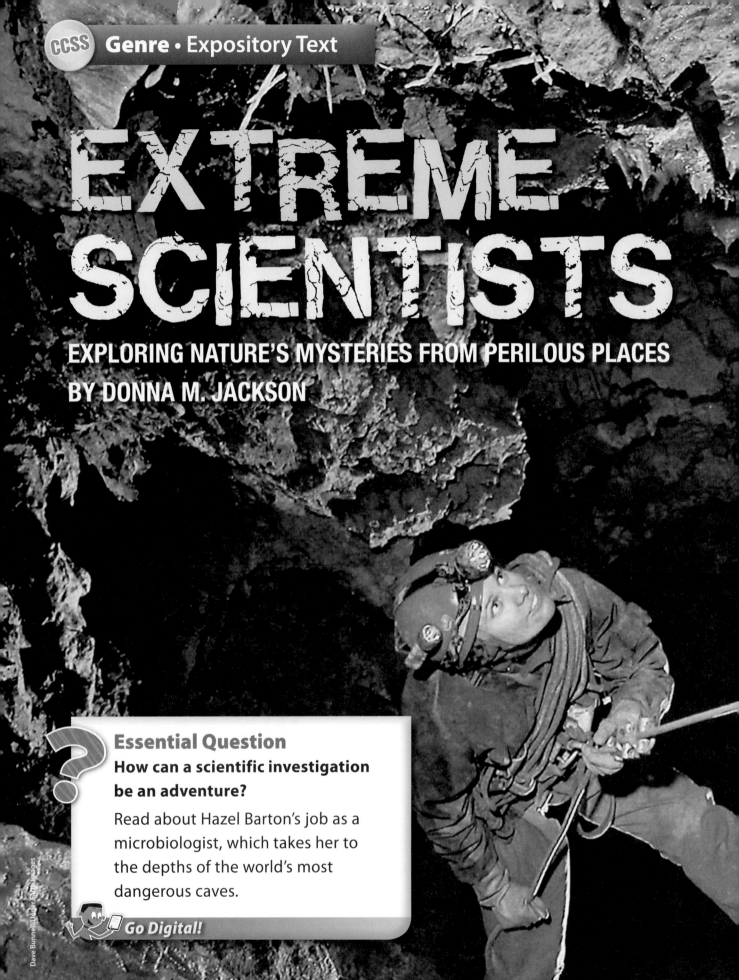

Essential Question

How can a scientific investigation be an adventure?

Read about Hazel Barton's job as a microbiologist, which takes her to the depths of the world's most dangerous caves.

Go Digital!

Dave Bunnell/Under Earth Images

CAVE WOMAN
HAZEL BARTON:
Mining Microbes

Nichol Creek Cave winds seven miles beneath a sleepy Kentucky mountain. Lush **foliage** and a fifty-foot rock cliff camouflage its secret, watery entrance. Looking to explore the cave's inner beauty and biology is British-born Hazel Barton, a microbiologist at Northern Kentucky University. Hazel hunts the earth's hidden frontier—from glacial ice caves in Greenland to underwater caves deep in the jungles of Mexico—for some of its tiniest inhabitants. These single-cell organisms, called microbes, include bacteria and fungi. They live everywhere—from in the air we breathe to inside our bodies—and are considered the oldest form of life on earth.

Some hardy microbes thrive in places never before thought possible, such as searing-hot ocean springs and the bottom of bitter-cold Antarctic lakes. Scientists refer to these super-resilient creatures as "extremophiles." They believe the microbes' ability to flourish under extreme conditions may provide insights to everything from life on Mars to cleaning the environment. Hazel Barton studies extremophiles that live in caves—dark, dank environments with little food—and does whatever it takes to reach her cavernous laboratories, from rappelling off vertical cliffs

Hazel rappels down a drop in the Pandora's Boxwork area of Black Chasm Cavern, Amador County, California. The cave is noted for its helictites—cave formations that grow as small twisted structures projecting at different angles.

463

to scuba diving in underwater passageways. "Caves are incredibly starved," says Hazel. "They're sealed off from the surface so there's no photosynthetic energy [sunlight] getting in."

How do cave microbes adapt to such harsh conditions and manage to survive?

Scientists aren't exactly sure, but Hazel thinks the microbes create a community that works together to stay alive. In developing her theory, Hazel collected a sample of cave-dwelling microbes living on a rock and grew, or cultured, them in a laboratory. "We grow most microbes in the lab with about fifteen grams of nutrients," she says. "You know, a couple of packets of sugar. But these microbes live on one-thousandth of one grain of sugar per liter of water, so (the nutrients they need are) tiny, tiny amounts in comparison."

The cave "bugs" also reproduce more slowly than the norm. "If you grow *E. coli* bacteria in the lab, you'll see a colony [a cluster of microorganisms] in sixteen to eighteen hours," explains Hazel. "But with these guys, it may take two or three weeks." When the extremophiles in Hazel's lab finally multiplied, they surprised researchers at the other end of the microscope.

"We thought that we would find two or three species that are very, very good at making a living when there's no energy around," says Hazel. "But we found five hundred species—species that we wouldn't expect to see. Individually, it didn't make any sense, but when you put them together as a group, you've got organisms that can take energy and nutrients from the air. You've got organisms that can take nutrients and energy from the rock, and you've got organisms that can break down the tiny amounts of energy that are percolating out of soil into the cave.

Hazel Barton and Jason Gulley collect samples of microbes living on a rock in Lechuguilla Cave, which is located at Carlsbad Caverns National Park in New Mexico. Lechuguilla Cave is among the longest caves in the world and is the deepest limestone cave in the United States.

"Put it all together, and you have a community that gets energy from multiple sources," she says. "It's like Cincinnati. If you had a million people who did one kind of job, the city wouldn't work. But you have people who take the trash, you have people who teach, you have people who bring the food in, sell it, and everybody has his role to make the city function. In caves, the energy levels are so low that you can't make it on your own. But when you're willing to share, there's enough to go around."

Hazel developed her "community-driven" energy hypothesis about cave microbes some years ago and has been researching it ever since. "We're not exactly sure how they work together as of yet," she says. Extremophiles could be sharing byproducts, detoxifying toxic compounds, or turning over nutrients as other bacteria die. These are a few of the possibilities.

"Some people have a hard time accepting there are multiple explanations to what we're seeing," she says. "This is my **hypothesis**, so I'm testing it. Others have come up with **alternative** ideas as to how it could be working."

Grand Beginnings

Hazel's interest in science developed early, with a little help from her grandfather. "He was always bringing me chemistry kits, and we would blow things up in the garage," she says. He also encouraged her to read books and to watch a British television series about life on earth. At the start of every program, the host pointed to the millions of animals and plants in the world and how each found its own unique way of surviving. He then went on to share a few of their stories.

After Hazel collects cave microbes, she grows the bugs in her laboratory by feeding them special nutrients so they'll reproduce and multiply into a colony. Extremophiles grow very slowly compared with other microbes.

STOP AND CHECK

Summarize Summarize what makes certain microbes different from all other forms of life on earth.

Donna M. Jackson

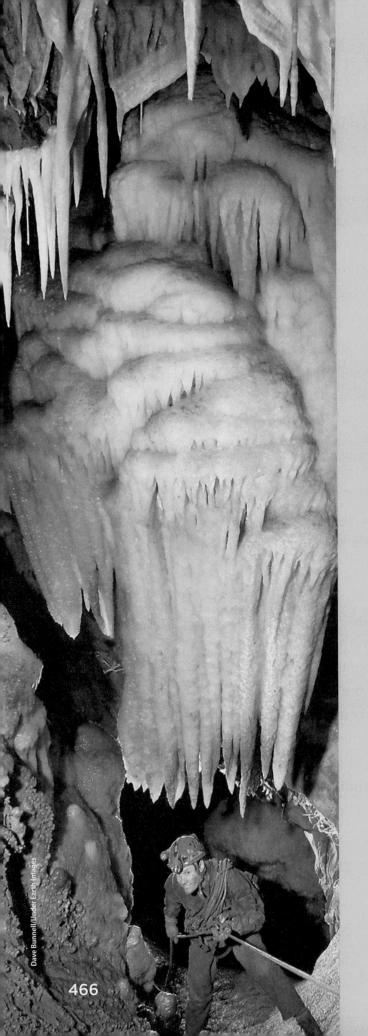

It wasn't long before Hazel knew she wanted to become a biologist. She just didn't know what type. "Then when I was fourteen, we did a lesson in biology in which they gave us petri dishes, and we got to brush our hair over them, stick our fingers in, and do all kinds of things and then come back and look at them the next day to see what grew. And something fell out of my hair and landed in the dish. The next day, this gross yellow thing grew, and it was just amazing to me. . . . From that point on, I knew I wanted to do microbiology."

Around the same time, the self-described "homebody" took an outdoor adventure class that included a caving trip. "Until that point, I'd never gone camping or orienteering or done any hiking," she says. While most of her peers were "terrified" during the excursion, she notes, "I was absolutely fascinated."

Through the years, caving became a relaxing hobby for Hazel, providing her with "the ability to explore the unknown and travel to places that no one had ever been before." Still, she kept caving separate from her work. That is, until she joined the lab of Dr. Norman Pace at the University of Colorado at Boulder. A lifelong caver

Hazel rappels under the "Dragon's Teeth" in Black Chasm Cavern in California.

and world-renowned environmental microbiologist, Dr. Pace encouraged Hazel to combine her interests and make caves her living laboratories.

"You always have to do what your heart says," notes Dr. Pace, who continues to collaborate with Hazel on projects. "Microbial organisms basically run the planet. Yet we know very little about them . . . and cave microbiology."

Since then, Hazel has traveled around the world—from Belize to New Zealand and Greece to Guatemala—exploring hundreds of caves and discovering new species. She's been featured in a movie in which she descends deep into a glacial ice crevasse in Greenland and dives into the treacherous waters beneath the rainforests of Mexico. The "rock star" also traveled to Venezuela. There she surveyed caves formed in large part by microbes.

Courtesy of Max Wisshak

STOP AND CHECK

Summarize Summarize the experiences that led Hazel to pursue a career as a microbiologist.

Hazel gazes at the delicate soda straw formations in Hollow Hill Cave, New Zealand. Soda straws are thin, hollow tubes that look like icicles. They form when water seeps into a limestone cave and drips from the ceiling.

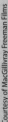

Hazel cave dives in the waters of Mexico's Yucatan Peninsula during the filming of a feature. Underwater caves offer scientists new opportunities to collect extremophiles—super-resilient microbes—that may one day result in powerful new medicines. The main drawback? Cave diving is as dangerous as it is exciting. A number of divers have died after losing their way in the passageways and running out of oxygen.

Life on the Rock

Endless questions—and a fascination with harvesting the unknown—draw Hazel to microbes. "People know how cars work, because they build them," she says. "But no one knows how microbes work."

While plants and animals may look different on the surface, they have the same basic chemistry, explains Hazel. "Microbes all look the same, but they do things different chemically. That's why they can live in extreme environments." Microbes also vary more genetically, with 200 million or more species inhabiting our world. This diversity arms them with more problem-solving strategies.

In Greenland, Hazel and a team of explorers descended deep into a glacial ice cave during the making of a movie. Buried beneath layers of blue and white ice—blue representing summer ice and white for winter—lay microorganisms frozen in time and waiting to be thawed back to life. Some of the samples Hazel collected from the wall of an ice cave to examine for extremophiles were chipped from ice estimated to be about two hundred years old.

"If something goes wrong and you only have a couple of ways to deal with it, chances are you may not survive," says Hazel. Microbes, though, have multiple options. Some may trade pieces of genetic material called DNA (deoxyribonucleic acid), she says, "or mutate and change their own information and recode it." For example, they may change the function of a **protein** so it performs under different temperatures.

When fending off rival organisms for food, cave microbes produce poisons to attack their foes. Scientists think certain strains of the toxins may potentially benefit humans by killing bacteria that cause infections. "When some of these species grow, we see

Courtesy of MacGillivray Freeman Films

LEFT: Sometimes the most dangerous part of caving is making it to the cave. Here Hazel (at right) and fellow caver Nancy Aulenbach rappel three hundred feet in 112-degree weather to reach an unexplored cave hidden in Arizona's Grand Canyon.

BELOW: Hazel scrapes corrosion residue from a wall in Lechuguilla Cave, New Mexico. The soft material is residue from what had been solid limestone. The corrosion appears to be the work of bacteria eating away at the rock.

little drips of liquid that **correspond** to antibiotics," says Hazel. One of her goals is to identify and **extract** these agents so scientists can produce more powerful disease-fighting drugs.

Another objective is to continue to work with NASA (the National Aeronautics and Space Administration) to uncover clues as to how life may exist on other planets. If there's any life on Mars, for example, it would probably be in the subsurface, says Hazel. "We know that there's volcanic activity on Mars. We know there has been water there in the past and that there's a bit of evidence for present water. And we know that underground, whenever there's water and an energy source, you have a lot of microorganisms." By studying extremophiles and the chemistry of caves on earth, scientists hope to one day make it easier to identify and locate signs of life on other planets.

Evidence of possible water sources on the planet Mars, such as these gully channels found in a crater, indicates the potential of life.

Buried Treasures

Millions of uncharted caves await exploration beneath the earth's surface. Nichol Creek Cave is a recent discovery, most likely formed a million and a half years ago. It's an epigenic cave, which means it was created by rainwater that seeps through cracks in the soil. As water flows through the fractures, it picks up carbon dioxide, which turns it into a weak carbonic acid—"like cola," Hazel says—that eats away at the rock. Over thousands of years, cavities form and gradually grow into channels and passages people can explore.

On a crisp October day, Hazel and her team prepare to journey into Nichol Creek. Before venturing in, they huddle near the cave's entry and double-check their gear and supplies. Helmets, wet suits,

Hazel and research student Eric Banks carefully pack lab equipment into a waterproof case before the team heads out to Nichol Creek Cave for the day.

boots, gloves, rope, three sources of light, extra batteries, cameras, tripods, notebooks, pens, snack bags, and a waterproof case for the lab equipment. . . . Ready to go.

Today's mission: to gauge the activity of microbes that have eaten into the cave's rock and measure the conditions they live in, including the humidity and acid levels, to better understand and recreate them in the lab.

One by one, the seven cavers squeeze through the narrow passageway leading several feet to the main cave. For two hours, they slosh forward—often on hands, bellies, and knees—in the "wet" cave before spending another hour hiking on dry land and climbing rocks to their ultimate destination. When the team reaches the testing site, lab technician Brad Lubbers sets up the microprobe equipment under a putty-like substance on the ceiling. Everyone else breaks out the snacks.

"See the rock and how soft it is?" Hazel whispers. "We've done some chemistry on it, and it's calcite [a common mineral and the main component of limestone]. That's what the cave's made of. We think a flood came through and the clay got stuck on the ceiling. When that happened, it stopped water from coming in," she says. "Water's always dripping into the cave, but when it can't come through the clay layer the calcite becomes **saturated**. When it becomes saturated, it has a lot of moisture and energy in it, and we think the microbes use it to produce an acid." The microbes excrete out the acid in the form of waste after consuming the water, and it's believed this acid eventually turns the rock to mush.

Hazel studied a sample of the soft rock in her lab and found it "absolutely packed with microbes." Next, she shipped it off to NASA. "We sent them a sample to figure out what chemistry the microbes were using, and we think they're using something called methane cycling. There's a constant energy being produced and

472

The entrance to Nichol Creek Cave is hidden beneath lush foliage and a fifty-foot rock cliff. Experienced cavers—such as Janeen Sharpshair and her son Aeron Horton, shown here—wear wet suits, boots, and gloves to get them through their first two hours of sloshing underground.

Cave Cricket: Many animals live in caves. Some, called troglobites, adapt to the total darkness and spend their entire lives in caves. Others, such as this cave cricket, which measures about three quarters of an inch, can live in or out of caves. They're referred to as troglophiles.

Popcorn formations, such as those pictured here in South Dakota's Wind Cave, abound in Nichol Creek Cave. Also referred to as cave coral, popcornlike speleothems are made of clusters of the mineral calcite.

consumed," she says. "The microbes take energy from the rock, breathe it in, and then breathe out methane. Then another organism, such as methanotroph [a bacteria that uses methane to grow], breathes that in . . . We think that's how they're getting their energy. What makes this unusual is that this would be the first terrestrial, or land, environment where that's been seen. It's usually found deep in the ocean."

Once the equipment's set up, Brad and assistant Eric Banks activate a robot controller that pushes a microprobe into the soft rock about forty times a minute. The probe measures oxygen amounts as well as moisture content. After countless attempts, however, it appears the researchers will have to try again on another trip. The fragile probe used to take measurements breaks each time it's pressed into the rock.

All in a day's work for Hazel. She knows patience and persistence will pay off in discoveries at a later date—in the lab and beneath the earth.

"Going into a cave, pushing and seeing where the cave goes and making the cave go farther than anyone else has made it go—that's man-on-the-moon exploration," says Hazel. Then there are unexpected scientific discoveries: "Like going into a cave that shouldn't exist and seeing things that shouldn't exist . . . such as weird and wonderful formations." You try to figure out why they're there and how they formed, she says. "You hypothesize and test."

STOP AND CHECK

Ask and Answer Questions Why is it important to seek out and investigate many different kinds of caves in the search for microbes?

QUICK QUESTIONS

Q: How does it feel to explore underwater caves?

A: It feels like flying. . . . If you want to go look at something, you kind of kick off, or just glide toward it. Psychologically, it's a lot harder than other types of caving. You have to really be secure in your equipment and know what you're doing. If something goes wrong—such as getting lost or tangled in the line—you only have a couple of minutes to deal with it as opposed to in a regular cave, where you have days before you really start getting into trouble. You can't fool around when you're cave diving.

Q: Where are the best caves in the world?

A: France, the United States, and Borneo. It depends what you're looking for . . . Mexico has some great underwater caves.

Q: What's been your most exciting moment in a cave?

A: One of the most exciting was the discovery of the Lunatic Fringe Room in Wind Cave in South Dakota. We were doing this exploration, and we were pushing and pushing and pushing, and we found this tiny hole. So we pushed through it, and we got into this room that had a big hole in the floor. We couldn't see a way down, so we came back a month later with a rope. It turned out to be a sixty-foot pit that dropped into a room about the size of a cathedral, lined with crystals.

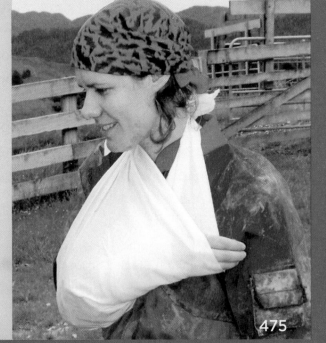

Hazel nurses an injured arm received when a boulder broke loose in a New Zealand cave. After surgery and thirty-seven stitches, she soon returned to caving.

Q: Have you ever been caught in a narrow opening?

A: No. I mean, you don't want to put yourself in that situation—that comes with experience . . . I've certainly crawled into things, and I've thought, "Oomph, it will take a lot of work to get back out." But if you panic, then you get stuck. The trick is to stay relaxed. I've pulled people out who've been trapped, as well as a guy who slipped. He was in a wide crack, and he slipped and fell into a narrower crack. So we had to pull him out, and that took about six hours because he was struggling. When you struggle, you get bigger. So I've never felt trapped in a squeeze. You really don't want to go into something if you don't know whether you can get back out.

Q: Have you been seriously injured in a cave?

A: Yes. I was in New Zealand on a photo trip . . . and we were in a stream passage where you could either walk through the passage or climb up to the ceiling and stay dry. Now, photography trips are notorious for being very slow and very long, and you get really, really cold. I didn't want to get wet and cold, so I decided to climb up to the ceiling and stay dry. There was a big boulder in the passage, so we climbed on top of it and then climbed up to the ceiling and traversed. What I didn't know was that there had been a flood in the cave the day before that undermined the rocks underneath and loosened the boulder. So when I stood on it, it went *pheww* and started to move. I jumped and got free, but it gave a blow to my wrist. If I didn't have the caving experience and hadn't jumped as soon as the boulder moved, I would have lost my arm.

TOP: Hazel squeezes into a new room discovered in Black Chasm Cave in California.
BOTTOM: Hazel examines specimens in her lab.

476

Q: What are some of the steps you recommend to keep safe?

A: There are a number of rules that adult cavers never break, or break at our peril.

- Get the appropriate training: caves are inherently dangerous.
- Wear a helmet.
- Have three sources of light.
- Tell someone where you're going and when you'll be back.
- Wear appropriate clothing for the cave.
- Leave nothing but footprints: everything that goes into a cave must come out—including human waste.
- Take nothing but pictures.
- Kill nothing but time.

Hazel descends to Lake Slytherin on the day of its discovery in an area of California's Black Chasm Cavern called the "Chamber of Secrets."

ABOUT THE AUTHOR

Donna M. Jackson

has always wanted to know the *who*, *what*, *where*, *when*, *why*, and *how* of things. When she was grow up in Massachusetts she loved reading mysteries and books about science. Later, as a member of h school newspaper staff, Donna enjoyed having th opportunity to interview people and share their stories with readers.

When Donna wrote an article about the experience of a deaf man who had been misdiagnosed, her story was so well-received sh decided to pursue writing and journalism as a career. Today Donn is the award-winning author of many science books such as *The Bo Detectives*, *The Bug Scientists*, and *The Elephant Scientist*, in which s examines the work of American scientist Caitlin O'Connell and he discoveries about how elephants communicate. Donna lives in Col with her husband, son, and their dog, Shadow.

AUTHOR'S PURPOSE

In *Extreme Scientists*, Donna Jackson profiles Hazel Barton. What format does Jackson use to present information about Hazel in Hazel's own words? How does this information reinforce and add to the ideas that Jackson presents in the rest of the selection?

RESPOND TO READING

Summarize

Find the most important details from *Extreme Scientists* to summarize the work Hazel Barton does as a microbiologist. Information from your Main Idea and Key Details Chart may help you.

Main Idea
Detail
Detail
Detail

Text Evidence

1. Identify two features from *Extreme Scientists* that help you identify it as an example of expository text. **GENRE**

2. In the opening section of text under the subhead "Mining Microbes," identify the key details in the text and then categorize and classify them in order to identify the main idea. **MAIN IDEA AND KEY DETAILS**

3. Use context clues to determine the meaning of the word *searing* on page 463. **CONTEXT CLUES**

4. In the text under the subhead "Grand Beginnings" that starts on page 465, the author describes how Hazel Barton became interested in science. Write about the details that support the main idea in this part of the text. **WRITE ABOUT READING**

Make Connections

Talk about how Hazel Barton's work as a microbiologist is also an adventure. **ESSENTIAL QUESTION**

How does scientific investigation into microbes and how they survive improve life for people? **TEXT TO WORLD**

Making The SCIENTIFIC METHOD Work For You

Scientist Hazel Barton travels to remarkably inhospitable environments in search of extremophiles. Her goal is to understand how these hardy, **resilient** microbes can adapt and survive. Hazel's research involves a multi-step approach to scientific investigation that is called the scientific method. You can follow this method as you conduct an experiment and record your own scientific research with a partner.

Your experiment will focus on one aspect of the human nervous system. The human nervous system is made up of a brain, a spinal cord, and a huge network of nerves that weave throughout the body carrying messages to and from the brain. The nervous system controls every aspect of a person's body, from the senses to body movements. A person wouldn't be able to breathe, walk, think, feel, taste, or dream without a central nervous system.

Your ability to react to stimuli—for example, how quickly you retract your hand if something you touch is too hot—is called "reaction time." Many factors can affect how long it takes you to remove your hand when you reach for a hot pot, laugh at a funny joke, or wiggle your nose when someone touches it with a feather. Scientists study people's reactions to various situations in order to learn more about the nervous system. You'll be doing that, too, in this experiment.

What is a Hypothesis?

A **hypothesis** is a possible explanation that is based on known facts and can be used as a basis for further investigation. For example, Marta plays in a softball league. Unlike many players, Marta is a switch hitter. This means she can bat both right-handed and left-handed. Usually, right-handed batters hit better against left-handed pitchers and vice-versa. So if a right-handed pitcher is playing on the opposing team, Marta's coach sometimes sends her onto the field to bat left-handed.

Still, Marta writes with her right hand, so her right hand is said to be her "dominant hand." She has also noticed that she hits more home runs when she bats right-handed. Based on further observation and a number of trials, she developed the following hypothesis: "While I get hits batting left or right-handed, if I bat with my dominant hand all the time then I will get more hits."

Using the following experiment, you can investigate the connection between response time and agility by comparing a person's left or right hand, and how it reacts, depending on which hand is dominant.

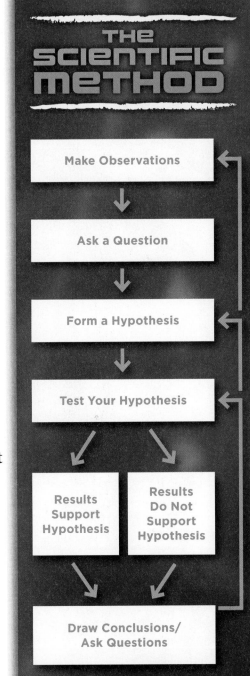

THE SCIENTIFIC METHOD

Make Observations

Ask a Question

Form a Hypothesis

Test Your Hypothesis

Results Support Hypothesis

Results Do Not Support Hypothesis

Draw Conclusions/ Ask Questions

THE EXPERIMENT

You will perform the reaction time experiment with a partner. For the sake of this experiment, you and your partner will need to choose one of these hypotheses:

1. Reaction time is faster when people use their dominant hand.

2. Reaction time is the same no matter what hand people use.

Testing a Hypothesis

1. To perform a trial, one partner holds the ruler near the 30 centimeter mark and lets it hang vertically. This is the "tester." The other partner, the "subject," puts one hand at the bottom of the ruler without touching it.

2. After saying "Now," the tester lets go of the ruler. The subject tries to catch the ruler as quickly as possible with his or her dominant hand.

3. After the subject catches the ruler, look at the mark on the ruler just above the subject's first finger where the ruler was caught. Create a three-column chart like the one below and record the results in the "Control" column.

4. Test the subject five times and then calculate the average of his or her results. You can do this by adding all five numbers together and then dividing by five.

materials

A 30 cm. (12 in.) soft, plastic ruler

A notebook

A pencil

SUBJECT'S REACTION TIME

	CONTROL	VARIABLE
Trial 1		
Trial 2		
Trial 3		
Trial 4		
Trial 5		

In a scientific experiment, *Control* means a factor which always remains the same. A *Variable* is something that can vary according to the situation. When you have finished recording your scores in the "Control" column, you need to test the subject's reaction time with his or her non-dominant hand. This is the variable. Then switch places. The subject becomes the tester, and the tester becomes the subject. Compare reaction times in both control groups with those in the variable groups. You may want to add other variables.

When you finish, you can generalize and interpret the data. Then you need to decide if your results support the hypothesis, or if the research suggests that you need to go back and generate a new hypothesis. Either way, congratulations! You have finished an experiment using the scientific method.

Make Connections

How can testing a scientific hypothesis be similar to an adventure? **ESSENTIAL QUESTION**

How is this experiment different from others you've read about? Which steps are the same? **TEXT TO TEXT**

Essential Question

What can scientists reveal about ancient civilizations?

Read how one of the greatest boats of the ancient world came to be built— and then rebuilt!

Go Digital!

PHARAOH'S BOAT

WRITTEN AND ILLUSTRATED
BY DAVID WEITZMAN

The pharaoh, Cheops, is dead, the people lament. *Now we are like a ship adrift without oars. There will be only chaos, and the sun will not appear in the sky tomorrow.*

Pharaoh, the Egyptians believed, was divine: all knowing, all powerful, in word and deed perfect in every way. The moment Cheops became pharaoh he also became a deity, a son of Re, the sun god. "Thou art like Re in all thou doest," his subjects would say upon entering the royal presence, foreheads to the ground. "Everything happens according to the wish of thy heart."

And everything did. In preparation for his own death, Cheops, like his father before him, ordered an enormous pyramid built to shelter everything he would need in the afterlife. But his pyramid would be even grander. Over the next twenty years, a hundred thousand workers cut, finished, and transported some 2,300,000 stone blocks weighing as much as fifteen tons, and raised them up to create a pyramid almost five hundred feet high.

On the day Cheops died, 4,600 years ago, it was ready for him. But there was one more task to be done.

Djedefre, Cheops's son, succeeded his father as pharaoh, and his first concerns were the rituals that would assure his father's safe passage into the afterlife. He ordered the construction of two magnificent ships: one to guide Cheops safely through the dark, perilous underworld of night, and the other to carry him up across the sky to **embark** on his eternal journey with the sun.

ABOVE, RIGHT: *Re—sometimes in his human form, sometimes as a scarab beetle, and sometimes with the head of a hawk—ferried the boat of the rising sun through the heavens.*

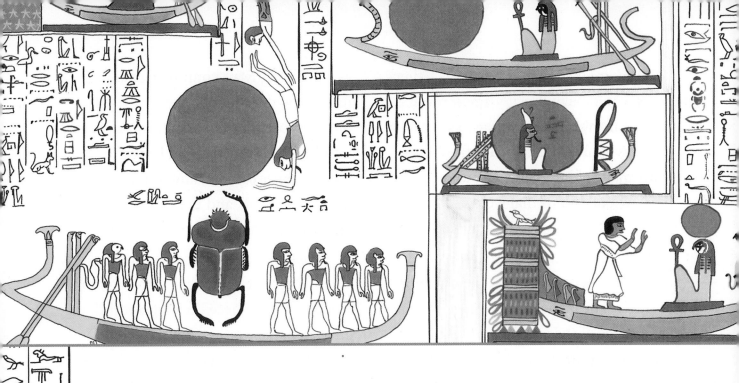

Travel by boat was so **intrinsic** to the Egyptian way of life that it shaped the people's beliefs about this world—and the next. When the Egyptians looked up into the sky, they saw a vast sea, a heavenly river. During the day, the sun sailed across this sea on a ship guided by Re. At night they imagined millions of little boats floating across the black waters with bright lanterns—the moon and the stars—at their bows.

Re's sun boat was crewed by pharaohs who upon their death were judged by the gods to be worthy of eternal life. Inscribed on the inside of their coffins were texts from the Book of the Dead, which protected them on their perilous journey to the afterworld and explained their service to Re. The pharaoh might help row the sun westward, chanting, "I take my oar; I row Re," or as captain, navigate the solar boat by the stars, saying, "I command the god's bark for him; steer his bark; I will fare upstream at the bow; I will guide the voyages."

Like many cultures, the ancient Egyptians believed the dead had to journey across a body of water, a "winding waterway," to arrive at the afterlife. And so, to reach the sun god there on the other side, Cheops, like other pharaohs before him, would need boats of his own.

487

Djedefre could be sure that his father's boats would be built with time-proven craftsmanship. The Egyptians were expert builders of all kinds of boats, from little skiffs made of bundled papyrus reeds to huge wooden ships that were powered by woven cotton sails and leaf-shaped oars.

Instead of a rudder, two large steering oars at the stern controlled the direction of travel. The boats fairly skimmed over the surface of the water, with the rowers at their oars, or the crew clambering aloft to work the lines and the billowing papyrus sails, and the captain at the helm.

Few trees big enough for ships' timbers grow in Egypt. But the Nile River served as a great highway, connecting cities along its bank with other peoples and goods on the shores of the Mediterranean Sea. Trading fleets sailed far and wide to bring back cedar, sycamore, and acacia trunks for shipbuilding, and the very finest were selected for Pharaoh's boat.

When the timbers arrived, the master shipbuilder needed no plans to begin his wooden masterpiece. In his powerful, gnarled hands was the knowledge of centuries of boat building tradition. He simply took up his "pencil," a twig dipped in charcoal, and drew the outline of the first plank on a cedar log.

STOP AND CHECK

Summarize Reread and summarize the initial steps that were taken to build Cheops's funerary boats.

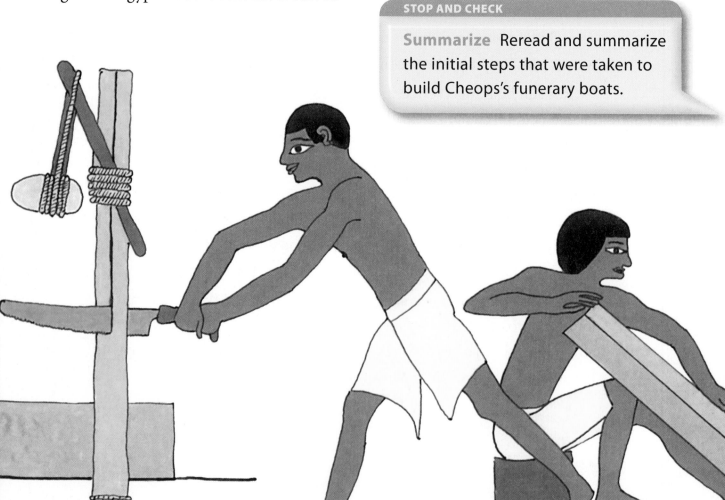

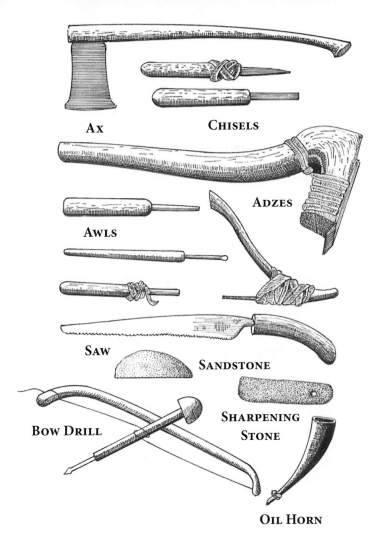

AX

CHISELS

ADZES

AWLS

SAW

SANDSTONE

BOW DRILL

SHARPENING STONE

OIL HORN

As Cheops's boats neared completion under the watchful eye of Vizier Hemiunu, Overseer of All the King's Works, the shipwrights' craft was visible in every curve and joint of the golden cedar hull. Every plank formed two curves—the roundness of the hull and the long curve fore to aft—and every surface and edge was angled just so. The result was a smooth, graceful, river-worthy boat meant to last through the ages.

While Cheops's funerary ships were being finished, workers carved two pits—each a hundred feet long, eight feet wide, and eleven feet deep—out of the solid limestone **bedrock** at the base of his pyramid.

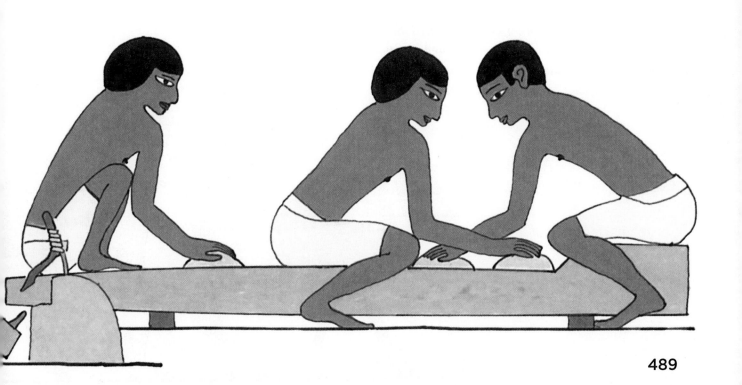

Workers easily moved the heavy stones by placing logs—which acted as little wheels—in front of and under the stones as they were moved across the sand.

As soon as the boats were completed, they were taken apart and placed in the pits. To help Pharaoh reassemble them in the afterlife, the pieces were laid in thirteen orderly layers aligned with the path of the sun's travel—bow to the west, stern to the east. Starboard beams and planks were placed to the right, port beams and planks on the left. The workers even included lengths of rope to bind all the pieces together, woven matting, and a few tools.

When moving the stones on clay, workers heaved the stones up onto sleds and made the ground underneath slippery by pouring water just in front of the skids. In this way, immense stones could be moved great distances.

Meanwhile, throughout the construction period, the priests responsible for the dead had been **meticulously** following the rituals that prepared Cheops's body for life after death. Hundreds of artisans had been working to finish the wooden case that would hold his mummy, the paintings and bas reliefs in his tomb, furniture, chariots, weapons, miniature granaries, and workshops—everything he would need in the afterlife. His body purified and preserved, Cheops would soon be making his last journey in this world, from his palace down the Nile to his pyramid tomb at Giza, where his boats would be waiting for him.

As the boat pits were being prepared at the foot of Cheops's pyramid, stonemasons labored to cut the huge blocks that would cover them. Copper and bronze chisels were too soft to cut through the rock, so the quarrymen used tools of dolerite, an extremely hard stone.

Each block was pried away from the rock face and then all the sides made flat. The quarrymen then "signed" the stones by chiseling their personal marks, as well as Djedefre's, into each block. Then the stones were moved to the boat pits.

One by one, the limestone blocks were set in a row over Cheops's ships, and every crack sealed with mortar. Although the air temperature in the desert is often hotter than one hundred degrees Fahrenheit, the air in the limestone pit stayed twenty or thirty degrees cooler. And because the limestone bedrock wicks moisture from the groundwater below, the decay-resistant royal cedar can survive for thousands of years in this damp environment.

Finally, to protect the boats from robbers, the blocks were covered by a boundary wall encircling the pyramid. Here, if all went well, Cheops's ships would remain, available to him through all eternity.

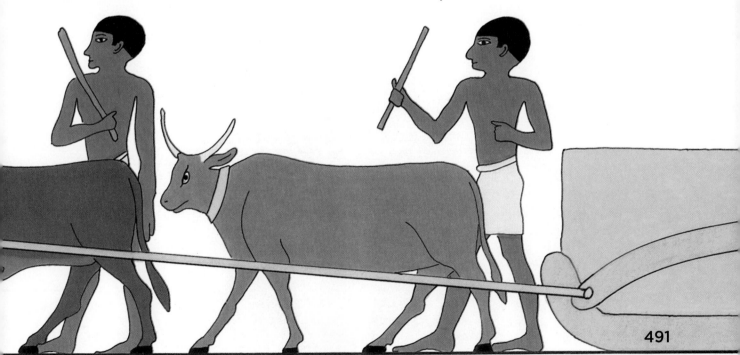

That might have been the end of the story were it not for one of those accidents to which archaeologists owe so much. In 1954, workmen were removing heaps of sand blown against the south face of the pyramid and piles of rubble left from earlier archaeological digs. They dug not with bulldozers but slowly and carefully with shovels, trowels, and their hands, alert for any artifacts that might still be buried. That's when they discovered the old boundary wall where they least expected to find it. The other three boundary walls were precisely 23.6 meters from the base of the pyramid; this southern wall was 5 meters closer.

Kamel el Mallakh, the Egyptologist supervising the work, found this **intriguing**. The ancient Egyptian builders were always so precise about their measurements; why, then, this variation? Continuing to dig down to what should have been bedrock, workmen instead found two rows of massive limestone blocks. Because the blocks were arranged in long rows, Mallakh was certain they covered boat pits.

Chipping away at the mortar between two of the blocks, Mallakh cautiously dug a small hole down, down, down, until suddenly he broke through to the darkness below. "I smelled incense," Mallakh later recalled. "I smelled time, I smelled centuries, I smelled history. And then I was sure the boat was there." What he smelled was cedar as fragrant as if it

had been placed there the year before. Reflecting the sun's light down into the pit with his shaving mirror—"the beam of Re," he says—he caught the first glimpse of a leaf-shaped oar.

Ahmed Youssef Moustafa, chief of the Restoration Department of the Egyptian Antiquities Service, was chosen to direct the recovery, preservation, and reconstruction of the huge ancient ship— an almost impossible task that no one had ever undertaken before.

When he was young, most of the archaeologists working in Egypt were foreigners, and Ahmed had dreamed of being one of the first Egyptians to explore and recover Egypt's glorious past. While still a teenager, Ahmed earned a first-class degree at Cairo's Institute of Applied Arts. Working on his own, he also taught

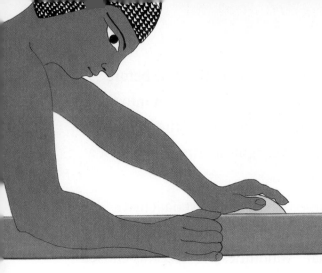

himself the exacting work of restoration. But when he presented himself at the Egyptian Antiquities Service, hoping to be offered work as a restorer, he was handed a broom! He often asked to be allowed to try his hand at restoration. The answer was always no. Instead, he was given little plaster statuettes of Queen Nefertiti to paint and to be sold later in the gift shop. Still, he persisted. "I made trouble at the department," he recalled years later with a smile and a twinkle in his eye.

No longer able to tolerate the young man's unending questions and insistence on helping, the museum's curator gave him a box containing a clod of dirt-caked fragments of wood, ivory, and glazed pottery. The curator sent him away and instructed him not to return until he made something of the pieces, confident— Ahmed believed—they had seen the last of him.

At home he carefully cleaned the chips and arranged them in different patterns. He made drawings of his reconstructions, tried new arrangements, made more drawings. A month later he returned to the museum and placed in the curator's hands an exquisite little ebony box inlaid with tiny pieces of blue pottery and ivory. The Akhenaten Box, as it became known, is on display at the Cairo Museum, considered one of Egypt's treasures.

Over the next twenty years Ahmed became an expert restoration specialist, recording and restoring important tombs. And now he was about to take on one of the most important projects in the history of Egyptian archaeology.

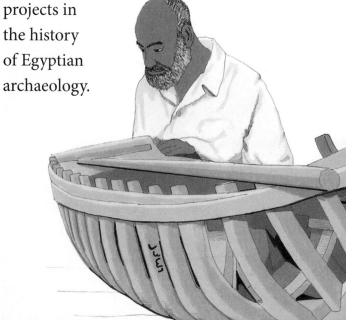

[I have come] to the conclusion that the only way to assure success was to pretend to be the ancient maker, to retrace his steps, and do again what he did long ago in moulding his masterpiece.

—Hag Ahmed Youssef Moustafa

Ahmed was confident he was up to the task, but he realized he would need to know more about building boats. "Since I knew carpentry and woods, it was more a problem of understanding a shipwright's way of thinking." Neither he nor any scholars of the day had any idea how the ancient shipwrights built boats. Now it would be up to Ahmed to find out. It was, he often remarked, like trying to complete a jigsaw puzzle without having the picture on the box.

So Ahmed apprenticed himself to some local boat builders. He visited their boatyard, watched, asked questions, made sketches, and took a turn doing some of the work. Then he hired one of the men to look over his shoulder while he built scale models of their market boats. Later, the scale model he built of the pharaoh's boat would help him solve difficult problems of reconstruction.

STOP AND CHECK

Summarize Summarize the events that led to the discovery of Cheops's boats and the selection of Ahmed to restore them.

Whenever he was stumped by a construction detail, Ahmed would visit his Nile boat builders. He enjoyed the thought that they were building boats just as generations of shipwrights had done before them. But something had changed over the centuries, and he would take several wrong turns before discovering what that was.

During the early reconstructions, Ahmed carefully considered each of the pieces of wood, expecting to find the heavy timbers that would form the frame. He assumed Cheops's shipwrights, like the men he watched on the banks of the Nile, built a frame,

a skeleton, of heavy timbers and then attached the planks forming the hull to the outside. This is the way boats had been built for many centuries now.

But where were those timbers? Again and again he looked over all the large

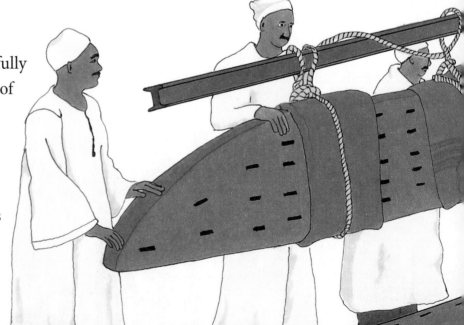

pieces that now lay in piles just as they had been in the pit, but there were none that seemed to work as a frame. Finally, after several attempts at putting the hull together, he realized his mistake. In the way of ancient boat builders all around the Mediterranean, indeed all over the world, this boat wanted to go together shell first. Then, only after the hull planks had given the boat its shape, would a frame be added inside. Pharaoh's boat had revealed to Ahmed an ancient Egyptian shipbuilding secret.

Like the hull and frame, the deck beams presented a real problem for Ahmed. "I must have rearranged them unsuccessfully fifty times. Finally, the boat builders told me how they arrange deck beams today, and when I tested it on Cheops's ship it worked. The pattern had not changed in forty-five hundred years!

He recalled seeing deckhouses like Cheops's in tomb paintings, covered with brightly colored woven-reed mats. It was his guess that the crew would douse the mats with river water, which, as it evaporated, cooled the deckhouse and royal passengers. Forward of the deckhouse, he reconstructed an open framework, where more wetted mats were hung to protect the oarsmen from the withering sun.

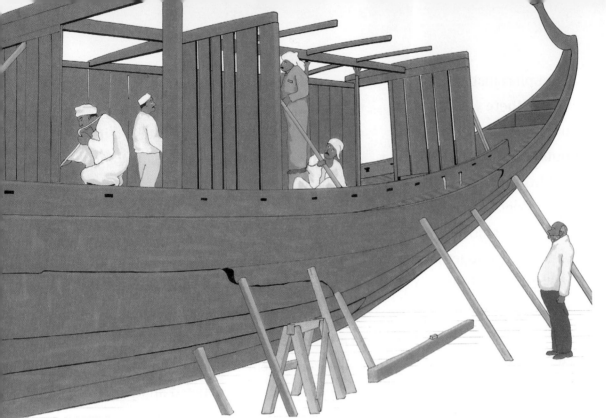

One of the interesting details of the ship's construction that Ahmed learned about from his scale model was the fit of the elegant stem- and sternposts, made to resemble the tied ends of traditional papyrus boats. During the final assembly, the posts slid, like the finger of a glove, over the tapered ends of the hull.

Before Ahmed was satisfied that the boat was assembled correctly, it had been put together and taken apart five times. In all, 1,224 pieces needed to be placed to complete the boat. But with each reconstruction, the team gained a better understanding of the ancients' shipbuilding techniques, and better appreciation of their skill. The first attempt at reconstruction took two years. In 1970, when they installed the ship in its new museum next to Cheops's pyramid, the assembly took just three months. Along the way, Ahmed and his team had

Other periods have their high points, but none compete with [Cheops's time] for beauty and for knowing when to stop. The workmanship and finish were of the finest level, and yet the craftsmen achieved a simplicity of detail and line that is an inspiration.

-Hag Ahmed Youssef Moustafa

pioneered new techniques for the recovery and preservation of ancient wooden boats.

Imagine Ahmed's satisfaction as the last piece was put into place and the boat was finished. What at first was only a jumble of timbers now emerged like an **exquisite** butterfly from its cocoon.

Afterword

The pharaoh's shipwrights had done their job well. Cheops's ship remains today the oldest, largest, and most complete in all the world. It is also considered, thanks to the pioneering work of Hag Ahmed and his staff, a miracle of preservation. The boat is on display in a museum built especially for it over the pit where it was found.

STOP AND CHECK

Ask and Answer Questions How did modern Nile boat builders help Ahmed rebuild Cheops's boat?

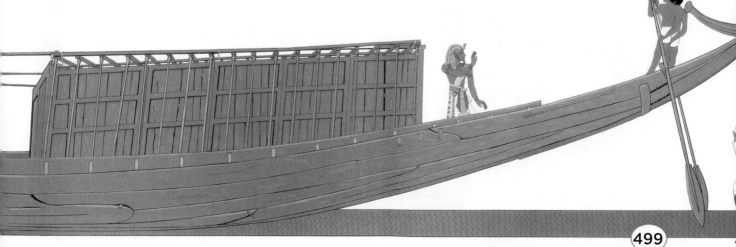

DAVID WEITZMAN

has written and illustrated numerous nonfiction books on technology and forms of transportation that were used in the past, such as steamships. A lifelong lover of history and archaeology, as a child Weitzman spent as much time as he could looking at Egyptian artifacts at museums in his hometown, Chicago. He even managed to teach himself about hieroglyphics from an old book he found. When Weitzman later visited Egypt, he knew almost instantly that he would write about the discovery and rebuilding of Pharaoh Cheops's boat, a remarkable find that had been buried at the foot of the Great Pyramid of Giza.

David says his stories "are quilted together from bits and pieces of history"—including sources such as tattered snapshots and historic photographs, rusty machines, hand-written letters and diaries, book illustrations, paintings, documents, engravings, and old workplaces.

Although he grew up in Illinois, today Weitzman lives in California, where he combines "bits and pieces of history" and other information on the solar powered computer where he writes his books.

AUTHOR'S PURPOSE

David Weitzman says that many different sources, such as paintings, documents, and tales from long ago, help him to "quilt" his stories together. How do these varied sources contribute to the style he uses to make events come alive in *Pharaoh's Boat*?

RESPOND TO READING

SUMMARIZE

Use key details from *Pharaoh's Boat* to summarize what you learned about the building and reconstruction of this ancient vessel. Information from your Sequence Chart may help you.

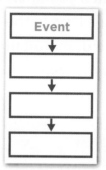

Event
↓
↓
↓

TEXT EVIDENCE

1. List two or more details that help you identify *Pharaoh's Boat* as an example of expository text. **GENRE**

2. As soon as the boats were completed, two events took place simultaneously. What were these events, and what signal words help you know that they took place at the same time? **SEQUENCE**

3. The word *archaeology* comes from the Greek root *arkhaiologia,* which means "the study of ancient things." What does the word *archaeologists* mean on page 492 of the selection? **GREEK ROOTS**

4. Write about the steps Ahmed took to prove himself at the Egyptian Antiquities Service, and how this led to his becoming a restoration specialist. **WRITE ABOUT READING**

Make Connections

What mystery did scientists reveal and solve by repeatedly assembling and disassembling pharaoh's boat? **ESSENTIAL QUESTION**

Identify one interesting fact that the author revealed about ancient Egypt. What can people learn about the past through the work of a restoration specialist such as Ahmed Youssef Moustafa? **TEXT TO WORLD**

501

Compare Texts
Read about a young visitor who spends time in the restoration department of a major museum and solves a mystery.

The **Mystery** of the **Missing Sandals**

James Bentley

This summer, like most summers, I got to hang out at the city museum where my mom works—she's the curator of the Egyptian wing there. That means she's pretty much responsible for organizing the exhibits, making sure the artifacts are correctly labeled, stuff like that. She likes to think that maybe someday I'll follow in her footsteps, and get a degree in Egyptology or archaeology, but I have other plans— plans that involve performing magic.

Starting in June, the museum had started getting pretty crowded because it had a traveling exhibit on King Tutankhamun. That's King Tut to you. The exhibit is filled with incredible artifacts, even an alabaster jar with a sculpture of the king on top that once held King Tut's mummified stomach. In case you don't know, Tut was sort of a minor king, but the ancient Egyptians still buried him in style in a tomb archaeologist Howard Carter unearthed in 1922. The reason Tut is so famous today is because, unlike so many other kings' tombs, Tut's wasn't robbed. The **excavation** of his tomb revealed countless treasures.

When I was a little younger I loved hearing about the discovery of the tomb. My mother read to me from Carter's own account. At first, he wrote, he could see nothing after he opened a small hole in the door to the tomb, and the hot air escaping the chamber caused the candle he had inserted to flicker. But presently, as his eyes grew accustomed to the light, details of the room began to emerge from the dark, and he saw images of strange animals, statues, and gold—everywhere the glint of gold. It sounded magical to me.

Hmmm. Maybe becoming an Egyptologist wouldn't be such a bad idea.

One Tuesday in late May, my mom was running around like a hamster in one of those exercise wheels, getting ready for the exhibit opening the next day. She was more frantic than I had ever seen her. "I'm truly losing my mind," she muttered. "Tut's golden sandals have gone missing, and I have searched everywhere! He was buried with them on his feet, so they are priceless and irreplaceable! My career will be finished if they don't turn up soon! How could they possibly have gotten lost with all the security we have? I'm sure they've just been misplaced, but where could they be?"

I thought I could help find the missing sandals, but my mom had other ideas. "Please, just stay out of my way today," she insisted. "I wish I could pull off a magic trick, like George in the restoration department, and make those sandals magically appear." Then she hurried away.

I ambled over to the restoration area of the museum. I like hanging out with the restorers who work there because they use all kinds of computers and machines to analyze bits and pieces of ancient artifacts. They clean and fix stuff, make sure it's authentic, that sort of thing.

George had been teaching me magic tricks ever since I first started going to the museum. We began with finding-a-quarter-in-your-ear tricks and moved on to bigger stunts. One of the magic books he loaned me even showed how to construct a false wall to make objects seem to disappear, and that training will come in handy in my career as a magician.

George had his head buried in what appeared to be a volume about the ancient ziggurats of the city of Ur, and he ignored me when I walked in. His feet, clad in flip-flops, tapped nervously under his desk. That's one of the cool things about working in a museum: the people in the back offices can wear jeans and sandals instead of a jacket and tie. Partly hidden by his briefcase, I could see an Egyptian model boat, one of the largest I had ever seen. It looked big enough to carry a small dog or cat on a trip down the Nile.

Alice, who works with George, was using a cotton swab to wipe 3,500-year-old dirt from another, much smaller boat, and I couldn't help admiring how the restorers are so **methodical** in the way they work,

James Bentley

analyzing and fixing up objects that were excavated in the desert.

"Nice boat," I said.

"Oh, hi Scott," Alice answered as she looked up. "It's one of several boats in the collection from King Tut's tomb, and I'm just giving it a final inspection for the exhibit. This is the smallest one. And I've uncovered this amazing detail—see this extra hole on the deck? I'm guessing there might have been another mast on this boat that was broken off long ago."

"Why were there so many boats found in the tomb?" I wondered aloud. "Wasn't Tutankhamun buried in the desert?"

"Boats were extremely important to the Egyptians," Alice answered. "The Nile River was their lifeblood. Boats were essential for transportation, and they floated all manner of things up and down the Nile, including materials for the pharaohs' tombs. The pharaohs were thought to join the gods after they died, and people believed they would use model boats similar to this—filled with all their possessions—to travel to the afterlife."

George coughed, finally acknowledging my presence, and said suddenly, and in an annoyed tone of voice, "We've got an awful lot of work to finish before the exhibit opens." There was no mistaking his "Get lost, kid" message. His feet continued to dance nervously on the floor by the boat.

I turned to leave the office. George's tapping toes were getting on my nerves anyway. He wasn't acting at all normal. Then it hit me. He knew all about how to make things appear to disappear. And he really liked sandals—even in January, he would slip off his boots when he got to work and put sandals on.

I waited until George and Alice went on lunch break. Then I sneaked back in and examined the boat that sat under George's desk. Just as I suspected, the boat had a false bottom! I carefully slid it back and discovered two ancient golden sandals that had once graced the feet of King Tut!

Now my mom tells everyone I saved her neck and her career. She also mentioned there's an opening in the restoration department, but I'm not old enough to apply. Maybe I'll work in a museum someday, but solving art thefts might be even more interesting. I suppose I could always do magic tricks on the side.

Make Connections

What can scientists reveal about ancient civilizations by uncovering and examining ancient artifacts? **ESSENTIAL QUESTION**

How is the work of restorers different from the work of archaeologists? **TEXT TO TEXT**

505

Essential Question
Why is taking a break important?
Read how poets reflect on the importance of taking a break —to rest, to think, to dream.

Go Digital!

Ocean/Corbis

506

To You

To sit and dream, to sit and read,
To sit and learn about the world
Outside our world of here and now—
    our problem world—
To dream of vast horizons of the soul
Through dreams made whole,
Unfettered, free—help me!
All you who are dreamers, too,
Help me make our world anew.
I reach out my hands to you.

—Langston Hughes

ODE TO PABLO'S TENNIS SHOES

They wait under Pablo's bed,
Rain-beaten, sun-beaten,
A scuff of green
At their tips
From when he fell
In the school yard.
He fell leaping for a football
That sailed his way.
But Pablo fell and got up,
Green on his shoes,
With the football
Out of reach.

Now it's night.
Pablo is in bed listening
To his mother laughing
To the Mexican *novelas* on TV.
His shoes, twin pets
That snuggle his toes,
Are under the bed.
He should have bathed,
But he didn't.
(Dirt rolls from his palm,
Blades of grass
Tumble from his hair.)

He wants to be
Like his shoes,
A little dirty
From the road,
A little worn
From racing to the drinking fountain
A hundred times in one day.
It takes water
To make him go,
And his shoes to get him
There. He loves his shoes,
Cloth like a sail,
Rubber like
A lifeboat on rough sea.
Pablo is tired,
Sinking into the mattress.
His eyes sting from
Grass and long words in books.
He needs eight hours
Of sleep
To cool his shoes,
The tongues hanging
Out, exhausted.

— Gary Soto

RESPOND TO READING

SUMMARIZE

Use important details from "Ode to Pablo's Tennis Shoes" to summarize the poem. Information from your Theme Chart may help you.

Detail
↓
Detail
↓
Detail
↓
Theme

TEXT EVIDENCE

1. Is "To You" a kind of lyric poem or is it an ode? Explain your answer. **GENRE**

2. Why do you think the poet uses repetition in "To You"? **LITERARY ELEMENTS**

3. How does the poet use hyperbole to help create imagery in "Ode to Pablo's Tennis Shoes"? Explain what this device adds to the poem. **FIGURATIVE LANGUAGE**

4. Reread "Ode to Pablo's Tennis Shoes." Use details from the text to explain the message the author is trying to communicate to the reader. **WRITE ABOUT READING**

Make Connections

The speaker of each poem reflects how important it is to take a break in order to rest or dream. What are some other worthwhile activities you can do when taking a break? **TEXT TO WORLD**

Compare Texts

Read how two poets write about the importance of just watching and listening.

Drumbeat

Listen. . . . . . .
There! Do you not hear them?
Come away from your
    overcrowded city
To a place of eagles
And then perhaps you will hear.
Be still this once;
Hold the yammering
Of your jackhammer tongue.
Take your stainless steel hands
From the ears of your heart

And listen.
Or have you forgotten how?
They are there yet
Through these hundred centuries
And all your metal thunder
Has not silenced them.
The wind in messenger,
Heed the whispering spirit.
Now. . . . the drums still talk,
From the grizzly bear hills,
Across the antelope plains,
In the veins of your blood:
The heartbeat
Of the Mother Earth.

— Carol Snow

TEXT: Carol Snow, Seneca Indian Artist and Writer; Natalie Fobes/Riser/Getty Images

Sittin' on the Dock of the Bay

Sittin' in the morning sun,
I'll be sittin' when the evening comes,
Watching the ships roll in.
Then I watch 'em roll away again, yeah.
I'm sittin' on the dock of the bay,
Watching that tide roll in,
Just sittin' on the dock of the bay
   wastin' time.

— Steve Cropper and Otis Redding

TEXT: (Sittin' On) The Dock Of The Bay Words and Music by Steve Cropper and Otis Redding. Copyright © 1968, 1975 IRVING MUSIC, INC. Copyright Renewed. All Rights Reserved. Used by Permission. Reprinted by Permission of Hal Leonard Corporation.

Make Connections

In what ways do "Drumbeat" and "Sittin' on the Dock of the Bay" both offer an incentive to take a break from the activity in our lives and enjoy some recreation? **ESSENTIAL QUESTION**

In what ways do each of the poems you have read differ in their approach to taking time out from your routine? **TEXT TO TEXT**

511

Glossary

A glossary can help you find the meanings of words in a
book that you may not know. The words in a glossary are
listed in alphabetical order.

Guide Words

Guide words at the top of each page tell you the first and last
words on the page.

anticipation/barbecue

First word on the page

Last word on the page

Sample Entry

Each word is divided into syllables. The way to pronounce
the word is given next. You can understand the
pronunciation respelling by using the pronunciation key.
Sometimes an entry includes a second meaning for the word.

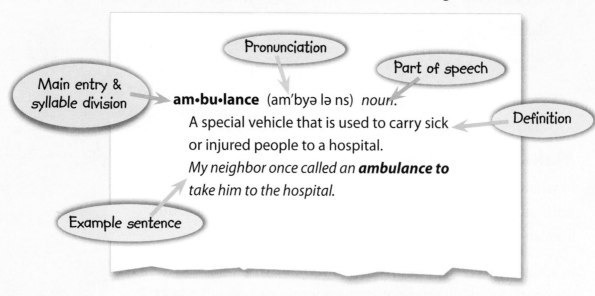

Pronunciation

Part of speech

Main entry &
syllable division

am•bu•lance (am′byə lə ns) *noun.*
A special vehicle that is used to carry sick
or injured people to a hospital.
*My neighbor once called an **ambulance to**
take him to the hospital.*

Definition

Example sentence

Pronunciation Key

You can understand the pronunciation respelling by using this **pronunciation key**. A shorter key appears at the bottom of every other page. When a word has more than one syllable, a dark accent mark (') shows which syllable is stressed. In some words, a light accent mark (') shows which syllable has a less heavy stress.

Phonetic Spelling	Examples	Phonetic Spelling	Examples
a	**a**t, b**a**d, pl**ai**d, l**au**gh	d	**d**ear, so**d**a, ba**d**
ā	**a**pe, p**ai**n, d**ay**, br**ea**k	f	**f**ive, de**f**end, lea**f**, o**ff**, cou**gh**, ele**ph**ant
ä	**fa**ther, c**a**lm		
âr	c**are**, p**air**, b**ear**, th**eir**, wh**ere**	g	**g**ame, a**g**o, fo**g**, e**gg**
e	**e**nd, p**e**t, s**ai**d, h**ea**ven, fr**ie**nd	h	**h**at, a**h**ead
ē	**e**qual, m**e**, f**ee**t, t**ea**m, p**ie**ce, k**ey**	hw	**wh**ite, **wh**ether, **wh**ich
i	**i**t, b**i**g, g**i**ve, h**y**mn	j	**j**oke, en**j**oy, **g**em, pa**g**e, e**dge**
ī	**i**ce, f**i**ne, l**ie**, m**y**	k	**k**ite, ba**k**ery, see**k**, ta**ck**, **c**at
îr	**ear**, d**eer**, h**ere**, p**ier**ce	l	**l**id, sai**l**or, fee**l**, ba**ll**, a**ll**ow
o	**o**dd, h**o**t, w**a**tch	m	**m**an, fa**m**ily, drea**m**
ō	**o**ld, **oa**t, t**oe**, l**ow**	n	**n**ot, fi**n**al, pa**n**, **kn**ife, **gn**aw
ô	c**o**ffee, **a**ll, t**au**ght, l**aw**, f**ou**ght	ng	lo**ng**, si**ng**er
ôr	**or**der, f**or**k, h**or**se, st**or**y, p**our**	p	**p**ail, re**p**air, soa**p**, ha**pp**y
oi	**oi**l, t**oy**	r	**r**ide, pa**r**ent, wea**r**, mo**r**e, ma**rr**y
ou	**ou**t, n**ow**, b**ou**gh	s	**s**it, a**s**ide, pet**s**, **c**ent, pa**ss**
u	**u**p, m**u**d, l**o**ve, d**ou**ble	sh	**sh**oe, wa**sh**er, fi**sh**, mi**ss**ion, na**ti**on
ū	**u**se, m**u**le, c**ue**, f**eu**d, f**ew**	t	**t**ag, pre**t**end, fa**t**, dress**ed**
ü	r**u**le, tr**ue**, f**oo**d, fr**ui**t	th	**th**in, pan**th**er, bo**th**
ů	p**u**t, w**oo**d, sh**ou**ld, l**oo**k	<u>th</u>	**th**ese, mo**th**er, smoo**th**
ûr	b**ur**n, h**urr**y, t**er**m, b**ir**d, w**or**d, c**our**age	v	**v**ery, fa**v**or, wa**v**e
		w	**w**et, **w**eather, re**w**ard
ə	**a**bout, tak**e**n, penc**i**l, lem**o**n, circ**u**s	y	**y**es, on**i**on
b	**b**at, a**b**ove, jo**b**	z	**z**oo, la**z**y, ja**zz**, ro**s**e, dog**s**, house**s**
ch	**ch**in, su**ch**, ma**tch**	zh	vi**si**on, trea**s**ure, sei**z**ure

Aa

a·bun·dant (ə bun′dənt) *adjective.* More than enough; present in great quantities. *We had an **abundant** supply of vegetables after the harvest.*

a·dept (ə dept′) *adjective.* Very skilled, proficient, expert. *The **adept** dancer displayed her skills in the talent show.*

ad·just·ment (ə just′mənt) *noun.* The act of making a change to correct or improve something. *The car ran better after we made an **adjustment** to the engine.*

ad·ver·si·ty (ad vûr′ si tē) *noun.* A difficult time or situation; hardship; a condition of misfortune. *Our team faced **adversity** due to the number of players who were out sick.*

ad·vo·cates (ad′və kits) *noun, plural.* People who support or speak in favor of a cause. *The project's **advocates** held a rally in the park to raise awareness.*

ag·i·tat·ed (aj′i tāt əd) *adjective.* Excited, disturbed, shaken up. *Dad became **agitated** when the dogs wouldn't stop barking.*

al·cove (al′kōv) *noun.* A small space or room that opens out from a main area. *The cats liked to curl up and sleep in the **alcove**.*

a·lign·ment (ə līn′mənt) *noun.* The state of being aligned or set in a proper position. *The wheels on the car are out of **alignment**.*

al·li·ance (ə lī′əns) *noun.* An agreement between two or more people, groups, or countries to work together toward a common goal. *The three clubs formed an **alliance** to help reach their fundraising goals.*

al·ter·na·tive (ôl tûr′nə tiv) *adjective.* Being or giving a choice between two or more things. *The **alternative** schedule allowed for more free time after school.*

an·swer·able (an′sə r ə bəl) *adjective.* Accountable; responsible; likely to be called upon. *The new teacher was **answerable** to the principal.*

ap·pli·ca·tion (ap′li kā′shən) *noun.* The act of putting something on or to use. *We used an **application** of wax to make our model boat waterproof.*

a·ris·to·cra·cy (ar′ə stok′rə sē) *noun.* A class of people with higher social standing than others due to privileges of birth, wealth, power, or achievement. *The group worked hard to preserve the benefits of the **aristocracy**.*

ar·ti·fact (är′ti fakt) *noun.* An object made in the far past by human beings. *The ancient **artifact** was now on display in the museum.*

as·pir·ing (əs pīr′ing) *verb.* Seeking ambitiously; trying strongly to achieve a goal. *The flute player was **aspiring** to be in a symphony orchestra one day.*

as·sess (ə ses′) *verb.* To set the value or ability of something. *The teacher would **assess** our skills before assigning projects.*

au·dac·i·ty (ô da′sə tē) *noun*. Boldness; daring marked by confidence or arrogance. *My sister showed **audacity** when she challenged the referee during the game.*

a·vail·a·ble (ə vā′lə bəl) *adjective*. Possible to get; ready for use or service. *We gathered all the **available** wood for our campfire.*

Bb

ba·si·cal·ly (bā′sik ə lē) *adverb*. In a simple, fundamental way or manner. *I studied hard and **basically** felt confident about the test.*

bed·rock (bed′ rok) *noun*. Unbroken, solid rock beneath the soil. *The thick layers of **bedrock** made it difficult to dig a new well.*

ben·e·fac·tor (ben′ə fak tər) *noun*. A kind person who gives money or services. *The park benches were a gift from a **benefactor**.*

ben·e·fit (ben′ ə fit) *noun*. An advantage or gift; something that helps a person. *An employee discount is one **benefit** of my job.*

Cc

cal·am·i·ty (kə lam′ə tē) *noun*. A disaster causing great damage, pain, sorrow, or suffering; catastrophe. *A flood would cause **calamity** for communities along the river.*

ca·pac·i·ty (kə pas′i tē) *noun*. The maximum amount that can be received or held. *The room has a **capacity** of 500 people.*

cas·cad·ed (kas kād′əd) *verb*. Flowed down like a waterfall. *The colorful leaves **cascaded** down from the tree.*

ca·tas·troph·ic (ka′tas trô′ fik) *adjective*. Sudden, extensive, and disastrous. *The lightning bolt caused **catastrophic** damage to our old oak tree.*

chat·ter·ing (chat′ər ing) *verb*. Talking quickly and without serious thought; making sudden, quick, speechlike sounds. *The toddler was **chattering** all through the movie and annoying the audience.*

clas·si·fi·ca·tion (klas′ ə fə kā′ shən) *noun*. The act of sorting things into groups or classes. *We made a chart to show the **classification** of the various plants we had observed.*

col·leagues (kol′ēgz) *noun, plural*. Fellow workers or associates. *Her new supervisor and **colleagues** wished her well on her first day of work.*

col·lec·tive (kə lek′tiv) *adjective*. Characteristic of or involving a group or gathering. *We took a **collective** vote to elect a group leader.*

---

at; āpe; fär; câre; end; mē; it; īce; pîerce; hot; ōld; sông; fôrk; oil; out; up; ūse; rüle; pùll; tûrn; chin; sing; shop; thin; **th**is; hw in white; zh in treasure.

The symbol ə stands for the unstressed vowel sound in about, taken, pencil, lemon, and circus.

com·mem·o·rate (kə mem′ə rāt′) *verb.* To honor or maintain the memory of; celebrate. *This statue will* **commemorate** *the founder of the park.*

com·merce (kom′ərs) *noun.* The buying or selling of goods; trade; business. *The business leaders discussed ways to increase* **commerce.**

com·mo·di·ty (kə mod′i tē) *noun.* Something that can be bought or sold. *The apple pie was the most popular* **commodity** *at the bake sale.*

com·mon·place (kom′ən plās) *adjective.* Ordinary and unremarkable. *Sandstorms are* **commonplace** *in a desert.*

com·mun·al (kə mū′nəl) *adjective.* Shared by the members of a group or gathering. *The town felt a* **communal** *sadness after their team's loss.*

com·part·ment (kəm pârt′mənt) *noun.* A separate division or section. *I place my glasses in a special* **compartment** *of my desk for safekeeping.*

com·pen·sate (kom′pən sāt′) *verb.* To make up for something; to pay for. *The diner's owner will* **compensate** *us for the delay with a free dessert.*

com·pu·ta·tions (kom′ pū tā′shənz) *noun, plural.* A calculation or determination made by mathematical means. *Her* **computations** *showed that we would arrive at our destination in less than an hour.*

con·fine·ment (kən fīn′ ment) *noun.* The state of being limited, restricted, or kept in a place. *The fresh air and sunlight felt good after a day of* **confinement** *indoors.*

con·ser·va·tive·ly (kən′ sûr′ və tiv lē) *adverb.* In a cautious or riskless manner; in a way that will not change things a great deal. *The mayor acted* **conservatively** *by not supporting new spending on playing fields.*

con·so·la·tion (kon sə lā′shən) *noun.* Something that provides comfort in a time of grief or loss. *As a* **consolation** *for our loss, the neighbors offered to cook our meals for the next week.*

con·tem·plate (kon′ təm plāt′) *verb.* To think about or consider carefully for a period of time. *I need to* **contemplate** *whether I should remain on the football team after my injury.*

cor·res·pond (kôr′ ə spond′) *verb.* To agree, match; to be similar. *The new prices will* **correspond** *to the actual cost of the items.*

cru·cial (krü′ shəl) *adjective.* Very important; decisive. *Our principal made a* **crucial** *decision to cancel classes due to the coming storm.*

Dd

de·cep·tion (di sep′shən) *noun.* A trick or lie meant to fool someone or hide the truth. *The magician used a simple* **deception** *to make the cup appear to vanish.*

de·duc·tion (di duk'shən) *noun*. A conclusion based on what is known to be true. *My Dad's shortened hair led me to the* **deduction** *that he had visited the barber.*

deft·ly (deft'lē) *adverb*. In a skillful, nimble, clever way. *The leaping player* **deftly** *caught the ball with one hand.*

de·ployed (di ploid') *verb*. Arranged and utilized strategically. *Our newspaper* **deployed** *three reporters to cover the major event.*

de·ri·sion (di rizh'ən) *noun*. Ridicule; contempt. *The movie star faced much* **derision** *for choosing to wear the crazy costume to the ceremony.*

de·rived (di rīvd') *verb*. Traced or coming from a source; originated. *Mom's new recipe was* **derived** *from one that her own mother had used.*

des·ig·nate (dez'ig nāt') *verb*. Mark or point out; select. *Our class will* **designate** *a new leader with next week's vote.*

des·o·late (des'ə lit) *adjective*. Deserted, without people; miserable or cheerless. *No one wanted to build a home in the* **desolate** *neighborhood.*

de·ter·i·or·at·ed (di tîr'ē ər āt'əd) *verb*. Made or became steadily worse. *The bike was left out for a year and slowly* **deteriorated**.

de·vas·ta·ting (dev'ə stāt'ing) *adjective*. Capable of or causing ruin or destruction. *The huge, powerful waves had a* **devastating** *effect on the shoreline.*

dil·em·ma (də le'mə) *noun*. A hard choice to make between two or more things. *I had a* **dilemma** *because I needed to be in two places at the same time.*

dis·posed (di spōzd') *adjective*. Having certain inclinations or tendencies. *She was more* **disposed** *to giving gifts during the holiday season.*

dis·tri·bu·tion (dis'trə bū'shən) *noun*. The process of delivering and spreading out goods. *I could make more money on my newspaper route if I increased my* **distribution**.

do·cu·men·ta·tion (dok'ū mən tā'shən) *noun*. Work that proves or provides information about a claim. *The judge asked for* **documentation** *that proved she was the owner of the car.*

do·mes·tic (də mes'tik) *adjective*. Of or pertaining to one's home, country, or family. *My father prefers* **domestic** *news over foreign reports.*

dom·i·nant (dom'ə nənt) *adjective*. ruling, governing, or having authority. *Ancient Rome was the* **dominant** *political force in the Mediterranean 2,000 years ago.*

---

at; āpe; fär; câre; end; mē; it; īce; pîerce; hot; ōld; sông; fôrk; oil; out; up; ūse; rüle; pull; tûrn; chin; sing; shop; thin; this; hw in white; zh in treasure.

The symbol ə stands for the unstressed vowel sound in about, taken, pencil, lemon, and circus.

drones (drōnz) *verb.* Makes a low, continuous tone. *As we approached the airport, I could hear the **drones** of the planes' engines.*

dy•na•mic (dī na'mik) *adjective.* Having or showing a lot of energy; active; forceful. *The audience cheered wildly after the **dynamic** dance performance.*

Ee

eaves (ēvz) *noun.* The overhanging, lower edges of a roof. *We noticed spider webs up along the **eaves** each spring.*

eaves•drop•ping (ēvz' drop ing) *verb.* Secretly listening to a conversation. *Mom warned my brother to stop **eavesdropping** on my phone calls.*

e•clipse (i klips') *noun.* An astronomical event in which one object is obscured or darkened by another. *During the **eclipse** the moon passed in front of the sun.*

ed•i•ble (ed'ə bəl) *adjective.* Fit or safe to eat. *The tree's fruits are **edible** but the leaves should be avoided.*

el•e•vat•ing (el'ə vāt ing) *verb.* Raising or lifting up. *The cheerleaders were **elevating** the spirits of the crowd at the game.*

em•bark (em bârk') *verb.* To start or set out, as on travels. *We will **embark** on our cross-country journey right after school ends.*

em•ber (em'bər) *noun.* A piece of wood or coal that is still glowing in the ashes of a fire. *She blew on the **ember** to make it hot enough to ignite the new pieces of wood.*

em•pa•thy (em'pə thē) *noun.* The act of experiencing or being sensitive to the feelings, thoughts, or attitudes of another. *His **empathy** for his grandmother led him to volunteer with the elderly.*

en•deav•or (en dev'ər) *noun.* A serious effort or attempt. *My father's new business **endeavor** was featured in the newspaper.*

en•gulfs (en gulfs') *verb.* Swallows up or covers completely. *Mom drives more carefully when fog **engulfs** the car.*

en•tail (en tāl') *verb.* To cause or involve by necessity or as a consequence. *The school closings in winter will **entail** extra days to be added in the spring.*

en•thralled (en thrôld') *verb.* Held the attention and interest of someone completely. *The street performer **enthralled** everyone who stopped to watch him in the park.*

ex•ca•va•tion (ek'skə vā'shən) *noun.* An area in which something has been exposed or uncovered for investigation. *The major **excavation** forced the road to be closed for weeks.*

ex•erts (eg zûrtz') *verb.* Makes use of; makes a great or strenuous effort. *Our coach **exerts** his voice calling plays and can barely speak after a game.*

ex·ot·ic (eg zot' ik) *adjective.* Foreign; strange; unusual. *My father would like to visit en **exotic** island location for our next vacation.*

ex·per·tise (ekz' pûr tēs') *noun.* Mastery of a skill or craft. *I enrolled in a class to increase my cooking **expertise**.*

ex·ploits (eks'ploits) *noun.* Notable deeds; heroic achievements. *My grandfather enjoys telling tales of his **exploits** as a ship captain.*

ex·qui·site (ek skwiz' it) *adjective.* Of great beauty or perfection; of high quality. *My mother admired the jewels and craftsmanship on the **exquisite** necklace.*

ex·ten·sive (ek sten'siv) *adjective.* Far-reaching, thorough, comprehensive; large, broad. *The town performed **extensive** research before adding another parking lot.*

ex·tract (eks trakt') *verb.* To take, get, or pull out. *The dentist had to **extract** the poorly developed tooth.*

Ff

fac·tors (fak'tərz) *noun, plural.* Things that contribute toward a result. *The teacher reviewed the **factors** that would lead to success in the class.*

fal·low (fal'ō) *adjective.* Unused but capable of yielding crops. *Wild grasses grew in the **fallow** fields.*

fee·bly (fē'blē) *adverb.* In a manner lacking strength. *She **feebly** pushed against the door, but it wouldn't open.*

flanked (flankd) *verb.* To be found at the side of something. *Cheering crowds **flanked** the street as the parade passed by.*

fluc·tu·ate (flək'chə'wāt) *verb.* To shift back and forth in an uncertain way. *We felt the temperature **fluctuate** as clouds kept passing in front of the sun.*

flu·ent (flü'ənt) *adjective.* Effortless, with smoothness and ease. *Because she was from Spain, my grandmother spoke **fluent** Spanish.*

fo·li·age (fō'lē ij) *noun.* The leaves on a tree or plant. *We enjoyed seeing the brightly colored **foliage** in the fall.*

for·lorn (fôr lôrn') *adjective.* Lonely and sad, as if forsaken or forgotten. *The **forlorn** dog awaited its owner at the door to the building.*

for·mu·la (fôr'myə lə) *noun.* A set of rules or methods for preparing or doing something. *We followed the **formula** to mix up some plaster for the repairs.*

for·ti·tude (fôr'tə tüd) *noun.* Mental and emotional strength. *She showed great **fortitude** as she overcame the challenges.*

---

at; āpe; fär; câre; end; mē; it; īce; pîerce; hot; ōld; sông; fôrk; oil; out; up; ūse; rüle; pull; tûrn; chin; sing; shop; thin; this; hw in white; zh in treasure.

The symbol ə stands for the unstressed vowel sound in about, taken, pencil, lemon, and circus.

foun·da·tion (foun dā'shən) *noun.* Basis; something that supports or justifies. *Our ability to improve was the **foundation** of our success as a team.*

fu·tile (fyü'təl) *adjective.* Incapable of producing a result; ineffective; useless. *The tiny hammer was **futile** for pounding in the larger nails.*

Gg

gal·ax·y (gal'ək sē) *noun.* A large group or system of stars. *The telescope allowed us to see the closest **galaxy** to our own.*

gen·er·at·ed (jen'ə rā'təd) *verb.* Brought about or produced; made. *The new posters **generated** a lot of talk about the upcoming event.*

glim·mer (glim'ər) *noun.* A subtle or faint perception; a dim glow. *At first the approaching headlights were just a **glimmer** down the road.*

Hh

hei·nous (hā'nəs) *adjective.* Shockingly bad or evil. *In the movie, the **heinous** villains were finally brought to justice.*

hor·i·zons (hə rī'zənz) *noun.* The range or limit of experience or knowledge. *Our parents encouraged us to go on the camping trip to expand our **horizons**.*

hy·po·the·sis (hī pôth'ə sis) *noun.* A guess or opinion based on facts and precedents to direct an investigation. *We will test my **hypothesis** that people buy more food if they shop while hungry.*

Ii

im·pen·e·tra·ble (im pen'i trə bəl) *adjective.* Unable to be broken through; difficult to understand. *The number of complicated scientific terms made the book **impenetrable** for most readers.*

im·ple·ment (im'plə ment) *verb.* To put into action; to carry into effect. *Our teacher will **implement** a new attendance policy next week.*

im·pov·er·ished (im pov'ər ishd) *adjective.* Having few resources or little wealth. *The group provided helpful services to people who lived in **impoverished** neighborhoods.*

im·pu·dence (im'pyə dəns) *noun.* The state of being rude, bold, or disrespectful. *The player yelled at the referee with **impudence** and was thrown out of the game.*

in·cen·tive (in sen'tiv) *noun.* Something that motivates or induces. *As an **incentive**, our parents promised us a free movie pass if we made the honor roll.*

in·con·ven·ience (in kən vēn'yəns) *noun.* Something that causes a lack of comfort or ease; something that causes trouble. *The closed hallways were a major **inconvenience** for the students at school.*

in•de•ci•sion (in′di si′zhən) *noun.* The inability to make up one's mind, determine, or decide. *His* **indecision** *about what to wear made us late for the performance.*

in•dis•pen•sa•ble (in′ di spen′ sə bəl) *adjective.* Absolutely necessary, essential. *The star players are* **indispensable** *to our team's plans for victory.*

in•dus•tri•al (in dus′trē əl) *adjective.* Using technology or machinery for production, usually on a large scale. *Many people came to work in our town during its first* **industrial** *period.*

in•ef•fi•cient (in′ə fish′ənt) *adjective.* Unable to use time, effort, or money wisely. *The man's* **inefficient** *plans led him to waste hours getting nothing done.*

in•fi•nite (in′fə nit) *adjective.* Immeasurable, exceedingly great. *We tested my mother's* **infinite** *patience by asking her so many questions.*

in•flict•ed (in flikt′əd) *verb.* Caused harm or damage; imposed upon. *The wildfire* **inflicted** *great destruction on many acres of forest.*

in•ge•nu•i•ty (in′jə nü′ i tē) *noun.* Cleverness and imaginativeness; resourcefulness. *My teacher was impressed with my* **ingenuity** *at solving the problem.*

i•ni•tial (i nish′əl) *adjective.* Coming at the beginning; first. *We returned to the new restaurant because our* **initial** *meal there was quite good.*

in•scrip•tion (in skrip′shən) *noun.* Writing that is carved, cut, painted, or impressed into or onto a hard surface. *The* **inscription** *on the door explained it was a sacred space.*

in•sight (in′sīt) *noun.* Special understanding about something. *The results of the scientists' test might give* **insight** *to why no plants will grow in the patch of soil.*

in•su•la•tion (in′ sə lā′shən) *noun.* Material that slows or prevents the transfer of heat, cold, sound, or electricity. *My wool coat provides* **insulation** *against the cold.*

in•trigu•ing (in trēg′ing) *adjective.* Arousing curiosity or intense interest. *I enjoy a good mystery novel with an* **intriguing** *plot.*

in•trin•sic (in trin′zik) *adjective.* Belonging to the nature or character of a thing. *Curiosity seems to be an* **intrinsic** *characteristic of this breed of cat.*

in•va•sive (in vā′səv) *adjective.* Tending to spread and take over areas. *Before long, the* **invasive** *weeds covered half of the garden.*

in•ven•to•ry (in′vən tôr′ē) *noun.* Goods and assets that are accounted for. *The clerks spent the weekend counting the* **inventory** *of the store's products.*

---

at; āpe; fär; câre; end; mē; it; īce; pîerce; hot; ōld; sông; fôrk; oil; out; up; ūse; rüle; pull; tûrn; chin; sing; shop; thin; <u>th</u>is; hw in white; zh in treasure.

The symbol ə stands for the unstressed vowel sound in about, taken, pencil, lemon, and circus.

ir•ra•tion•al (i rash'ə nəl) *adjective.* Not logical or sensible. *My father has an* **irrational** *fear of foods that are orange.*

Ll

leg•a•cy (leg'ə sē) *noun.* Something handed down from the past. *These beautiful journals are my grandmother's* **legacy** *to her children.*

lounge (lounj) *noun.* A place for sitting, waiting, or relaxing, especially a public space. *The passengers sat in the* **lounge** *and waited for their flight.*

Mm

mag•net•ic (mag net' ik) *adjective.* Having the power of magnets to attract or repel physical objects within their fields. *He used a* **magnetic** *device to separate the metal from the scrap paper.*

ma•jes•tic (mə jes'tik) *adjective.* Having a lofty, imposing, or grand aspect or style. *The show's host welcomed us with his* **majestic** *voice.*

ma•neu•ver•ing (mə nü'vər ing) *verb.* Moving or managing skillfully or cleverly. *The driver took his time* **maneuvering** *around the fallen branches.*

ma•nip•u•la•tion (mə nip'yə lā'shən) *noun.* Clever or skillful control or management. *Her* **manipulation** *of the clay resulted in a beautiful sculpture.*

man•u•fac•tured (man' yə fak'chərd) *adjective.* Made or processed, usually in quantity and with machinery. *Cars and trucks are types of* **manufactured** *vehicles.*

men•tor (men'tôr) *noun.* An influential counselor, guide, or teacher. *My* **mentor** *will help me to do well on the upcoming tests.*

me•thod•i•cal (mə thä'di kəl) *adjective.* In a systematic, regular, routine way. *After a* **methodical** *search from the kitchen to the laundry room, we finally found the lost cat in the clothes hamper.*

me•tic•u•lous•ly (mə tik'yə ləs lē) *adverb.* Very carefully; with great attention to detail. *The artist* **meticulously** *painted the smallest details of the scene.*

mil•len•ni•um (mə len' ē əm) *noun.* A period of 1,000 years. *The stone artifacts in the museum are over a* **millennium** *old.*

mod•i•fi•ca•tion (mod' ə fi kā'shən) *noun.* An alteration or change. *I made a slight* **modification** *to my jacket to make it fit better.*

mul•ti•tude (mul'ti tüd) *noun.* A great number of people or things; a crowd. *The performers thanked the cheering* **multitude** *that had come to see them.*

mu•tat•ed (mū'tāt əd) *verb.* Changed or transformed, usually genetically over time. *We read that the insects had* **mutated** *to adapt to the warmer climate.*

Nn

ne·go·ti·ate (ni gō'shē āt') *verb.* To deal with or make a bargain, to bring about a settlement. *We will **negotiate** with the teacher for an extra day of studying.*

no·mad·ic (nō mad'ik) *adjective.* Moving about over time; wandering from place to place. *The **nomadic** people were prepared to pack up and move on a moment's notice.*

nu·tri·ents (nü' trē ənts) *noun.* Substances needed by plants and animals for life and growth. *The doctor recommended a diet rich with **nutrients**.*

Oo

ob·li·ga·tion (ob'li gā'shən) *noun.* A sense of duty or responsibility. *I have an **obligation** to help my grandparents on weekends.*

ob·liv·i·ous (ə bliv' ē əs) *adjective.* Unaware, inattentive; lacking mindfulness or memory. *The sleeping man on the beach was **oblivious** to the gathering rainclouds.*

ob·scure (əb skyůr') *verb.* To hide; to make hard to see or understand. *Clinging snow might **obscure** the words on the road signs.*

ob·so·lete (ob'sə lēt') *adjective.* Outdated, no longer useful. *She traded in her **obsolete** phone for the newest model.*

op·tim·al (op' tə məl) *adjective.* Best, most satisfactory. *We settled on an **optimal** time for everyone to attend the meeting.*

or·nate (ôr nāt') *adjective.* Elaborately adorned or decorated. *The **ornate** frame was quite different from the simple picture it contained.*

Pp

per·cep·tion (pər sep'shən) *noun.* Mental or physical awareness or understanding. *As I grew tired, my **perception** of events began to lessen.*

pe·ri·od·ic (pîr'ē od'ik) *adjective.* Happening at regular intervals of time. *The school has **periodic** fire drills to prepare for an emergency.*

pe·riph·er·al (pə rif' ər əl) *adjective.* Of or pertaining to the outer edges of something, such as the field of vision. *Mom's strong **peripheral** vision allowed her to keep track of all three children at once.*

---

at; āpe; fär; câre; end; mē; it; īce; pîerce; hot; ōld; sông; fôrk; oil; out; up; ūse; rüle; půll; tûrn; chin; sing; shop; thin; <u>th</u>is; hw in white; zh in treasure.

The symbol ə stands for the unstressed vowel sound in about, taken, pencil, lemon, and circus.

per·se·ver·ance (pə r'sə vîr'əns) *noun*. A steady and continuous course of action, especially in spite of difficulty. *We thanked the firefighters for their **perseverance** in battling the huge blaze.*

per·sis·tent (pər sis'tənt) *adjective*. Continuing firmly and steadily despite challenges. *After our **persistent** complaints, the town finally fixed the sidewalk.*

pho·bic (fō' bik) *adjective*. Having a specific fear or aversion. *The **phobic** traveler washes his hands at least ten times a day.*

plum·met·ing (plum'ət ing) *verb*. Falling at a fast rate of speed. *The roller coaster was **plummeting** from the top of its highest hill.*

pop·u·lous (pop'yə ləs) *adjective*. Having a lot of people, crowded. *The stores were very **populous** just before the holidays.*

po·ten·tial (pə ten' shəl) *noun*. Possibility; capacity to become something. *Because he is tall, my brother has the **potential** to do well at basketball.*

pre·ced·ed (pri sēd'əd) *verb*. Went before or ahead of. *A bolt of lightning **preceded** the rumble of thunder.*

pre·sumed (pri zümd') *verb*. Assumed, supposed, believed without question. *We **presumed** the dog was hungry because he was pushing his bowl around.*

pre·vail (pri vāl') *verb*. To succeed over time; to win. *Our team hopes to **prevail** throughout the season and head to the championships.*

prin·ci·pal (prin' sə pəl) *adjective*. First in importance; greatest. *Safety is the **principal** concern in our science lab.*

pro·duc·ti·vi·ty (pro' duk ti' və tē) *noun*. The rate at which goods, services, or commodities are made. *The new worker was quickly promoted because of her **productivity**.*

pro·longed (prə lôngd') *adjective*. Lengthened in time; extended. *We **prolonged** our visit to the museum until the rain storm had passed.*

prom·i·nent (prom'ə nent) *adjective*. Easily noticeable; standing out in some way. *There is a **prominent** statue in the park that people often use as a landmark.*

pro·mote (prə mōt') *verb*. To help in doing something, such as growing. *Fruits and vegetables will **promote** good health.*

pro·por·tion (prə pôr' shən) *noun*. The relation between things or parts with regard to size, number, or amount. *Our class has an equal **proportion** of boys and girls.*

pro·tein (prō' tēn) *noun*. An organic molecule found in all living cells of animals and plants and essential for growth and life. *The scientists studied how the human body uses **protein** to build muscle.*

pul·ver·ize (pəl'və rīz) *verb*. To crush, grind, or pound. *The chef decided to **pulverize** the stale bread to make bread crumbs.*

Rr

rap·port (ra pôr') *noun.* A connection of understanding; special relationship. *His rapport with animals makes him a good vet.*

re·coiled (rē koild') *verb.* Fall back under pressure or shock; moved away quickly. *I recoiled when I saw the snake on the path.*

rec·re·a·tion (rek'rē ā'shən) *noun.* Something done for relaxation or amusement, or enjoyment. *The resort hotel at the ocean has many options for recreation.*

reg·u·la·tion (reg'yə lā'shən) *adjective.* Required; meeting stated standards or guidelines. *We practiced with a small ball, but used a regulation ball.*

rem·i·nisce (rem ə nis') *verb.* To recall the past with longing. *My grandmother likes to reminisce about her childhood in Africa.*

re·plen·ished (rē plen' ishd) *verb.* Resupplied; refilled. *I fed the dog and replenished his water twice a day.*

re·sem·blance (ri zem'bləns) *noun.* A recognizable similarity. *There is a close resemblance between my sister and me.*

re·sil·ient (ri zil'yənt) *adjective.* Capable of recovering from adversity; durable. *The resilient players kept their spirits up and tied the game in the final minute.*

re·strict (ri strikt') *verb.* To confine; to keep within limits. *The lifeguards restrict the use of the pool during bad weather.*

re·tal·i·a·tion (ri tal' ē ā' shən) *noun.* An act that returns like for like; revenge. *We feared our opponent's retaliation after we scored so many points against them.*

re·trieved (ri trēvd') *verb.* Recovered, regained. *My brother retrieved the baseball from the nearby yard.*

re·u·nites (rē' ū nīts') *verb.* Brings together again. *Our family reunites with our old neighbors for dinner once a year.*

rig·ors (rig'ərz) *noun, plural.* Extreme hardships, challenges, or severities. *My brother was exhausted from the rigors of soccer camp.*

roused (rouzd) *verb.* Stirred from sleep or rest; awakened. *After dozing off, we roused ourselves when the train arrived in the station.*

Ss

sal·a·ries (sal'ə rēz) *noun, plural.* Fixed amounts of money paid to someone at regular times for work done. *Due to our hard work, the company increased our salaries at the start of the year.*

---

at; āpe; fär; câre; end; mē; it; īce; pîerce; hot; ōld; sông; fôrk; oil; out; up; ūse; rüle; pull; tûrn; chin; sing; shop; thin; this; hw in white; zh in treasure.

The symbol ə stands for the unstressed vowel sound in about, taken, pencil, lemon, and circus.

sar·cas·tic (sär kas'tik) *adjective.* Using sharp and contemptuous words meant to insult, demean, or make fun of someone. *No one enjoyed doing business with the* **sarcastic** *store clerk.*

sat·u·rat·ed (sach' ə rāt' əd) *adjective.* Become completely filled or soaked with a liquid. *We wiped up the spill until the towel became too* **saturated** *to absorb any more.*

scald·ing (skôld'ing) *adjective.* Extremely hot or boiling; capable of burning. *The waiter warned that the tea was* **scalding** *hot.*

shards (shärdz) *noun, plural.* Sharp, often pointed fragments. *We swept up the* **shards** *of glass after the window broke.*

share·crop·per (shâr'krop ər) *noun.* A farmer who pays a portion or share of his crop to rent the land or farm he uses. *The old* **sharecropper** *showed us pictures of the day he first began planting on the farm.*

sig·nif·i·cant (sig nif' i kənt) *adjective.* Important, having special meaning or consequence. *We spent a* **significant** *weekend with my cousins before they moved away.*

skewed (skūd) *verb.* Took an indirect course. *Because of the wind, our sailboat* **skewed** *to the left.*

smol·der·ing (smōl'dər ing) *adjective.* Burning with few or no flames. *We doused the* **smoldering** *campfire with water.*

smug·gle (smug'əl) *verb.* Brought into or out of secretly or illegally. *My sister was sent home after she tried to* **smuggle** *a kitten into the classroom.*

sol·i·tude (sol' i tüd) *noun.* The state of being alone. *I enjoy listening to music in* **solitude** *and without interruption.*

som·ber (som' bər) *adjective.* Dark or gloomy; dismal; depressing. *My parents frowned as they read the* **somber** *news .*

sparse (spârs) *adjective.* Thinly distributed; not living or growing close together. *It was hard to find shade among the* **sparse** *trees in the desert.*

spe·cies (spē'shēz) *noun.* A group of related living things with very similar characteristics. *The colors on their wings made it easier to identify the* **species** *of insects.*

spec·ta·tors (spek'tā tərz) *noun, plural.* People who observe or watch something but do not take part. *The* **spectators** *cheered as the performers danced across the stage.*

spec·u·la·tion (spek'yə lā'shən) *noun.* Deep thought or reflection; wonderment. *There was some* **speculation** *that the injured player might not return to the game.*

spind·ly (spind'lē) *adjective.* Oddly tall or long and thin, usually frail. *The lobster crept forward awkwardly on its* **spindly** *legs.*

sta·tion·er·y (stā'shə ner'ē) *noun.* Paper, envelopes, and other materials used for writing. *I took out my* **stationery** *to write thank you notes after the party.*

stead·fast (sted' fast) *adjective.* Dedicated to a purpose, unwavering; loyal and trustworthy. *I told the secret only to my most* **steadfast** *friends.*

sti·fling (stī′fling) *adjective.* Suffocating, oppressively close. *We opened the windows to lessen the **stifling** heat in the room.*

stoop (stüp) *noun.* A platform with steps outside a home or building's door. *I liked to sit on the **stoop** and watch for the mail carrier to come.*

stur·dy (stûr′dē) *adjective.* Strongly built, robust, hardy. *The library needed **sturdy** shelves to hold the heavy reference books.*

sub·merged (səb mûrjd′) *adjective.* Underwater or covered with liquid; beneath the surface. *We steered the boat around the **submerged** rocks.*

sub·se·quent·ly (səb′ si kwent′ lē) *adverb.* Occurring or coming after; following; later. *I tripped and **subsequently** spilled the drinks on the stairs.*

sum·mit (sum′ it) *noun.* The highest point, as of a hill or mountain. *The hikers took pictures of the view from the mountain's **summit**.*

sum·mon (sum′ən) *verb.* To call upon for specific action; to ask to come. *I became nervous when I heard my teacher **summon** me to the school office.*

sur·plus (sûr′ plus) *noun.* An amount that is greater than what is used or needed. *After paying the bills, we set aside the **surplus** for our vacation fund.*

sus·tain (səs tān′) *verb.* To support; to keep going. *I wondered how long the singer could **sustain** the high note without breathing.*

sym·me·try (sim′i trē) *noun.* Beauty of form; a balanced grouping of parts on either side of a line or around a center. *We admired the **symmetry** of the shapes in the painting.*

Tt

te·nac·i·ty (tə na′ sə tē) *noun.* The characteristic of being stubborn or persistence. *The man's **tenacity** made it difficult to reach an agreement.*

ten·ta·tive·ly (ten′ tə tiv lē) *adverb.* In an uncertain, unsure manner; not confidently or decisively. *We **tentatively** stepped onto the new ice before deciding it was safe for skating.*

thresh·old (thresh′hōld) *noun.* A gate or door; a point of entry or crossing over. *They greeted us at the **threshold** with hugs and handshakes.*

trail·blaz·er (trāl′ blā′ zər) *noun.* A leader who leaves a path for others to follow into new or unfamiliar territory or endeavors. *Each year we honor the **trailblazer** who founded and settled our town.*

---

at; **ā**pe; f**ä**r; c**â**re; **e**nd; m**ē**; **i**t; **ī**ce; p**î**erce; h**o**t; **ō**ld; s**ô**ng; f**ô**rk; **oi**l; **ou**t; **u**p; **ū**se; r**ü**le; p**ù**ll; t**û**rn; **ch**in; si**ng**; **sh**op; **th**in; **th**is; **hw** in **wh**ite; **zh** in trea**s**ure.

The symbol ə stands for the unstressed vowel sound in **a**bout, tak**e**n, penc**i**l, lem**o**n, and circ**u**s.

Uu

ul•ti•mate•ly (ul′ tə mə t′ lē) *adverb.* In the end. *I studied hard and **ultimately** passed.*

un•daunt•ed (un dônt′əd) *adjective.* Not discouraged, not giving in to fear or challenge. *The **undaunted** hiker continued along the trail despite the rain.*

un•di•min•ished (un′ di min′ishd) *adjective.* Not lessened or decreased. *Our excitement for the show was **undiminished** by the long wait.*

un•earthed (un ûrthd′) *verb.* Uncovered; dug up out of the earth. *The dog **unearthed** a bone he had buried weeks ago.*

un•fet•tered (un fe′tərd) *adjective.* Released from physical or mental bonds; free and unrestrained. *Our **unfettered** pet bird likes to fly around the apartment.*

un•seem•ly (un sēm′lē) *adjective.* Inappropriate or improper; rude. *Mom made me apologize for the **unseemly** remark I had made.*

up•heav•al (up hē′vəl) *noun.* A strong, sudden, or violent change or disturbance. *The erupting volcano caused an **upheaval** in the land around it.*

ur•gen•cy (ûr′jən sē) *noun.* An insistence of need; a demand for immediate action. *Dad treated the cut with **urgency**.*

u•ti•lize (ū′tə līz) *verb.* To make use of. *We will **utilize** the new computer to produce the school newspaper.*

ut•most (ut′mōst) *adjective.* Greatest or highest. *I have the **utmost** respect for our town's firefighters.*

Vv

val•iant (val′yənt) *adjective.* Bold, courageous, noble, or brave. *The **valiant** soldier risked his life to bring the general the important message.*

vast•ness (vast′nes) *noun.* A very great size or extent. *The **vastness** of the ocean amazed early sailors.*

ver•i•fy (ver′ə fī) *verb.* To prove the truth of. *The delivery person had to **verify** my identity before she would give me the package.*

Ww

wind•swept (wind′swept′) *adjective.* Exposed to and subjected to the wind. *The **windswept** grasses bent and swayed across the field.*

with•stood (with stŭd′) *verb.* Held out against; resisted the effects of. *The strong sea wall **withstood** the pounding waves of the high seas.*

Yy

yields (yēldz) *noun.* The amounts produced; the crops or results of cultivation. *Doubling the recipe **yields** twice as many biscuits.*

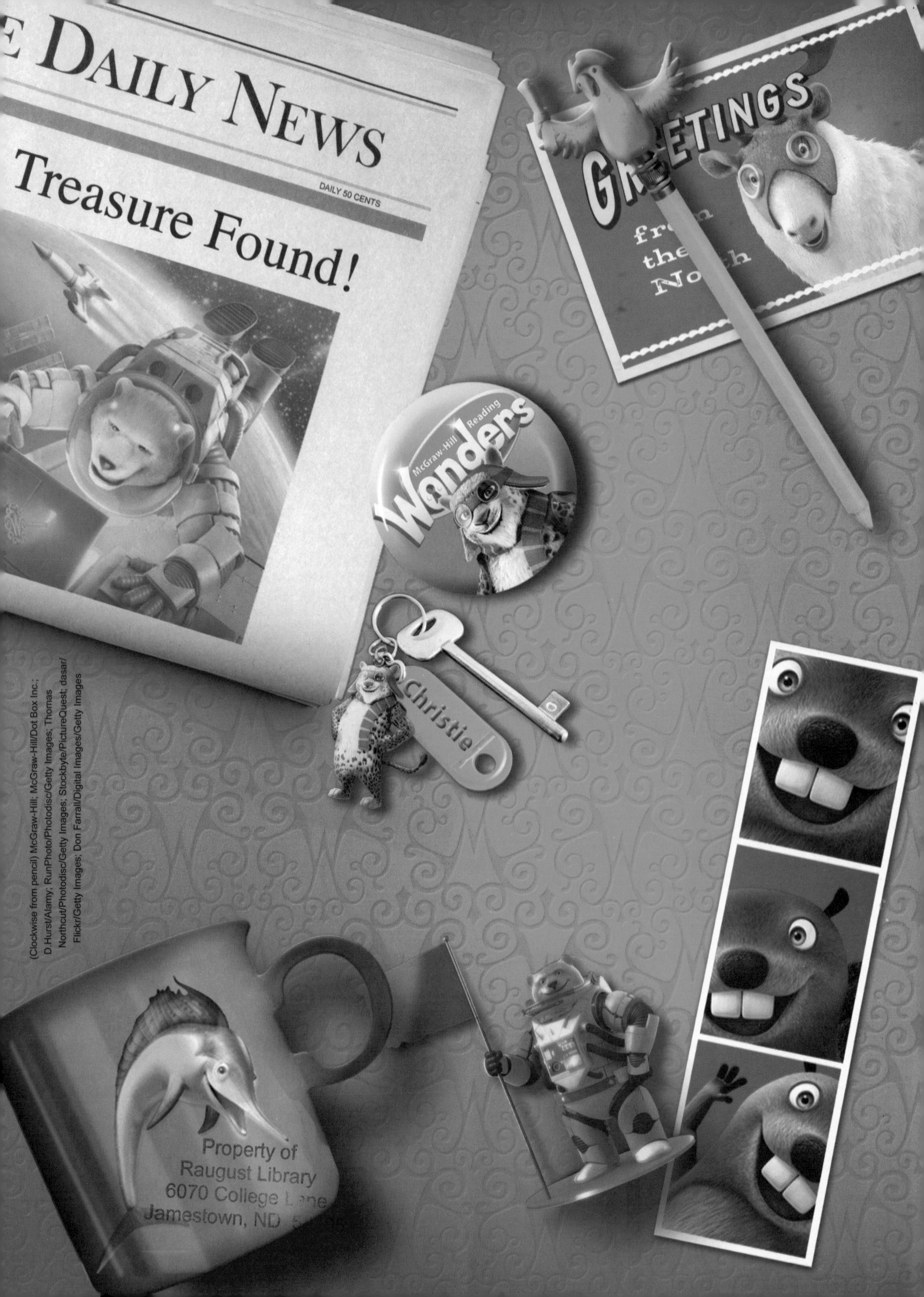

E DAILY NEWS
DAILY 50 CENTS
Treasure Found!
GREETINGS
from the North
McGraw-Hill Reading
Wonders
Christie
Property of
Raugust Library
6070 College Lane
Jamestown, ND

(Clockwise from pencil) McGraw-Hill; McGraw-Hill/Dot Box Inc.; D.Hurst/Alamy; RunPhoto/Photodisc/Getty Images; Thomas Northcut/Photodisc/Getty Images; Stockbyte/PictureQuest; dasar/ Flickr/Getty Images; Don Farrall/Digital Images/Getty Images